CALVIN:

Revolutionary, Theologian, Pastor

CALVIN:

Revolutionary, Theologian, Pastor

Williston Walker

Copyright © 2005 Christian Focus Publications Ltd

Paperback ISBN 978-1-84550-104-4
epub ISBN 978-1-78191-564-6
mobi ISBN 978-1-78191-565-3

10 9 8 7 6 5 4 3 2

First Published 1906 as
John Calvin: The Organiser of Reformed Protestantism 1509-1564

This edition published in 2005 and reprinted in 2014
by Christian Focus Publications Ltd.,
Geanies House, Fearn, Tain,
Ross-shire, IV20 1TW, Great Britain.

www.christianfocus.com

Cover Design by Alister MacInnes

Printed and bound by
Nørhaven, Denmark

Contents

1

CALVIN'S SPIRITUAL ANTECEDENTS

Calvin belongs to the second generation of the reformers. His place chronologically and, to a large extent, theologically, is among the heirs rather than with the initiators of the Reformation. At his birth Luther and Zwingli were already twenty-five years of age, Melanchthon was about to take up a student's career at the University of Heidelberg, and Henry VIII had just begun his eventful reign. None of these leaders had entered, indeed, upon his reformatory work; but the thorough development of the Reformation in Germany and in German-speaking Switzerland was achieved before Calvin reached the activities of manhood. Yet, in spite of his lateness in point of time, Calvin must be ranked among the most influential leaders in the gigantic struggle of the sixteenth century. He could not have done his work had not Luther and Zwingli gone before, but he was far more than a builder on other men's foundations. That work had its antecedents and was made possible by many predisposing influences. A brief glance, therefore, at the state of the land in which Calvin grew to manhood may be of service as exhibiting the soil and the atmosphere in which his early intellectual and religious life was nurtured.

The kingdom of France, at the beginning of the sixteenth century, had many claims to eminence among the states of Christendom. In consciousness of national unity, in efficiency of governmental organization, and in consequent influence on the politics of Europe, it could challenge favorable comparison with any of its contemporaries. Not so worldwide in the activities of its inhabitants as the newly significant kingdom of Spain, then feeling the fever stimulus of the great discoveries which marked the close of the fifteenth century, its growth was more natural, solid and unforced than that of its portentous southern rival. Though the neighboring kingdom of England could show the forms at least of more popular governmental institutions, the physical strength of England was reckoned far inferior to that of France. The great Holy Roman Empire, rich in commerce, cities and soldiers, was much less able to use its strength than France by reason of its divisions and its lack of a national spirit. Though far from having attained the organic development of a modern state, France, in the early sixteenth century, was, with the possible exception of England, the most advanced of any European kingdom on the road toward modern national life.

The national tendencies characteristic of the French monarchy of that age had conspicuous embodiment in Francis I (1515–1547), contemporary with whom Calvin was to do the formative portion of his work. A ruler of unbounded military ambition, anxious to win for France the post of highest influence in Europe, his personal charm, ready wit, eloquence, tact, and appreciation of scholarly and artistic merit gave him deserved popularity. His social talents attracted a splendid court, but his easy morality and entire want of personal religion or of ethical seriousness unfitted him to appreciate the fundamental significance of the gigantic religious struggle which convulsed Europe during his reign. France, under him, had an aggressive though largely unsuccessful military policy, a brilliant court, and a high degree of national unity and internal prosperity.

The relations between the French Church and the monarchy had for centuries been close and cordial to a degree hardly equaled elsewhere in Europe. Church and King had aided each other against the nobility. While thoroughly orthodox, as the Middle Ages understood orthodoxy, and bitterly opposed to "heretics" at home like the Cathari and Waldenses, the French Church felt a greater hostility toward extreme papal claims than was general in other branches of Western Christendom. It possessed a strong sense of corporate unity, and of national or "Gallican" rights, which even the papacy ought not to infringe. But the growing strength of the crown was leading to increasing control by the sovereigns over the Church, and this control was decidedly strengthened when, in 1516, Francis I and Leo X entered into the famous Concordat. The King was henceforth to nominate to the higher administrative and monastic posts in the realm. To the sovereign the Concordat brought a firmer grasp on the French Church; to the papacy it secured an increase in revenue. But though the rights of the Church were thus in a measure sacrificed, it was exempt from many papal interferences and exactions that bore heavily on other lands. There was not, therefore, in France that popular hatred of the Roman *curia* which was so widespread in Germany and there made possible the rapid growth of the Lutheran revolt.

It would be an error to suppose, however, that the spiritual state of the French Church was superior to that existing in lands where the crown enjoyed less influence. The same evils of externalism in the conception of religion, of emphasis on acts done, penances performed, pilgrimages accomplished, and indulgences won, rather than on the inward state of the soul and on the ruling purpose of the life existed in France that were to be found elsewhere in Latin Christendom; and whatever of criticism may justly be passed upon the Roman Church of this period as a whole attaches equally to that of France. The growth of the power of the monarchy brought far less aid to the spiritual interests of the French Church than did a similar increase of royal authority south of the Pyrenees to that of Spain, since no French sovereign of the fifteenth or sixteenth centuries manifested a religious zeal comparable with that of Isabella of Castile or even with that of the emperor, Charles V. The French kings enjoyed the control of the Church which their share in the appointment of its prominent officers afforded. They appreciated its possibilities as a source of revenue. They were ready enough to oppose changes which would in any serious way alter a fabric so useful to them. But they gave to political considerations the chief weight in ecclesiastical appointments; and the great evils of the possession of office by the morally unfit and the heaping up of benefices in the hands of favorites,[1] who, however well-intentioned, could give them no adequate spiritual care, continued to flourish unrelieved by any counteracting influence from the throne. France, as a whole, seems to have been fairly well content with its religious situation at the beginning of the sixteenth century and, as compared with Germany or Spain, its sense of the need of betterment was undeveloped.

Foremost among the intellectual forces of France was still to be placed the University of Paris. That eminent seat of mediaeval learning, to which all other universities of northern Europe looked up as their archetype, had enjoyed high academic fame since the beginning of the thirteenth century. Within its walls Aquinas, Bonaventura, Duns Scotus, William of Occam, d'Ailli and Gerson had taught. Its repute as a center of theological instruction had, indeed, been considerably dimmed by the beginning of the sixteenth century, but was still great. It theological faculty, known popularly as the Sorbonne, from the large concentration of its instructors in the Collège founded in 1253 by Robert de Sorbon, regarded itself as being, and was widely reputed, of unimpeachable orthodoxy. Nor was it wanting in courage and independence. Its

---

[1] Henry C. Lea, in *The Cambridge Modern History*, i. 659, gives a striking instance of pluralism contemporary with Calvin's life. Jean, son of Duke René II of Lorraine, was born in 1498. In 1508 he entered into possession of the revenues of the bishopric of Metz; 1517 saw him Bishop of Toul; 1518 brought the addition of Térouanne; 1521 added Valence and Die; 1523, Verdun. In 1524 he became Archbishop of Narbonne. The year 1533 added the archbishopric Reims and made him primate of France. In 1536 he became Bishop of Alby, and the next year Archbishop of Lyons. He then gained the bishoprics of Macon, Agen, and Nantes. Several of these posts he resigned to relatives; but many he continued to hold till his death in 1550. In addition, he was in possession of the "abbeys of Gorze, Fécamp, Cluny, Marmoutiers, St. Ouen, St Jean de Laon, St Germer, St Médard of Soissons and St Mansuy of Toul."

opposition to the Concordat, as recently as 1516, bore witness to the jealous concern of the University for the liberties of the French Church. But it was, nevertheless, on the whole a hindrance to progress. It stood strongly opposed to innovations in learning or in doctrine. Not that it wholly neglected the new learning that was crossing the Alps from Italy: Greek had been taught within its walls, though for a brief period, as early as 1458. In 1508 new interest in the Attic tongue had been awakened by the coming of Girolamo Aleandro, afterwards famous as an opponent of Luther at Worms. But, in spite of this measure of approval, the friends of classic studies felt that the University was hostile to them, that its dominant spirit was scholastic and its methods antiquated. Its leaders looked upon Greek as the "language of heresies," and they condemned the teachings of Luther in terms of the utmost abhorrence.[2]

Yet, in the early years of the sixteenth century, the new learning was rapidly winning its way in France. In 1507, the printing of books in Greek was begun in Paris, and two years later the leader of native French Humanists, Jacques Le Fèvre, already famed for his studies on Aristotle and in mathematics, published his exposition of the Psalms which Luther was to use in his early years of teaching at Wittenberg. Among many distinguished pupils of Le Fèvre, none was more eminent for scholarship than Guillaume Budé, whose *Commentary on the Greek Language* of 1529 gave him a European fame. To Budé's influence with Francis I was due the establishment, in 1530, of the Royal Lecturers (*Lecteurs royaux*), at Paris, to give instruction in Greek, Hebrew and mathematics, wholly in the spirit of the Renaissance, and with a zeal for the new learning that roused the hostility of the Sorbonne. From this royal foundation the Collége de France was to grow. Indeed, under the reign of Francis I, the new learning had become distinctly fashionable. The King was conspicuously its supporter, and the roll of

---

[2] See the letters of Henri Lorit and Valentin Tschudi in A. L. Herminjard, *Correspondance des réfromateurs dans les pays de langue francaise*, i. 31, 38; Abel Lefranc, *Histoire du Collège de France*, pp. 60–63, 68.

scholars, architects and artists who found in him a patron is an ornament to his reign. Even more committed to the support of Renaissance men and methods was Francis' elder sister, Marguerite d'Angoulême, whose increasing liberalism was ultimate to carry her into real, though not publicly announced, sympathy with Protestantism.[3] In Marguerite, men of liberal ideas generally had a determined defender; and she afforded to many efficient protection, especially after her marriage, in 1527, to Henri d'Albret, King of Navarre, had put her at the head of a little court at Nérac. With Francis, however, support of the new learning was based on admiration for humanistic scholarship rather than on conviction, and it ceased whenever the new leaven threatened the constitution or the doctrine of an organization so useful to the French monarchy from a political and financial point of view as the French Church.

It was true in France, as elsewhere in Europe, that the new learning was leading to criticism of the existing state of the Church. From its standpoint the Sorbonne was amply justified in its opposition. The spirit of the Renaissance was that of a return from the scholarship of the later mediaeval period to the sources. Begun with a revived interest of the writers of classical antiquity, it soon led men to investigate anew the sources of religious truth, and to go back of d'Ailli, Occam, Scotus, and Aquinas, to Augustine, and, even further, to the New Testament. The attempted return did not usually involve any hostile intention toward the established Church. Men like Erasmus, Ximenes, or Reuchlin believed that sound learning, the study of the Scriptures and of the Fathers, and earnest opposition to the superstition, ignorance, and maladministration rampant in the Church would effect all that was necessary for its betterment. They had no wish for revolution. In France this humanistic spirit of reform had its conspicuous embodiment in Le Fèvre who, both by reason of his own services to the cause of the religious awakening and the disciples whom he aroused to similar or even greater zeal,

---

[3] Abel Lefranc, *Les idées religieuses de Marguerite de Navarre*, Paris, 1898, p. 123.

deserved the first place among the religious leaders of his native country in the generation that preceded Calvin, and prepared the way for Calvin's more positive work.

Born at Étaples in Picardy about the middle of the fifteenth century,[4] Jacques Le Fèvre was early attracted to Paris, where he learned Greek from a fugitive from Sparta, George Hermonymus. A journey to Italy, in 1488–1489, quickened his humanistic zeal, and his religious spirit was no less manifest in a sympathy with the mystical type of piety. A little man, modest, kindly, gentle, of a life that did honor to his priestly vows, he won friendship by his personal qualities as he attracted admiration by his zeal for scholarship. His disciples were destined for the most various parts in the Reformation struggle, but they seem to have held him in singular affection. Among those who honored him as their teacher were: Guillaume Briçonnet, sprung from one of the eminent noble houses of France, and to be Bishop of Meaux; Guillaume Budé, instrumental, as has been seen, in the establishment of the Royal Lecturers; François Vatable, one of the first teachers of Hebrew on that foundation and to be Calvin's instructor; Gérard Roussel, the later confessor of Marguerite d'Angoulême and Bishop of Oloron, for a time Calvin's friend; Louis de Berquin, destined to die at the stake for his Protestant faith; and Guillaume Farel, to be the fiery preacher of evangelical doctrines in French Switzerland, and Calvin's intimate associate.

It was by reason of Briçonnet's appointment as abbot of the great Parisian monastery of St Germain-des-Prés in 1507, that Le Fèvre came to make that religious foundation his home for the next thirteen years. There, aided by its noble library, he turned to the study of the Bible in a singularly fresh spirit. In 1512 he published a Latin translation of and commentary

---

[4] The usual and more probable date is "about 1455," e.g. G. Bonet-Maury in Hauck's *Realencyklopädie für protestantische Theolgie*, v. 174; but Professor E. Doumergue, *Jean Calvin, les hommes et les choses de son temps*, Lausanne, 1899, seq., i. 539–541, has an interesting argument favouring the conclusion that at his death, in 1536, he was 100 years old.

upon Paul's Epistles which shows clearly the development of his thought. Le Fèvre did not break with the Roman Church as an organization– that he never did. He still held to many of its characteristic doctrines. Yet, five years before Luther's theses, he had come to deny the justifying merit of good works, to hold salvation to be a free gift from God, to doubt the doctrine of transubstantiation, and to imply a belief in the sole authority of the Scriptures.[5] But these assertions, though clear, were the utterances of a quiet, scholarly mystic, who saw no incongruity between his views and a cordial support of the Church as it then existed; and it is no wonder that few perceived what he failed to see. His book made no sensation, and he continued his peaceful career, holding with ever-increasing firmness the affection of his friends and pupils, and gaining, through the good offices of Briçonnet, the regard of Francïs I and of Marguerite.

Meanwhile, Luther was beginning his reformatory work in Germany, and by 1519 that land was filled with the noise of the battle. His books soon reached France. The Sorbonne, under the lead of its syndic, Noël Béda, condemned his views in April, 1521. Criticisms of the Church which had passed well-nigh unnoticed now appeared dangerously "Lutheran." Le Fèvre himself came under suspicion. In 1517 and 1518 he had put forth a scholarly study denying the identity of Mary Magdalene with Mary the sister of Lazarus and the Mary who anointed the Savior's feet. In itself, this might seem an academic question, but it denied the current teachings of the Church, it practically asserted the right of private biblical interpretation, and it was an invasion by one who was only a master of arts of a field of thought to be fittingly open only to a doctor of theology. Under the suspicion which the rise of Luther had instilled, Le Fèvre was now attacked by Béda, and his opinion on the problem of the Marys was condemned by the Sorbonne about seven months after it had denounced the Saxon reformer.

---

[5] For discussions from somewhat divergent points of view of the extent of Le Fèvre's Protestantism, see Herminjard, *Correspondance*, i. 239; and Doumergue, *Jean Calvin*, i. 81–86, 542–551.

About a year before the condemnation of his book, however, Le Fèvre had left Paris for the friendly home of Briçonnet, who, since 1516, had been Bishop of Meaux. The bishop was a worthy disciple of Le Fèvre in purpose. He saw the need of reform, and held the humanistic belief that a return to the sources – the study of the Bible and the preaching of biblical truth – would right the evils of the Church. He perceived no need of revolution, nor did he, any more than Le Fèvre, grasp the seriousness of the situation. But he was willing to do much more than most humanists to use the remedies in which he believed, and in his reformatory convictions and his efforts alike, he had the powerful sympathy of Marguerite. He now began the work in earnest. Under his encouragement and that of Marguerite, Le Fèvre published in 1523 a translation of the New Testament which grew by 1530 to a version of the whole Bible. This was, indeed, far from being the first translation of the Scriptures to be made or printed in France, but those that had gone before had been marked by the abbreviations and modifications popular in the Middle Ages. Le Fèvre now gave a careful version of the Vulgate, enriched here and there by comparison with the Greek.[6] Though in no sense a great translation, Le Fèvre's work undoubtedly furthered extensive reading of the Scriptures in France.

Briçonnet was inaugurating, meanwhile, an active campaign of preaching in his diocese, aided by Roussel, Vatable, Farel, and Michel d'Arande, all of whom had caught their inspiration from Le Fèvre; but he soon found himself in great difficulties. By the champions of the existing order he was looked upon as little better than a Lutheran. On the other hand, the new preaching could not be confined to simple expositions of the Scriptures. The humanistic reformatory course was one almost impossible to hold in practice, save as an individual attitude. Farel inveighed against the papacy, and was probably dismissed by Briçonnet

---

[6] Reuss and Berger in Hauck, *Realencyklopädie*, iii. 126–131; Doumergue, i. 98; *The Cambridge Modern History*, ii. 283. The New Testament had been printed in French at Lyons about 1477, and the whole Bible, modified as above mentioned, at Paris about ten years later.

in 1523. But iconoclastic acts, wholly distasteful to Briçonnet, Roussel, and most of his friends, soon occurred. In December 1524, Jean Le Clerc, a wool-carder of Meaux, tore a copy of a papal bull from the cathedral door and affixed instead a declaration that the Pope was Antichrist.[7] Briçonet denounced the acts of Le Clerc and his possible associates in January 1525,[8] but the political situation soon made his position impossible. The great defeat of the French at Pavia in February was followed by the captivity of the King in Spain, whither Marguerite went to join him in August. The Parlement of Paris was now able to oppose Briçonnet unhindered. His preachers were forbidden and Le Fèvre's translations ordered burned.

Briçonnet felt that the situation was beyond his solution. He was not a man of the highest courage, but had he been more daring than he was he might well have thought that his mild reformatory efforts had resulted in attempts more revolutionary than he anticipated or relished. He now issued, on October 15, 1525, two synodical decrees[9] condemning Luther's doctrines and books and deploring the "abuses of the Gospel" by those who denied purgatory and rejected prayers to the saints. His reformatory work at Meaux was over. The same month Le Fèvre and Roussel were compelled to fly for safety to Strassburg; but Briçonnet himself continued in possession of his office till his death in 1534. Fortunately the royal favor followed the fugitives. On his return from Madrid in 1526, Francis recalled them. To Le Fèvre he gave the post of teacher to his children and librarian of the Château of Blois. Here the aged scholar labored on his translation of the Bible, but the growing tension of the ecclesiastical situation led the ever-kindly Marguerite to effect his transfer to the safety of her court at Nerac in 1530, and there Le Fèvre died six years later. Roussel did further work as a reformatory preacher in

---

[7] He was whipped and branded at Paris. On July 22, 1525 he was burned at Metz for the destruction of a shrine.

[8] Letter to the clergy of Meaux, Herminjard, i. 320.

[9] Herminjard, i. 153, where they are dated 1523, though with hesitation. On the true date see Doumergue, i. 110.

France and, as will be seen, influenced Calvin at a crisis in that reformer's history; but he was even more of a mystic quietist than Le Fèvre. Like Le Fèvre and Briçonnet he saw the need of reform, without desiring or appreciating the necessity of revolution, or being willing to pay the cost.[10] Aided by Marguerite, he accepted the bishopric of Oloron and died about 1552 in good repute for fidelity in the spiritual administration of his diocese.

Yet if Le Fèvre, Briçonnet and Roussel were thus disposed only to a humanistic type of reform that did not break with Rome, and proved inadequate to the struggle, there were those who entered into the spirit of the German revolt and wished to effect a similar revolution in France. Most of these radical reformers were from the mercantile and wage-earning classes, but a few men of learning and rank were also to be found among them. Of Le Fèvre's stormy pupil, Guillaume Farel, something has already been said, and there will be abundant occasion to speak further of him in this narrative. The most eminent in station among the early uncompromising reformers of France was Louis de Berquin, a noble of Artois, and, like Farel, a disciple of Le Fèvre. A man of dignified bearing, scholarly attainments and high character, Berquin won the friendship of Marguerite and Francis I, and became a member of the royal council. A little later he gained the rather timid regard of Erasmus.[11] A translator of Erasmus and Luther, and himself a writer in favor of reform, he was an object of attack from 1523 onward, but was at first saved by the friendship of Marguerite and of her royal brother. That favor Francis I failed to extend to Berquin at last, probably because he became convinced that Berquin's attack on so useful an institution as the crown found the French Church to be was too serious, but his end came in death by fire on April 16, 1529, on condemnation by the Parlement of Paris – sentence hastily passed and executed to prevent possible interference by the King. When a nobleman of such connections and influence was thus made to suffer, it was

---

[10] Letter to Farel, August 24, 1524, Herminjard, i. 271.

[11] His story is well told by H. M. Baird, *History of the Rise of the Huguenots*, i. chap. iv. For Erasmus' estimate, see Herminjard, ii. 188.

evident that scant mercy could be expected from the French courts by heretics of lower social rank. In the death of Berquin French Protestantism of the thorough-going type lost its most conspicuous representative. Yet he cannot be called a leader; he was no organizer. He seems to have had little missionary force. He fought largely alone, and he left the Reform movement little stronger save for the courage of his example.

The vast majority of the radical reformers of France were, however, from the humbler walks of life, and their conduct in many instances was such as to exasperate rather than attract. Iconoclastic excesses, such as had been exhibited at Meaux, were repeated in many places, notably at Paris in 1528. The Gallic spirit is more impulsive than the German, and though iconoclasm was common enough in many lands during the Reformation age, it showed its injudicious, aggravating face nowhere more plainly than in France, where the image-breakers, instead of representing, as in some lands, a popular revolution, were but a handful as yet among a hostile and angered population.

By 1530 the French Reform movement, in both its types, was slowly and somewhat irregularly growing. Its humanistic form appealed to men of culture. Where the new learning had penetrated, in the court and among student circles, there was not a little sympathy with such efforts as Le Fèvre had led. A critical attitude toward mediaeval doctrines and practices, that yet did not break with Rome, was extensive, especially among the younger race of scholars. The radicals found little sympathy among the humanistic reformers. If the latter were inadequate to their task, the former were as yet incapable of widely commending their cause. The great lack of the French reformatory movement was a leader whose controlling mind could knit its scattered and divergent forces. Such a leader must appeal to the world of scholarship, and yet go further in opposition to Rome than the humanists had done. He must be as firm as the radicals in hostility to the papacy, and yet be able to show that iconoclastic excesses were incidental, not characteristic. He must present a type of theology congenial to non-German religious thought. Such a leader it was to find for the first time in Calvin. That the intellectually and politically divided forces opposed to Rome, or to Roman abuses, not merely in France, but ultimately in Switzerland, the Netherlands, Scotland, and to a large degree in England, also, were knit into spiritual unity; that the theology of the Reformation was given an interpretation congenial to the non-German mind; and that a great type of ecclesiastical independence characteristic of Romanism, but forfeited by most of the reformers, was preserved, and combined with a lay participation in church government unknown to the Latin Church, were to be the results of his work.

2

CHILDHOOD AND EARLY STUDENT DAYS, 1509–1527

The venerable episcopal city of Noyon lies on the little river Verse, about a mile above the entrance of that short-coursed tributary into the much larger Oise, and some fifty-eight miles to the north-northeast of Paris. Its situation is one of no marked strength to resist military attack under the conditions of mediaeval and even of sixteenth-century warfare, but its chief natural advantage has always been the great fertility of the surrounding soil. Never a place of large population,[1] it has yet had a distinctive character. First known as a station on the Roman road from Reims to Amiens,[2] probably in the fourth century of our era, it gained ecclesiastical distinction when, about the year 531, St Médard transferred his see thither from the town which was afterwards to be known as Saint-Quentin, and inaugurated a succession of bishops that continued at Noyon till the French Revolution brought it to an end. The significance of the city in the eighth century is attested by the coronation there in 768 of Charlemagne as joint king of the Franks, and it is almost certain that Noyon beheld the similar consecration to royal office of Hugh, the first sovereign of the Capetian line, in 987. The political developments of the twelfth century brought about the comparatively peaceful

---

[1] At present 7,443 inhabitants.

[2] Many of the facts in this paragraph are due to Abel Lefranc's *Histoire de la vile de Noyon*, Paris, 1887, and to Doumergue's *Jean Calvin*, vol. i.

organization of its citizens into a commune in 1108 or 1109, but by the end of the next century the power thus obtained had largely slipped from the grasp of the burghers, and authority had either been regained by the ecclesiastics or passed into the hands of officers representing the rapidly growing might of the King. The commune persisted in name, however, and in the time of Calvin still chose burghers to its fellowship and elected a mayor and councilors, to whom some vestiges of authority still clung.

In the early years of the sixteenth century, as throughout the Middle Ages, Noyon presented the aspect of a very clerical town. The absence of any considerable trade or manufacture, which then even more than now marked the little city, left the field the more open for the development of its ecclesiastical interests. The architectural evidences of this priestly dominance give a distinct quality to the appearance of Noyon even at the present day, when the bishopric that there had its see has ceased for more than a century, combines the strength of Romanesque architecture with some of the graces of the Gothic style which was then just developing in the region. It yet stands a witness to the zeal and sacrifice of those who erected it. But, besides this imposing monument of mediaeval piety, Noyon still preserves a graceful thirteenth-century chapter-house wherein the canons of the cathedral once transacted their business, while the library, of sixteenth-century construction, and still remaining fragments of the bishop's house, attest the now vanished dignity of its prelates. That secular rights were not utterly forgotten is evidenced by the quaint Renaissance City Hall, built in 1486, and on which, as upon the other structures of which mention has been made, Calvin's eyes must often have rested.

In the sixteenth century Noyon's most conspicuous resident was its bishop, by office one of the twelve peers of France, and in his dual capacity as count and spiritual lord the largest landed proprietor of the region. The occupant of this honored post from 1501 to 1525, and therefore during Calvin's boyhood, was Charles de Hangest,[3] sprung from a family eminent among the nobles of

---

[3] On the family of Hangest see A. Lefranc, *La jeunesse de Calvin*, Paris, 1888, p. 186; and Doumergue, i. 536.

Picardy. His successor was his nephew, Jean, whose episcopate of fifty-two years extended beyond Calvin's death, and whose stormy nature involved him in quarrels with his Chapter over so trifling a matter as his right to wear a beard, while his indifference to the religious questions of the day laid his soundness in the faith open to Rivalries were, indeed, far from uncommon between the bishops at Noyon and the fifty-seven canons who constituted its assertive and tenacious Chapter – a body possessed of much landed property and ancient rights, and able to contend for its claims oftentimes on equal and sometimes on superior terms. And besides these two ecclesiastical powers that centered round the cathedral, Noyon was marked by its parish churches, its well-endowed monastic establishments, and other abundant evidences of the presence and importance of churchly interests. Education, moreover, had been remembered and Noyon possessed an ancient school founded by Canon Robert LeFèvre in 1294,[5] of which Calvin was himself to be a pupil, nicknamed that of the *Capettes*, from the dress which distinguished its beneficiaries. Altogether, judged by sixteenth-century standards, Noyon must have been a pleasant place in which to live for those in the service of the Church or laymen not dependent on a trade. It had its own local interests and debates, besides the questions that forced their way in from the great world outside. Its proportion of men of some education and of assured position must have been large. Even if its controversies were often petty, they must have stimulated intelligence.

Geographically, Noyon belonged to Picardy, and its inhabitants exhibited the characteristics of the Picard race. Eager, controversial even to fanaticism, enthusiastic, dogmatic and persistent, they have fought on all sides in the controversies by which France has been divided, but have never been lukewarm or indifferent. They are capable of producing men of leadership and ready to carry principles to logical consequences. A territory that has given birth to Peter the Hermit, the philosophers Roscelin and Ramus, and the revolutionists Desmoulins and Baboeuf, to mention no others,

[4] Doumergue, i.18

[5] Lefranc, *Jeunesse*, p. 12.

was a land where the reformatory ideas of the early sixteenth century could not fail to find response,[6] and Picardy contributed significant names, besides that of Calvin, to the list of French religious reformers. Le Fèvre, Olivétan, Roussel and Vatable were among its sons. It was then true, as an eleventh-century bishop of Noyon[7] had declared of the land in his day, that it was a "country fertile in warriors and in servants of God."

The family from which Calvin was to come was one rising in worldly success and in the social scale during the closing years of the fifteenth century. Its roots did not run back to Noyon itself, but to the little neighboring village of Pont-l'Évêque, where the Cauvins – for so they spoke the name – had long had their home, and whence they went forth to the exercise of their ancestral occupation as boatmen on the Oise.[8] Calvin's grandfather, whose Christian name seems not to have been preserved, is said to have added the cooper's trade to that of riverman;[9] or possibly he may have undertaken the more sedentary occupation when years counseled a life of less exposure than that on the water. But his sons, of whom it seems uncertain whether there were two or three,[10] were all ambitious of a larger place in the world, or at least of membership in a more populous community, than their father had enjoyed. One of these sons, Richard, and a second, also Jacques, if there were really three of them, found a home in Paris and there followed the iron-worker's trade.[11] The remaining son, Gérard, whose story most concerns us, established himself in Noyon before 1481[12] as a man of professional employment rather than as a

---

[6] Compare Lefranc, *Jeunesse*, pp. 23–25; Doumergue, i. 4.

[7] Rathobod II, bishop 1068–1098; see Lefranc, *Hist. De la ville de Noyon*, 27.

[8] The facts have been gathered by Lefranc and Doumergue.

[9] So Le Vasseur, *Annales de l'église de Noyon*, Paris, 1633; Doumergue, i. 5.

[10] The matter is discussed by Doumergue, i. 6, 7. It seems more probable that Richard and Jacques were son and grandson of the cooper-boatman of Pont-l'Évêque, rather than both sons.

[11] See a geneology of Calvin from the Dupuy Collection, in the National Library at Paris, in Henry, *Das Leben Johann Calvins*, Hamburg, 1835–1844, iii. 174.

[12] His name first appears in a legal document of September 20, 1481, Le Vasseur, p. 1170; Lefranc, *Jeunesse*, p. 2.

manual laborer like his ancestors and brothers. Here his skill in legal and administrative business soon won him standing, and to the post of one of the registrars of the government of Noyon which he had attained by 1481 he added gradually the duties and emoluments of solicitor in the ecclesiastical court, fiscal agent of the county, secretary of the bishopric, and attorney of the Cathedral Chapter. By 1497 he was reckoned sufficiently one of the leaders of the Noyon community to be admitted a member of its somewhat exclusive *bourgeoisie* and thus given a political stake in the city. We may readily credit the statement of Beza[13] that he was a man of judgment and ability, and he must also have been of attractive personal qualities for he won the friendship of that powerful family of Hangest which was the most influential noble house of the region, and which gave two bishops in Gérard Cauvin's lifetime to the Noyon diocese. This friendship, in turn, may well have helped his early rise; and as the quarrel between the Chapter and the younger of these prelates waxed fierce, may have been no inconsiderable source of the troubles of his later years.[14]

Here at Noyon, at some uncertain date, but not improbably about the time of his admission to the *bourgeoisie*, Gérard Cauvin married Jeanne Le Franc, the daughter of a well-to-do retired innkeeper, Jean Le Franc, who, having prospered in business in Cambrai had settled at Noyon, and was received into its *bourgeoisie* in 1498, where he soon attained the distinction of membership in the city council.[15] Of the mother of the future reformer little is known. In spite of attempted, and wholly baseless, detraction by later religious partisanship, she seems to have been a woman marked by earnest piety of the Roman type, and she lived in local tradition as possessed of unusual beauty. Her influence on the training of her children was brief, however, for she died before

---

[13] *Life*, in *Opera*, xxi. 121.
[14] A suggestion due to Principal A. M. Fairbairn, *The Cambridge Modern History*, ii. 350.
[15] The facts regarding the Le Francs have been investigated by Abel Lefranc, *Jeunesse*, pp. 5–7.

any of them reached maturity, though the year is not known. Her husband married again, but the personality of this stepmother of the reformer is yet more shadowy than that of his mother. It is probable that she died before Gérard Cauvin, and even the name of this second wife has perished.[16]

Gérard Cauvin and his wife, Jeanne, lived in a comfortable house on the lively Place au Blé, where the dwelling of the Le Francs, from which the bride had come, was also situated. Though the greater part of this home of the Cauvins has long since been replaced by other structures, it seems probable that an inner portion still remains, so that it is quite possible that the room in which the future reformer first opened his eyes on the world may yet be seen by the visitor to Noyon.[17] Within its walls, five sons, apparently, were born to Gérard and Jeanne Cauvin,[18] three of whom grew to maturity. Antoine and François died in childhood. Charles, the eldest of the sons who reached manhood, ran his brief career in priestly orders at Noyon and in its vicinity to its tragic end in 1537, as there will be occasion to note. The youngest son to grow up to man's estate, who was also the second who bore the name Antoine, was to accompany his brother, John, to Geneva, and was to live there, a respected citizen, in spite of much distress caused to him and to his relatives by the scandalous conduct of his first wife, till his death, February 2, 1572. Besides these sons, Gérard Cauvin had two daughters, both apparently by his second

---

[16] Le Vasseur, p. 1152. There is no mention of her in the probate proceedings after the death of her husband given, ibid., p. 1169, and quoted by Lefranc, pp. 201–203. She was a widow when she married Gérard Cauvin.

[17] Lefranc, in *Le bulletin de la société de l'histoire du protestantisme francais*, for 1897, pp. 371–376; Doumergue, i. 9. It is known as the "Maison de Calvin."

[18] Nicolas Colladon, in his *Life of Calvin* (1565), *Opera*, xx. 53, gives to Calvin four brothers. As the name "Antoine" is ascribed to two of them, one then living and another dead in childhood, many have seen in this repetition a confusion on Colladon's part, and have reckoned Calvin's brothers as three instead of four, e.g. Lefranc, *Jeunesse*, p. 7; Doumergue, i. 22; but there is nothing uncommon in the repetition of a beloved name, the first bearer of which had been removed by death, and therefore no real ground to doubt Colladon's accuracy.

wife, and therefore John's half sisters. One of them, Marie, like her brothers John and Antoine, ultimately made her home in Geneva, where it would seem she married. The other half sister, whose name is unknown, became the wife of a resident of Noyon.[19]

John Calvin, to give the familiar anglicized form of his name, was the second of the sons of Gérard Cauvin and Jeanne Le Franc to grow to maturity.[20] Born on July 10, 1509, he was taken for baptism, doubtless speedily thereafter, to the little church of Sainte-Godeberte, to the parish of which his parents belonged and which then stood in the Place au Blé opposite the Cauvins' home. Here he had as godfather Jean de Vatines, one of the canons of the Noyon cathedral, and it is possible that he received his Christian name out of compliment to this sponsor whose place in the little episcopal city was undoubtedly one of dignity. Of the events of his boyhood only scanty memorials have been preserved. Gérard Cauvin was ambitious for his sons. He was determined that they should have the best education that was in his power to obtain for them; therefore, Charles, the eldest of the boys, was sent by his father to the endowed school known as that of the

---

[19] John Calvin, in his will of April 25, 1564, left a bequest to "Jeanne, daughter of Charles Costan and of my half-sister on the paternal side"; French version, *Opera*, xx. 300. The Latin version, ibid., xxi. 163, is less definite, calling her simply *affinis*; but the French is earlier and was printed by Beza in the year of Calvin's death. The reference to "Maria Paludana," in Calvin's letter of January 18, 1532, in which Herminjard (*Correspondance des reformateurs*, ii. 397) saw a Latinized form of the name of a supposed husband, is probably not to her. Marie was more probably unmarried when she came to Geneva with Calvin in 1536 and her marriage to Charles Costan was probably during Calvin's first stay in the city, though of this nothing is certainly known. See Doumergue, iii. 676–679. For the nameless sister see Lefranc, pp. 8, 183. That both were half sisters is made probable by the absence of mention of them in the legal proceedings instituted by Charles, John and Antoine Calvin regarding the disposition of the property of their late mother. Ibid., pp. 202, 205; Doumergue, iii. 678. That Calvin had a sister Catherine who became the wife of William Whittingham, Dean of Durham, as often alleged, is an error. Doumergue, iii. 666–675.

[20] According to the genealogy from the Dupuy Collection, Henry, iii. 174, John was the third son. All other authorities place him second. See Lefranc, p. 8.

Capettes, of which mention has already been made. Thither John and Antoine followed him in due course, and though his later fame may have colored the tradition, one can readily believe that the impression which existed two or three generations later was correct, that even here John Calvin manifested so eager a spirit and so retentive a memory as to give him an easy superiority over his youthful schoolfellows.[21]

Quite as influential in the development of the boy's life as this instruction in the schoolroom of the *Capettes* were the friendships which he formed with his contemporaries among the sons of the noble family of Hangest, notably with those of Louis de Hangest, lord of Montmor, and of his brother, Adrien, Lord of Genlis.[22] To Claude, son of the nobleman last named, Calvin was years later to dedicate his first book, when Claude had become abbot of Saint-Éloi at Noyon. With Joachim and Ives, and a brother of theirs whose name is now lost, sons of the seigneur of Montmor, Calvin stood in intimate school fellowship; and his relations to these households of Montmor and Genlis seem, indeed, to have been much closer than merely those of the schoolroom. To Claude he could later gratefully describe himself as "a child brought up in your house, initiated with you into the same studies."[23] Such an association was doubtless in large part a result of the high estimate in which Calvin's father was held by the family of Hangest, but not wholly so, for neither of John's brothers seems to have enjoyed this friendship in a similar degree, so that some share in its growth must be ascribed to the attractive qualities of the boy himself. Yet it was as no dependent on the bounty of those higher in station that Gérard Cauvin encouraged or the boy fostered a relationship which the early death of his mother may have rendered even more homelike and attractive. His education,

---

[21] So Papire Masson, writing about 1583, *Elogia*, Paris, 1638, ii. 409; and Jacques Desmay, between 1614 and 1621, *Remarqués considerables sur la vie et moeurs de Jean Calvin*, Rouen, 1621. See, also, Doumergue, i. 35.

[22] On the members of this family see Lefranc, *Jeunesse*, p. 186; and Doumergue, i. 536.

[23] *De Clementia*, in *Opera*, v. 8.

as Beza definitely affirms, was at his father's charges;[24] and he never forgot the relative simplicity of his own origins, describing himself in the dedication from which quotation has just been made as "a man of the people," in contrast to the noble house whose friendship he enjoyed. Of the value of that friendship to the future reformer there can be no question. It probably determined his father to send him to the University of Paris, and it certainly gave to Calvin an acquaintance with the ways of polite society such as few of the reformers enjoyed, in an age when the gulf between the manners of those in high station and of the mass of the people was far greater than at present.

Though Gérard Cauvin was too independent by nature to permit his sons to solicit the gifts of friendly noblemen, he had no hesitation in employing his influence with the bishop and Chapter of Noyon to procure for them appointments to lucrative ecclesiastical positions as a means of aiding their studies. This was a not infrequent practice, and conveyed to the popular mind little of the impression of an abuse that would now attach to it, when it is remembered that the youthful recipients of office were not themselves of age or position to discharge the duties thus nominally assumed, but were compelled to have the actual service performed by those in clerical office and of maturer years who would be willing to undertake the labor for a fraction of the stipend. Gérard Cauvin first procured this means of support for his eldest son. On February 24, 1519, Charles was put in possession of a chaplaincy attached to the altar of *La Gésine* in the cathedral of Noyon – a charge which he exchanged in November, 1520, for a similar post in the same church. May 19, 1521, saw the same office which Charles Cauvin had received two years before bestowed on his brother, John, who still lacked nearly two months of having reached 12 years of age when thus given an ecclesiastical charge. He doubtless received the tonsure – the only sign of membership in a clerical order which Calvin ever attained in the Roman Church – but there could be no question of ordination of the youthful incumbent, whose connection with

---

[24] *Life*, of 1575, in *Opera*, xxi. 121.

the office was purely financial. Chief of the revenues which it brought its schoolboy holder were taxes in grain, payable by the neighboring territories of Voienne and of Eppeville (Espeville). To this benefice in the Noyon cathedral John Calvin added, on September 27, 1527, the pastorate of Saint-Martin de Martheville– a curacy which he exchanged on June 5, 1529, probably for family and pecuniary reasons, for that of Pont-l'Évêque, the ancestral home of the Cauvins. His claim on the altar of *La Gésine* John relinquished, on April 30th, of the year last mentioned, in favor of his younger brother, Antoine, but resumed it again not quite two years later, on February 26, 1531.[25] In this matter all three brothers received similar advantages, Charles becoming pastor at Roupy in 1527, and Antoine at Tournerolle about two years later. With the income thus provided, John Calvin and his brothers were enabled to carry on their studies and make their start in life.

This wish to do the best possible for the education of his children doubtless was the prime moving cause that induced Gérard to send John to the University of Paris in August 1523, when the boy had just passed his fourteenth birthday. But certain special considerations made the parental decision easy at the time. The plague was raging in Noyon,[26] rendering that city an unsafe place of residence. His three friends of the house of Montmor were going to the University under the charge of a tutor, whose instruction and guidance, all insufficient as it proved,[27] he could share. The residence of an uncle, Richard, gave the boy the certainty of friendly supervision during the trying beginnings of his student life. It may well have been agreeable to Gérard's independent spirit that his son, while enjoying the advantages of study and companionship with his noble friends, should not be in any way indebted to their father's bounty for his living, but should find a home with his uncle, near the church

---

[25] Extracts from the Registers of the Chapter are given by Lefranc, *Jeunesse*, pp. 194–201; see also ibid., pp. 9–12; and Doumergue, i. 37–39. On these dates see Karl Müller, *Calvins Bekehrung*, in the *Nachrichten von der königl. Gesellschaft der Wissenschaften zu Göttingen*, for 1905, pp. 220–222.

[26] Lefranc, *Jeunesse*, p. 13.

[27] Calvin calls him "*homo stolidus*," Letter to Cordier, *Opera*, xiii. 526.

of Saint-Germain l'Auxerrois, separate from that in which they were domiciled.

To the boy of fourteen, the transfer to Paris brought almost complete separation from the city in which his childhood had been spent. Thenceforward he was to be rarely and but for brief sojourns in Noyon; but his interest in the fortunes of the town and of its inhabitants always continued keen, and his relations to the friends who still lived there show the depth and permanency of his affection for the city of his nativity.

The University of Paris, in which Calvin now became a student, had long been reputed, as has already been noted, the most eminent seat of learning in Europe. It had not maintained its ancient leadership in the world of thought. In the educational transition which the rise of the new learning was effecting, it had clung for the most part to the older methods which humanism would revolutionise, and even these traditional conceptions of education were inefficiently applied. Doubtless the scorn of the humanists for its teaching, its prevailingly mediaeval Latinity, and its hair-splitting dialectics was not wholly deserved, but it had a very considerable basis of truth. Yet an institution that was, through one of its instructors, to develop Calvin's Latin style, and by its classrooms was to train his dialectic skill, cannot have been without strength even in its comparative decay. Though it prevailingly resisted the new learning, Calvin was to find a representative of that classic revival within its walls. In general, however, the intellectual outlook of the University of Paris was unquestionably mediaeval.

Judged by modern standards, the University was a seat of secondary as well as of higher instruction.[28] Its Faculty of Arts, under which the student began his course, was divided, according to the nativity of those under instruction, into the four "nations" of France, Germany, Normandy, and Picardy. Above this Faculty of Arts were the higher Faculties, or, as we should now say, graduate schools, of Theology, Law, and Medicine – that first named being of great strength, for Paris was primarily noted

---

[28] Doumergue has treated the University with great wealth of detail, i. 49–77.

as a seat of theology and philosophy, while the two latter were weak. These "nations" of the Faculty of Arts were administrative divisions – the work of the students being chiefly carried on in "colleges," in which a great portion of the student body also lived. These colleges in origin were charitable foundations to aid indigent scholars, but had extended by the time of Calvin to the University as a whole. In many of these colleges the life of the student was marked by an asceticism in food that now seems almost incredible,[29] while the filth, the severe hours of study and recitation, beginning at five in the morning, and extending with but four hours' intermission for food and play till eight in the evening, and the constant employment of corporal punishment, made his lot a hard one from the point of view of modern education. To a certain extent, as an out-student living in the home of an uncle, Calvin must have been protected from the temptations and spared the more trying physical experiences that then beset student life, and there is no evidence that he ever regarded his way as peculiarly difficult; but the path to knowledge must have been a painful one at best.

The preparation in Latin, already gained by Calvin at Noyon, was but a beginning, insufficient to enable him to enter any class higher than the fourth,[30] in which the rudiments of the language were studied. But here a piece of great good fortune awaited him. Though still, and for some time to come, under the direction of the unsatisfactory tutor who had guided him and his friends the Montmors, and had accompanied them to Paris, he now became a student in the comparatively inconspicuous Collège de la Marche, where Mathurin Cordier then served as one of the two "regents in grammar." Moreover, Cordier, who had been teaching the first, or most advanced, class with success, disgusted with the insufficiency of current grounding in Latin, had, in the year of Calvin's coming to Paris, taken up voluntarily the instruction of the comparative beginners of the fourth class.[31]

---

[29] Compare Doumergue, i. 68–73.

[30] *Opera*, xiii. 525.

[31] *Opera*, xiii. 525.

To be under Cordier's tuition was to enjoy the best introduction to the study of Latin that France had then to offer. About forty-four years of age when Calvin became his pupil, Cordier had been as a young man a priest in Rouen, of which region he was probably a native,[32] but for ten years he had taught at Paris. Convinced that the prime task of the teacher, especially of young scholars, is to arouse interest for study in pupils, he put aside, in large measure, the formal and arbitrary methods of instruction then generally in vogue. To make the language live in the thought of the pupil, rather than to fill the young student's mind with a mass of mechanically acquired detail, was his aim. That it should be accomplished, he devoted great attention to the acquisition of a correct and elegant conversational use of the ancient tongue. He strove to weed out current barbarisms, of which student usage afforded only too plentiful illustration. His kindly spirit, no less than his clear pedagogical insight, led him to oppose the constant use of the rod, and to urge the establishment of familiar and friendly relations between teacher and scholars, whose moral development, no less than whose intellectual training, the teacher, he held, should regard as a duty. Not a little of this kindliness of relationship to his young pupils by which Cordier effectually put into practice his enlightened ideas of education was the fruit of his simple, unaffected piety of heart.[33] A lovable as well as a very helpful man, he may well have aided in the religious, as he certainly did in the intellectual, development of the boy who now came under his moulding influence and found in him a teacher to admire and revere. Calvin always remembered with affection this instructor under whom he began his student days at Paris, and ascribed to Cordier his initiation into effective methods of study.[34] When, in turn, thirteen years later, Cordier found France dangerous ground for the Protestant sentiments which he had then embraced, he followed his former pupil to

---

[32] He was from Normandy or le Perche, Doumergue, i. 537.

[33] His ideas were set forth in his *De Corrupti Sermonis Emendatione*, of 1531; see, also, Doumergue, i. 60, 61.

[34] *Opera*, xiii. 525, 526.

Switzerland, was welcomed by Calvin, taught at Neuchâtel, lived in Geneva and died in the latter city in the same year as Calvin, at the advanced age of 85.

Calvin's stay at the Collège de la Marche, and consequent training under Cordier, was but for a few months at most. His studies were still regulated by the tutor who directed him and his three friends of the house of Hangest, and by what Calvin seems afterward to have regarded as the tutor's caprice he was transferred to the Collège de Montaigu.[35] It may have been true, however, that his father's intention that he should be fitted for a career in the Church, and the wishes of the canons of Noyon, by whose favor he held the benefices that defrayed the expenses of his student days, were factors in the decision, for Montaigu was a much more ecclesiastically flavored, as well as more noted, Collège than La Marche.[36] The Collège of which Calvin now became a member bore the name of Pierre de Montaigu, Bishop of Laon, by whom it had been reconstituted in 1388, seventy-four years after its foundation by Gilles Aiscelin, Archbishop of Rouen. But its fame in Calvin's day was primarily due to the work of Jean Standonch, by whom it had been brought to a flourishing condition, and given a series of rules of exceeding ascetic and scholastic strictness which were completed in the year of Calvin's birth.[37] Erasmus had been one of its scholars half a generation before Calvin entered its halls, and Ignatius Loyola was to follow immediately after Calvin's departure. Nor was the head of the Collège de Montaigu in Calvin's student days in any way unworthy of his fame. Its principal for many years had been Nöel Béda, a conservative theologian of power, the determined enemy of all modifications of Roman doctrine or usage. In 1521 he had led the onslaught on Le Fèvre which had resulted in the condemnation by the Sorbonne of that mild-tempered scholar's criticism of the current identification of Mary Magdalene with Mary, the sister of Lazarus, and with the woman "which was a sinner." Not content with this achievement,

---

[35] *Opera*, xiii. 526.

[36] Lefranc, *Jeunesse*, pp. 63, 64, makes this suggestion.

[37] Félibien, *Histoire de Paris*, iii. 727–728; compare Doumergue, i. 66–73.

Béda, five years later, attacked Le Fèvre and Erasmus in print,[38] and showed the courage of convictions which were bringing upon him, by reason of their extremely reactionary character, the hostility of King Francis I, and at a later period (1533) were to lead to his exile from Paris. It was no weak or insignificant champion of mediaeval scholarship and theology that ruled the Collège de Montaigu while Calvin was numbered in its student body.

Calvin's immediate instruction in the classroom on his entrance into the Collège de Montaigu was from an unnamed learned Spaniard, the vehicle being of course the Latin tongue, for the use of French was not permitted in the Collège. So effectively did the work supplement that had already been begun under Cordier that Calvin soon surpassed those who had been his companions in the preliminary studies of grammar and rhetoric, and was promoted,[39] doubtless as the result of the successful passage of the examination then required, to what were regarded as the more important disciplines of philosophy and dialectics, which constituted the backbone of the course then pursued under the Faculty of Arts. Any calculation of the date of this event is, of course, conjectural; but if, as is probable, Calvin followed the philosophical course for the three years and a half then considered its normal length,[40] his promotion from grammatical studies would have occurred in the autumn of 1524, a little over a year after his entrance to the University. Such facility in the mastery of Latin reveals the young scholar as giving brilliant promise not merely of success in the usual student career of the University, but of conspicuous humanistic attainments as within his ultimate grasp. Of his course in the college little can be definitely affirmed. The institution was famous for its learned disputations, and there is every reason to believe not merely that Calvin's own powers of argument were developed and strengthened by these intellectual wrestling-matches, but that he soon came to excel in argumentative force as he had already in linguistic ability. The discipline thus undergone must have been

---

[38] Herminjard, i. 78, 402, 436.

[39] Beza, *Life*, of 1575, *Opera*, xxi. 121.

[40] Bulaeus, *Hist. Univ. Paris.*, v. 858–859.

of great value in training those keen powers of logical analysis
and constructive reasoning of which he was afterwards to make
remarkable use. Here at the Collège de Montaigu his course of
study continued till the close of 1527, or, more probably, the
opening weeks of 1528, when he would naturally attain the rank
of licentiate of arts. That he received this degree is not a matter of
record, but without it he could not have entered upon the higher
studies that he then immediately began.[40]

If it is impossible to recover many details of Calvin's early
student career, we are fortunately not in ignorance as to some of
the friendships he then continued or formed which throw some
light on his character at this critical period of his life.[41] With the
three boys of the Hangest family he had come to the University,
and the friendship begun in Noyon remained steadfast. There is no
evidence that any of them was conspicuous for scholarship, and
two of the three were to die early in the profession of arms,[42] but to
their cousin, the third of the group,[43] Calvin was warmly to dedicate
his first book, as has already been noted. A younger brother of the
two first mentioned was, years later, to throw in his lot with Calvin
at Geneva, and the family of Hangest was to contribute a number of
its representatives to the Protestant cause.

Besides these companions of his boyhood home, Calvin
became intimately acquainted at Paris, with the household of
Guillaume Cop,[44] first physician to the King and an eminent

---

[40] Herminjard, ii. 279, note. He is described as a "magister" in the records of
the Noyon Chapter of April 30, 1529, Lefranc, *Jeunesse*, p. 177.

[41] The subject is discussed by Lefranc, *Jeunesse*, pp. 67–71; Doumergue, i. 75–77;
and Fairbairn, *The Cambridge Modern History*, ii. 351.

[42] Joachim and Yves were killed at the storming of Saint-Pol in 1537. Lefranc,
ibid., p. 68.

[43] Claude, then abbot of Saint-Éloi at Noyon.

[44] Haag, *La France Protestante*, 2nd ed., iv. 615–617. Calvin's letter of June 27,
1531, to François Daniel, Herminjard, ii. 346, shows that his acquaintance
with the Cops did not begin with his second stay at Paris, and therefore
probably dates back to this undergraduate period. Müller (*Icalvins
Bekehrung, p. 203*) thinks that Nicolas Cop may have first met Calvin
in Orléans or Bourges, or the Cops and Calvin may have been brought
together by Wolmar.

member of the Faculty of Medicine. A Swiss from the liberal and humanistic city of Basel, Cop enjoyed the friendship of Erasmus and Reuchlin, and was not merely of high fame in his profession, but possessed of considerable interest in letters.[45] The elder two of Cop's four sons were perhaps too old to be well acquainted with the student from Noyon,[46] but to Nicolas, the third of these brothers, Calvin was attached by the closest ties of friendship. Four years Calvin's senior, and of such brilliant scholarly attainments that he received a professorship of philosophy in 1530 in the Collège Sainte-Barbe of the University, Nicolas Cop was to be associated with Calvin in the crisis of his own scholarly career, on terms of intimacy the exact extent of which there will be occasion later to examine. With the fourth of Guillaume Cop's sons, Michel, Calvin was almost as closely associated as with Nicolas; and this friend was later to follow Calvin to Geneva, and enter the Reformed pastorate. A further close acquaintance of Calvin's Parisian student days was one whom he may have met at Noyon while a schoolboy, Pierre Robert, who bore the scholastic nickname of Olivétan. Older by a few years than Calvin, he was not only a fellow townsman from Noyon, but the son of one who, like Gérard Cauvin, was a solicitor in the ecclesiastical court, and linked to Calvin by family relationship.[47] Of his later relations to Calvin's religious development there will be not a little to be said; but the fact of his friendship may now be noted in trying to form some picture of Calvin's circle at the University.

Besides the more intimate friends already mentioned, it is probable that Calvin's membership in that portion of the student body known as the "nation" of Picardy would bring him into

---

[45] Erasmus called him, in 1498, "*Musarum cultorem*," *Letters*, ed. Le Clerc, iii. 1, 26.

[46] This has been disputed, Herminjard, ii. 348; Doinel, *Bulletin* xxvi. 176; Doumergue, i. 75.

[47] Just what the relationship was it is impossible to say, but Beza and Colladon witness to the fact, *Opera*, xxi. 29, 54, 121. On him in general see Herminjard, ii. 451, v. 228, 280; Lefranc, *Jeunesse*, 28, 99–104; Doumergue, i. 117–125; Bonet-Maury in Hauck's *Relencyklopädie für prot. Theologie*, xiv. 363.

close touch with all students or instructors of prominence who regarded his native region as their home. But, as these relations are inferential rather than a matter of proof, it is easy to insist upon them too much.[48] It is evident, however, from such friendships as have been described, most, if not all, of which were now formed, that the young student at Paris must have been of more than ordinary attractiveness and charm. To win the regard of such a man as Cordier, to hold the affections of young noblemen like those of the house of Montmor-Hangest, who assuredly were under no obligation to continue a friendship had it proved irksome, above all to gain the goodwill of a family of distinguished station and scholarly eminence like that of Cop, bespeak unusual winsomeness in a student of relatively humble birth, with little save himself to offer. Nor is the quality of his friendships less illuminative as to his personal character. To attract a Cordier or the household of a Cop certainly indicates a nature attuned to the better and finer side of life. No student of low impulses, unrefined tastes, or of a misanthropic, uncompanionable disposition could have won the permanent regard or made the lasting impression that Calvin did upon those whose friendship it was an honor to possess.

Yet legend, reflecting it may be the severer traits of his later life, has ascribed to the student Calvin a censoriousness of judgment in his relations to his companions, and an unsociability of temper, that, if true, would paint for us a very different portrait of the young scholar whose experiences at the University of Paris have just been reviewed. A story, credited by Le Vasseur[49] to Calvin's brilliant renegade one-time friend and disciple, but afterward enemy and calumnist, François Baudoin (1520–1573), relates that his fellow students called him "the accusative case," because of his denunciatory spirit. It is unnecessary, however, to weight the question of Baudoin's degree of truthfulness, as the statement is

---

[48] Lefranc, ibid., pp. 68, 69, and Doumergue, i. 76, give the names of some into relations with whom he was probably brought.

[49] *Annales de l'Église de Noyon*, Paris, 1633, p. 1158; see also Kampschulte, *Johann Calvin*, i. 225; and Doumergue, i. 73–75.

not to be found in his own published controversy with Calvin, and has no real foundation. A degree of plausibility is given to it, it is true, by Beza's declaration regarding the friend whose biography he was writing that, as a student at Paris, Calvin was not merely very religious, but a strict censor of all vices among his associates (*severus omnium in suis sodalibus vitiorum censor*).[50] Student life, as is abundantly witnessed not merely by the satires of Rabelais, but by the sober letters of Erasmus and of many less distinguished scholars, was apt in that day to be lawless and vicious enough; and an earnest, religious and scholarly youth of refined tastes, such as Calvin was, could have had little sympathy with its cruder excesses. But that he was misanthropic, of unfriendly spirit, or was regarded by his associates with aversion, there is no adequate evidence. The facts point to an opposite conclusion; and he appears at the completion of his course under the Faculty of Arts, in his 19th year, a student of high personal character, great linguistic and dialectic promise and able to make and keep friends whose interest in him must have been primarily due to the attractive qualities of head and heart which he revealed to them. The report of his successes at the University must have pleased his old patrons, the canons of the cathedral at Noyon, for in September 1527, they added to his ecclesiastical holding the curacy of Saint-Martin de Martheville. The increase in his income was considerable, and the purpose which impelled the gift can have been naught else than a desire to aid a brilliant young fellow townsman in his studies, for the relations of Gérard Cauvin to the Chapter were already such that the benefice cannot have been given for the father's sake. Certainly the young student from Noyon was well treated by friends who had known him in his boyhood town and, in turn, must have possessed qualities which commanded their regard.

---

[50] *Opera*, xxi. 121.

3

Uncertainty as to His Work in Life, 1528–1533

The completion, late in 1527 or early in 1528, of what would now be called in America his undergraduate course under the Faculty of Arts, brought Calvin face to face with the question of his life-work and the consequent further direction of his studies. The time for technical preparation for a profession had come. His father had long intended him for the Church and had strongly desired that he should specialise in theology,[1] but his father now insisted with equal positiveness that he should turn to the study of law. It was an age in which those expert in legal knowledge and practice had become the chief recipients of important civil offices from the crown, and a successful lawyer was well-nigh certain of high distinction. The Church had long since ceased to be the path to royal favor that it had been in the Middle Ages. An ambitious father, and certainly Gérard Cauvin deserves so to be described, may well have regarded the law as offering the "surest road to wealth and honors."[2] Gérard Cauvin, though an officer of the Church, was concerned wholly with its secularities and in no sense a clergyman. Had he received a full legal education, such as his clever son might now enjoy, could he not have risen to yet higher "wealth and honors"?

---

[1] Calvin in Preface to *Commentary on the Psalms*, *Opera*, xxxi. 22; Colladon and Beza, *Lives*, *Opera*, xxi. 54, 121.

[2] Beza (ibid.), gives this as his reason; Calvin (*Opera* xxxi. 22), speaks only of wealth.

But whatever weight these considerations may have had with Gérard Cauvin, other reasons, of a more personal nature, seem to have had their share in affecting his decision so radically to alter his son's prospective career. His own relations to the Chapter at Noyon had been rapidly changing for the worse.[3] The precise cause is difficult fully to define. It may have been pecuniary embarrassment leading to mishandling of trust funds which aroused the antagonism of the Chapter. His conduct in this respect was certainly irregular and blameworthy. But the case cannot have been very serious in the amount involved at least since his sons had, apparently, little difficulty in persuading the Chapter that they could adjust it after his death. One suspects that Gérard Cauvin and the Chapter had other grounds of quarrel than merely pecuniary questions, and that the matters of accounting were demanded and refused in a spirit of ill will on either side. If this was the case, the most probable explanation is to be sought in Gérard Cauvin's devotion to the family of Hangest. Charles de Hangest, who had held the bishopric of Noyon since 1501, was a man of high character, much practical insight and skill; but on his resignation in 1525, he was succeeded by his nephew, Jean de Hangest, older brother of Calvin's friend and fellow student, Claude. Jean was, indeed, too young to enter on the full duties of his office for several years, during which he traveled and studied. He was arbitrary, rather petty, and quarrelsome, to say nothing of suspicions entertained at a later time as to his orthodoxy and it was not long before his relations to the Chapter were strained. As an ardent supporter of the house from which the new bishop-elect sprang, Gérard Cauvin may have shared in his unpopularity with the Chapter. However, this may have been the records of the Chapter show that on June 27, 1527 Gérard Cauvin was ordered to make an accounting as executor of the estate of Nicolas Obry, a deceased chaplain of the cathedral at Noyon. This he failed to do and on May 15, 1528 he was again directed to make returns on this estate, as well as on that of Michel Courtin, who had held a

---

[3] The pertinent records are given by Lefranc, *Jeunesse*, pp. 196–199; see also ibid., pp. 15–22.

similar office. His refusal led to repeated action by the Chapter, and ultimately to his excommunication. He was under the ban at the time of his death, and it was only at the intercession of his sons that his body was allowed burial in holy ground. One thus in open quarrel with the ecclesiastical authorities of his city would certainly be disposed to see in some other profession than the service of the Church the best road of advancement for his son.

How the young student himself regarded the change of plans thus effected is a question not altogether easy to answer. His earliest biographers, Beza and Colladon, affirm that his mind had already been turned from scholastic theology and that he had begun to read the Scriptures and feel that the Roman worship was superstitious, thanks to the influence of his friend and relative, Pierre Robert Olivétan.[4] But Calvin's own statement regarding his entrance upon the study of law[5] implies that he did so in obedience to his father's wishes rather than from any desire of his own.

The decision that Calvin should study law led to a change of universities, for Paris had no teacher of jurisprudence worthy to be compared with Pierre Taisan de l'Estoile, the leading lawyer of France,[6] who had been an ornament of the Faculty of the University of Orléans since 1512 and was now forty-eight years of age. A man of strongly conservative opinions, of profound learning, and thorough Catholic orthodoxy, the death of his wife had led him into clerical orders, while continuing his professorship; and, in February 1528, just as Calvin was about to go to Orléans, he had been urgent in demanding repressive action against the rising Protestants at the Council of Sens.[7] The jealousy of the University of Paris, proud of its theologic eminence, had prevented the establishment of chairs of divinity at Orléans, with the result that law was there vigorously cultivated, no less than eight "doctors,"

---

[4] *Opera*, xxi. 29, 54, 121. The fact or the extent of the influence thus ascribed to Olivétan will be discussed in considering Calvin's conversion.

[5] *Opera*, xxxi. 22; see, also, Kampschulte, i. 226.

[6] Beza, *Opera*, xxi. 121, 122.

[7] Lefranc, *Jeunesse*, p. 72; Doumergue, i. 130.

of whom l'Estoile was by far the most noted, being charged with its exposition.

In sharp contrast to the clerical, and often ascetic, atmosphere of the University of Paris, such as had surrounded Calvin at the Collège de Montaigu, the University of Orléans had the repute of being a delightful and rather easygoing place of study.[8] Certainly this unascetic atmosphere, and the advanced character of his own studies, permitted Calvin to regulate his life more as he might wish than had been possible in the undergraduate days and under the severer discipline of the Collège de Montaigu at Paris. Yet if Calvin was now released from the stricter rules imposed on undergraduate life at Paris, he was strenuous far beyond what was wise in his employment of his own time. Nicolas Colladon recorded[9] in 1565 that those then living who had known Calvin at Orléans remembered that, after a very light supper, he often studied till midnight and then waking early in the morning would lie abed recalling and thinking over what he had learned the evening before. Undoubtedly, as Beza[10] as well as Colladon points out, these protracted vigils strengthened his remarkably retentive memory as well as greatly enlarged his erudition, but they also gave rise to dyspepsia[11] which ever after pursued him, and was the prime cause of the ill health of his later life. Brilliant as a student, his keen and ready powers of argument, his clearness of analysis and charm of diction won him distinction in debate, and his repute was speedily such that on several occasions he took the place of one or another of his instructors, who found themselves unable to meet their classes.

While thus winning reputation by his success in the study of law, Calvin found time, however, for the development of his knowledge of the classics. The humanistic spirit of the age strongly moved him. His intercourse with Cordier and the Cops at Paris must have served as a powerful antidote to the scholasticism of

---

[8] Lefranc (*Jeunesse*, p. 74), compares it to Heidelberg, Jena, or Göttingen.

[9] *Opera*, xxi. 55.

[10] Ibid., 122.

[11] "*Ventriculi imbecillitatem contraxit,*" says Beza, ibid.

Béda and the Collège de Montaigu. That interest in letters now probably attracted the friendship of one to whose stimulus Calvin was to owe much – Melchior Wolmar. A German by nativity, having been born in 1496 in Rothweil, a town of Württemberg, Wolmar had studied at Bern, Freiburg and Paris, where he was greatly distinguished, being first on the list of Licentiates of Arts.[12] His religious opinions which were, apparently, inclined to Lutheranism, made Paris an uncomfortable place to sojourn,[13] and he established a boys' boarding school in the freer atmosphere of Orléans, of which the nine-year-old Theodore Beza became one of the pupils in 1528. To Wolmar Calvin subsequently owed his initiation into Greek literature. His possible indebtedness to this kindly German teacher for his religious development will be discussed later in our story, but to Wolmar, no less than to Cordier, Calvin looked back with grateful recollection as to one who had been powerfully influential in his scholarly development.

Busied with the law course and continuing doubtless his studies in the field of letters, Calvin's days at Orléans can have left him little leisure. But even when thus burdened, he was no hermit. Though his intimate circle of acquaintances at Orléans seems to have been limited, a warm attachment united him to those friends whom he came to know at this epoch, François Daniel and François de Connam, fellow students, and a somewhat older young lawyer, Nicolas Duchemin, with whom he lodged during at least part of his stay at the University. Connam was from Paris, where his father was one of the Masters of the Chamber of Accounts. Daniel was a well-to-do native of Orléans, having two brothers and several sisters who formed a pleasant family circle into which Calvin was welcomed. To these friends Calvin's earliest surviving letters were addressed, and in them he expresses himself in terms of warmest affection.[14] His relations were evidently more than a common interest in the same studies, which was doubtless the connecting link with which the

---

[12] Herminjard, ii. 280, 281, note.

[13] Bulaeus, *Hist. Univ. Paris.*, vi. 963.

[14] E.g. *Opera*, xb. 3, 9–30.

acquaintances began; and though their separate walks in life, and the fact that these friends remained in the communion of the Roman Church led to the cessation of this correspondence after a few years, Calvin improved an opportunity to do a service to a son of François Daniel, as an occasion to renew the correspondence with the father, in 1559 and 1560, on the old friendly footing.[15]

Though Calvin thought highly of the instruction given by Pierre de l'Estoile, his interest was aroused by the reports that became current among the students at Orléans of the teaching given by the great Italian jurist Andrea Alciati (1492-1550), who had begun his work in the University at Bourges on April 29, 1529.[16] Just when he made his transfer thither is unknown, but the very probable suggestion has been made by one of his most recent biographers that the autumn of 1529 saw him matriculated at Bourges and in Alciati's classroom.[17] His friend Daniel made the same change of universities, and the satisfaction of his stay there was doubtless much enhanced when Wolmar removed thither, also late in 1530. The University of Bourges was a comparatively recent foundation, having been privileged in 1463 and 1464. It had greatly declined; but under the fostering care of Marguerite d'Angoulême, mistress of the duchy of Berry, of which Bourges was the capital, able teachers like Alciati and Wolmar were being induced to settle there, an atmosphere of considerable intellectual and religious freedom prevailed and the scholastic reputation of the University was rapidly rising. Alciati, in particular, was a real reformer in juridical science. Law was not for him; as for l'Estoile, a mere dry matter of arbitrary detail, it was capable of explication by great general principles, and of illumination by history and literature. In his teaching it became a science rather than a mere mass of knowledge. Such a training must have been of the highest value in supplementing the teaching which Calvin had received at Orléans. Yet, contrary to one's presuppositions as to what would have been the case, Calvin preferred the severely churchly and

---

[15] *Opera*, xvii. 585, 681, xviii. 16.
[16] *Opera*, xxi. 55, 122; Doumergue, i. 141–143.
[17] Doumergue, i. 141.

rather mediaeval instructor at Orléans to the brilliant innovating Italian at Bourges. In the controversy that sprang up between their partisans, his friend Duchemin published a defence of l'Estoile, and Calvin contributed to the volume a brief preface – his first writing to appear in print.[18]

Calvin's work seems to have gone forward at Bourges on the same lines as at Orléans, and he now began with Wolmar the study of Greek.[19] His time was still divided between the law and literature, and he regarded anything that took him from his studies with impatience. But an event of no little significance occurred in the spring of 1531. Calvin had been in Paris, probably during vacation, in March of that year, and had thence apparently gone to Noyon, either for a visit or summoned by bad news from home. From his native city he wrote to his friend Duchemin under the date of May 14th that he was detained by the illness of his father, which, though at first not hopeless, was now evidently fatal.[20] Twelve days later Gérard Cauvin's death occurred. The baldness with which he announces the news to his friend gives the reader a sense of shock. The contrast between the bare statement of his father's approaching mortality and his address to Duchemin as "my friend, dearer than my life," is striking. Yet it must be remembered, in partial explanation at least, that Calvin had seen little of his father since he left home, a boy of fourteen, nearly eight years before; and there can have been no very deep sympathy between the highly studious, sensitive, cultivated young lawyer and his ambitious, acquisitive, self-made father. Yet he owed a great debt to Gérard Cauvin, whose highest and

---

[18] Duchemin's work was written in 1529, and published in 1531 at Paris under the title *Antapologia adversus Aurelii Albucii Defensionem pro And. Alciato contra D. Petrum Stellam.* Calvin dated the Preface from Paris March 6 (1531), and saw the book through the press for his friend. The Preface is given in Herminjard, ii. 314–318; also *Opera*, ix. 785.

[19] Calvin's dedication of his *Commentary on II Corinthians* to Wolmar in 1546, *Opera*, xii. 364, 365, makes it evident that it was but a beginning. On the time see Beza, *Life*, of 1564, ibid., xxi. 29, 30; and Müller, *Calvins Bekehrung*, pp. 194, 201.

[20] *Opera*, xb. 8; Herminjard, ii. 332.

most unselfish desire seems to have been to secure for his sons advantages which he had not enjoyed.

The death of Calvin's father removed from him the parental pressure that had kept him to the study of law, but not till that course had been substantially, if not wholly, completed; for a legal document of February 14, 1532 describes him as *licentié ès loix*,[21] and this degree may have been obtained some months earlier. An obscure passage in a letter written by his friend François Daniel in the previous December implies that Daniel, at least, had hopes that Calvin might obtain some appointment befitting his legal talents from an unnamed bishop – probably his acquaintance, Jean de Hangest, Bishop of Noyon. But meanwhile, within a month of his father's death, Calvin had betaken himself to Paris and now devoted himself to the study of the classics with all the zeal of an eager disciple of the "new learning." Many reasons have been given for this change of the scene of his studies. It is certain that his pursuit of the law was due to his father's desires rather than to his own, and it has been suggested that he recoiled from public conflicts at the bar;[22] that he found no suitable opening as a lawyer;[23] or that he wanted to give himself to the solution of personal questions, primarily those of religion.[24] A sufficient reason may be seen, however, in his desire to avail himself of the revolution in teaching that had just taken place at Paris. Moved by Guillaume Budé and by Guillaume Cop, both earnest humanists, Francis I had appointed in March 1530, a group of "Royal Lecturers," to give instruction in Greek, Hebrew, and mathematics. This event, which, as has already been noted, is regarded as the foundation of the Collège de France,[25] was of capital significance in the history of French education. It was the triumph of the "new learning," which thus made a place for itself such as it had never before possessed in France. And who would

---

[21] Le Vasseur, *Annales*, p. 1169; Lefranc, *Jeunesse*, p. 202.

[22] Henri Lecoultre, in the *Revue de theologie et de philosophie*, Lausanne, for 1891, p. 53.

[23] A. Lang, *Die Bekehrung Johannes Calvins*, Leipzig, 1897, p. 8.

[24] Doumergue, i. 196.

[25] *Ante*, p. 7.

be more willing to avail himself of the privileges thus offered by the royal bounty than a student whose interest in Latin had been awakened by a Cordier, and who had found time amid the exactions of a course in law to pursue Greek with a Wolmar?

At Paris Calvin now lodged in the Collège Fortet, opposite his familiar Collège de Montaigu.[26] Under the guidance of the marvelously widely read "Royal Lecturer," Pierre Danès, he pursued eagerly the study of Greek, and with Danès' colleague, François Vatable, he began that of Hebrew.[27] Engaged in congenial studies, his life in Paris must have been very pleasant, in spite of the ill health from which he occasionally suffered. He was in constant communication with Duchemin and Daniel, and saw them from time to time in the city. His younger brother, Antoine, was a resident of Paris. With Nicolas Cop he had a warm friendship. It was an agreeable and relatively large circle of young humanists and jurists of which Calvin now made a part. But, while Calvin thus rejoiced in a circle of friends so considerable that the mere visits of greeting filled four days on his arrival in Paris,[28] his nature was sensitive and exacting, and he seems to have been quick to feel any real or fancied want of friendliness on the part of those dear to him.[29] Yet, aside from these occasional slight lacerations of a somewhat demanding friendship, and the limitations due to his uncertain health, Calvin's chief worry in this relatively unburdened portion of his life must have been caused by the affairs of his older brother, Charles, who had remained at Noyon. So negligently did Charles discharge his duties as Calvin's business representative in the collection of income due from the Parisian students' ecclesiastical holdings, and in the settlement of their father's estate, that Calvin, on one occasion at least, had to borrow from Duchemin[30] – a thing evidently galling to his pride to do.

---

[26] Lefranc, *Jeunesse*, p. 89.

[27] Doumergue, i. 205; A. J. Baumgartner, *Calvin hébraïsant*, Paris, 1889, p. 14.

[28] *Opera*, xb. 9.

[29] See Lefranc, *Jeunesse*, pp. 95, 96; *Opera*, xb. 11, 13, 21, 26, etc.

[30] *Opera*, xb. 17.

Charles' financial slowness was a lesser cause of anxiety, it may be believed, than the difficulties into which he fell with the Chapter at Noyon, which began before the death of Gérard Cauvin, and continued in growing aggravation till his own decease.[31] The cause seems at first to have involved no question of religious opinion. Excited, it may be, by the discussions arising from his father's quarrel with the Chapter, though of this there is no definite proof, he had a personal encounter with Antoine Tourneur, a beadle of the Noyon cathedral, regarding which event the Chapter ordered an investigation on February 11, 1531. Only two days later he was again under discipline for having struck one of the clergy. By this act the quick-tempered young man incurred excommunication; this was his condition when his father died, also excommunicate. Apparently he made no attempt to remedy it, but treated the Chapter with contempt, procuring ordination to the sub-diaconate in spite of his want of ecclesiastical standing. On September 15, 1531, when his brother John had been in Paris engaged in humanistic studies for about three months, Charles was forbidden entrance to the cathedral by the Chapter, with which he continued in full quarrel. So the matter remained during the rest of John Calvin's student days, but in May 1534, a month of great importance in the younger brother's life, as there will be occasion to see, Charles was accused of a heretical opinion, regarding which such secrecy was observed that it is impossible to say how far his revolt against the Roman Church may have gone. In its maintenance Charles persisted; and at his death, October 31, 1537, he refused the Roman Sacraments and was, in consequence, buried beneath the gallows at Noyon. Charles Cauvin's "heresy" did not manifest itself till after his brother had broken with the Roman Church; it was quite as probably due to John's influence over him as in any way a cause of John's adhesion to Protestantism. He seems to have been of coarser fibre than his more famous brother. He had none of John Calvin's capacity for

---

[31] The matter has been discussed by Lefranc, *Jeunesse*, pp. 18–21, 197–201, 210, where extracts from the registers are given. Doumergue, i. 22–25. On the dates, see Müller, *Calvins Bekehrung*, pp. 220–223.

leadership. And his earlier, and more personal, quarrels with the Noyon Chapter, which occurred while John was still a student, show the contentious rivalries of administrative jealousy in a small city, or at most a filial participation in his father's quarrel, rather than the presence of deep religious conviction such as was to lead John Calvin to his break with Rome.

During these months at Paris in the latter half of 1531 and the beginning of 1532, Calvin had not only been studying Greek and Hebrew under Danès and Vatable, he had been hard at work upon his first book – his *Commentary on Seneca's Treatise on Clemency*.[32] Calvin's attention seems to have been called to the theme by Erasmus' edition of Seneca's works, published in 1529, in which the great humanist has expressed a critical and, as it seemed to Calvin, a too disparaging judgment of the Roman Stoic philosopher.[33] All the eagerness of a young scholar's enthusiasm – the author was not yet twenty-three – went out to it, as it came from the press in April 1532. The expense, which he had paid from his own pocket, had been a heavy draft upon his means, and he sought the good offices of his friends to secure the distribution of copies in influential quarters, and to let him know its reception.[34] The impression upon the scholarly world which his volume might make was to him a matter of great, and natural, concern. Calvin's *Commentary* is a work of 156 pages in quarto. Beginning with the dedication to his boyhood companion and student friend, Claude de Hangest, to which reference has already been made, there follows a short life of Seneca, "compiled from good authors," and then a series of brief chapters, each having at its head a consecutive section of the text of Seneca's essay, but being made up chiefly of notes on the passage quoted. These comments are of all kinds: explanatory, historical, critical, exegetical, but

[32] It bore the title of *L. Annei Senecae, Romani Senatoris, ac Philosophi Clarissimi, Libri duo de Clementia, ad Neronem Caesarem: Joannis Calvini Noviodunaei Commentariis Illustrati*. Paris, 1532. It is printed in *Opera*, v. 1–162.

[33] *Opera*, v. 6, 7. Henri Lecoultre has a very valuable discussion of the whole work, *Revue de théol. Et de philos.*, Lausanne, 1891, pp. 57–77.

[34] *Opera*, xb. 19–22.

chiefly philological and philosophical, and illustrative by constant quotation of the linguistic usage of the Roman philosopher. From the point of view of scholarship the young author had nothing to fear. Written in a Latin style of singular clarity and brilliancy, with not a little of the lawyer's sense for lucid presentation and cogent argument, his book showed a range of reading almost marvelous in a man of Calvin's years. This impression of precocity is but intensified when it is remembered how comparatively recently he had begun the study of Greek. The text is illuminated by citations from fifty-six Latin and twenty-two Greek classical writers, seven Fathers of the Church, and the humanists of his own age.[35] Many of these references are to a number of works by the same author, for instance to thirty-three of the orations, treatises, and letters of Cicero, or to five of the plays of Terence. Certainly those long hours of study and reflection at Orléans and Bourges, and of work under the "Royal Lecturers" at Paris, had had their abundant fruitage in the erudition of which the young humanist revealed himself so easily the master. Nor is the work less remarkable for its maturity and poise of judgment. There is in it almost no suggestion of a youthful effort. Perhaps an exception is to be seen in a slap at his former teacher, Alciati,[36] whom he and his friend Duchemin had criticized; but the opinions expressed are, almost universally, those of one who seems to have thought long and wisely.

Conspicuous throughout the volume are Calvin's high sense of moral values, and conception of the sinfulness of conduct not in accordance with them. His sympathies are drawn to the Roman writer who laid such stress on moral action. It is because Seneca is so conscious of the importance of right ethical principles in human life that Calvin is attracted to him. Clemency and justice, he holds, are virtues of the first order; and, however exalted the prince or magistrate, it is only as he illustrates them in his conduct that he proves himself the friend and not the enemy of

---

[35] Lecoultre, op. cit., pp. 76, 77, gives an approximately full list, and remarks (p. 59), "*c'est en effet un puits d'érudition.*"

[36] *Opera*, v. 146.

those whom he judges or rules. Moreover, with all his sympathy for Seneca, Calvin has sufficient independence sharply to criticise the Stoic philosophy. He finds its insensibility abhorrent to the general sentiment of mankind. It is human, he declares, to be affected by grief, to feel, to resist, to receive consolations, to shed tears. The individual isolation of Stoicism he dislikes. Even to follow conscience is not sufficient, if such following leads a man to neglect the good name and welfare of his neighbor – a doctrine which Calvin declares to be the teaching of "our religion," that is, of Christianity. Here, then, is the treatise of one who knows and admires the world of classical antiquity, but who feels the compelling force of moral law, is desirous to apply it to his own age, and is convinced that union and mutual dutifulness, not isolation, even that of individualistic philosophic rectitude, are the proper conditions of mankind.

Did Calvin have any purpose in writing this remarkable treatise beyond that of illuminating an author who, he felt, had not been rightly appreciated, and winning for himself, in so doing, an honorable name in the world of scholarship? From the time that Papire Masson wrote his sketch of Calvin (about 1583)[37] to the present there have been those who have asserted that a further purpose was to move Francis I to a more kindly treatment of his Protestant subjects. This is the view of Henry,[38] and, in a modified form, of Domergue.[39] On the other hand, Kampschulte,[40] the Strassburg editors of Calvin's works,[41] Lecoultre,[42] and Fairbairn,[43] see in it no evidence of any such ulterior or disguised purpose. In that conclusion the writer must agree. Had it not been for Calvin's later history no one would probably have seen in this noble *Commentary* more than the work of an unusually high-minded, ethically strenuous humanist. Nor would one have looked

---

[37] *Elogiorum*, pars secunda, Paris, 1638, p. 403; Doumergue, i. 214, 529.

[38] *Das Leben Johann Calvins*, i.52–55.

[39] I. 215, 216.

[40] I. 238.

[41] *Opera*, v. xxxii.

[42] Op. cit., p. 72.

[43] *The Cambridge Modern History*, ii. 352.

upon its author as specially interested in religious problems. The Bible is cited but three times, and then in a relatively incidental manner. It may be too much to say, with one of the most careful of recent students, that Calvin then knew only the Vulgate;[44] but it is not unwarranted to affirm with him that the Bible had no such attraction for the youthful commentator on Seneca as was possessed by the great writers of classical antiquity. There is no impression that can be traced unmistakably to the burning religious controversies of the hour. If Calvin was interested in them at the time that he wrote this volume that interest does not appear in its pages.

Calvin's life during the months immediately following the publication of the *Commentary* just considered is difficult to trace in detail; but one or two features are fortunately made evident by letters and documents which have survived. The correspondence with his friend, Daniel, shows that in May 1532, Calvin was planning soon to make the journey to Orléans, and to bring with him a copy of the Bible – possibly Le Fèvre's translation, which had been printed at Antwerp late in 1530.[45] Had these letters been all the evidence, a stay at Orléans longer than a brief visit would hardly be conjectured. But documents in a legal action dated May 10 and June 11, 1533[46] show not merely that he was then at Orléans, but that he was holding the office of *Substitut Annuel de Procureur* for the nation of Picardy – one of the ten "nations" in which the students of the University of Orléans were organized, and composed, of course, of those from Calvin's native region of France. As annual representative of the Attorney, or, more properly, Dean, of the Picard students, Calvin presumably remained some months at Orléans, and as he was present at a meeting of the Cathedral Chapter at Noyon on August 23, 1533, when prayers were ordered

---

[44] A. Lang, *Die Bekehrung Johannes Calvins*, p. 29; but comp. Doumergue, i. 219.
[45] *Opera*, xb. 20–22; Herminjard, ii. 388, 418–421; *Hauck's Relencyklopädie für prot. Theologie*, iii. 130, 131.
[46] Doinel, *Le bulletin de la doc. de l'histoire du Prot. francais*, for 1877, pp. 174–179; Lefranc, *Jeunesse*, pp. 105, 203, 204.

on account of the plague,[47] and had settled once more in Paris by the following October,[48] the supposition seems well-nigh certain that he prolonged his stay and spent a year, from the early summer of 1532 to that of 1533, once more as a student at Orléans. It was probably further discipline in the law that attracted him; for the opportunities to continue his humanistic studies were much better at Paris. It has been suggested that he desired the degree of doctor; he may have wished to be with his friends Daniel and Duchemin, but all is conjecture. The only fact that can be confidently affirmed is that Calvin had not yet found his life-work, and some reasons why this discovery was not easy at this time will appear in the consideration of his conversion. The law and the path of classic scholarship he had tried successively and alternately. He had greatly distinguished himself in both, but he was not yet satisfied in his own mind. He had not yet come to peace with himself as to what his path in life should be.

It was while serving as a representative of the Picard students of the University of Orléans that Calvin became engaged in his official capacity in a curious lawsuit illustrative of surviving mediaeval conditions. A count of Beaugency, having recovered from a severe illness three-quarters of a century before Calvin's sojourn, had then attributed his cure to the favor of St Firmin, a missionary martyr of the seventh century, often called the "Apostle of Picardy." In recognition of the blessing received,[49] he had acknowledged himself the vassal of the saint for certain properties near Beaugency. Of the revenues thus pledged by the count, a portion came ultimately to be paid to the "nation" of Picards at Orléans, which held St Firmin in reverence as its patron. Payment was due annually on January 13, in the form of a *maille d'or de Florence*, that is a medal or specially struck coin of a fixed weight of gold, bearing the fleur-de-lis as well as an image of John the Baptist. It was of no great intrinsic value, but its reception was the occasion of a much-prized and

---

[47] Dionel, Lefranc, *Jeunesse*, p. 200.

[48] *Opera*, xb. 27–30.

[49] For the whole matter, see Bimbenet, *Mémoires de la Société des Antiquaires de Picardie*, x. 398–474; Lefranc, *Jeunesse*, 105, 106, 203, 204; Doumergue, i. 299–304.

rather Bacchanalian student festival in which Picardy was duly glorified with oratory and feasting. For some reason, payment was refused in January, 1533 and a legal action, which ultimately proved successful, was therefore begun by the Picard students before the Parlement of Paris, authority being given by successive meetings of the "nation" under Calvin's chairmanship. The expenses were in part paid by a tax on the students, but also in part by the sale of two silver vases which belonged to the "nation" and were not improbably used in the services of the Church of Nôtre-Dame des Bonnes-Nouvelles which it regarded as its headquarters. The full legal record of the authorisation of this sale still exists,[50] but an absurd and slanderous legend, after Calvin had become an object of attack, and was no longer living so that a reply was impossible from him, twisted this clear transaction into a story that he abused his position at Orléans to steal a silver chalice belonging to the Picard nation, in order to pay the personal expenses of a long journey.[51]

While other positive intimations of Calvin's life during the last half of 1532 and the first seven months of 1533 are lacking, save the important legal records just considered which show his presence and official position in the University of Orléans, a letter of Calvin's has been preserved, undated as to the year, but written, apparently from Noyon, on a September 4th, to the eminent German reformer, Martin Bucer (1491-1551) of Strassburg, commending to that theologian's favor a French refugee who "could no longer bow the neck to that voluntary bondage which even yet we bear."[52] This epistle was assigned to the year 1532 by Conrad Hubert in the sixteenth century, and this traditional date, which was followed by the older historians, was retained, though with much hesitation, by the Strassburg editors of Calvin's works. It has a recent though cautious defender in Professor Doumergue.[53] If this view is correct, we have not merely

---

[50] Doinel, *Bulletin*, etc., for 1877, p. 179; Lefranc, *Jeunesse*, p. 203.

[51] Jacques Desmay, *Remarques...sur la vie...de Jean Calvin*, published at Rouen, in 1621, reprinted in Cimber and Danjou's *Archives curieuses de l'histoire de France*, v. 393; Doumergue, i. 303.

[52] *Opera*, xb. 22–24.

[53] I. 297–299, 556.

an additional indication as to Calvin's whereabouts during the period in question, but what is vastly more important: clear proofs of his relations to the great Strassburg reformer, and of his own evangelical opinions, as early as September 1532. But weighty reasons serve to throw doubt on the correctness of this dating. The letter itself, as the Strassburg editors pointed out,[54] implies a previous intimacy, of which there is no proof if 1532 be the date; and its tone is strikingly, and one may say from the point of view of that age shockingly, familiar, if used by a youthful student toward a scholar of European reputation. Herminjard would, therefore, put it in 1534 or possibly 1533,[55] and Lefranc accepts the former date;[56] but whatever may be urged as possible in view of Olivétan's relations to Bucer, or Calvin's later indebtedness to Bucer's theological writings, it seems difficult to the present writer to avoid the conclusion reached by Lang, that while we cannot certainly fix the date of this letter as 1534, it must unquestionably be considerably later than 1532.[57]

When we next encounter Calvin after his presence in the meeting of the Chapter at Noyon, on August 23, 1533, of which mention has already been made, he is settled once more in Paris and is writing to his friend, François Daniel, at Orléans, under date of the 27th of the following October. Calvin had come to Paris at an interesting juncture. The year was one of hope in the history of the reformatory movement in France as none previous had been and none for a long time to come was to be. And of the hope Paris was the center. Under the kindly patronage of Marguerite d'Angoulême, who represented her brother, the King, in his long absence from the capital, the humanistic reformers of the school of Le Fèvre were in high favor, and their opponents had some reason to fear that this goodwill would lead to the countenancing of teachers of a much more radical policy.

---

[54] *Opera*, xb. 23.

[55] Herminjard, iii. 204; Doumergue, i. 557.

[56] *Jeunesse*, p. 46.

[57] *Die Bekehrung Johannes Calvins*, pp. 16, 17. Müller (*Calvins Bekehrung*, pp. 245–253) inclines to put it in 1538, or possibly from Nyon, on Lake Geneva, in 1537, 1542 or 1543–1547.

Calvin's letter[58] shows him deeply interested in the discussions of the capital, among which the religious questions of the hour had a large place. He is evidently on cordial terms with Gérard Roussel, the intimate disciple of Le Fèvre who, like his master, was never to break with the Roman Church outwardly, but who was far enough removed from its dominant spirit. Roussel, whom Marguerite d'Angoulême had long admired for his mystical piety and humanistic conceptions of reform, had been secured by that Queen and her husband, the King of Navarre, in the absence from Paris of Francis I, as Lenten preacher for 1533. His sermons had led to that outbreak of hostility on the part of the theologians of the University which King Francis had checked in May by banishing Beda and his associates, the representatives of an unbending Roman conservatism which the King was willing for the time being to oppose in the interest of fashionable humanistic learning.[59] Calvin could now speak of Roussel as "our G.[érard]," and circulate his writings confidentially.[60] It must have been with keen satisfaction that Calvin was able, in this letter, to refer to his friend Nicolas Cop as "now rector" of the University, an office to which Cop had been chosen only seventeen days before; and Calvin unquestionably shared the pleasure of his humanistic friends, Roussel and Cop, when, just as he was writing, the interference of the King had compelled the conservatives of the University to disavow any intention to condemn Marguerite d'Angoulême's *Le miroir de l'âme pécheresse.*[61]

---

[58] *Opera*, xb. 25–30. For the general situation see Bourrilly and Weiss, *Jean du Bellay, les Protestants et la Sorbonne*, in the *Bulletin*, lii. 193–231 (1903).

[59] Herminjard, iii. 54–61.

[60] *Opera*, xb. 26; Herminjard, iii. 105.

[61] An expression in Calvin's letter has given rise to much perplexity. He said, "*Visum est statui pessimum exemplum eorum libidini qui rebus novis inhiant,*" etc. (*Opera*, xb. 27). Those "who gape after new things" are regarded by Herminjard, Lecoultre, Stähelin, and Doumergue as the reformers. If so, it is hard to explain Calvin's remark in view of his evident sympathy with Roussel and Cop. Müller (*Calvins Bekehrung*, p. 198) interprets them more truly as a criticism of those who were "making trouble," i.e. of the conservatives by whom the reformers were opposed.

Five days after this letter, Cop pronounced his rectorial address in the Church of the Mathurins, using possibly, though hardly probably, the words of Calvin, and giving utterance to sentiments of an unmistakably evangelical character, drawn from Protestant sources.[62] With his friend Calvin undoubtedly sympathized. It is evident that by November 1, 1533, Calvin, whether in his own estimate a Protestant or merely an earnest humanistic reformer of the school of Le Fèvre, had come to religious convictions generally associated with Protestantism, and had been mastered by an interest in religion of which there is no evidence in his *Commentary on Seneca* or in his earlier correspondence. Whether he then knew it or not, and probably he had yet little conception of its significance, Calvin had found his life-work. This crisis properly challenges the questions of Calvin's religious development and of the nature of that transforming experience which he himself styled his "conversion."[63]

---

[62] This address will be considered in the next chapter.
[63] *Opera*, xxxi. 21.

4

Religious Development and Conversion, 1528–1533

In approaching the subject of the religious development and conversion of Calvin, a theme of much difficulty is encountered. Not that the final result is in any way obscure. No religious leader of the Reformation age stands more clearly defined than he in all the traits of the spiritual character of his maturer years. But the process by which Calvin passed from the status of a student supported by funds drawn from Roman ecclesiastical foundations, and reckoned as of the Roman clergy even if in no clerical orders, to that of a leader of Protestantism, is exceedingly difficult to follow in detail, partly by reason of Calvin's own reticence in regard to all that concerned his inward experiences, partly because his earliest biographers unintentionally, but none the less effectively, distorted the facts of his early religious life, and partly, also, in consequence of the varying interpretations which modern historians have placed on such scanty indications of the stages of his spiritual development as have survived. Nor are those who have recently treated of the matter at one as to what they understand by his "conversion." Is that to be regarded as implying simply his attainment of views now considered distinctive of Protestantism, or can nothing be properly given that name that does not involve a deliberate separation from the Roman communion? The answer given to this question makes not a little difference in the dating assigned to this crucial episode in Calvin's religious history.

Calvin's most distinct account of his spiritual development was written in middle life and occurs almost incidentally in the Preface to his noble *Commentary on the Psalms*, published in Latin in 1557 and in French the following year. It is at nearest almost a quarter of a century later than the experiences that it pictures. The struggles of the writers of the Psalms, especially of David, recall to him his own combats and induce him to compare his own trials with those of the Jewish poet-king:[1]

"It is true that my estate is much humbler and lower [than David's], and there is no need that I should stop to demonstrate the fact; but as he was taken from caring for beasts and raised to the sovereign rank of royal dignity, so God has advanced me from my humble and lowly beginnings so far as to call me to this most honorable office of minister and preacher of the Gospel. From the time that I was a young child, my father had intended me for Theology; but afterwards, because he perceived that the science of the Laws commonly enriches those who follow it, this hope caused him promptly to change his plan. That was the reason why I was withdrawn from the study of Philosophy, and why I was set to learning Law. Though I forced myself to engage faithfully in it in order to obey my father, God finally made me turn about in another direction by his secret providence.

And, in the first place, because I was so obstinately addicted to the superstitions of the papacy that it was very hard to draw me from that deep slough, by a sudden conversion He subdued and reduced my heart to docility, which, for my age, was over-much hardened in such matters. Having consequently received some taste and knowledge of true piety, I was forthwith inflamed with so great a desire to reap benefit from it that, although I did not at all abandon other studies, I yet devoted myself to them more indifferently. Now I was greatly astonished that, before a year passed, all those who had some desire for pure doctrine betook themselves to me in order to learn, although I myself had done little more than begin. For my part, I commenced to seek some hiding-place and means of withdrawing from people,

[1] *Opera*, xxxi. 21–24. The Latin and French versions are there given in parallel. Both are thought to be from Calvin's pen. I quote from the French.

since I have always loved quiet and tranquillity, being by nature somewhat shy and timid; but so far was I from succeeding in my wish that, on the contrary, all retreats and places of retirement were as public schools for me. In short, while I have always had this aim of living privately without being known, God has so led me and guided me by various vicissitudes that He has never let me rest in any place whatever, but, in spite of my natural disposition, He has brought me forth into the light, and, as the saying is, has thrust me onto the stage.[2] And, in fact, when I left the land of France I came to Germany of set purpose to the end that there I might live in some inconspicuous nook as I have always wished."

Earlier in date of composition, though much less definitely of a biographic character, are certain passages in Calvin's brilliant *Reply to Jacopo Sadoleto* of 1539. The Roman cardinal had pictured a Catholic and a Protestant as rendering account of their religious principles and motives before the bar of God's judgment, to the decided disadvantage of the reformer.[3] Calvin takes up the same figure and puts into the mouths of a Protestant minister and of a common member of his flock most skillful defences of Protestant principles, written with consummate literary art and by no means to be considered wholly autobiographic,[4] yet of such spiritual earnestness and verisimilitude that they are undoubtedly to a considerable extent drawn from his own religious experience.

Called to answer before God, the minister may make reply:[5]

They charged me with two of the worst of crimes – heresy and schism. And the heresy was that I dared to protest against dogmas which they received. But what could I have done? I heard from Thy mouth that there was no other light of truth which could direct our souls into the way of life than that which was kindled

---

[2] An English equivalent is lacking for Calvin's expression "et fait venir en jeu, comme on dit."

[3] *Opera*, v. 379–381.

[4] Lang, *Bekehrung*, pp. 31–36; but comp. Doumergue, i. 347–350.

[5] *Opera*, v. 408; Henry Beveridge's translation, *Tracts*, Edinburgh, 1860, i. 50.

by Thy Word. I heard that whatever human minds of themselves conceive concerning Thy Majesty, the worship of Thy Deity, and the mysteries of Thy religion, was vanity. I heard that their introducing into the Church instead of Thy Word, doctrines sprung from the human brain, was sacrilegious presumption. But when I turned my eyes towards men, I saw very different principles prevailing. Those who were regarded as the leaders of faith neither understood Thy Word, nor greatly cared for it ...They had fabricated for themselves many useless frivolities, as a means of procuring Thy favor, and on these they so plumed themselves that, in comparison with them, they almost condemned the standard of true righteousness which Thy law recommended – to such a degree had human desires after usurping the ascendancy, derogated, if not from the belief, at least from the authority, of Thy precepts therein contained. That I might perceive these things, Thou, O Lord, didst shine upon me with the brightness of Thy Spirit; that I might comprehend how impious and noxious they were, Thou didst bear before me the torch of Thy Word; that I might abominate them as they deserved, Thou didst stimulate my soul.

The solemn justification ascribed to the layman by Calvin bears fewer marks of the author's personal struggles. Some of its touches, especially regarding the Bible, reflect the experience of the "common man of the people" rather than that natural to an inquisitive student at Paris and Orléans. But it would seem to be the order-loving, legally trained, precedent-seeking Calvin that speaks for himself these words:[6]

When, however, I had performed all these things [i.e. had sought forgiveness for sin in accordance with the teachings of the Roman Church], though I had some intervals of quiet, I was still far off from true peace of conscience; for, whenever I descended into myself, or raised my mind to Thee, extreme terror seized me – terror which no expiations nor satisfactions could cure. And the more closely I examined myself, the sharper the stings with which my conscience was pricked, so that the only solace that was left to me was to delude myself by obliviousness.

---

[6] *Opera*, v. 412; *Tracts*, i. 56.

> Still, as nothing better offered, I continued the course which I had begun, when, lo, a very different form of doctrine started up, not one which led us away from the Christian profession, but one which brought it back to its fountain-head, and, as it were, clearing away the dross, restored it to its original purity. Offended by the novelty, I lent an unwilling ear, and at first, I confess, strenuously and passionately resisted; for (such is the firmness or effrontery with which it is natural to men to persist in the course which they have once undertaken) it was with the greatest difficulty that I was induced to confess that I had all my life long been in ignorance and error. One thing, in particular, made me averse to those new teachers – viz. reverence for the Church. But when once I opened my ears, and allowed myself to be taught, I perceived that this fear of derogating from the majesty of the Church was groundless. For they reminded me how great the difference is between schism from the Church and studying to correct the faults by which the Church herself was contaminated.

A hint as to one of Calvin's earliest acquaintances with Protestant discussion, and as to a difficulty which operated with others to set him in opposition toward Protestant claims, appears to be contained, also, in the following passage from his *Second Reply to Westphal*, published in 1556, many years after the experience to which it refers:

> For when I was beginning to emerge from the darkness of the papacy, having gained a slight taste of sound doctrine, I read in Luther that nothing was left of the Sacraments by Ecolampadius and Zwingli save bare and empty figures. I confess that I was so alienated from their books that I long abstained from reading them. Afterwards, before I undertook to write, they moderated something of their former vehemence, having discussed together at Marburg, so that the thicker fog was somewhat scattered even if it was not yet fully clear weather.

The implication would seem to be that Calvin had run across one of Luther's discussions of the Supper, before the Marburg Colloquy – that is before October 1529.

From Calvin's positive statements regarding his religious experience several conclusions may with confidence be drawn. It is evident that he regarded his "conversion" as the sovereign work of God. Nothing less, he felt, than divine power could have wrought the change which he recognized as having taken place in him. It had been brought about by an immediate and transforming intervention of God Himself. Nothing stood or could stand between his soul and God. Equally plain is it, also, that this transformation in the fundamental habit of his mind by a power outside himself had been, in his apprehension, "sudden." It had been a change of view no less unlooked for than supernatural in its origin. And it is clear, too, that, within the year following this experience, Calvin had become a leader in evangelical, or at least humanistically reformatory, circles in the community in which he was. This publicity, to whatever extent it may have reached, was distasteful to him, and he would have preferred a life of literary ease; but the same divine power that had effected the initial transformation in him now, as it seemed to him, forced him into conspicuity and increasing leadership. If to these positive details drawn from his Preface to the *Commentary on the Psalms* the less certainly autobiographic intimations of the *Reply to Sadoleto* may properly be added, it is clear that this "sudden conversion" had as an important factor – probably as its central experience – the recognition of the Scriptures, and of the Scriptures alone, as the very voice of God. God speaks, and he can but listen. And this speaking for Calvin is through the Word – not through the Church, or even primarily within, though it will be found that in his developed theology Calvin gives weight to the inward testimony of the Spirit. This strenuous conviction regarding the absolute and exclusive divine authority of the Scriptures, characteristic of the Reformation generally, but held by Calvin more clearly, perhaps, than by any other of the reformers, is the logical outcome of that return to the sources which was the ground-note of the Renaissance. With most of those who had thus far sought a betterment of religious conditions in France its full significance was but dimly apprehended; with Calvin it was fundamental. But one can well believe that, before his order-loving mind could feel that only in the Scriptures is final divine truth to be found, Calvin had to struggle with that "reverence for the Church" and sense of the sanctity of accepted views of the Sacraments which were part of his race-inheritance. His lawyer-grasp must have a document on which to base its deductions. The authority must be tangible and objective, and this he found in the Scriptures; but before he could deny to the Roman Church any authoritative interpreting function, or reject its long series of precedents and decisions, he must needs pass through a struggle the outcome of which seemed to him the intervention of a power no less than that of God. It is fair, also, to infer from the *Reply to Sadoleto* that a sense of sinfulness and of the inadequacy of the common mediaeval theories of the way of salvation, ending in glad acceptance of relief from the burden through the way known as justification by faith alone, was an integral part of the experience which he called his "conversion." In a measure, at least, his pathway was similar to that of Luther, though a comparison to Augustine would perhaps be truer.

But, if the general features of Calvin's religious development are thus made at least presumptively plain by his own statements, very weighty questions yet remain unanswered. When and where did this great transformation occur? Who were the human instruments, if any, in it? Was its power that of a revolution in the whole spiritual man leading to immediate action, or was it a sudden energizing of a will thus far lacking strength to put into vital practice convictions already long held as intellectual verities? To these queries most various answers have been and are still given by competent scholars.

According to the representations of Calvin's friends and oldest biographers, Beza and Colladon,[7] Calvin's transition to Protestantism began with the influence of his relative, Pierre Robert Olivétan, and was already so advanced by the time that he entered on the study of law at Orléans, early in 1528, as to be an important factor in that decision to substitute jurisprudence

---

[7] Lives, of 1564, 1565, and 1575, in *Opera*, xxi. 29, 54, 55, 121, 122.

for theology. Influenced by Olivétan, the youthful Calvin began the study of the Scriptures and withdrew himself, in a measure at least, from the Roman worship. According to their representation, this must have happened before Calvin was nineteen years old. Arrived at Orléans, Calvin vigorously continued his study of the Bible, and made himself a leader among those seeking religious reform. While a student at Bourges he preached at Lignières and on coming to Paris where he wrote his Seneca, he became acquainted with all the reformers there and his relations with Estienne de la Forge, the noble evangelical merchant who was to seal his faith by martyrdom in 1535, and with Nicolas Cop are cited as examples of this reformatory activity.

A modification of this interpretation of the beginnings of Calvin's Protestantism was presented by the Catholic historian, Florimand de Raemond.[8] Anxious to find in Germany rather than in his native land the source of Calvin's "heresy," he affirmed that its initiation was due to Melchoir Wolmar at Bourges. Among more modern historians Henry was firmly of the opinion that Wolmar was the prime human factor in Calvin's conversion.[9] It is easy, moreover, to combine the report of Beza with the representation given by Raemond, and to hold, as Merle d'Aubigné and many other historians have done, that Olivétan began and Wolmar ably continued the evangelical development of the reformer.

Within the last third of a century, and especially during the last twenty years, Calvin's statements, the affirmations of his earliest biographers and such hints as can be derived from his letters and the *Commentary on Seneca* have been subjected to much patient scholarly analysis. Yet the conclusions reached exhibit great variety of critical deduction.

To the Old-Catholic German historian, F. W. Kampschulte, writing in 1869, the "traditional view" seemed "wholly erroneous that Calvin had been completely won for the Reformation during his university years, and had even stood forth with great success

---

[8] *La naissance, progrèz et décadence de l'hérésie*, Paris, 1605, p. 882. The author died in 1601.

[9] *Leben Johann Calvins*, i. 38 (1835).

at its defender and furtherer."[10] The evidence of the letters shows the contrary. Kampschulte reaches the conclusion:[11]

"We recognise that Calvin long found himself in a state of uncertainty and vacillation regarding religious questions. His earlier dependence on the religion of his fathers had been shattered by the impressions which he had received during his university days, as well as by his theological studies. The former peace was gone; the forms and spiritual remedies of the Catholic Church no more gave him full satisfaction. What he experienced in his family was not fitted to strengthen him in the faith of the Church. His father died, excommunicate. His older brother, Charles by name, although a clergyman, fell into conflict with the spiritual authorities and was laid under ecclesiastical censure by them. One of his nearest relatives, Robert Olivétan, was devoted to the principles of religious innovation, and early sought, it is said, to win him for them. It was hard permanently to withstand so many points of attack ...There were already in the capital and elsewhere actual congregations of Evangelical believers, who had wholly broken with churchly tradition and were ready to pledge property and life for their new religious convictions. At Paris Calvin came into close relations with some of them, notably with a respected and well-to-do merchant, de la Forge, whom he extolled in his later writings. Should he have less courage than these men, and persist in his determination to lead a quiet life? Without acting against his conscience he could not...It is difficult to determine the date of this decisive change. Yet we shall not think ourselves in error if we place it in the second half of the year 1532."

Twelve years after Kampshculte published his volume, a Dutch scholar, Allard Pierson, put forth the most radical criticism of the accepted view of Calvin's conversion yet offered – a criticism that has secured comparatively few followers.[12] Not only does he deny to Calvin the authorship of Cop's inaugural discourse of November 1, 1533, but he finds no certain proof of Calvin's

---

[10] *Johann Calvin*, i. 233.
[11] Ibid., pp. 240, 241.
[12] *Studien over Johannes Kalvijn*, Amsterdam, 1881, pp. 58–109.

Protestantism before August 23, 1535 – the date of the Preface to the *Institutes*.

In 1888 Abel Lefranc, now Professor in the Collège de France at Paris, presented in his remarkable study of Calvin's youth an interesting modification of the traditional view, and supported it with great learning. His investigations marked a decided advance in the knowledge of Calvin's family and early environment. Calvin's transition to Protestantism, he concluded, was a very gradual process, however sudden in its decision at the end, for which the way was prepared by his native surroundings and family experiences.[13] His father's excommunication and his elder brother's breach with the Noyon clergy aroused in Calvin the spirit of protest which was natural to the Picard character, and had its illustration in Le Fèvre, Roussel, and others from the same territory. To these influences were added the positive evangelical exhortations of Olivétan from 1528 onward. That young reformer, who had had to seek protection in Strassburg by May of the year just mentioned, was the cause, Lefranc held, of a gradual and mysterious propagation of reformed ideas at Noyon, which soon won such following that the Chapter did not dare too vigorously to oppose it. But while the way was made ready for Calvin's Protestantism by the influences that came from his native city, as well as by the experiences of the University, it was long before he became fully an adherent of the new faith, or could engage in a "great stroke" on its behalf such as *Cop's Address*, Calvin's authorship of which Lefranc fully accepts:

> "The truth is that, long before inclined by his own nature, prepared by his education, the situation of his family, his relations, his studies, he did not declare himself openly a Huguenot until the time when all these circumstances unitedly forced him to do so almost against his will, and when, so to say, he could no longer do otherwise.
>
> Calvin's decisive conversion was above all a question of logic and reflection, in which sentiment had no part ... In all probability, and

---

[13] *Jeunesse*, pp. 21, 24, 31, 37, 39, 41, 97–99, 112, etc.

as far as it is possible to determine so intimate a growth of ideas, this change must have taken place in the second half of the year 1532."[14]

Two years after Lefranc, in 1890, Henri Lecoultre, a young Swiss scholar, now no longer living, took up the problem once more.[15] In criticism of Lefranc he rejected the thought of any direct influence tending toward Protestantism upon Calvin derived from the family or early environment at Noyon. Gérard Cauvin's troubles were pecuniary, not religious; Charles Cauvin's "heresies" did not appear till 1534; nor is the existence of a Protestant movement in Noyon demonstrable before that year, by which time Calvin was a decided adherent of evangelical views. Possibly Gérard Cauvin's insistence that his son should study law may have been, in its consequences, a step of high importance toward ideas of reform; but it was in no way so intended by the father. But Lecoultre agrees with Lefranc in admitting the influence of Olivétan and the Calvinistic authorship of *Cop's Address*. With Lefranc he holds that Calvin was long intellectually convinced of the truth of Protestant doctrine before being willing to break with the Roman Church, but he differs from the scholar just named in refusing to see conclusive evidence of that conversion in any act earlier than Calvin's formal breach with the ancient Communion by his resignation of his benefices in May, 1534:[16]

"What was the day of that sudden conversion? What was its immediate occasion? We do not know; perhaps we may never know. But its meaning need not be doubtful; it is neither a conversion of intellect, nor a conversion of feeling, but a conversion of will. It did not give him conviction regarding Protestant dogmas – that he possessed already; it did not inspire in him a warm interest for the things of the kingdom of God – he was already filled with it; it made vital an arrested resolution to conform his conduct scrupulously to his convictions, and to break all connection with the errors which he had already abjured in the depths of his heart. The first external evidence

---

[14] *Jeunesse*, pp. 41, 97, 98.
[15] *Revue de théologie et de philosophie*, Lausanne, 1890, pp. 5–30.
[16] Ibid., pp. 27, 28.

of this conversion, the first at least known to us, is a sacrifice of which Calvin never boasted, and of which Theodore Beza seems to have had no knowledge. The archives of Noyon prove that on May 4, 1534, Calvin resigned, in his native city, all his ecclesiastical benefices. This act, the natural consequence of which was voluntary exile, was needed to make of Calvin a real Protestant, for genuine Protestantism does not consist only of the doctrines of justification by faith and of the supreme authority of the Scriptures. It implies, as its name indicates, an energetic protest, formulated in the name of these doctrines, against ecclesiastical abuses of every kind.

The careful sketch of Calvin's life by the late Rudolf Stähelin, printed in 1897,[17] without entering as deeply into the question as the discussions just cited, expresses disbelief in his authorship of *Cop's Address*, and concludes, in view of Calvin's letter written on October 27, 1533, of which some account has been given,[18] that the future reformer "cannot have come to the break with the Catholic Church ... before the first months of the year 1534."

But during the same year that Stähelin's biographical article appeared, a no less able German-speaking scholar, August Lang of Halle, published one of the most thorough investigations of the circumstances of Calvin's conversion yet attempted.[19] In Lang's opinion, as in that of Lecoultre, influences from Noyon can have had little direct connection with Calvin's conversion. And, furthermore, the allegations of Beza and Colladon, made much of by Lefranc and accepted by Lecoultre, regarding the instrumentality of Olivétan, Lang regards as resting "on very unsafe ground." Wolmar's share in Calvin's religious transformation is quite as unsupported. Calvin thanked him for initiation into the knowledge of Greek, yet he said nothing regarding any indebtedness to his old teacher for religious instruction. In fact, as a student Calvin exhibited no special interest in religion. His letters and the *Commentary on Seneca* show that "the Bible is still a closed book for Calvin because his heart

---

[17] *Hauck's Realencyklopädie für protestantische Theologie und Kirche*, iii. 654–683.
[18] *Ante*, p. 67.
[19] *Die Bekehrung Johannes Calvins*, Leipzig, 1897.

does not beat for it. We must, therefore, lay aside all attempted explanations which would place the beginnings of the conversion of the great Biblical theologian in his student years as thoroughly astray. Before the year 1532, and we may go yet further, to perhaps the middle of 1533, the religious question is as good as non-existent for him." But a "change first appeared in the second half of the year 1533," and it had its most conspicuous early manifestation in *Cop's Address*, Calvin's authorship of which Lang strongly defends. That transformation is best explained as occasioned by the activity of the Reform party in Paris in 1533, and especially by the acquaintance of Calvin with Gérard Roussel, who, though never breaking with the Roman Church, was preaching doctrines to all intents Protestant. It is inconceivable also, Lang thinks, that a man of iron will and strenuous conscientiousness, as Calvin always was, could have remained for years intellectually convinced of the truths of Protestantism and yet not subject his action to his conviction, as Lefranc and Lecoultre would have it. His was no mere conversion of the will. Calvin's own statements that he "was obstinately addicted to the superstitions of the papacy," and that his "heart was over-much hardened,"[20] show that both intellect and will were active in the transformation. "As soon as his understanding was convinced, the newly-won knowledge must almost of itself arouse the will to eager activity." To Calvin, his conversion appeared the direct work of God, the results of which were "the certainty that God speaks in the Scriptures, and the recognition that all truth is contained in them; and that therefore their study and their dissemination are the worthiest object of the talents and zeal of a man's whole life." This conviction made of the humanist a Bible theologian.

The problem has not, however, rested with the solution that Lang has offered, for the traditional view, in a somewhat modified form it is true, has found a defender of great learning and force in Émile Doumergue, Professor of the Theological Faculty at Montauban in France, the first volume of whose monumental biography of Calvin appeared in 1899.[21] To Doumergue the statements of

---

[20] See *Ante*, p. 49.
[21] See i. 116, 117, 181–183, 337–352.

Beza and Colladon as to Calvin's evangelical beginnings carry great weight. Olivétan initiates him into evangelical principles as early as 1528. This was Calvin's "sudden conversion." It was, indeed, but a beginning; but it led Calvin to the study of religious questions, and to read, for instance, the Lutheran exposition of the Lord's Supper earlier than the Colloquy at Marburg (1529). At Orléans and even more at Bourges, Calvin came into contact with Wolmar and, though Calvin speaks only of Greek as the subject of their study, it is probable that they read the Greek Testament together and inconceivable that they could do so without religious instruction being given by the teacher to the pupil. Wolmar's influence Doumergue views as "decisive." It confirmed and greatly extended the work begun by Olivétan. Doumergue furthermore holds that Calvin's statement, "Before a year passed all those who had some desire for pure doctrine betook themselves to me in order to learn,"[22] refers to his student days at Orléans and to his friends there like Daniel and Duchemin, at whose instance it may be believed he preached, not as a Protestant, but as a reformatory Catholic at Lignières. Evidence of Calvin's interest in religion Doumergue sees in his citation of the Scriptures and of the Fathers in the *Commentary on Seneca* as well as in his purchase of a Bible for Daniel; and he thinks there would have been a good many more such tokens had not Calvin's correspondence been searched after the *Address* of Cop. But Calvin's religious development appears to Doumergue gradual, taking him through the stage of the partial Protestantism of a Le Fèvre; and it was not till the views were reached that are shown in *Cop's Address*, in Calvin's authorship of which Doumergue is fully confident, that his conversion, suddenly begun years before, was evidently completed. The termination of the gradual process of Calvin's conversion, suddenly begun years before, was evidently completed. The termination of the gradual process of Calvin's conversion by his arrival at the full Protestant position Doumergue would place apparently in the months immediately following the publication of his *Commentary on Seneca* – that is, in 1532.

---

[22] *Ante*, p. 72.

Calvin's conversion still proves a theme rewarding study, and in 1905 an elaborate monograph appeared from the pen of Professor Karl Müller[23] of Tübingen, not only discussing the whole subject anew, and with much dissent from Doumergue, but subjecting the claim that Calvin wrote *Cop's Address* to a painstaking examination leading to its denial. Müller holds it as probable that Olivétan influenced Calvin in the direction that Le Fèvre represented as early as Calvin's undergraduate days, and brought him into connection with evangelical circles at Orléans. Wolmar, in Müller's opinion, may later have been the agent through whom Calvin was led during his second or third stay in Paris into association with similar reformers there. But his "sudden conversion," Müller believes, may have taken place in connection with the Roman services held on account of the pest in which he shared in Noyon on August 23, 1533, when he may have seen the inconsistency of his principles with participation in Roman worship. The chief element in that conversion he regards as a submission of Calvin's will to that of God.

Yet the discussion has not rested here, for in the early part of 1906 Professor Paul Wernle of Basel has taken it up,[24] examining principally the sources of Beza and Colladon's *Lives of Calvin*. He concludes that their assertions regarding Calvin's religious development are simply their interpretations of the scanty allusions in Calvin's own writings, and that almost nothing of original value on this question is to be derived from them. In his opinion we have no direct knowledge of Calvin's religious history during his studies in law at Orléans or Bourges, nor can any connection of Wolmar or Olivétan with that development be proved from the sources at our disposal.[25] Wernle inclines to Müller's association of Calvin's "conversion" with the inward

---

[23] *Calvins Bekehrung*, in *Nachrichten von der königl. Gesellschaft der Wissenshcaften zu Göttingen*, pp. 188–255.

[24] *Noch einmal die Bekehrung Calvins*, in the *Zeitschrift für Kirchengeschichte*, xxvii. 84–99.

[25] Wernle would trace Beza's statement regarding Olivétan's influence simply to Calvin's allusion to his acquaintance with that reformer as "*vetus nostra familiaritas*" in his Preface to Olivétan's translation of the Bible (*Opera*, ix. 790).

questionings aroused by participation in the Roman service of August 1533, at Noyon.

It must be clear that a main cause of the wide divergency of these conclusions regarding the time and nature of Calvin's conversion is to be found in the scantiness of the evidence. Calvin's own reticence, to say nothing of the remoteness of the time at which he wrote from the events to which he cursorily alludes, the even greater removal in point of time of his earliest biographers, and the fragmentary remains of his correspondence, leave much room to conjecture and give but an imperfect foundation for the erection of a structure of solidly buttressed historical facts. To the present writer none of the careful interpretations just cited is wholly satisfactory, but he can offer his own attempted reconstruction only with the consciousness that it is equally tentative and fallible.

It would seem that Calvin's family experiences must have done not a little to loosen the hold of the Church upon him, even if it be thought that Lefranc has claimed too much. To have a father and a brother fall into open conflict with the ecclesiastical authorities, even though the causes were only financial and disciplinary, must certainly have disposed a boy just passing into manhood toward an attitude of criticism. This need not have gone far; but it must have left the mind in some degree open to discussion of the claims of the establishment with which his relatives were in controversy, even though that controversy was with a local Chapter and in no sense with the Church as a whole. Furthermore, the statement of Beza and Colladon that Calvin's initiation into Reformed sentiments was effected by Olivétan is so definite that it must reflect the impression prevalent among Calvin's friends during his later life, and have some probable basis in fact. Mistake here is far less likely than regarding the date and extent of Calvin's early religious activity. The long acquaintance of Calvin with Olivétan is witnessed by Calvin's own description, in 1535, of their friendship as *vetus nostra familiaritas*.[26] It is difficult to find a place for this

---

[26] Preface to Olivétan's French Bible, *Opera*, ix. 790. This seems to the writer a sufficient justification for Beza's conslusion even if it is, as Wernle believes, only Beza's conjecture from the phrase itself.

influence later than 1528, except on the improbable supposition that it was by letters of which we have now no hint, written after Olivétan had fled from Orléans to Strassburg in the spring of that year. Supposing Olivétan's influence to fall in Calvin's early days at the University of Orléans, it came at a time when the young scholar was not merely escaping from the severities and mediaevalism of the Collège de Montaigu into greater liberty of advanced student life, and the more humanistic atmosphere of Orléans, but at a season when Gérard Cauvin's difficulties with the Chapter at Noyon had developed and that ambitious father had determined that his son should exchange theology for law. The statement of Beza that Calvin turned to the study of law partly because of opposition to the old Church, receives, however, no confirmation from Calvin's own writings, which represent it as a step taken merely in deference to his father's wishes. Yet Olivétan, or some other impelling cause, seems to have led Calvin, if one can judge from his declaration to Westphal,[27] to look into one of Luther's fiery discussions of the Lord's Supper at this time, though with the result that he was more antagonized by such Protestant polemics than attracted. He began to know something now of the questions at issue, but to hold as Doumergue does, that this initiation, slight even in that historian's opinion, deserves the name of a "sudden conversion" seems an error.

At Orléans and at Bourges, Calvin undoubtedly found himself in an atmosphere favorable to the humanistic ideas of churchly reform. Sympathy with the thought of a betterment of the Church by education, preaching, purer morals, and, above all, by a return from mediaevalism to the sources of Christian truth, such as Erasmus had urged, was widespread in France and nowhere more so than in the universities. It involved no intention to break with the historic Roman Church. The Cops at Paris, and Daniel and Duchemin at Orléans, to speak only of Calvin's friends, were of this way of thinking. Le Fèvre, Briçonnet, Roussel, and Marguerite d'Angoulême had even made it fashionable. Calvin must have felt its influence about him, and undoubtedly sympathized

---

[27] *Ante*, p. 76.

with it. It is quite possible that Wolmar may have contributed to the development of these reformatory sympathies, but proof is wanting of any further service on his part to Calvin than instruction in Greek. Earnest and serious-minded always, and the holder of an ecclesiastical benefice, it is not impossible that some basis of truth may underlie the report of Beza and Colladon that he preached on occasion at Lignières, though, if so, it could not have been, as even Doumergue has pointed out, as a Protestant.[28]

But to regard Calvin as a center of evangelical religious activity during his stay at Orléans and Bourges, as Beza does, and as the spiritual guide of Daniel and Duchemin as Doumergue interprets Beza's statement, seems unwarranted for several reasons. Calvin himself says that his activity as a religious instructor was after his "sudden conversion"[29] – an event which, it will be seen, took place not about 1528, but subsequent to his first period of study at Orléans with which we have now to do. Moreover, Beza apparently drew from Calvin's own statement just referred to his knowledge of the activity which he mistakenly ascribed to this period.[30] And, chief reason of all, the remains of Calvin's correspondence show him in no such light. It is not a sufficient answer to say with Doumergue[31] that the search and seizure of Calvin's letters which Beza and Colladon report as having taken place, to the peril of

---

[28] I. 191, 192.

[29] *Ante*, p. 72.

[30] Compare Calvin with Beza, *Opera*, xxxi. 22 with xxi. 122.

CALVIN	BEZA
Itaque aliquo verae pietatis gustu imbutus tanto proficiendi studio exarsi, ut reliqua studia, ouamvis non abjicerem, frigidius tamen ssectarer. Necdum elapsus erat annus quum omnis purioris doctrinae cupidi ad me novitium adhuc et tironem discendi causa ventitabant.	Interea tamen ille sacrarum literarum studium simul diligenter excolere, in quo tantum etiam promoverat ut quicunque in ea urbe aliquo purioris religionis cognoscendae studio tangebantur ad eum etiam percontandum ventitarent.

[31] I. 354, 355.

his friends, after *Cop's Address*, proves the existence of letters of a different sort and that what remain are the "non-Evangelical," and therefore harmless residuum. To say little of the fact that the existence of letters showing evangelical activity late in 1533 would prove nothing as to such activity in 1528–1531, Calvin's letters sent to his friends were not seized with his papers, since they were not in his, but in the friends' possession. It is well-nigh a moral impossibility that side by side with the cordial student-like, but religiously colorless letters which have survived of Calvin's earliest correspondence, there could have been another series in which the writer took the totally different role of religious advisor. Nor is Calvin's interest in religious questions any more actively evident in his *Commentary on Seneca*. True he quotes the Bible three times – and three times only – but the passages thus relatively few in proportion to the mass of his citation are of no significance as bearing on the burning religious problems of the times.[32] In fact Lang's contention seems sustained that certainly till after the publication of the commentary just cited, in April 1532, Calvin's interest in religious questions was inconsiderable compared with his zeal for humanistic scholarship.

But between that publication and *Cop's Address* of November 1, 1533, a great change had taken place in Calvin, and the query naturally arises whether it is not this change that he describes as his "sudden conversion." His account of that experience shows that he regarded it as a crisis of the utmost significance, wrought by nothing less than divine power. Can that "conversion" have been only the beginning of a long period of gradual development, as Doumergue would have it, an experience to be dated in 1528? It is Doumergue's opinion that Calvin states distinctly, in the passage already often cited,[33] that his conversion occurred while engaged in the study of law under his father's command. The phrase used does not seem to

---

[32] He cites Proverbs xvi. 14, as illustrative of royal anger; Romans chapter xiii., as proving that "the powers that be are ordained of God," and I Peter ii. 18, as enjoining duties on masters toward their servants.

[33] *Ante*, p. 72; Doumergue, i. 344.

the present writer to demand that interpretation. He says that God "finally" (*finalement, tandem*) turned him. It is as if Calvin anticipated the reader's question why, if he studied law, he was not a lawyer. God "at length" interfered, but he speaks as if much had happened before that interference occurred. Be this as it may, the conclusion is much more certain that is to be drawn from Calvin's statement, in the same passage, that, "before a year passed, all those who had some desire for pure doctrine betook themselves to me in order to learn, although I myself had done little more than begin. For my part, I commenced to seek some hiding-place and means of withdrawing from people." Calvin here speaks not as a student attendant on classes, but as one able to find a home for himself where he will. His search for a quiet resting place fits in much more naturally with the months of wandering after *Cop's Address* than with student life at Orléans or Bourges. Furthermore, the relative indifference which Calvin declares he felt after his conversion to studies other than religious, is hard to conceive as previous to the publication of the *Commentary on Seneca*, which reveals on every page unwearied zeal in the mastery of the Greek and Latin classics. A just conclusion seems to be that Calvin's conversion must have occurred between the completion of that commentary and the delivery of *Cop's Address*, and probably toward a year before the latter date, that is late in 1532 or early in 1533.

Calvin's conversion, moreover, does not appear to have been, as Lefranc and Lecoultre hold, one of the will only. It was – whenever it occurred – an enlightening of the understanding, no less than a determination to act. Henceforth to the eager young humanist, religion became the chief concern. If we ask for the human agents in this transformation, however, the answer is difficult. The situation in Paris in the summer and autumn of 1533 was extremely favorable to the spread of Reformed opinions. Lang's suggestion of the Paris Lenten preacher of that year, Gérard Roussel, as Calvin's guide into the freer faith is not impossible. Roussel and Calvin were certainly friends in 1533, and on the strength of this friendship, Calvin upbraided

Roussel in 1537 for lack of courage to refuse a bishopric and leave the Roman communion.[34] But, if our conjecture as to the date of the conversion is at all justified, it may more probably have taken place at Orléans during Calvin's second sojourn there, when representative of the Picard "nation"; and as to its human agents, if any, it is in that case hard to say. Calvin himself referred it to the agency of God and, if we have understood his letter to Sadoleto aright,[35] it was the conviction that God spoke directly to him through the Scriptures that formed the central element in that experience. That conviction might have come to such a man as Calvin in the quiet of his study with no less force than if impressed upon him by public discourse or friendly exhortation.

If, then, Calvin had come, by November 1533, to doctrinal positions now universally recognized as characteristic of Protestantism, and the logical outcome of which was soon to be separation from Rome, it by no means follows that he recognized the full consequences of his beliefs or regarded himself as a Protestant. On August 23, he was present at a meeting of the Chapter at Noyon. On October 27, he could express himself to Daniel in a way that showed that he held himself in full sympathy with the humanistic reformers.[36] He also sent to Daniel a treatise of Roussel for confidential circulation, and he may well have shared Roussel's hope that the Church of France might be reformed from within by purer preaching and truer doctrine, without breach of its historic continuity. Nothing more radical than this is necessarily involved even in *Cop's Address*. Certainly it was not till the following May, that Calvin resigned his benefices.

It was an ancient custom of the University that the newly elected incumbent of the annual office of rector should give an inaugural oration before the academic world and such of the general public as chose to be present in the Church of the

---

[34] *Opera*, v. 279–312; xxi. 127.

[35] *Ante*, p. 73.

[36] *Ante*, p. 68.

Mathurins on All Saints'. The new rector, Nicolas Cop, Calvin's warm friend, had sufficiently followed his distinguished father's profession to have graduated as Bachelor in Medicine, but since 1530 he had taught philosophy in the Collège Sainte-Barbe. The brief rectorate of only twenty-one days since his election had seen him actively intervening in the religious questions of the hour as a supporter of Marguerite d'Angoulême and of the freer type of preaching which she countenanced. When the conservatives of the University had desired to condemn that queen's *Le miroir de l'âme pécheresse*, and had been called to account by King Francis, as has been already narrated,[37] Cop had summoned the Faculties to consider the royal letters on October 24, and had shown himself a determined and successful defender of the queenly author in the heated debate that followed. He had therefore already entered the lists as a champion of reform as represented by Marguerite d'Angoulême, and he now determined to make his inaugural oration tell in the same cause. He would make a declaration of significance against conservatism and in favor of reform; and so bold was the utterance, considering the time and place of its delivery, that it became at once the sensation of the hour.

Pierson has, indeed, queried whether *Cop's Address* is really known to us.[38] His criticism has, however, been destructively answered by Lang.[39] A letter of Bucer, probably in January 1534, to Ambrose Blaurer of Constance, speaks of the delivery of an oration by Cop, with such insistence on justifying faith as to cause his flight.[40] Consonant with this contemporary testimony as to the nature of *Cop's Address* are the statements of Colladon in his *Life of Calvin* of 1565.[41] That the *Address* which we now have is that pronounced by Cop is furthermore attested by an annotation in a sixteenth-century hand on the manuscript of a portion of it

---

[37] *Ante*, p. 68.

[38] *Studien over Kalvijn*, pp. 72–78.

[39] *Die ältesten theologischen Arbeiten Calvin's*, in the *Neue Jahrbücher für deutsche Theologie*, ii. 273–282 (1893).

[40] Herminjard, iii. 129.

[41] *Opera*, xxi. 56.

now in the Library of Geneva,[42] and is borne out by its contents. There is, therefore, no reasonable question that Cop's academic oration of November 1, 1533 has been preserved.

While *Cop's Address* is therefore well known, Calvin's authorship of it is by no means certain. In favor of that authorship may be urged the facts that Colladon evidently believed the work to be that of Calvin when, about 1570, he prepared Calvin's papers for the press,[43] – but, above all, that the fragment of the *Address* now in the Library in Geneva is indisputably in Calvin's handwriting.[44] Against it are the considerations that the style seems hardly equal to Calvin's usual brilliant Latinity; that Colladon, in his *Life* of 1565, speaks only of Calvin's friendship with Cop, not of any authorship of *Cop's Address*; and that only in his final *Life*, that of 1575, does Beza declare that "Calvin furnished it."[45] These facts raise the question whether Colladon's attribution of authorship to Calvin, witnessed by his inscription on the manuscript, was not simply a deduction from a discovery, after his *Life* of 1565 was written, of that manuscript in Calvin's well-known handwriting. Professor Müller, to whom this striking suggestion is due, has furthermore presented evidence that the complete form of the *Address* preserved in Strassburg is not a perfected oration based on Calvin's manuscript as its first draft, as Lang held, but that both are copies of a now lost original.[46] Calvin may simply have desired to preserve his friend's work.

Whether Calvin actually composed any part of *Cop's Address* is therefore at best doubtful. The weight of evidence certainly now

---

[42] The hand is certainly that of Nicolas Colladon, Herminjard, iii. 418; Müller, *Calvins Bekehrung*, pp. 226, 228. The fragment at Geneva, containing the first sheet, is printed in Herminjard, iii. 418–420; *Opera*, ix. 872–876; and given in photographic facsimile by Müller, op. cit. The whole *Address* is printed (poorly) from a manuscript in the *Thomas-archiv* (now *Stadtarchiv*) at Strassburg, in *Opera*, xb. 30–36.

[43] So even Müller holds, p. 231.

[44] Herminjard, iii. 420; *Opera*, ix., Preface, lxxii; Lang, op. cit., p. 274; Müller, p. 224, who cites the emphatic testimony of the present director of the Geneva Library, M. H. V. Aubert.

[45] *Opera*, xxi. 123.

[46] Lang, op cit., p. 28; Müller, pp. 231–237.

inclines to the negative side. But of Calvin's hearty interest in the *Address* there can be no question – the existence of the manuscript in his handwriting is sufficient evidence of that, if of no more. Even though not his composition, it can hardly have been delivered without consultation between the two friends. It is impossible to suppose Calvin ignorant of it. In view of his intimacy with Cop it may therefore properly be cited as a witness to the religious development which Calvin had attained at the date of its delivery. It is no less interesting in its revelation of the books by which the spiritual life of the circle of which Cop and Calvin were members had been fostered.

Its form is that of a sermon. The *Address* opens with an apostrophe to "Christian Philosophy," – that is to the gospel, as ascertained by a study of its sources, and distinguished from current scholastic theology. As Lang has discovered,[47] both the phrase and the treatment are borrowed from Erasmus. The thought and not a little even of the language of this introduction rest back on Erasmus' Preface to the third edition of his Greek New Testament, published in 1524. This "Christian Philosophy," the orator declares, shows us that we are sons of God. To proclaim it, God became man. Those who have its knowledge exceed other men, as men in general are superior to beasts. It is the worthiest of sciences. It reveals the remission of sins by the mere grace of God. It shows that the Holy Spirit, who sanctifies the heart and guides to life eternal, is promised to all Christians. It gives peace to distressed minds and leads to good and happy living. Having thus praised the gospel as a whole, the speaker remarks that some selection from its wealth must be made if the limits of a discourse are to be observed, and he therefore takes as his text a verse from the Gospel read in the appointed service of the day: "Blessed are the poor in spirit." The introduction concludes with a brief invocation of the aid of Christ as "the true and only intercessor with the Father," that the discourse to follow "may praise Him, may savor of Him, may breathe Him, may call Him to mind." Having said this, it adds the then customary salutation to the Virgin – a combination that illustrates the partially developed status of the Reform movement at Paris.

---

[47] *Bekehrung*, pp. 44–46; *Opera*, xb. 30–31.

If the writer of the discourse thus reveals the influence of Erasmus in his introduction, the first part of the body of the *Address* which follows shows even greater use of a sermon preached by Luther, on occasion of the same church festival, probably in 1522, in which the German reformer, in treating of the Beatitudes, had discussed the relations of Law and Gospel.[48] Thanks to a Latin translation, by Martin Bucer of Strassburg, of the collection of Luther's sermons in which this has a place, it had been accessible to the learned world since 1525, and later editions had been issued in 1528 and 1530. Though not expressly mentioned, it may have been one of the volumes of the reformers, which Berthold Haller found more or less openly for sale at Paris in August, 1533.[49] In words modeled on this discourse of Luther the Parisian speaker tells his hearers: He encounters, as Luther does, the objection that Christ had said in the passage under consideration, "For great is your reward in heaven." Are not the Beatitudes then a new Law, the keeping of which earns a reward? No, they set forth the gospel; and the author explains with an illustration all his own, likening him who lives deserving of the Beatitudes to a son who has striven in a father's lifetime to do that father's pleasure, and who receives an inheritance, which may be called a reward of faithful sonship, though in no sense a debt due for filial service. The author then pays his respects to the "sophists" – unquestionably the conservative Roman theologians of the University of Paris – who "contend perpetually about trifles" to the neglect of "Christian Philosophy."

The speaker invokes the blessing of the peacemakers on the controversies of the time. "Would that in this our unhappy age we restore peace in the Church by the Word rather than by the sword." But the orator evidently foresees the impossibility of the fulfillment of his desire, and exclaims: "Twice blessed are they who endure persecution for righteousness' sake" and he closes with a fervently expressed wish that God "may open our minds that we may believe the Gospel."

---

[48] Lang, *Bekehrung*, pp. 47–54; *Opera*, xb. 31–33.
[49] Herminjard, iii. 75.

That this lofty and spiritually minded *Address* was a carefully planned manifesto on behalf of Protestantism is an opinion that has often been expressed. Of its boldness there can be no question. But its wisdom, under the circumstances of its delivery, is not so evident. The Reform movement had been growing by the tolerance of the King and the support of his gifted sister, largely because it had not, at Paris, greatly passed the bounds of orderly discussion. True, it had had its martyrs like Berquin, but the favorable situation of the movement in the year 1533 was due in no small degree to a comparative moderation which had not forfeited the goodwill of the King. Anything likely to exasperate the situation was, we can now see, certain to lead to repression of the innovating forces. But that was not then so apparent. Cop may have believed that the royal authority would support him as it had already aided Roussel through Marguerite d'Angoulême.

Much more probably there was no deep and farsighted plan behind the *Address*. It grew, almost on the moment, out of the impulsive enthusiasm of a young man who, suddenly called to a great position in the University, had found himself a leader in resistance to an attempt to discipline the scholarly, reformatory, and popular Queen of Navarre, and the humanistic reformers whom she favored. The opportunity to continue before a larger public the discussion of the principles involved in the University session of October 24, of which their minds were full, and in which the young rector had borne a conspicuous part, is a sufficient explanation of Cop's action and of Calvin's aid if such aid was given. Protestant in doctrine as the *Address* is, and opposed to the "sophists" of the Sorbonne, it betrays no evidence that its author thought that he was putting himself outside the communion of the Roman Church. Ideas and expressions are borrowed from Luther, but the German reformer is not mentioned, and it is his doctrine of the way of salvation, not his breach with the papacy, that interests him. Yet the *Address* clearly shows the sources from which Cop and probably Calvin were drawing their spiritual life. The New Testament, Erasmus, and Luther had already made Calvin a Protestant in most of his beliefs, and would inevitably place him on the Protestant side when lines of division should be more closely drawn.

5

Flight for Safety in
Concealment and Voluntary Exile, 1533–1535

The effect of Cop's bold *Address* was to show that the strength
of the conservative party in Paris was greater than its speaker
and his friends could have anticipated, if, as is unlikely, they
had deliberately counted the cost before its delivery on the 1st
of November. They doubtless expected the resentful hostility
of the Theological Faculty, which he had so severely arraigned.
But a more formidable adversary almost immediately appeared
in the great judicial court, the Parlement of Paris. Aroused
not improbably by the efforts of two Franciscan monks, the
Parlement now began proceedings against Cop for heresy. He
answered at once by summoning a session of the Faculties of
the University, which met on November 19 in the same Church
of the Mathurins in which his discourse had been delivered.
Before this academic assembly the young rector urged that the
proceedings of his accusers and of Parlement were an invasion
of the privileges of the University, which should have had at
least primary jurisdiction in the matter of the alleged heresy of
its officers. The contention would ordinarily have been effective;
but, thanks probably to a vastly prevailing want of sympathy
with his radical theological opinions, Cop found but a divided
support. The Faculties of Medicine and of Arts took his side,
those of Theology and of Law were opposed; and no action by

the University as a whole could be had.[1] Cop felt the ground slipping from under his feet. On November 26, proceedings were begun by the Faculty of Theology which resulted in the arrest of Roussel and of a preacher whom we shall meet at Geneva, Élie Coraud.[2] The same day the Parlement stated the situation to the King, and on December 10, he wrote from Lyons enjoining strict suppression of "the Lutheran sect."[3] Many of the Reform party were thrown into prison. Cop himself avoided this fate by flight – apparently before November 26,[4] – and ultimate refuge in the shelter of the Protestant city of Basel, which had, years before, been his father's home. Soon a reward of 300 crowns was offered for his capture alive or dead.[5]

These experiences of his friend must have filled Calvin with well-grounded anxiety for his own safety. His relations to Cop had been so intimate as to involve him in suspicion. The authorities, probably late in November, therefore went to his room in the Collège Fortet which had been his home when in Paris since 1531, hoping to effect his arrest. News of this intention reached him in season to effect his escape.[6] His papers were seized, to the peril of his friends, but he himself found refuge, according to a late but not impossible report at Noyon,[7] whither the same account says, with much greater likelihood of legendary embellishment, that he made his way disguised as a vine-dresser. Calvin cannot, however, have been as conspicuously before the public as an advocate of reform as Cop, Roussel, or Coraud; and his self-imposed exile from Paris was brief at this time. Marguerite

---

[1] Bulaeus, *Hist. Univ. Paris.*, vi. 239.

[2] Herminjard, iii. 146, note.

[3] Ibid., 114.

[4] King Francis, whose information probably came from the letters of Parlement, speaks of his flight in his order of December 10th. Ibid., 117. He reached Basel January 25, 1534. Doumergue, i. 354.

[5] Herminjard, iii. 130.

[6] P. Masson, *Elogiorum*, p. 414, alleges that he escaped by a window, but Beza and Colladon, *Opera*, xxi. 56, 123, simply say that he was not found at home. Compare Doumergue, i. 354.

[7] Jacques Desmay, in *Archives curieuses*, v. 393.

d'Angoulême is said to have interested herself on his behalf. Proceedings against Calvin were dropped, and he returned to Paris perhaps to be received honorably by this benefactress who had a welcome for scholars of the new learning and humanistic reformatory impulse.[8] Even the friendliness of this reception, if it took place, gave Calvin no sense of security; and, partly because Paris was a place of peril, partly also to seek the peace and scholarly retirement which he loved, he soon left the city. If a conjecture may be hazarded where the chronology is so obscure, this second departure was in the opening month of 1534, or even possibly in the last days of 1533.

Fortunately an agreeable asylum opened for him at once at Angoulême, some 250 miles southwest of Paris, in the home of a young clerical friend, Louis du Tillet, seigneur of Haultmont, canon of the cathedral of Angoulême and rector also of the village church of Claix about ten miles out of the city. The du Tillets were of a family of Angoulême which had risen into prominence in the service of the State. The father had been Vice-President of the royal Chamber of Accounts at Paris. Of Louis' three older brothers, one had held and another was now holding the office of chief Registrar of the Parlement of Paris, and a third had, like Louis, entered the Church in which he was to become, at a much later period (1562), Bishop of Meaux. The family was no less conspicuous for its learning; the home at Angoulême held a remarkable library, said to have contained 3,000 or 4,000 manuscripts and printed books.[9] How Calvin's friendship with the young canon may have been begun there is no certain information; but he seems to have been about Calvin's age, and the conjecture lies close at hand that they were fellow students. The du Tillets, like the Cops, belonged to the class that had profited by royal favor and had also welcomed the new learning. Among such people the humanistic conceptions of reform as advocated by Erasmus, Le Fèvre, and Roussel, found ready hearing. Calvin and Louis du Tillet had many studious

---

[8] Beza, in *Opera*, xxi. 123. The whole matter is doubtful. Compare Müller, p. 214, and Wernle, p. 93.

[9] Florimond de Raemond, *Naissance*, etc., p. 885.

tastes in common,[10] and a good deal of religious sympathy; but du Tillet, as compared with Calvin, was a man of weak courage, and of convictions which, though inclining him to throw in his lot with the reformers for a season, led him ultimately back into the Roman communion. At this time, however, he and Calvin were undoubtedly in substantial religious agreement.

Here at Angoulême, and at the neighboring Claix, Calvin, as he told his friend Daniel in a letter intentionally indefinite as to his whereabouts and occupations,[11] found not merely a kind "patron" in du Tillet, whose generosity he recognizes in the warmest terms, but opportunity for study. The letter shows that he is valued by his host not merely as a friend, but for what he has to give; and the religious note now dominant in Calvin's life sounds clear in his expression of gratitude to God to whose wise providence he cheerfully entrusts his future. Calvin's note to his friend implies that he was aiding du Tillet in literary studies, and this intimation gives countenance to the statement of Flormond de Raemond, published more than seventy years later, but probably written at a period considerably less remote, that Calvin instructed his friend in Greek.[12] According to the same writer, he was popularly nicknamed "the Greek of Claix," from the name of the country parish where du Tillet was beneficed, and where apparently he resided a portion of the time. At du Tillet's home, or, if Florimond de Raemond was correctly informed, at Girac, a house belonging to the prior of Bouteville, Antoine Chaillou, outside of Angoulême, on the road to Claix, Calvin was accustomed to meet with the prior just named, with the abbot of Bassac, with du Tillet, and du Tillet's cousin, the seigneur de Torsac. Among Calvin's acquaintances at Angoulême was also, by his own testimony,[13] the young brother of the scholar last named, Pierre de la Place, later to be an eminent Huguenot lawyer and one of the victims of the

[10] Calvin said of du Tillet to Daniel, probably in March, 1534, "the kindness of my patron ... is such that I readily understand that it is shown for the sake of letters, not for myself," *Opera*, xb. 37.

[11] *Opera*, xb. 37.

[12] *Naissance*, etc., pp. 883–885; see also Doumergue, i. 370–373.

[13] *Opera*, xiii. 681.

massacre of St Bartholomew. In this company Calvin discussed not merely congenial topics relating to classical learning, but matters of religion; and evidently with sympathetic appreciation, for Beza as well as Colladon report that, at du Tillet's request, he wrote evangelical sermons for the use of certain pastors of the region who had caught something of the reformatory spirit.[14]

Of greater significance for his future was the beginning, in this period of retirement at Angoulême, of the studies which were to result in the first edition of his *Institutes*. How far they had made progress by the time he was to leave France there is no means to determine, but a careful examination of such hints as Calvin's own writings afford confirms at least enough of Florimond de Raemond's assertion that Calvin wrote part of the *Institutes* at Angoulême to carry the conviction that Calvin must have planned and made preparation for this great service to Protestantism while du Tillet's guest, and doubtless with the aid of du Tillet's notable library.[15]

Calvin's friendship for Gérard Roussel has already been mentioned. Warmly committed to the Reform movement which Roussel had represented at Paris and for which that eloquent mystic had been suffering a brief imprisonment during the stormy days after the delivery of *Cop's Address*, it was natural that Calvin should desire to make the acquaintance of Roussel's venerable master, the leader of the humanistic reformers of France, Jacques Le Fèvre. The aged scholar was spending his last days under the protection of Marguerite d'Angoulême at Nérac, the little capital of French Navarre; and thither Calvin journeyed for a brief visit to the kindly old man.[16] The journey may be placed, with considerable probability, about the beginning of April 1534, and if so, is interestingly coincident with the publication, at Antwerp, early in the same month, of Le Fèvre's corrected and revised edition of his translation of the Bible into French.[17]

---

[14] Ibid., xxi. 56, 57, 123.

[15] The whole subject is carefully discussed by the Strassburg editors, *Opera*, iii., Introduction, pp. xi–xiv.

[16] Beza and Colladon, *Opera*, xxi. 57, 123; Doumergue, i. 380–415.

[17] Doumergue, i. 380, 401.

Calvin's work, in this period, was still that of the retiring scholar rather than of the preacher or public reformer. That he was yet to become, but not till circumstances were to force him into a role foreign to his natural disposition. He was already planning his great exposition of Christian doctrine, though it was but a brief handbook that he yet had in mind. He was already a leader in the little circles which he quietly influenced. His power to make friends, especially among those of good position and scholarly tastes, was remarkable. But the public evangelical activity traditionally attributed to him before his departure from France, and illustrated in popular nomenclature by so-called "Calvin's pulpits," at Bourges, Nerac, Clairac[18] – places destined later to suffer for their acceptance of the Protestant position in religion – and elsewhere, is greatly exaggerated. What he did for the evangelical cause – and his work was not small – was still by inconspicuous and personal relations. Unjustified as was the taunt thrown at Calvin in December 1538 by du Tillet, then returned to the Roman communion, this former intimate friend witnesses at least to the private character of Calvin's efforts in this period when he says: "It is before those to the greater part of whom you know your doctrine to be pleasing that you maintain it, not elsewhere, for you have abandoned your country because you did not dare to set it forth and maintain it publicly there."[19]

Calvin's development since the commotion aroused by *Cop's Address* had compelled him to leave Paris was leading him to a decision which would sever formally his connection with the Roman Church. He had held benefices at Noyon since May 1521. He was now approaching the age of twenty-five, the normal time for ordination to the priesthood, when a decision as to his personal relations to the ecclesiastical duties thus far discharged by his deputies was to be expected.[20] These motives counseled a determination of his own future. Should he go forward, like Roussel, du Tillet, or other of his humanistic reformatory friends,

---

[18] Doumergue, i. 416.

[19] *Opera*, xb. 299.

[20] Doumergue, i. 426.

holding doctrines in many respects evangelical, but refusing to break with the Church which they hoped to reform from within, and accepting promotion in its service? Or should he come out from it altogether? The decision must have been a difficult one. Honors, literary opportunity, even possibly greater usefulness, might easily seem to sway the balance in favor of a conclusion to remain. Exile, poverty, and struggle could alone, apparently, result from separation from the Roman Church. But Calvin's mind was determined. On May 4, 1534, the first certain date in Calvin's career since that of *Cop's Address*, his chaplaincy at the cathedral at Noyon, vacant by Calvin's resignation, was transferred to another by the Chapter;[21] at or about the same date Calvin laid aside his rectorship at Pont-l'Évêque.[22] Probably he had taken the long journey across France from Nérac to Noyon to make the resignation in person; certainly he was in Noyon later in the same month.

The time was one of excitement and apprehension in the city. On January 19 previous, a procession had been held in expiation of the heretical disorders of the age; on May 6, two days after Calvin's resigned benefice had been given to his successor, an investigation based on a charge of heresy was begun, as secretly as possible, by the Chapter against his quick-tempered and contumacious older brother, Charles. John Calvin himself could hardly hope to escape suspicion under such circumstances, however circumspect he had thus far been in avoidance of publicity in the advocacy of Reformed doctrines. It is of great interest therefore to find that Calvin was imprisoned at Noyon on May 26 "for uproar made in the church on the eve of Holy Trinity," three days before.[23] The place of his confinement, the prison of the Chapter known as La Porte Corbaut, is still standing, a little building strongly barred, and containing a small courtroom, below which are two dungeons and above which are two cells of less forbidding aspect.[24] From this confinement Calvin was released on the eighth day of incarceration, only to be

---

[21] Records, in Lefranc, *Jeunesse*, p. 201.

[22] Desmay, in *Archives curieuses*, p. 395; Doumergue, i. 425.

[23] Records, in Lefranc, *Jeunesse*, p. 21.

[24] Doumergue, i. 25, 427.

rearrested and again imprisoned on June 5, two days later. How long this second confinement may have lasted, or under what circumstances he was finally set free, there is no means at present of forming an opinion, but in view of the very considerable activity which he was yet to show before leaving France, and the time that it must have required, his second imprisonment cannot have been more than a few weeks in duration at longest. It may, like his first, have been for a few days only.

Unfortunately little can definitely be affirmed regarding the circumstances of Calvin's arrest in his native city. Lang's view that the "uproar" in church was due to an attempt to proclaim evangelical doctrine[25] has been effectively criticized by Doumergue, who points out that such action would have been little in consonance with Calvin's character. Nor does the vacillation of the Noyon authorities regarding Calvin's imprisonment indicate that they had any clearly defined charge against him, such as would have been furnished by a public attack on Roman worship or doctrine. The conjecture would seem more probable by far that popular opinion judged Calvin to be a "heretic" and found expression in an outbreak in the Church. His arrest followed; but the charges against him very probably did not seem sufficiently warranted to be pressed, though suspicion availed to place him twice for a brief period in custody. Fortunately for the future reformer his arrest and imprisonment did not prove the road to the stake.

With this imprisonment two of the most careful of recent students of Calvin's history, Lefranc and Doumergue, connect whatever slight shred of fact may have served as a thread on which to hang one of the most baseless and absurd, as well as one of the most persistent of the calumnies by which Calvin's memory has been assailed. In the bitter controversies of the sixteenth and seventeenth centuries, Calvin was charged, especially after his death and that of the generation that had known him, with drunkenness, licentiousness, and, strangely enough, with ignorance.[26] These

[25] *Bekehrung*, p. 13; compare Doumergue, i. 427.

[26] E.g. Laingey, *De Vita et Moribus atque Rebus gestis Haereticorum nostri Temporis*, Paris, 1581. Doumergue, i. 429.

contumelies were too often in that age the weapons of all shades of theological controversialists, when vituperation was employed to an extent now almost inconceivable. The more specific charge, to which reference is now made, was formulated thirteen years after Calvin's death by Jérôme Hermès Bolsec, a one-time Carmelite monk of Paris who settled about 1550, as a Protestant and a physician at Veigy, near Geneva. Falling into a controversy with Calvin, of which an account will be given on a later page, he was banished from Geneva in December 1551, and ultimately returned to the Roman Church. He naturally felt bitterly toward Calvin's memory, but the revenge which he now took is one which recoils on himself through the revelation of his own unscrupulous character. According to Bolsec's allegation[27] he had seen a report prepared by a "Bertelier" (probably Philibert Berthelier is meant), and legally attested by the most prominent people of Noyon, whither he alleges Bertelier had been sent by Genevans desirous of investigating Calvin's early life, witnessing that Calvin had been convicted of heinous moral turpitude,[28] the punishment for which was then death by fire, but that the Bishop of Noyon had commuted the extreme penalty into branding a fleur-de-lys with a red-hot iron, as a perpetual mark of infamy, on the future reformer's shoulder. No evidence has ever been produced of the existence of such a document as Bolsec alleges. Jacques Desmay, the earnest Catholic writer who used his stay as Advent and Lenten preacher at Noyon in 1614 and 1615 to learn all he could of Calvin's life there by records and tradition, found nothing of it.[29] An equally determined Roman historian of Noyon, Jacques Le Vasseur, in his *Annales* of 1633, expressly repudiated it,[30] and careful modern Roman Catholic scholars, such as Kampschulte[31] and Paulus,[32]

---

[27] *Histoire de la vie, moeurs, actes, constance, et mort de Jean Calvin*, Lyons, 1577, chap. iv.; Lefranc, *Jeunesse*, p. 176.

[28] Genesis xix. 5.

[29] Pp. 15, 16; in facsimile in Doumergue, i. 434, 435.

[30] Pp. 1172; in facsimile in Doumergue, i. 438.

[31] I. 224.

[32] *Luther Lebensende*, 1898, p. 48; Doumergue, i. 435.

reject it as "unworthy of serious refutation." When repeated in the name of Cardinal Richelieu, in a volume published after the death of that statesman-prelate, it was the immediate cause of the elaborate and scholarly defence of Calvin's memory by Charles Drelincourt;[33] and its utter worthlessness has been recently exhibited in examples of historical criticism as brilliant as they are convincing by Lefranc[34] and Doumergue.[35] Whatever explication of the growth of such a fable may be found beside the malignant invention of theological controversialists, is to be discovered in the obscurity of the circumstances of Calvin's imprisonment – the first instance of which is, however, expressly declared in the records to have been "for uproar made in the church" – and to the remarkable coincidence of name, reported by Desmay and Le Vasseur.[36] They report that in 1550 or 1552, when Calvin had long been a well-known resident of Geneva, another John Calvin, whom they carefully distinguished from the reformer, was disciplined by the Chapter at Noyon for a breach of the law of chastity less heinous than that charged at Bolsec. The whole calumny would be unworthy of discussion had the accusation not been repeatedly renewed by a certain class of controversialists during the last century – in one instance as recently as 1898.[37]

The same uncertainty as to the date and order of events in Calvin's life which attaches to the period from *Cop's Address* to the resignation of his benefices extends from the beginning of his second imprisonment at Noyon to his departure from France. How long that imprisonment lasted is unknown, but Beza and Colladon speak of a perilous visit to Paris,[38] which may most probably be placed between this imprisonment and the outbreak of persecution consequent upon the posting of Antoine Marcourt's Placards against the Mass in the October following. According to the early

---

[33] *La defense de Calvin contre l'outrage faite à sa mémoire par le Cardinal de Richelieu*, Geneva, 1663–1667.

[34] *Jeunesse*, pp. 48–52, 175–181.

[35] I. 428–440; iii. 516.

[36] *Remarques*, p. 16; Annales, p. 1170; Doumergue, i. 435, 436.

[37] Doumergue, i. 432.

[38] *Opera*, xxi. 57, 123.

biographers just cited, the most important incident of this brief and carefully guarded sojourn was an attempted conference with Servetus, at a house in the Rue Saint-Antoine, which failed by reason of the neglect or inability of the radical Spanish theologian to keep his appointment. At Paris Calvin not improbably found a lodging on the Rue Saint-Martin in the home of that earnest Protestant merchant, Estienne de la Forge, who was to give his life for his faith in the February following Calvin's visit. Under la Forge's roof he may have been a witness to that discussion with a member of the sect of "Libertins" of which he gave an account in his attack upon that party of extreme radicals published in 1545.[39] Of la Forge, whom Calvin knew well, the future reformer was accustomed to speak in high praise as a man of character, sincerity, and piety.[40]

If it is at least probable that Calvin's visit to Paris, which has just been described, was on his way southward from Noyon toward the friendly shelter of Angoulême immediately after his final release from imprisonment, no such comparative plausibility of conjecture applies to the course of his movements during the next few months. He probably returned, at some time in this period, to Angoulême, for when he leaves France it is in company with Louis du Tillet; he was certainly at Orléans, for he dates from there the first Preface to his *Psychopannychia*; and Florimond de Raemond gives an account of activity at Poitiers that must have some basis in fact beneath it. As to the relations of these several sojourns one to another, or their length, there is no adequate means of forming a conclusion; and the stay at Orléans may perhaps, though less probably, have occurred before, rather than after, Calvin's imprisonment at Noyon and visit to Paris. Of these three brief halts before leaving his native land, that at Poitiers was significant as marking a new stage in Calvin's relations to Protestant worship, while that at Orléans reveals a new consciousness of his mission as a defender of evangelical doctrine.

Florimond de Raemond, writing indeed at a distance in point of time which causes his testimony to be received only with

---

[39] *Contre la secte phantastique des Libertins, Opera*, vii. 185.
[40] Colladon, *Opera*, xxi. 56.

much uncertainty as to its value in detail, represents[41] Calvin as entering, largely at first through the gateway of a common interest in letters, into more or less intimate friendship, at Poitiers, that religious city, with a little group of learned men of high station: François Fouquet, prior of Trois Moutiers, with whom he lodged; Charles le Sage, Professor of Law; Antoine de la Duguie, afterward prominent in the Faculty of Law; Albert Babinot, Lecturer at the University; Philippe Véron and Jean Vernou, all three to be prominent teachers of the Reformed faith, and the last named to give his life in martyrdom; Jean Boisseau, sieur de la Borderie, and even the lieutenant-général, François Doyneau, seigneur de Sainte-Soline. With them Calvin is said to have held long conversations on religious as well as scholarly themes, and over a number of them he acquired much influence. The representation given by Florimond de Raemond certainly has much verisimilitude to what we know of Calvin otherwise at this period. Not by public preaching, but by private intercourse with the friends that his high scholarship, agreeable manners, and spiritual earnestness readily secured did he now try to advance the reform which had mastered him. But, if the same historian is to be trusted, Calvin now took a step in advance of any progress he had thus far made in the direction of Protestant worship. With some of these friends, in the shelter of a cave outside the city, he observed the Lord's Supper. It was Florimond's opinion that the simple, primitive rite practiced by the early Protestants of Poitiers which he describes, had been taught them by Calvin. In its observance the leader read a passage from the Gospels describing the institution of the Sacrament, the Roman Mass was then denounced, and those present were invited to the table with the words, "Brethren, let us eat the Lord's bread in memory of His death and passion." Breaking the bread, the leader then gave a fragment to each of those seated with him, and all ate in silence; in the same way the wine was received. Then, after a prayer of thanksgiving by the leader, all repeated the Lord's Prayer and the Apostles' Creed in Latin, and with that the simple service

---

[41] *Naissance*, etc., pp. 891–911; Doumergue, i. 458–464, 580–583.

closed.[42] In this fashion, it may be believed, Calvin ministered to
the little company; and he justified his rejection of the Roman
worship by an appeal to the Scriptures. To Jean Boisseau, sieur de
la Borderie, who lived till 1591, Florimond de Raemond attributed
the narrative – which he may not improbably have heard from
Boisseau himself – that Calvin, in a debate on the Mass held with
Charles le Sage during this stay at Poitiers, pointed to the Bible
before him with the exclamation:[43]

> There is my Mass, and throwing his cap on the table, lifting his
> eyes toward heaven, he cried: Lord, if on the day of judgment
> Thou rebukest me because I have not been at Mass and have
> forsaken it, I shall justly say: Lord, Thou hast not commanded it;
> here is Thy law, here is the Scripture which is the rule that Thou
> hast given me, in which I could not find any other sacrifice than
> that which was offered on the altar of the cross.

Certainly the story sounds very like a probable incident in the
history of that Calvin whose religious development has thus far
been followed. It speaks the same confidence that the Scriptures
are the direct voice of God, and that they are the only law fully
and implicitly to be obeyed, which had been so large factors
in Calvin's conversion. But, whether Florimond de Raemond
is correct in these details or not, it is fair to conclude from his
account that Calvin began the exercise of Protestant ministerial
functions soon after the resignation of his benefices, though
only in the comparatively secure company of his friends. Calvin
had never been ordained in the Roman Church; he was never
to be set apart for the ministry by the imposition of Protestant
hands. He regarded his pastoral labors as a task to which he was
called of God – a call witnessed by his own clear consciousness
of the divine guidance in appointing him his course in life.[44] His
entrance on the pastorate was therefore gradual, but its clear

---

[42] *Naissance*, p. 911; Doumergue, i. 460, 525.

[43] *Naissance*, p. 906; Doumergue, i. 460.

[44] The matter forms a chief part of his correspondence with du Tillet in 1538,
Opera, xb. 241, 269, 290; see also Doumergue, ii. 407–409.

manifestation may, with no little probability, be connected with his stay at Poitiers.

The chief significance of Calvin's stay at Orléans is to be seen in the completion there of his first distinctly theological treatise, the *Psychopannychia*. That Calvin's sojourn in Orléans was long enough to allow time for the composition of the whole tract[45] it is not necessary to suppose; but certainly a brief Preface to the little work was written and dated there.[46] The treatise, which was not printed till 1542, and then apparently in a revised form, is a refutation, by arguments drawn almost entirely from a careful examination of a great number of biblical passages, of the opinion that the soul "sleeps without memory, without intelligence, without sensation, from death till the day of judgment, when it will awake from its slumber." The year in which Calvin wrote was one of widespread dread, in more conservative circles, of the rapidly growing Anabaptist movement which was just coming to its most fanatical manifestation in the establishment of what was proclaimed to be the kingdom of God on earth at Münster. The view which he combated was one to be met with among the Anabaptists, though it had neither the prominence among them, the significance in itself, nor the large number of adherents that he ascribes to it. It is difficult to see why Calvin should have selected this relatively insignificant fragment of Anabaptist speculation for refutation unless it had been more than ordinarily discussed in the little group of friends among whom he was in some sense the leader. But, though the treatise belongs distinctly to the minor writings of Calvin, its original Preface, preserved apparently in unchanged form, is of value as revealing something of his mind just before leaving France. Calvin feels that he is called to be a teacher of Christian doctrine. "If in such need I am silent or dissimulate," he says, "I do not see why I should not be called a betrayer of the truth." He must speak in its defence. It may be charged, however, that by so doing he fosters schism in the Church and offends charity, but "it may be answered, that

---

[45] Doumergue, i. 466, so holds.

[46] *Opera*, v. 170, 171.

we recognise no unity, save in Christ; no charity, save that of which He is the bond; therefore the prime thing in maintaining charity is that the faith should remain inviolate and unchanged among us." The emphasis on purity of doctrine is characteristic of the reformers generally. Luther had set a similar importance upon it in his discussions with Zwingli. Nor is the feeling that by maintaining God's truth, as he saw it, he was purifying rather than dividing the Church, anything peculiar to Calvin, but it is evident that in every way the year 1534 was one of growth in Calvin's religious experience and in recognition of what he believed to be a divine call to a leadership which we may give him credence was in many ways repugnant to his shy and scholarly nature.

As the year 1534 drew toward a close, however, France became increasingly a difficult region of sojourn for a Protestant. The rash and violent placards against the Mass, prepared by Antoine Marcourt, and posted on the night of October 17 or 18, aroused a strenuous, though not long continued, policy of repression. Calvin had been careful in the public manifestation of his opinion; he was not a man to court needless risks, but he had already suffered practical banishment from Paris, and imprisonment at Noyon. His views were well known to many at Angoulême, Poitiers, and Orléans. His friend Louis du Tillet felt no more safe than he. The situation counseled flight from the kingdom if his work was to be continued or his life preserved. And, therefore, in company with du Tillet, aided by two servants, and at least two horses – largely, it is probable, at du Tillet's expense – Calvin made his way through Lorraine to Strassburg and thence to Basel, where he arrived about the beginning of 1535, having experienced no more misadventure on the road than the theft of most of the money of the party and of one of the horses near Metz by an unfaithful servant.[47] Calvin's friend Cop had found a refuge in the same hospitable city just about a year earlier; and his presence there may have been a main reason in inducing Calvin to make it his home.

---

[47] Beza and Colladon, *Opera*, xxi. 57, 124. Calvin was somewhat aided pecuniarily at times by du Tillet, ibid., xb. 272.

6

The "Institutes," Italy and Arrival in Geneva,
1535–1536

At Basel Calvin found a lodging in the home of Catherine Klein, who seems for years to have received student guests, in the eastern suburb of the city – that of St Alban.[1] Here, as Calvin himself says, he "lived as it were concealed and known to few people,"[2] hidden under the name of Martinus Lucanius. The city afforded not merely a safe retreat, but abundant opportunities for study and publication. The reasons which had induced the now-aged Erasmus to make it his home, availed to attract many a less-known scholar. Under the leadership of Johannes Ecolampadius, whose death had occurred more than three years before Calvin's arrival, Basel had been thoroughly committed to Protestantism, and the work thus begun was being ably continued by the chief pastor, Oswald Myconius. Here, though living very quietly, Calvin began some important friendships – with Myconius, with Pierre Viret, to be his associate in the reformation of French-speaking Switzerland, and with Heinrich Bullinger, Zwingli's noble successor in the spiritual leadership of Zürich. Calvin was also in friendly relations with Farel, though this ultimately momentous acquaintance may have been earlier begun. He studied Hebrew, it

---

[1] Peter Ramus, in Doumergue, i. 488.
[2] *Opera*, xxxi. 24.

is probable, under the eminent guidance of Sebastian Münster.[3] Meanwhile he stood in cordial fellowship with Pierre Robert Olivétan, whose relations to his conversion have given rise to so much discussion. Olivétan had been laboring since 1532 among the Waldenses who found protection in the valleys of the southern Alps, and he had been preparing with their approval and at their expense a translation of the Bible into French. When its printing was completed at Neuchâtel in June 1535, it appeared with two commendatory Prefaces from Calvin's pen.[4]

Yet the chief event of Calvin's stay at Basel was the completion and publication of the first edition of the *Institutes*, the preparation of which had been begun at Angoulême. As it was to be put forth after considerable delay at the printer's, in its original Latin dress, in March 1536, it was not merely[5] a handbook of theology which marked its young author as the ablest interpreter of Christian doctrine that the Reformation age had produced, but it was prefaced by a bold yet dignified and respectful Letter addressed to King Francis which at once placed Calvin at the head of French reformers and revealed him in the highest degree as a man of leadership. French Protestantism had had its mystics, its fanatics, its compromisers, and its martyrs, but it had been lacking in men who could speak soberly, convincingly, and boldly in its name. In Calvin, such a leader made himself heard through the Letter to the King. That letter bore the date of August 23, 1535, and as it is evident that its composition was subsequent to the practical completion of the doctrinal treatise to which it was prefixed, it is plain that the manuscript of Calvin's notable volume was essentially finished when he was not yet two months entered on his 27th year.

To judge from his own statements, Calvin would have been content to have labored peacefully at Basel on the production of the *Institutes* longer than was to be the case, and to have issued

---

[3] Doumergue, I, 488, 489, 505; Baumgartner, *Calvin hébraïsant*, p. 20.

[4] *Opera*, ix. 787; Herminjard, ii. 451–454; iii. 294, 348.

[5] The circumstances of its publication, etc., are best discussed by Doumergue, i. 589–595; see also *Opera*, iii. vii–xlvii.

them at last as a practical, dispassionate treatise setting forth the Christian system as he saw it revealed in the Scriptures. The purpose of the *Institutes* was expository. Calvin was above all else, in his own view, an expounder of the Word of God. Writing in 1541, he said of his treatise:[6]

> Although the Holy Scriptures contain a perfect doctrine, to which nothing can be added ... still every person, not intimately acquainted with them, stands in need of some guidance and direction as to what he ought to look for in them ... This cannot be better done in writing than by treating in succession of the principal matters which are comprised in Christian Philosophy. For he who understands these will be prepared to make more progress in the school of God in one day than any other person in three months ...With this view I have composed the present book.

As it came forth, it was not merely a calm doctrinal exposition, but thanks to the Letter prefixed, a noble, dignified – yet none the less passionate – defence of a persecuted cause. The desire to defend that cause and its supporters by the Letter determined the author to issue his volume when he did without waiting for its further elaboration. He must vindicate the character and faith of his associates. Once more, as it seemed to Calvin, the providence of God had thrust him into a publicity which he could not avoid and still be faithful to his duty.

The severe repression with which the King followed the posting of the placards was viewed with disfavor by the Protestants of Germany, whose goodwill Francis wished to retain as possible allies in his rivalries with Charles V. To justify his persecution of French Protestants in the eyes of their German fellow believers, Francis issued a public letter on February 1, 1535, addressed to the estates of the Empire,[7] in which he charged the Protestants of France with anarchistic aims designing an "overthrow of all things." Any government must resist such a "contagious plague that looked toward the foulest sedition." The whole tone of the

---

[6] Preface to the French ed., Beveridge's translation.

[7] Text in Herminjard, iii. 250–254.

royal argument implied that there was a vast gulf between the sober, orderly German Protestants and the rabid revolutionists of France. Calvin must have had rise before his imagination, as he reflected on this presentation, the martyred figure of his Parisian friend, that generous, peaceful, honorable merchant, Estienne de la Forge, who had suffered sixteen days after the date of the King's Letter. He could not leave such calumnies unanswered. Writing twenty-two years after the event, he thus described the publication of the Institutes:[8]

> "Leaving my native country, I removed to Germany, planning that, concealed in some obscure corner, I might enjoy long denied peace. But while I was in retirement at Basel, evil and lying pamphlets were spread abroad to suppress the indignation that the fires in which many pious men had been burned in France excited here and there among the Germans, to the effect that those so cruelly treated were no other than Anabaptists and turbulent men who would overturn by their perverse insanities not religion only, but all political order. Seeing this done by the tricksters of the Court, I felt that my silence would be treachery and that I should oppose with all my might not only lest the undeserved shedding of the innocent blood of holy martyrs should be concealed by false report, but also lest they should go in future to whatever slaughter they pleased without arousing the pity of any. These were my reasons for publishing the *Institutes*: first, that I might vindicate from unjust affront my brethren whose death was precious in the sight of the Lord; and, next, that some sorrow and anxiety should move foreign peoples, since the same sufferings threatened many. Neither was it that thick and elaborate work it now is, but only a little hand-book that then appeared, nor had it any other aim than to witness to the faith of those whom I saw evilly reviled by impious and faithless flatterers."

It was, indeed, as Calvin said, relatively a small volume as originally issued. Yet it numbered 519 pages. Their dimensions being, however, only six and a quarter by four inches, it could be readily carried in a fair-sized pocket. In typography, it was a

---

[8] Preface to *Psalms, Opera*, xxxi. 23.

credit to the printers, Thomas Platter and Balthasar Lasius, and to the publisher, Johann Oporin, who stood behind them. Its sale was considerable, for in March 1537, a year after its publication, Oporin could report to Calvin that so much was it in demand that no copies remained at Basel, and not more than fifty at Frankfurt, whither a supply had been sent for sale at the great fair. A new edition was being eagerly sought.[9]

The Letter to King Francis is one of the few masterpieces of apologetic literature. Courteously and respectfully, yet as one aware of his legal rights as a subject, and conscious that his sovereign has duties as a ruler which have not been fulfilled, Calvin argues the case for himself and his Protestant fellow believers. It is no cringing seeker for toleration that here speaks, nor is it a fanatic uttering a tirade against persecutors; but the voice is one convinced of the justice of his cause and skilled to reply to criticisms of it with carefully trained and lawyer-like acuteness and cogency of statement. It is as convincing as it is brilliant.

The Protestants, who have been so cruelly slandered, Calvin tells the King, are being condemned on mere rumor. However humble their persons, justice demands that the sovereign examine into their cause the more urgently because it involves:[10]

> Such mighty interests as these: how the glory of God is to be maintained on earth inviolate; how the truth of God is to preserve its dignity; how the kingdom of Christ is to continue amongst us compact and secure. The cause is worthy of your ear, worthy of your investigation, worthy of your judgment-seat ... Take but a cursory view, most valiant King, of all the parts of our cause, and count us of all wicked men the most iniquitous, if you do not discover plainly that "to this end we labor and suffer reproach, because we put our hope in the living God;" because we believe it to be "life eternal" to "know the only true God and Jesus Christ" whom He has sent. For this hope some of us are in bonds, some beaten with rods, some made a gazing-stock, some proscribed,

---

[9] Herminjard, iv. 208.
[10] *Opera*, i. 11, 13, 14, Beveridge's translation slightly amended.

some most cruelly tortured, some obliged to flee; we are all pressed with poverty, loaded with dire execrations, lacerated with abuse, and treated with the greatest indignity. Look now at our adversaries... The true religion which is handed down in the Scriptures, and which ought to have stood unchanged among all men, they readily permit both themselves and others to be ignorant of, to neglect and despise; and they deem it of little moment what each man may hold concerning God and Christ, or may not hold, provided he submits his opinion with implicit faith to the judgment of the Church ... Nevertheless, they cease not to assail our doctrine, and to accuse and defame it in what terms they may, in order to render it either hated or suspected. They call it new, and of recent birth; they carp at it as doubtful and uncertain; they ask by what miracles it has been confirmed; they query if it be fair to receive it against the consent of so many holy fathers and the most ancient custom; they urge us to confess either that it is schismatical in giving battle to the Church, or that the Church must have been almost dead during the many centuries in which nothing of the kind was heard. Lastly, they say there is little need of argument, for its quality may be known by its fruits, namely, the large number of sects, the many seditious disturbances, and the great licentiousness which it has produced.

Having stated his opponents' criticisms Calvin proceeds, like an able attorney, to refute them in order. The doctrine he defends is not new, save to his enemies; it is the very Word of God. It is not doubtful, save to those that are ignorant of it. It needs no fresh miraculous confirmation, since it is the same gospel, "the truth of which is confirmed by all the miracles which Christ and the Apostles ever wrought." The Fathers, at least of a purer age, though not without much human error, are even more on the side of the reformers than those who pretend to do them special reverence; and in numerous instances, which Calvin cites, they have opposed doctrines or practices now obtaining in the Roman Communion. Custom is no fitting test of truth, for "human affairs have scarcely ever been so happily constituted as that the better course pleased the greater number." Nor do Protestants hold the Church to have been dead; those who seek reform have a truer definition of what the Church really is than their opponents:[11]

> The hinges on which our controversy turns are these: first, in their contending that the form of the Church is always visible and apparent; and, secondly, in their placing that form in the see of the Church of Rome and its hierarchy. We, on the contrary, maintain that the Church may exist without any apparent form; and that the form is not ascertained by that external splendor which they foolishly admire, but by a very different mark, namely, by pure preaching of the Word of God and rightful administration of the sacraments.

In so defining the "notes of the Church," Calvin stood on the general Protestant basis, expressed, for instance, six years before in the Augsburg Confession. To the allegation that the new preaching brought disorder, he replies: "The blame of these evils is wrongfully charged upon it, which ought to be ascribed to the malice of Satan" and he concludes with the appeal:[12]

> Magnanimous King, be not moved by the absurd insinuations with which our adversaries are striving to frighten you into the belief that nothing else is wished and aimed at by this new gospel (for so they term it) than opportunity for seditions and impunity for all vices. God is not the author of division, but of peace; and the Son of God, who came to destroy the works of the devil, is not the minister of sin. We are undeservedly charged with desires of a kind for which we have never given even the smallest suspicion …[Your] good will, we are confident, we should regain, would you but once, with calmness and composure, read this our confession, which we wish to serve with your majesty instead of a defence. But if the whispers of the malevolent so possess your ears that the accused are to have no opportunity of pleading their cause; if those vindictive furies, with your connivance, are always to rage with bonds, scourgings, tortures, maimings, and burnings, we, indeed, like sheep doomed to slaughter, shall be reduced to every extremity; yet so that, in our patience, we will possess our souls,

---

[11] *Opera*, i. 20, 21.
[12] Ibid., 25, 26.

and wait for the strong hand of the Lord, which doubtless will appear in time, and show itself armed, both to rescue the poor from affliction, and to take vengeance on the despisers. Most powerful and illustrious King, may the Lord, the King of kings, establish your throne in justice and your rulership in equity.

Calvin had spoken the word which French Protestantism needed to have said in its defence, and henceforth no man could doubt his leadership in its cause.

The *Institutes* themselves, to which this Letter was prefixed, were, indeed, far from the perfection of logical treatment and inclusiveness of view which were to characterise the final form attained in the edition of 1559, but they were even now sufficiently significant.[13] Calvin's work follows the ancient popular order of religious instruction which had served Luther for an outline in drafting his short *Catechism* of 1529, and was determined in its sequence by the elementary teachings which every Christian child had long been expected to learn by heart. In the first four of his six chapters he therefore treats of the Law, as set forth in the Ten Commandments; Faith, as embodied in the Apostles' Creed; Prayer, as illustrated in that of our Lord; and the Sacraments of Baptism and the Lord's Supper. To these he joins two further chapters, one treating of the "False Sacraments" which Roman teaching had added to the primal two, and the other of "Christian Liberty, Ecclesiastical Power, and Civil Administration." This order of discussion was not only historically familiar, but it gave to Calvin's legally trained mind the advantage of basing much of his exposition on defined documents generally believed to be of absolute authority. Yet Calvin's treatment is far from being confined to an exposition of these documents alone. Its range is broad, and it deserves the description which the publishers, more probably than Calvin, placed on the title page of the first edition of the *Institutes* – that of "containing well-nigh the whole sum of piety." Between the first three chapters and their successors a certain

[13] Text in *Opera*, i. 27–252; for comparison with later editions see ibid., li–lviii, and also Köstlin, "Calvins Institutio nach Form und Inhalt," in *Theologische Studien und Kritiken*, for 1868, pp. 7–62, 410–486.

difference of style and atmosphere may also be noted. The earlier portion is less polemic, more simple, and calm; while the closing chapters are more vivacious and controversial in tone and reflect more strongly the heat of the quarrel with the ancient Church. The supposition is natural that they were written after Calvin's rising indignation at the misrepresentation of his fellow-believers had led him to modify his earlier plan of a peacefully wrought-out work of Christian instruction. Yet the whole volume is remarkably well-poised and exhibits everywhere great self-control on the part of its author. Its denunciatory epithets are much fewer than in its later editions. As compared with them, however, it shows more of a departure from the classics-loving Calvin who had commented on Seneca. Though Ambrose, Augustine, and Plato are quoted, Calvin makes far less use of the Fathers and the great writers of Greece and Rome than in the subsequent editions of the *Institutes*.

In its doctrinal outlook, the first edition of the *Institutes* might well appear a product of the German Reformation, especially as that movement had developed in the Rhine Valley. Most of the peculiarities of Calvinism are discoverable, but they are not so prominent or so sharply put as in later editions. Yet there is already in clear evidence that profound consciousness of the reality and authority of God which marks all Calvin's thought. Next in emphasis is its doctrine of salvation through reconciliation by faith in Christ. "All the sum of the gospel is contained in these two heads: repentance and remission of sins."[14] Election is briefly set forth as a basis of confidence of salvation and as determining membership in the invisible Church, but it is not given quite the central position that seems logically to belong to the doctrine, and reprobation is simply mentioned. From election, the perseverance of those thus chosen is clearly deduced.

The treatise begins, like the later editions of the *Institutes*, with the declaration that religious truth is almost entirely comprehended in the knowledge of God and of ourselves: of God, that He is infinite wisdom and goodness, and the source of all good everywhere, for whose glory all things are made, a just Judge and

---

[14] *Opera*, i. 149.

yet merciful to those that seek Him; of ourselves, that, since the loss of that original perfection in which Adam was created, the whole human race has been totally corrupt and justly exposed to the wrath of God. Hence any effort to merit righteousness is unavailing, but God forgives sins and gives a new heart to the humbly penitent, through and for the sake of Christ, if they accept His gifts with "certain faith." The Law, therefore, is not our rule of salvation, but a "looking-glass" which shows us our condition. Calvin then explains the several commandments and concludes that the Law has three main uses: it shows what God justly requires of us; it admonishes those whom nothing but fear of punishment will move; and it is "an exhortation to the faithful," furnishing them a rule for learning what is "the will of God" to which it is their purpose to conform. This third use of the Law as a discipline for Christian believers is a mark of Calvinism as distinguished from Lutheran interpretations. Though having no confidence in good works as of a saving value, the Christian will look for them in his life as "the fruit of the Spirit of God," done by God through him, and the evidence that he has "passed from the kingdom of sin to the kingdom of righteousness." His assurance of salvation is based on the divine election thus witnessed.

In his second chapter, "On Faith," Calvin distinguishes between an intellectual recognition of God's existence and of the historic truth of the Scripture narrative – a possession "unworthy of the name of faith" – and a belief which places "all hope and confidence in one God and Christ," "doubting nothing of the good-will of God towards us." The basis without which this faith cannot be sustained is declared to be the Scriptures. Calvin then discusses the Trinity, and proceeds to the explanation of the Apostles' Creed. The "holy catholic Church" he defines as "the whole number of the elect"; but, since this invisible Church cannot be exactly perceived by us, we may in the judgment of charity hold to be of it "all who by confession of faith, example of life, and participation in the sacraments confess the same God and Christ as we."

Since men have nothing of good in themselves, they must look to God for all blessings, and hence Calvin devotes his third chapter to prayer. Its first condition is humility, its next "certain faith." The merit is not in the prayer, nor in the dignity of him who offers it, but in the divine promise which will be fulfilled to him who prays in equal faith, as truly as to Peter or to Paul. It is to be offered to God in the name of Christ only – not to or through the saints, and public prayer should be in a tongue understood by all the congregation. Private prayer may be spoken or without words, but true prayer has always two elements – petition and giving of thanks. Calvin then expounds the Lord's Prayer as a model of what prayer should be.

With his fourth chapter Calvin takes up the Sacraments, which he defines as "external signs by which the Lord sets forth and attests his goodwill towards us in order to sustain the weakness of our faith." No sacrament is without the preceding divine promise, to which it witnesses. It is like the seal to a document, valueless in itself, but confirming that to which it is attached. Two sacraments only have been thus divinely instituted – Baptism and the Lord's Supper. Baptism serves to strengthen our faith in God's remission of our sins, and as a confession of Him before men. It is to be administered to infants as well as to adults, and in the simple way the Scriptures indicate. Whether by immersion or sprinkling may well be left to the usages of different countries. Like Baptism, the Lord's Supper is "an exercise of faith, given to maintain, excite, and increase it." It is the attestation and witness of God's promise. It gives assurance that whatever is Christ's is ours, whatever is ours is His. "All the energy of the sacrament is in these words, 'which is given for you.'" Having said this, Calvin brings to mind the "horrible dissensions" which had been manifested in the recent controversies between Lutherans and Zwinglians regarding the nature of Christ's presence in the Supper. His own view, which he argues with great acuteness, is that "the sacrament is something spiritual." It is the very condition of the existence of a physical body that it can be in but one place. Hence, in the Supper, Christ is "truly and efficaciously," but not physically, present: "not the very substance of his body nor the real and natural body of Christ is there given, but all things which Christ bestows as benefits to us by His body." Though asserting thus in the clearest terms that Christ's presence in the elements is one of spiritual power only, Calvin gives the impression of standing in closer sympathy with Luther than with Zwingli in his estimate of the nature and worth of the Supper. He then goes on to reject the Roman conception of the Mass in most energetic terms, and urges that Communion should be observed with simple ritual, and at least once a week – a fact which should be weighed by those who criticize the Sunday worship of Calvinism as too bare and too purely intellectual. If a much less frequent observation became the rule in the Reformed churches, it was not by Calvin's intention.

In his fifth chapter Calvin carries his warfare yet more vigorously against the Roman system, attacking with great vivacity of style and keenness of argument the claims of Confirmation, Penance, Extreme Unction, Orders, or Marriage to be called sacraments at all. As God alone can create a sacrament, since He alone can give the promise of which it is the witness, so His Word alone reveals the Sacraments that He has instituted; and tried by this test, the five just enumerated are found wanting. Calvin discusses each at length, and criticizing in its connection auricular confession, satisfaction, a treasury of good works, indulgences, and purgatory. Treating of orders, Calvin holds that the Scripture "recognizes no other minister of the Church than a preacher of the Word of God, called to govern the Church, whom it calls now a bishop, now a presbyter, and occasionally a pastor." Orders are simply this calling, which should be accomplished with the consent of the Church to be served, and the advice of one or two neighboring ministers as to the fitness of the candidate. Whether this consent of the Church should be expressed by a meeting of the whole congregation, or the votes of a few elders, magistrates, princes, or a city government, Calvin leaves to be determined by circumstances. Imposition of hands may properly be used in setting the minister apart for his work, but is in no sense a sacrament.

Calvin's concluding chapter takes up the theme of Christian liberty. It consists, he holds, in a freedom which raises the Christian above the "Law" as a test of obedience, though, since we are called to sanctification, the Law remains an admonishing and stimulating influence. From this principle it follows that Christian "consciences submit to the Law not as if compelled by the force of the law, but free from the yoke of the Law itself, they obey the will of God voluntarily." Hence, to the Christian, the Law is a rule of life. A third element in Christian liberty is freedom in the use of those gifts of God which are often called indifferent things. "Nor is it anywhere forbidden to laugh, or enjoy food, or to add new possessions to old and ancestral property, or to be delighted with musical harmonies, or to drink wine" – a phrase which reveals Calvin as anything but an ascetic – but he adds, "that is, indeed, true; but when the abundance of possessions leads one to be wrapped up in enjoyments and to immerse one's self in them, to intoxicate mind and soul with present pleasures and always to seek after new delights – these things are as far as possible from a proper use of the gifts of God." "The sum is, that 'We that are strong ought to bear the infirmities of the weak and not to please ourselves.'" For his proper guidance, man is placed in this world under a double government, spiritual and temporal. That spiritual kingdom has only one King, Christ, and one Law, the Word of the Gospel. Its officers are "ministers" of that Word, and have no right to add to or take from the prescriptions therein contained. "The Church is to be heard, they say. Who denies it, since she proclaims nothing save from the Word of God? If they demand anything more, they know that the words of Christ give no support to their demand." Of pastors, and all other Church officers, Calvin declares, "All their function is bounded by the ministry of the Word of God, all their wisdom by the knowledge of that Word, all their eloquence by its preaching." Holding this principle, Calvin necessarily finds no authority in the decrees of councils or in the promulgations of Church Fathers and bishops, save as they conform to this one divine standard of faith and practice.

Calvin then proceeds to vindicate civil government from the criticisms of it as no fit employment for Christian men, often directed against it by the Anabaptists and other radical reformers of his day. It is established by divine authority "to order our life for the society of men, to conform our conduct to civil justice, to reconcile us one with another, to nourish and preserve common peace and tranquillity." The duty of the magistrate is not merely to see that "public peace be not disturbed, and each safely possess his own," but to guard lest "idolatry, sacrilege against the name of God, blasphemies against His truth, or other public offences against religion should break out or be spread among the people." Severe punishments are often necessary, but clemency is the chief ornament of a ruler. The collection of taxes and the waging of just wars are not forbidden to the Christian magistrate, any more than the establishment of such laws as equity and the teaching of God's Word counsel. The punishments by which laws are sanctioned may vary with times and places, but their purpose is always the same. They condemn what God condemns. To these laws and magistrates, even to rulers of vicious and tyrannical character, full obedience is due, save where the command contradicts the revealed will of God. Where God has spoken, no other voice deserves the slightest heed.

Such, in the barest outline, is the remarkable handbook of Christian belief with which Calvin accompanied his defence of French Protestantism. Though greatly to be enlarged and improved in the later editions on which he was unweariedly to labor till within five years of the close of his life, it stood forth, even in this early form, not merely as by far the most significant treatise that the reformers of France had yet produced, but without a superior as a clear, logical, and popularly apprehensible presentation of those principles for which all Protestantism contended. It was far more than a theoretic exposition of Christian truth. Though in form not strictly a program for action, it could easily yield the basis of a new constitution for the Church, and of a regulation of the moral life of the community. The felicity of its style, the logical cogency of argument, the precision of statement which marked the volume, were Calvin's own. The moral enthusiasm which shines through it was a kindling force. As a treatment of Christian doctrine, it was fresh and original. But it was even more a carefully wrought-out exposition of the Christian life, novel and inspiring in its clearness and earnestness.

Such qualities do not exclude, however, a large degree of indebtedness to those who had thought before him on these themes, and especially to his immediate predecessors in the leadership of the Reformation. Calvin's mind was formulative rather than creative. Given the fundamental principles of the Reformation, he could carry them to their logical consequences with a keenness of insight and a clearness of statement such as none of his contemporaries could equal; but it may be questioned whether in the development of Christian doctrine he could have done the path-breaking work accomplished by the first generation of the reformers.

Calvin's indebtedness to Luther was, of course, great. It is Luther's doctrines of faith alone and of the way of salvation that the *Institutes* present, and, in spite of divergencies of the highest significance from the view of Christ's presence in the Supper taught by the Saxon reformer, it is Luther's conception of the Sacraments as attestations of the divine promise designed to strengthen our trust, that marks Calvin's definition of these Christian ordinances. Calvin's whole theological work was made possible only by the antecedent labors of Luther. But in many doctrinal details it is easy to trace an indebtedness not so much to Luther directly as to the German Reformation as it fashioned itself in the minds of the reformers of southwestern Germany. Calvin had little spiritual kinship to Zwingli. He stood nearer to Luther than to the reformer of German-speaking Switzerland. But he owed much to Martin Bucer of Strassburg.[15] Such a sympathy in interpretation of the principles of the Reformation was natural to a young frenchman by reason of the geographical proximity

---

[15] See R. Seeberg, *Lehrbuch der Dogmengeschichte*, Erlangen, 1898, ii. 379–383; and, especially, August Lang, *Der Evangelienkommentar Martin Butzer's*, Leipzig, 1900, *passim*.

of the Rhineland and consequent readiness of intercourse, but in Calvin's case it seems more than a general indebtedness to influences widely prevalent in the region of which Strassburg was the center. Views characteristic of Bucer, and which Bucer had put forth in his *Evangelienkommentar*, the first edition of which had appeared in 1527, Calvin had clearly made his own, so that there is reason to believe that Bucer's work had been used in his studies preparatory to the *Institutes*. Some color is given by this acquaintance to the claim that a correspondence had begun with the Strassburg reformer by Calvin before his flight from France, though reasons have already been adduced showing this opinion to be improbable.[16]

Calvin's centration of his theology about the two conceptions of the universal agency of God in salvation and of the divine predestination was of the essence of Bucer's thinking. Calvin's treatment of election, clearly apparent in the first edition of the *Institutes*, as the basis of that confidence enjoyed by those living the Christian life which distinguishes them from non-Christians, was already taught by Bucer, with whom, as with Calvin in the first edition of the Institutes, election was a doctrine to strengthen practical Christian living far more than an abstract explanation of the divine government of the universe. With Bucer, Calvin defined faith as "persuasio" – a certainty of conviction, and as with Bucer the "glory" or "honor" of God are phrases frequently employed to denote, for example, the purpose "for which all things in heaven and in earth are created." As with Bucer, man is powerless to achieve any good thing – all of worth is from God. But in Bucer and Calvin alike, by a kind of overriding of logic by the demands of an ardent practical piety, the Christian life is looked upon as a strenuous, warm hearted, self-denying effort to realize in one's self the blessings and the character which the divine election has made ours.[17] The whole Reformation age made much of election, as was natural in an epoch characterized by a mighty revival of Augustinianism, but the pietistic use of the doctrine as the

---

[16] *Ante*, p. 65.
[17] Compare Lang, op. cit., pp. 194, 195.

basis of confidence and the encouragement to struggle for high attainment in the Christian life was more markedly a trait of Bucer than of any of his contemporaries among the reformers of the first generation, and was to be made by Calvin a prime characteristic of the churches which felt his moulding touch.

But besides this indebtedness to older reformers who were still living when Calvin's *Institutes* were first published, the young thinker took much, consciously or unconsciously, from the later schoolmen. Thus he owed to Scotus, doubtless without realizing the obligation, the thought of God as almighty will, for motives behind whose choice it is as absurd as it is impious to inquire. To Scotus, also, was due the conception that the power of God accompanies, rather than exists in, the Sacraments. And from the general feeling of mediaeval Latin Christendom that the Church is independent of the State, Calvin probably derived the conviction which was to make his theory of the relation of the Church to organized political society one involving far greater freedom than that of any other of the reformers, whatever limitations that theory was afterwards to exhibit in Calvin's Genevan practice. To point out these obligations is, however, in no way to detract from the merit of the youthful theologian. He built his edifice of Christian thought with utmost skill, but in so doing he did not reject the plans on which older laborers had wrought or the materials which their patient efforts had gathered.

On the publication of the *Institutes* in March 1536, or perhaps on the completion of the revision of the proofs of the previous month,[18] Calvin set out from Basel, accompanied by his friend du Tillet, for a brief visit to Ferrara, the object of which was to meet the duchess, Renée, wife of Ercole II. He traveled under the disguised name of Charles d'Espeville, evidently reminiscent of the territory from which part of his ecclesiastical revenue at Noyon had been derived. The occasion and circumstances of this journey to Italy are obscure

---

[18] Beza and Colladon, *Opera*, xxi. 30, 58, 125. The literature treating of this journey, which is extensive and controversial, is well considered by Doumergue, ii. 3–94; see also C. A. Cornelius, *Historische Arbeiten*, Leipzig, 1899, pp. 105–123.

and have given rise to a mass of fable and conjecture, but a sufficient reason is to be seen in the existence of a state of affairs at the court of Ferrara which gave promise, for the time being, that the Reform movement would there find a welcome. To aid the cause he had at heart was doubtless Calvin's purpose in crossing the Alps.

Renée, who was almost the same age as Calvin, was the daughter of King Louis XII of France, and regarded her mission in Italy as the defence of French interests, even at the expense of long-continued disputes with her husband. Proud of her birth and nationality, she had a generous welcome for such Frenchmen as sought her aid, and was accustomed to reply to critics of her kindliness: "They are ... of my nation, and if God had given me a beard on my chin, and I were a man, they would all be my subjects ... if this evil salic law did not bind me too firmly."[19] In mental traits she much resembled her cousin, Marguerite d'Angoulême, possessing the same love of letters, the same desire to aid those who were advancing the cause of learning, and similar religious opinions, being probably largely an adherent of the newer views at heart all her life, as she openly became after her return to France as a widow. But, like Marguerite, she remained during her sojourn in Italy in outward conformity to the Roman Church, and was claimed by either side in the struggle. Like that of Marguerite, also, her court was a place of refuge for many whom the persecuting policy of Francis I compelled to fly from France; and in the spring of 1536 it sheltered, among others, the Protestant poet Clément Marot, whose name had been seventh on the list of those under suspicion as having guilty knowledge of the placards of October 1534, which had cost French Protestantism so heavily. The suspicion with which these fugitives were regarded by the churchly authorities at Ferrara was confirmed by an act of one of Marot's companions, like him suspected of connection with the Placards, a young singer known as Jehannet. On Good Friday, April 14, 1536, he had walked out of the church, at the time of the adoration of the cross, in evident disapproval of the service.[20]

---

[19] Brantôme, OEuvres, viii. 111.

[20] *Bulletin*, x. 36, 37; xxxiv. 291; Doumergue, ii. 52.

Arrested and examined by torture, he declared many of Renée's protégés adherents of the newer views. Most of those thus implicated promptly left Ferrara; but investigation continued, and on May 4 another of the French recipients of the duchess's bounty, Jean de Bouchefort, a clergyman who had come from the diocese of Tournay, was arrested under a charge of "Lutheranism." The court of Ferrara might well seem to an eager French reformer a hopeful field for sowing evangelical ideas, or even for inducing a duchess already so favorable to French refugees to take an open stand in support of the faith which many of them cherished. A young humanist, such as Calvin was, would moreover gladly embrace an opportunity of seeing Italy, and this desire Beza presents as one of Calvin's motives.[21]

How far Calvin's hopes may have reached or just what he attempted in Ferrara, it is impossible to say. His visit was brief. He was later wont to say that he had entered Italy only to leave it; and, though his stay has been variously estimated, it was probably at most from the middle of March to the latter part of April. The arrest of Jehannet appears to have induced him and du Tillet, as it did many other foreign visitors, to leave the dangerous city. Calvin was no rash seeker of peril. He met Renée, and made the acquaintance of others in her circle. It is inconceivable that he did not make plain his position to her, and labor to win her to a more positive evangelicalism, so far as brief opportunity permitted; but his character and mission were not generally revealed. The learned German physician at the court of the duchess, Johann Sinapius, with whom Calvin formed an acquaintance at Ferrara, remained in ignorance;[22] and, if he did not know, it is evident that Calvin kept his dangerous secret from the world at large. His departure from Ferrara was unhindered. The story of a seizure by the Inquisition and an escape from its clutches, first recorded by Muratori, and since often repeated, in dramatic form for instance by Merle d'Aubigné, and with greater care of investigation by Fontana, is legendary – the dates

[21] *Opera*, xxi. 125.
[22] Sinapius' letter, Herminjard, vi. 3; Cornelius, *Historische Arbeiten*, p. 107.

involved showing that, whatever the experience may have been, its hero was not Calvin.[23]

Though brief, Calvin's visit to Ferrara was not without result. His unusual power of attracting associates and rendering them friends was once more manifested. In spite of doubts cast upon the success of his intercourse with Renée,[24] it seems to have paved the way for the correspondence which, though not begun till at least a year later, was to continue till Calvin's death. But, if his success in turning the duchess to a public support of the evangelical cause was not what he may possibly have hoped, he won the devoted friendship of a brilliant young French lady of the little court, Francoise Boussiron, daughter of the lord of Grand-Ry in Poitou, and soon to become the wife of that Johann Sinapius of whom mention has been made. To her Calvin became a spiritual adviser, and with her, and soon with her husband, he remained in correspondence. Writing to Calvin from his later home in Germany, in 1557, more than two years after her death, Sinapius could say: "She honored you as long as she lived, and loved you, and you, in turn, regarded her as a sister."[25]

A frequent subject of Calvin's discussions with the little group into brief association with which he came at Ferrara must have been the proper attitude to assume toward the services of the ancient Church. That, he tells Renée in a letter written very possibly in 1537, had been a subject of conversation, unquestionably at Ferrara, between him and her almoner, the adroit and unstable François Richardot.[26] To Richardot he showed a "treatise," which may possibly have been the just-published *Institutes*, but which was more probably one of two burning letters of entreaty and denunciation written, so Colladon recorded, on this Italian journey,[27] though not

---

[23] Muratori, *Annali d'Italia*, 1749, x. 275; Merle d'Abugné, *La réformation en Europe au temps de Calvin*, v. 567; Fontana, Renata di Francia, 1889, passim; Doumergue, ii. 54–56.

[24] Cornelius, p. 107; compare Doumergue, ii. 57, 729–731.

[25] *Opera*, xvi. 375; Doumergue, ii. 66.

[26] Ibid., xi. 326; on date, Doumergue, ii. 729.

[27] Ibid., xxi. 60; see also Calvin's letter, Herminjard, vi. 200.

to be given to the public till they were put forth at Basel, early in 1537, by the same printers that had issued the *Institutes*.[28] The first of these letters, and probably the one shown to Richardot in manuscript, was addressed to an "excellent man and close friend" who has always been identified with Calvin's intimate associate at Orléans, Nicolas Duchemin, though it is evident that the author had in view the general body of those unwilling or afraid to carry Protestant convictions to what seemed to him their logical conclusions, rather than a single reader. He answers the question, certainly a very pressing one in those days of persecution, whether a man of evangelical convictions could give the sanction of an outward conformity to much of the Roman ritual, notably to "that head of all abominations, the Mass," with a decided negative. No man, he argues, can rightfully offer anything less than a conscientious obedience to God's commands as set forth in His Word. "This is specially forbidden you, that any one should see you sharing in the sacrilege of the Mass, or uncovering the head before an image, or supporting any superstition whatever of a nature whereby the glory of God is dimmed, His religion profaned, His truth corrupted." Such a position was undoubtedly logical and heroic, but one cannot wonder that many could not reach it, nor can one blame these "Pseudo-Nicodemites" as much as Calvin and his age were wont to believe they deserved. The martyr spirit is not given to all; nor had Calvin been the least cautious of men in avoiding danger by overt action in Catholic lands. Calvin's other letter was addressed "to an old friend, now a prelate," who was undoubtedly that eager humanistic reformer of 1533, Gérard Roussel, to whom Calvin himself had owed much, but who had recently received the bishopric of Oloron. Nowhere in his writings does Calvin show more passionate indignation. To him, evidently, Roussel was one who had turned from the good cause, and had made shipwreck by accepting office in a communion marked by greed and avarice. His friend had become a traitor. Calvin's indignation is easy to understand. Roussel had changed, however, far less than he supposed.

---

[28] The Preface was dated January 12, 1537. Both are given in *Opera*, v. 233–278; and are respectively entitled *De jugiendis impiorum sacris* and *De sacerdotio papali abjiciendo*.

The advance toward militant Protestantism had been in Calvin himself; and Roussel carried his always incomplete yet real evangelical ideas to his bishopric, where he continued to do much the same work as when Calvin had formed the now-despised friendship with him at Paris.

The change for the worse in the situation of the French refugees at Ferrara consequent upon Jehannet's overt action induced Calvin and du Tillet to leave a city that had now become dangerous, for the safety of Switzerland. By what route they made their way over the Alps, probably early in May 1536, we do not know, but a persistent tradition has asserted that Calvin engaged in evangelical missionary activity in Aosta, the southern terminus of the St Bernard pathway across the mountain barrier between Italy and the valley of the upper Rhone. Like all that relates to Calvin's Italian journey, this tradition has given rise to controversy.[29] Anything like a prolonged activity at Aosta is impossible; but the Alpine valley was the scene of much religious agitation in 1535 and 1536, and it is conceivable that Calvin may have chosen the St Bernard route and have made a brief stay at Aosta to see with his own eyes the religious situation and the prospects of the evangelical cause. At present it must remain a matter of conjecture, though Calvin's connection with Aosta is probably purely legendary. What is certain is that Calvin and du Tillet reached Basel in safety, and there separated, du Tillet going to Neuchâtel and Geneva, and Calvin taking his journey to Paris for a brief sojourn in France, that he might put in order his few business interests in that land and bring back his brother and sister with him, to find a home in the Protestant atmosphere of Strassburg or Basel.[30]

---

[29] Set forth and defended by Jules Bonnet in *Calvin au val d'Aoste*, Paris, 1861, the story was destructively and effectively criticised by Albert Rilliet, *Lettre à M. J.-H. Merle d'Aubigné*, 1864. The evidence is gone over anew by Doumergue, ii. 85–94. See also Eduard Bähler, "Calvin in Aosta," in the *Jahrbuch des Schweizer Alpenclub*, xxxix. 189–195; and the *Bulletin* for March and April, 1905, pp. 177–183.

[30] Colladon, *Opera*, xxi. 58.

That Calvin was thus able peacefully to return to a capital from which he had been compelled to flee less than three years before was due to the exigencies of French politics. Francis had entered but a few months on the persecutions following the placards when he turned largely from them to begin cultivating the German Protestants as possible allies in the new war with Charles V that was to break out early in 1536. In June, 1535 he invited Melanchthon to visit the French court. On July 16 following, he issued the Edict of Coucy, permitting those charged with heresy to return, provided they would desist from their errors and abjure them within six months. On May 31, 1536, these privileges had been confirmed.[31] Availing himself of this grace, Calvin was in Paris by June 2, 1536, for on that day he gave a power of attorney to his younger brother Antoine, who ten days later joined at Noyon with his elder brother, Charles, in a sale of lands which had belonged to their parents.[32] The granting of this power of attorney makes it well-nigh certain that Calvin himself did not go to Noyon. From Paris, his business completed, he set forth, accompanied by Antoine and his sister Marie, for Strassburg; but knowing, as he himself later recorded, that the direct route was barred by the war, Calvin made a long detour, probably by way of Lyons, reaching Geneva in the latter half of July, and intending to pass only a single night in the city before resuming his journey to the Rhineland.[33] Recognized by an acquaintance, in all probability du Tillet, his presence was made known to Guillaume Farel, who was struggling to maintain the evangelical cause in the recently reformed city. Farel, always fiery and eloquent, urged and adjured Calvin to stay and aid in the difficult endeavor. It was a moment of far-reaching decision, for Calvin recognized as he believed the divine call, and, if God had spoken, His voice was to be obeyed. "Farel kept me at Geneva," he said, writing of the event, "not so much by advice and entreaty as by a dreadful adjuration, as if

---

[31] *Opera*, xb. 55, 58; Doumergue, ii. 174.

[32] Documents in full in Lefranc, *Jeunesse*, pp. 205–208.

[33] Preface to *Psalms*, *Opera*, xxxi. 26. On time of arrival at Geneva see Herminjard, iv. 74, 75; Doumergue, ii. 7.

God had stretched forth His hand upon me from on high to arrest me."[34] That the task was hard and unexpected was no reason why that divine summons should be disregarded. God, he thought, had set before him the work to be done. He would enter on it.

---

[34] Ibid., *Opera*, xxxi. 26.

7

GENEVA TILL CALVIN'S COMING

No city in Christendom had had a more eventful or stormier history than Geneva[1] during the generation and especially during the decade preceding Calvin's coming. In none had more diverse forces contended for the mastery. Intermixed as political considerations were in all the religious struggles of the Reformation period, nowhere was the skein more tangled than at Geneva; and nowhere, also, did the field seem more difficult for the development of a movement predominantly religious in character.

Known certainly since the time of Julius Caesar, Geneva had been a town of importance under Roman rule, and had become the seat of a bishopric soon after the conversion of Constantine gave peace to the Church. The downfall of the Roman Empire saw Geneva the capital of the Burgundian kingdom and after various vicissitudes, it came, early in the twelfth century, under the overlordship of the Hohenstaufen emperors, and was known, perhaps not quite justly, as an "imperial city." The real possessors of power in the city during this period were, however, the counts of Geneva and its bishops; and between these spiritual and lay

---

[1] By far the best sketch in English is that of Prof. H. D. Foster, "Geneva before Calvin," in *The American Historical Review*, viii. 217–240 (1903), where the more important sources are indicated. More extended and very valuable are Kampschulte, *Johann Calvin*, i. 3–218; and Doumergue, ii. 97–149.

rulers constant struggles were waged, which resulted in the decided victory of the ecclesiastical lords. With the thirteenth century, a new lay force made itself felt – that of the rising, ambitious, and energetic house of Savoy. The Genevan bishops used its aid to rid themselves of the last remnants of the power of the Genevan counts, only to find that in the rulers of Savoy they were to meet a far abler enemy. In 1285 Amadeus V of Savoy entered into a compact to protect the burghers of Geneva against their bishop, and in 1290 the bishop was forced to yield as a fief to that energetic count of Savoy the appointment of the episcopal deputy for temporal administration, or *vicedominus* – a post which its new lords retained under their control till 1528, and with it a position of influence in Genevan affairs. Meanwhile the burghers of the city, who had been of sufficient significance to be courted in the aggressions of Savoy as early as 1285, were demanding recognition of their claims till after long struggles they forced from Bishop Adhémar Fabri in 1387 the *Franchises*, which gave constitutional sanction to their much-prized customs. By this charger the right of the citizens to gather in a General Assembly (*Conseil général*) for the choice of administrative officers was recognized. These functionaries were four "syndics" selected annually, and a treasurer elected for a term of three years. With the addition of the syndics of the previous year and of counselors selected by the syndics in office, there speedily developed the "Little Council" – at first of a variable number, but ultimately of twenty-five members, which constituted the inner consultative and executive body in the administration of the interests of the burghers. A second and larger Council, originally fifty, but speedily sixty in number, was established in 1457 to discuss matters not conveniently debatable in the General Assembly. The aristocratic tendencies of the Genevan citizenship are illustrated by the fact that, from 1459 onward, the members of this larger Council were designated by the "Little Council." The government of Geneva, by the end of the fourteenth century, was therefore shared by three powers: the bishop, the vicedominus, and the citizens, and this division of authority continued till the struggles of the third decade of the sixteenth century. The bishop, honored with the title "Prince of Geneva" and in theory sovereign of the city under the emperor, possessed the rights of leadership in war, of coining money, of hearing appeals, and of granting pardons. To the vicedominus fell the duties of defending the city, guarding the prisoners, executing criminals, and of exercising a restricted judicial function in civil and criminal cases. To the representatives of the citizens was ascribed the decision of all serious criminal charges against laymen. To them belonged the maintenance of good order at night by a suitable police force throughout the city, and they were charged with a watchful supervision lest the rights guaranteed by the Franchises should be infringed.

The population of Geneva, which may have numbered about 13,000 permanent residents, was as varied as the government of the city was divided. The situation of the city near the most frequented passes over the Alps made it a center of trade where products of France, Germany, and Italy were exchanged. Its merchants were prosperous, and its workmen skilled and widely famed. Its rank as a commercial city was high. As a center of ecclesiastical foundations, it was scarcely less conspicuous. Its bishopric was accounted one of the most desirable ecclesiastical posts in Western Christendom, its Cathedral Chapter was largely recruited from the noble families of the region. The city was divided into seven parishes, and monasticism was represented by strong establishments of Benedictines of the Cluny congregation, of Dominicans, Franciscans, and Augustinians, and a nunnery of the Clarissines. With its 300 clerics and nuns, its ornate churches, and its pilgrims to the ancient shrine of Saint-Victor, the ecclesiastical significance of the town was constantly in evidence, though unfortunately the character of its clergy was open to very serious reproach. A pleasant, bustling city, it was also a favorite place of residence for the lesser nobility of the neighboring lands, not a few of whom settled permanently within its walls. With so much that was attractive was combined, also, not a little that is less pleasing in life and manners. Geneva had the vices of a commercial city, situated on the highways of travel, and its population was undoubtedly more than usually pleasure-loving and luxurious. Its moral standards were low, and among those who set evil example to its dwellers were members of some of its most distinguished families, and many in priestly office or under monastic vows.

A city of contrasts and marked individuality, its inhabitants have been well characterized by a careful American student of its history:[2]

> The Genevans, in fact, were not a simple, but a complex, cosmopolitan people. There was, at this crossing of the routes of trade, a mingling of French, German, and Italian stock and characteristics; a large body of clergy of very dubious morality and force; and a still larger body of burghers, rather sounder and far more energetic and extremely independent, but keenly devoted to pleasure. It had the faults and follies of a mediaeval city and of a wealthy center in all times and lands; and also the progressive power of an ambitious, self-governing, and cosmopolitan community. At their worst, the early Genevans were noisy and riotous and revolutionary; fond of processions and "mummeries" (not always respectable or safe), of gambling, immorality, and loose songs and dances; possibly not over-scrupulous at a commercial or political bargain; and very self-assertive and obstinate. At their best, they were grave, shrewd, business-like statesmen, working slowly but surely, with keen knowledge of politics and human nature; with able leaders ready to devote time and money to public progress; and with a pretty intelligent, though less judicious, following. In diplomacy they were as deft, as keen at a bargain, and as quick to take advantage of the weakness of competitors, as they were shrewd and adroit in business. They were thrifty, but knew how to spend well; quick-witted and gifted in the art of party-nicknames. Finally, they were passionately devoted to liberty, energetic, and capable of prolonged self-sacrifice to attain and retain what they were convinced were their rights. On the borders of Switzerland, France, Germany, and Italy, they belonged in temper to none of these lands; out of their Savoyard traits, their wars, reforms, and new-comers, in time they created a distinct type, the Genevese.

---

[2] Prof. H. D. Foster, *American Historical Review*, viii. 239.

It is evident that the Genevan political situation contained elements of constant rivalry in the existence of divided authority. The house of Savoy sought unceasingly to increase its power over the city. Controlling the office of vicedominus from 1290 onward, and succeeding by purchase to the claims of the counts of Geneva in 1401 after the extinction of their direct male line in 1394, it also gained the bishopric, when, in 1444, Amadeus VIII of Savoy, the counter-pope of the Council of Basel, took upon himself that episcopal office. From his death in 1451 till 1490 the see was successively held by three of his grandsons, two of whom were scandalously young for entrance on their high office, and none of whom was of religious character. In the appointments of the succeeding bishops, Antoine Champion (1491–1495) and the seven-year-old Philip of Savoy (1495–1510), the influence of the rulers of Savoy was controlling, and their power was once more manifest in the establishment on the episcopal throne of John, the "Bastard of Savoy" (1513–1522), son of the third grandson of Amadeus VIII who had held the Genevan bishopric. To him Pierre de la Baume succeeded – a man of better personal life, but weak, luxurious, and unworthy of his office, against whom the burghers were to rise in successful rebellion.

These constant aggressions of the house of Savoy were met with growing hostility by the burghers of Geneva. Led by two men of very unlike character but of conspicuous force, Philibert Berthelier and Bezanson Hugues, the citizens on February 6, 1519 entered into an alliance for protection against Savoyard attack with the burghers of Freiburg, the party favoring the league being popularly known as "Eidguenots" (*Eidgenossen*), while their opponents who supported Savoy were known as "Mamelouks." The first struggle was, however, disastrous. Duke Charles III of Savoy forced the abandonment of the alliance. The power of the bishop was restored. In August of the same year, Berthelier was beheaded. With the change of bishopric from John of Savoy to Pierre de la Baume in 1522, much was hoped for by the citizens, but the new prelate proved without firmness, and his own historic rights no less than those of the burghers were

133

trampled upon by the duke, who was determined to make Geneva practically a Savoyard city. By the close of 1525, with the aid of his troops, the duke seemed to have accomplished his purpose, but his departure from the city showed the real weakness of his work and he was never again to set foot in the town. Unable to count on the bishop for help against Savoy, the citizens under the leadership of Bezanson Hugues now turned once more to Freiburg for aid, and to the most powerful of the Swiss cantons, that of Bern. By March 1526, Geneva was in formal alliance with her two neighbors, and the weak bishop, after vain protest, became apparently and professedly a hearty supporter of the new order. It was only for a brief season, however, that Pierre de la Baume stood on the patriotic side. In 1527 he left the city, never to re-enter it, save for a few days in the summer of 1533, and by 1528 he was fully committed to the interests of Savoy.

These successful assertions of Genevan independence led naturally to a modification of the constitution of the city, and to the growth to power of a more radical party than that of which Bezanson Hugues had been the leader. The year 1527 saw the erection of a new Council, that of the "Two Hundred," in imitation of Bern – a body chosen, certainly from 1530 onward, by the Little Council and practically absorbing the business of the still existing Council of Sixty. Within the next two years, the authority of the vicedominus was abolished, and new judicial offices were established by the General Assembly of the citizens. The Savoyards pressed Geneva and made travel unsafe on the roads leading to its gates, but military aid from Bern in 1530 relieved the situation. Thus far no serious thought of a religious revolution had entered into Genevan plans. The bishop might have kept much of his power had he sided permanently with the burghers, but he had chosen the part of their enemies, and hostility to Savoy involved more and more opposition to his authority also. In August 1533, the syndics denied to the bishop his historic right to exercise the power of pardon; and fourteen months later his office was declared by them to be vacant.

The later developments of this struggle were complicated by the beginnings of the Reformation movement in the city – a movement for which the attitude of the bishop more than any other single cause opened the way. From 1528 onward, Geneva was in a difficult situation in view of the religious controversies of the hour. Bern, the stronger of her two allies, accepted Protestantism that year, and thenceforward ardently furthered the Protestant cause. Meanwhile Freiburg, the less powerful but the earlier and more friendly member of the league, stood staunchly by the older Church. When Bernese troops occupied the city in 1530, Protestant preaching and Protestant attack upon the symbols of Roman worship accompanied their presence, but the people as a whole had, as yet, little sympathy with religious innovation. By June 9, 1532, however, there was enough Protestant feeling in Geneva to lead to the placarding of the public buildings of the city with an assertion of the Lutheran doctrine of justification by faith alone. The clerical leaders, the papal nuncio, and the Freiburg allies expressed their displeasure. The Genevan government, hard pressed between the diverse sentiments of its fellow leaguers, disclaimed any desire to modify the faith of the Fathers or to adopt Lutheranism, but at the same time requested the vicar to order preaching of "the gospel and epistle of God according to truth, without mingling with it any fables or other human inventions" – a vote which certainly went a considerable way toward neutralizing the declarations of adhesion to the Roman side, as it was doubtless intended to do. Though still relatively feeble, it is evident that enough anti-Roman feeling existed in Geneva by the summer of 1532, thanks to the attitude of Bern, popular hostility to the bishop, and, it may be, some real spiritual sympathy with the doctrines that Luther had made prominent, to insure a hearing for any bold preacher of Protestantism. In October following, such a proclaimer of reformed doctrine came in the person of Guillaume Farel.

Farel's history had indeed been stormy.[3] Born in 1489 of a family of distinction near Gap, about fifty miles southward of Grenoble

---

[3] Herminjard, I. 178; ii. 42, 79; R. Stähelin, in *Hauck's Relencyklopädie für prot. Theologie und Kirche*, v. 762–767; Doumergue, ii. 150–172.

in southeastern France, he was Calvin's senior by twenty years. From a devoted adhesion to the Roman Church he had passed, during his student years at Paris and under the influence of Le Fèvre, through the gateway of humanistic sympathies, to a full Protestantism. Of intense nature, his development had been at the cost of much inward struggle, and he became one of the most fiery and uncompromising advocates of the evangelical faith. After some preaching at Meaux under the countenance of Bishop Briçonnet, persecution compelled him to fly from France, and by 1524 he was vigorously aiding the success of the party of Reform in Basel, but the opposition of Erasmus forced his withdrawal. We next find him in a strenuous and polemic ministry of two years' duration at Montbéliard, about thirty-five miles westward of the Swiss city just mentioned. Some months of sojourn in Basel and Strassburg were followed, late in 1526, by the beginning of a stormy pastorate in Aigle, a town then under Bernese jurisdiction, situated on the Rhone a few miles above its entrance into Lake Geneva. Here he contributed not a little to the movement which won Bern for Protestantism in 1528, and he now received a roving commission to preach the evangelical faith in all towns under Bernese authority – chiefly of course those in which his native French was spoken. He became missionary of Protestantism to Romance Switzerland. Everywhere he went, notably at Neuchâtel, there was tumult; but his success was great. Opposition, danger, even wounds, but spurred him to more unsparing denunciation and more abundant activity. About three years of this itinerant evangelism had passed when his desire to aid the Reformed cause brought him early in October 1532[4] to the struggling and much-beset city of Geneva. He was a man fitted as few even of his polemic age to arouse attention and to stimulate controversy. Of stentorian voice, homely and forceful speech, and undaunted courage, men might approve or reject the messenger and his preaching, but indifference to him was scarcely possible. Accompanied by his friend Antoine

---

[4] The date is given in the interesting chronicle of the nun, Jeanne de Jussie, published as *Le levain du Calvinisme*, Chambéry, 1640(?), Geneva, 1865, pp. 46–51.

Saunier, and probably also by Pierre Robert Olivétan, with both of whom he had been laboring among the Waldenses, and armed with a letter from the Bernese authorities, he was cited before the bishop's vicar, and the Chapter. Here he met heated attack with characteristic intrepidity, but the populace and even the cathedral canons wished to throw him into the Rhone, gun burst as it was being fired at him, and he was kicked and struck in the face[5] by officers of the Church. The next day, October 4, he and his companions had to seek safety by flight up the lake from Geneva, landing near Lausanne, and going to Orbe, not quite twenty miles northward. Here, Farel found a younger fellow believer, Antoine Froment, and persuaded him to go to Geneva to attempt the work which opposition had made impossible for Farel.

Like Farel a native of Dauphiné, Froment was now about twenty-four years of age. He had early attracted the attention not only of Le Fèvre, but of Marguerite d'Angoulême. From 1529 he had aided Farel in the spread of Reformed doctrine in Switzerland. A man of slight frame, eager spirit, and undoubted courage, this portion of his life seems to have been entirely free from the stains with which his checkered career was later to be marked. He now began his work in Geneva in the guise of a schoolmaster eager to give instruction in French, but under the protection of this occupation he propagated evangelical doctrines to the utmost of his power. His hearers increased till on January 1, 1533 he ventured to preach in the square known as the "Molard."[6] The riot which followed led the Council of Two Hundred to forbid, by a vote passed the next day, any preaching without the permission of the syndics or of the bishop's vicar; but, though Geneva was still almost wholly Catholic, the beginnings of a Protestant congregation had been made. Bern urged its powerful influence in favor of the reformers by a letter received on March 25, 1533,[7] and

---

[5] Jeanne de Jussie, p. 49; Froment, *Les actes et gestes...de Genéve*, ed. 1854, pp. 6, 7.
[6] This has been called the "first public Protestant sermon in Geneva," but Megander had preached, in German, during the Bernese occupation in 1530.
[7] Herminjard, iii. 32.

three days later, a battle in the streets was narrowly averted by the syndics, while the Council of Two Hundred tried to keep peace by a truce which was really a partial compromise.[8] It availed little. At the Easter season the Protestants observed the Lord's Supper for the first time, and on May 4 following, in a riot, Canon Werly, one of their most determined opponents, was killed. He had been a citizen of Geneva's Catholic ally, Freiburg, and the government of that canton now persuaded Bishop Pierre de la Baume to return to Geneva as the best means of restoring ecclesiastical order. The prelate showed himself utterly incompetent, and on July 14 left the city – as it proved forever. The conflict was but intensified. Guy Furbity, a Domincan preacher of denunciatory zeal, was imported in the late autumn of 1533 to defend the Roman cause, and in December Farel once more ventured to come to Geneva. Freiburg and Bern now sent delegates to further their opposing religious interests, and with those of Geneva's Protestant ally came once more a pupil of Farel, who had already been for a brief time in the city ten months before, Pierre Viret, a Swiss of Orbe, of slender figure and low stature, now not quite twenty-three years of age, but already widely known no less for his skill as a preacher than for his sweetness of temper and personal modesty. On March 1, 1534, Farel and his supporters seized the chapel of the Franciscan monastery known as the "Rive," and held public worship. The distracted government, drawn in both directions, was forced to side with its Protestant political ally, Bern, as the stronger; and on May 15 the league with Catholic Freilburg was broken under Bernese pressure. Eight days later, an iconoclastic attempt showed the growing Protestant strength, and on the 24th of the following July, the Little Council formally voted that "the sole power is the Word of Christ and the sword which He has committed to the powers."[9]

Much of the late success of the Protestants had been due to the fatuous policy of Bishop Pierre de la Baume, who was earnestly supporting the Savoyard claims, and by the summer of

---

[8] Foster, *Am. Hist. Review*, viii. 224; Doumergue, ii. 118.

[9] Foster, op. cit., p. 224.

1534 was doing all he could to raise troops against the city. Under such circumstances, Geneva came increasingly under Protestant control, for its independence seemed bound up in resistance to its spiritual no less than to its ducal foes. On October 1, the Little Council, as already noted, declared the bishop's office vacant, yet Geneva was still far from Protestant by doctrinal conviction, and a Protestant observer, writing less than two weeks earlier, had affirmed that scarcely a third of its inhabitants could be counted against the bishop and the duke.[10] It was well-nigh impossible, however, to remain neutral in that strenuous age. The current now swept strongly on. An attempt, so it was widely believed, to poison the ministers, which nearly cost Viret his life on March 6, 1535, was followed by the execution of the woman who was thought its principal instrument; and being widely, though it is impossible to judge whether correctly charged to the instigation of the Roman clergy, it greatly increased the tension between the contesting factions.[11] The government took the ministers, whom it believed imperiled, under its protection and assigned them quarters in the monastery of Rive. Farel pressed for a public debate, such as had resulted favorably for Protestantism at Zürich, Bern, and elsewhere. The bishop forbade his followers to take part. With difficulty two already wavering champions of Rome were found in the persons of Jean Chappuis, a Dominican monk, and Pierre Caroli, a doctor of the Sorbonne who had already fallen into disrepute with the Roman authorities at Paris, and was later to incur Calvin's displeasure.

The result of this one-sided discussion, which lasted from May 30 to June 24, was of course claimed as a victory for the Protestant party, and Farel hastened to reap its fruits. On July 23, he seized the Church of La Madeleine and preached in it. The government tried to temporize. Its position was difficult; the city was still divided religiously. On July 30, the Little Council ordered the Protestants to limit this preaching to the monastery of Rive and the Church of Saint-Germain, but Farel felt victory was with

---

[10] Berthold Haller to Bucer, Herminjard, iii. 209.

[11] Kampschulte, i. 159; Doumergue, ii. 131.

him. He had the same day declared to the Council that "he must obey God rather than men." With the support of his friends he now seized successively the Church of Saint-Gervais, then that of the Dominicans, and finall on August 8, the Cathedral of Saint-Pierre itself. Image-breaking immediately followed. The churches were pillaged by the mob. The government bowed. On August 10, the Council of Two Hundred, by a majority vote, while ordering image-breaking to cease, also directed that the celebration of the Mass be suspended until further notice.[12] The downfall of the Roman party was evident. The revolution had taken place, and the Roman clergy, monks, and nuns[13] now generally left the city. It was during these dramatic events of August 1535, that Calvin, in his quiet retirement at Basel, was finishing the Letter to Francis I with which his *Institutes* was to be prefaced.

Protestant conviction and aggressive zeal, and episcopal hostility to the independence of the city, were not, however, the only causes of the downfall of the Roman cause in Geneva. The clergy as a body seems to have been ignorant and inefficient. Not a few of them were unworthy. If any monastic order had deservedly a reputation in Christendom above others for learning, it was that of St Dominic, but the Genevan Dominicans excused themselves from sharing in the debate of May 1535, on the ground that they had no learned man among them.[14] Jeanne de Jussie makes it apparent that the moral status of many of the clergy was scandalous, and recent investigation confirms the earlier testimony.[15] As Kampschulte has well said: "The Catholic episcopal city fell, since it must fall, like a fortress the defence of which is intrusted to the hands of the cowardly and the unfit."[16]

---

[12] *Registres du Conseil*, quoted by Foster, op. cit., p. 225.

[13] Jeanne de Jussie gives a picturesque account.

[14] Kampschulte, i. 171.

[15] *Le levain du Calvinisme*, p. 34. Compare Kampschulte, i. 90, 169; *Mémoires et doc. pub. per l'Académie Salésienne*, xiv. 175 (1891); Foster remarks, op. cit., p. 223, "on this point there is substantial agreement between Catholic and Protestant historians."

[16] I. 171.

While the later events just narrated were happening, Geneva was sustaining a difficult political struggle. The bishop, from his castle of Peney, a few miles down the Rhone, in co-operation with the Duke of Savoy, was raising troops, pillaging the environs of Geneva, cutting off its trade, maltreating such of its citizens as were captured, and pressing it sorely. Bern would give no help, doubtless by reason of the selfish expectation that hard-beset Geneva would come under Bernese jurisdiction as the price of its deliverance. When, in the autumn of 1535, Neuchâtel marched to the aid of Geneva, Bernese agents sent these helpers homeward after an auspicious success in battle at Gingins. And now, in December 1535, King Francis of France, about to attack the Duke of Savoy who had been won by the crafty policy of Charles V, for the imperial side in the great struggle for the headship of Europe, offered French protection to Geneva on terms which seemed to promise well-nigh full local freedom. Had they been accepted, Geneva would have become, ultimately, a French possession, and the course of Reformation history would have been profoundly altered. But Bern was now thoroughly frightened at the prospect. To have French influence established at Geneva would be to lose all Bern had hoped. On January 16, 1536, Bern, therefore, suddenly ended its halting policy and declared war against the Duke of Savoy. The Bernese army met no serious resistance. It pillaged the country of Geneva's enemies almost to the gates of the city, drove out the Catholic peasants from the country roundabout, and burned hostile castles. In February, it was in Geneva. In March, it completed the conquest of the Savoyard territories bordering on the Genevan lake by the capture of Chillon and the liberation of its prisoners. All effective resistance by the Duke of Savoy was now rendered impossible, for scarcely had the Bernese army done its work when he was independently attacked in another direction by the overwhelming power of France. Geneva was suddenly freed from a peril which had been the dread of years. Yet it was in great danger of losing its newly acquired freedom by reason of the claims of its ungenerous ally. On February 5, 1536, the Bernese commanders demanded the rights over the city which had once been exercised by the bishop and the vicedominus. That would have made Bern the real master. The syndics and councils refused with spirit. Geneva would not forfeit its hard-won liberties; and, at last, on August 7, 1536, Bern consented to a treaty by which Geneva retained all disputed rights lately enjoyed by the bishop and duke, and held the lands once belonging to the episcopal see, its Chapter, and the priory of Saint-Victor. The Genevan territories thus embraced not merely the city, but some twenty-eight adjacent villages ruled by officers appointed by the Little Council.[17]

The rejection of the authority of the bishop and the suspension of the Mass left the ecclesiastical administration of Geneva completely unsettled. But the citizens of Geneva evidently regarded themselves as a Church, and the city government at once showed its determination to succeed the deposed ecclesiastical authority in the moral and religious control of the city. In large measure it stepped into the bishop's place. In September, October, and November, 1535, the Council of the Two Hundred and the General Assembly used part of the monastic and ecclesiastical property to reform the older hospitals, establishing a large refuge for the sick in the former nunnery of the Clarissines, and an asylum for beggars, whose solicitation of alms was now forbidden. The prisons were unified. Early in April of the next year, under Farel's insistent urgency, preachers were sent to the outlying villages, the Mass forbidden in them, and their inhabitants ordered to attend the newly established sermons.[18] The day following this vote the Little Council showed its growing sense of its own ecclesiastical authority by declaring that it held as absolved the excommunicated parishioners of the village of Thiez.[19] The government assumed no less vigorous control over the moral status of the city and its dependent territory. Even before the Reformation, when episcopal power was recognized, the councils had exercised the right to regulate games, dances, and singing,[20] and

---

[17] Foster, op. cit., pp. 228, 229, where the literature is given.

[18] *Registres du Conseil, Opera*, xxi. 198; Foster, op. cit., p. 227.

[19] Herminjard, iv. 26; Foster, p. 227.

[20] Foster, p. 231, gives a series of enactments from 1481 to 1530; see also Doumergue, iii. 432–436.

now, by a vote of February 28, 1536, the Council of Two Hundred issued a series of prohibitions, soon placarded throughout Geneva, forbidding blasphemy, oaths, card playing, and strictly regulating the sale of intoxicants and the reception of strangers into taverns. Brides were soon after ordered to cover their heads. In June, presence at the sermon was required under penalty of a fine, and the recognition of any festival save Sunday prohibited. The same month a citizen who had had his child baptized by a priest was ordered banished; and, in July, Jean Balard, once a syndic and a man of peaceable disposition, was summoned before the Council, and, because conscientiously unwilling to listen to the new preaching, was given ten days to conform or leave the city.[21] It is evident that governmental regulation of faith and conduct at Geneva did not begin with Calvin. It was an inheritance in part from mediaeval functions of the city councils, in part from the episcopal authority to which those councils regarded themselves as having succeeded.

While the government of Geneva was far from a full democracy, most of its affairs being managed by the largely aristocratic and close-knit councils,[22] the full acceptance of Protestantism seemed

---

[21] *Registres du Conseil*, xxx. 32; *Opera*, xxi. 203.

[22] Foster, op. cit., p. 234–236, has pointed out that of the Little Council only five were elected by the General Assembly in any one year; viz. the four syndics and the treasurer. The syndics of the previous year remained members of the Little Council, and their sixteen associates were chosen annually by the Council of Two Hundred. The Two Hundred, composed of the Little Council and 175 others, were chosen annually after 1530 by the Little Council. Elections of syndics by the General Assembly occurred usually on the first Sunday in February; on the day after, the Little Council was chosen, and on Tuesday the Two Hundred. The syndics and Little Council were the legislative body and the supreme court in all ordinary cases. In serious cases of public policy the Two Hundred were called in, and they also had the right of pardon. The General Assembly chose the syndics annually and treasurer triennially; and also elected, from 1529 on, five judges – a lieutenant of justice and four auditeurs – who constituted the lower civil and criminal court. These judges were elected annually in November. The assent of the General Assembly was also needful in very important decisions, like the one to be described, but Geneva was only remotely a democracy in all ordinary matters of civic policy, though choosing her chief officers in democratic fashion.

a matter of so much moment as to require the General Assembly of the citizens. Urged by Farel, such a meeting gathered, on the call of the Little Council and of the Council of Two Hundred, on Sunday, May 21, 1536, at the sound of the bell and trumpet. The citizens of Geneva thus met, led by Claude Savoye, the first syndic, now voted, without expressed dissent, their "desire to live in this holy evangelical law and Word of God, as it has been announced to us, desiring to abandon all Masses, images, idols, and all that which may pertain thereto."[23] Those entitled to express an opinion in the Assembly may have numbered from 1,000 to 1,500 of the inhabitants of Geneva. This action undoubtedly voiced the conviction which the opposition of the bishop and the long political struggle in which Bern had played so significant a role, as well as the labors of Farel, Froment, and Viret, had forced upon them, that the only path of municipal safety lay in adhesion to the Protestant cause.

It was not this vote alone, however, that made this meeting of the General Assembly of Genevan citizens significant. Two days before, the Two Hundred, at the advice of the Little Council, had chosen Farel's friend, Antoine Saunier, head of the "great school," at a salary of 100 gold écus, and associated with him two "bachelors," as assistants in instruction. The General Assembly now voted that the education of the poor should be free, "and that every one be bound to send his children to the school and have them learn."[24] Universal popular education at Geneva was thus established, largely through Farel's influence, before Calvin's arrival, and a main feature of Genevan discipline was thus early inaugurated.

But, in spite of all that had been done, only a beginning had been made, if Geneva was to become the Protestant city that Farel wished, or even if its future Protestantism was to be secured. As matters were going, the utmost that could be expected was

---

[23] *Registres du Conseil*, xxix. 112; *Opera*, xxi. 201; English trans., Foster, op. cit., p. 235.

[24] *Registres*, ibid.; *Opera*, xxi. 200–202; Foster, ibid. There had been a municipal school since February 28, 1428.

that Geneva would develop along the lines of state-controlled ecclesiasticism according to the pattern already established in Bern and Zürich. Though its services doubtless approximated to the form which Farel had put forth, several years before, in his *Maniére et fasson quon tient en baillant le sainct Baptesme*, etc.,[25] the Genevan Church lacked all organization, save that the city government favored Protestantism, supported Protestant preachers, and exercised a kind of ecclesiastical control over Genevan territories. It had no creed, save the determination of the General Assembly to live according to "the Word of God," no separate discipline, no existence independent of the will of the civil rulers of the turbulent city.[26] Years later, in his farewell address, Calvin said with substantial truth regarding its state at his coming: "In this Church there was well-nigh nothing. There was preaching, and that is all ... All was in confusion."[27] There is no proof that Farel was not well content with the direction toward state control which the development had thus far taken, largely under his fiery discourses; but he doubtless felt that his abilities to plan were inadequate to the needs of the situation. The papacy and the ancient worship had been rejected; but an architect was needed if a new structure of solidity and strength was to take the place of the old. It is proof of Farel's insight into character, no less than of his personal unselfishness, that he believed that the leader Geneva required was to be found in the youthful author of the *Institutes* whom the chances of war, or, as he would have more religiously declared, Divine Providence, had unexpectedly sent to the city.

---

[25] Printed in 1533, though written earlier, perhaps nearly a decade; see J. G. Baum, *Le sommaire de Guillaume Farel*, Geneva, 1867, p. vi.

[26] Compare Foster, ibid., pp. 235–236.

[27] *Opera*, ix. 891.

8

CALVIN'S EARLY WORK AT GENEVA, 1536–1538

Calvin's sudden determination, reached in July 1536, under the potent exhortation of Farel, to make Geneva his home, was followed by a brief business trip to Basel. His return to Geneva, about the middle of August, saw him the victim of a sharp and painful illness,[1] so he can hardly have begun work before the end of the month. That inauguration was most informal. He did not become one of the preachers till nearly or quite a year later.[2] Under Farel's auspices, he began the exposition of the Pauline Epistles in the Church of Saint-Pierre, and it was as "Professor of Sacred Letters in the Church of Geneva" that he published at Basel, in January 1537, the two brief tracts on the proper attitude of evangelical believers toward Roman worship and offices of which mention has already been made as having probably been written during his Italian journey.[3] Farel, anxious that his friend should have an adequate livelihood, appealed on Calvin's behalf to the

---

[1] Calvin's letter to Daniel, Herminjard, iv. 87.

[2] Calvin said in his letter to Sadoleto (1539), "I discharged the duties first of a teacher, then of a pastor," *Opera*, v. 386. Colladon stated that "a little after, he was also chosen pastor," ibid., xxi. 58. But as late as August 13, 1537, the Council of Bern distinguished between Farel, "preacher," and Calvin, "reader in Holy Scripture," Herminjard, iv. 276. See also C. A. Cornelius, *Historische Arbeiten*, Leipzig, 1899, p. 129, of which I have made much use in this chapter.

[3] *Opera*, v. 233. *Ante*, p. 154.

Little Council on September 5, 1536, but so slight an impression had the newcomer then made on the city as a whole that the Secretary, in evident ignorance of Calvin's name, recorded the request as having been made on behalf of "that Frenchman." It was not till February 13 following that a modest grant was voted.[4]

From the first, however, Calvin exercised a profound influence over Farel, and his weight was soon felt in all the religious interests of Geneva. When the *Colloquia*, or meetings of the ministers of Geneva and vicinity, were established in November 1536, Calvin became a member, and in their name he spoke the admonition to Denis Lambert, the unsatisfactory pastor at Veigy, in the opening days of the following month.[5] Even earlier, services of a more public character had brought Calvin into notice. The victorious forces of Bern had entered Lausanne, the chief city of Vaud, where Viret was even then advocating the evangelical cause in March 1536. In spite of the prohibition of the nominal overlord, the Emperor Charles V, that aggressively Protestant canton, had determined to support the newer worship in Vaud, and, as a means to that end, appointed a public disputation at Lausanne for October 1. Thither Calvin went with Farel, and, though his part was relatively modest compared with the work of his elder companion and that of Viret, in the eight days' session that ensued he gained distinction by the learning and skill with which, fortified by abundant citations from the Fathers, he attacked the doctrine of the physical presence of Christ in the Supper and thus contributed to the overthrow of the feebly championed Roman party.[6] From Lausanne Calvin went to Bern, and was present from October 16 to 18 at a synod which considered inconclusively the recently drafted Wittenberg Form of Concord, which Bucer was urging on the Swiss as a means of uniting all the forces of Protestantism. Calvin was thus rapidly making the acquaintance of the Protestant leaders of southern and central Switzerland. Those of the north and of the adjacent Rhine Valley he largely knew already.

---

[4] *Registres du Conseil*, xxx. 51, 173; *Opera*, xxi. 204, 208.

[5] Herminjard, iv. 107, 123; Cornelius, p. 129.

[6] *Opera*, ix. 877–884; Doumergue, ii. 180–218.

Farel's expectation was that Calvin would be a force in the organization of the Genevan Church, and in this work the author of the *Institutes* immediately took the leadership, though popular judgment still continued to regard Farel as chief among the churchly guides of Geneva. The result of Calvin's work was the speedy preparation of Articles directive of Church government, of a Catechism for Christian instruction, and of a Confession of Faith for the whole Genevan community – the latter possibly by Farrel though expressing Calvin's thoughts. In them Calvin outlined not only the principles which had found expression in the *Institutes*, but many of the more essential features of his system of government as it was ultimately to develop.

Before Calvin's coming, on May 24, 1536, the Council had ordered that Articles[7] be drafted to secure the "unity of the State." In compliance, on November 10 following, Farel laid before the civil authorities certain propositions not now definitely known, which met with prompt approval.[8] Whether the articles then presented were those drafted by Calvin which have come down to us as of January 1537,[9] or were, as seems more probable,[10] simply anti-Roman ordinances, is impossible absolutely to determine. If the latter be the case, however, as the writer believes, then the Articles of January 1537 were not only entirely distinct from those of the previous November, but their presentation was an act unsolicited by the city government, and one illustrative not merely of Calvin's organizing abilities, but of his prompt and conscientious determination to make Geneva what he would have it. For, though the records of the Little Council describe the Articles read before it in January 16, 1537, as "given by G. Farel and the other preachers,"[11] the hand of Calvin and the familiar thoughts

---

[7] On this general subject see A. Rilliet and T. Dufour, *Le catéchisme francais de Calvin*, Geneva, 1878, pp. x–xxxiii; Cornelius, pp. 131–137; Doumergue, ii. 219-227.

[8] *Registres du Conseil*, xxx. 7, 87.

[9] E.g. Rilliet, Dufour, Doumergue.

[10] Cornelius.

[11] Xxx. 151; *Opera*, xxi. 206. The full text of the Articles may be found in *Opera*, xa. 5–14; and Herminjard, iv. 155–166.

and even language of the *Institutes* are unmistakable. Calvin had won the support of his colleagues, he would win the approval of the government for this first program for the construction of a Genevan Church as he desired that Church to be.

The Articles begin with a declaration that good churchly order demands the frequent and dignified observance of the Lord's Supper. Calvin's prime thought is evidently religious. As in the first edition of the *Institutes*, he advocates its observance at least every Sunday, yet "because the weakness of the people is such that there is danger that this holy and most excellent mystery may be despised if so often celebrated," he recommends its maintenance, for the present, once a month.[12] The dignity of this central feature of worship demands the exclusion of those of unworthy life and contemptuous conduct, and this consideration brings Calvin to the most significant element of the Articles – their provision for Church discipline. "For this reason our Lord has established in his Church the correction and discipline of excommunication."

The Articles then propose a systematic establishment of discipline, which had evidently fallen out of all use except as enforced by such sumptuary and moral enactments of the civil authorities as have already been noted:[13]

> To accomplish this we have decided to ask of you [the government] that your pleasure may be to appoint and choose certain persons of upright life and good reputation among all the faithful, likewise of firmness and not easily corruptible, who being divided and distributed in all the quarters of the city, shall have an eye to the life and conduct of each one; and if they see any notable fault to censure in any person they shall communicate with some one of the ministers to admonish the one in fault and exhort him fraternally to reform. And if it appears that such remonstrances are of no avail, he shall be informed that his obstinacy will be reported to the Church. And if he confesses, there is already a great profit in this discipline. But if he will not hear, it will be time for the minister, being informed by those who have this charge, to declare publicly

---

[12] *Ante*, p. 142; *Opera*, xa. 7, 8.
[13] *Opera*, xa. 10, 11.

in the assembly the effort which has been made to bring him to amendment and how all has been of no avail. When it is apparent that he wishes to persevere in hardness of heart, then it will be time to excommunicate him, that is to say, he shall be held as rejected from the company of Christians ... Such seems to us a good way to re-establish excommunication in our Church and to maintain it in its entirety; and beyond this admonition the Church cannot go. But if there are those of such insolence and so abandoned to all wickedness that they only laugh at being excommunicated and do not concern themselves about living and dying in such exclusion, it will be for you to judge whether you will suffer such conduct long to continue and leave unpunished such contempt and such mockery of God and of His Gospel.

With this recommendation was coupled another of well-nigh equal importance:[14]

It is certain that there is no greater division than concerning faith; and if those who agree in faith with us ought, nevertheless, to be excommunicated by reason of their ill deeds, with much more reason they ought not to be endured in the Church who are wholly contrary to us in religion. The remedy that we have thought of for this situation is to ask you that all the inhabitants of your city shall make confession and give account of their faith, so that it may be understood who of them agree with the Gospel, and who love better to be of the kingdom of the Pope than of the kingdom of Jesus Christ. It would therefore be an act becoming Christian magistrates if you, Gentlemen of the Council, each one for himself, would make confession in your council by which it may be understood that the doctrine of your faith is truly that whereby all the faithful are united in one Church. For by your example you would show what each one should do in imitation of you; and afterwards you should appoint certain of your body, who, being joined with some minister, should require each person to do the same. This should be for this time only, since it cannot yet be seen what doctrine each person holds, which is the right beginning of a Church.

---

[14] *Opera*, xa. p. 11.

Besides this sifting process by which those really in sympathy with the evangelical cause could be distinguished among the inhabitants of Geneva, and the maintenance of the purity of the Church by discipline, Calvin and his associates proposed the training of the young in religious truth as a third important means of securing the spiritual welfare of the city:[15]

> There should be a brief and easy outline of the Christian faith, which should be taught to all children, and at certain seasons of the year they should come before the ministers to be questioned and examined, and to receive more ample explication according as there shall be need in proportion to the capacity of each, until they are approved as sufficiently instructed. But may your pleasure be to order parents to exercise care and diligence that their children learn this outline and present themselves to the ministers at the time appointed.

Here, then, was a program of far-reaching significance, and of the utmost boldness as applied to a city like Geneva. All inhabitants were to be sifted by a creed test, which in the conditions of sixteenth-century life meant something different from such a test today. It was almost impossible to be non-partisan between Protestantism and Romanism, and Calvin intended that it should be absolutely impossible. Each inhabitant must choose one side or the other with all its consequences. He must live "according to the Gospel," or according to the papacy. But all inhabitants who accepted the evangelical side, were, by right of their acceptance, as well as of their baptism, members of the Genevan Church. Calvin does not say what shall be done with inhabitants who refuse Protestantism. He did not need to say. The Genevan authorities had already taken the position, in the month of Calvin's arrival, and without influence from him, that they must leave the city.[16]

This Church thus established must be maintained in purity not merely by education, but by discipline, and this discipline

---

[15] *Opera*, xa. p. 13.
[16] Case of Jean Balard, July 24, 1536, *Ante*, p. 178.

was to be applied not, as in most American religious bodies, to that relatively small portion of the population who have made a profession of Christian experience and have "joined a church," but to all inhabitants who professed adherence to the evangelical side, that is to all dwellers in Geneva after the sifting process should be completed. There was nothing novel in the idea of a strict watch by the civil government over the manners and morals of the citizens. Many regulations interfering with their conduct had been made before Calvin came, even in Roman days, nor were such supervisions peculiar in any way to Geneva.[17] Calvin's contribution was twofold, however. He would secure the appointment of lay inspectors, who should work in conjunction with the ministry – a real Consistory, if still in undeveloped form. Even more important, he would make the work of the inspectors a function of the Church, not of the State. To the point of excommunication, which he deemed the limit of spiritual functions, these inspectors and the ministers, though appointed by the government, should act as spiritual, not as civil officers. The independent self-government of the Church was thus Calvin's aim. That self-government was far from complete as presented in these Articles; but it was real. When discipline had done its utmost, and not till then, was the State to exercise its authority over the hopelessly incorrigible. The chief peculiarity of Calvin's recommendation is not therefore its regulation of private conduct – that existed before his work was begun – but this provision for an independent exercise of ecclesiastical discipline in a Church which was largely the creature of the State and over which the State exercised control. It was a first step toward the restoration, in a new and Protestant form, of that ancient ecclesiastical independence which the Reformation had almost universally sacrificed to its need of State support. Calvin's motive in thus asserting the principle of independent discipline was primarily pastoral, not theoretical, and grew out of his conception of the care of souls. As he declared, in 1538, in his Preface to the Genevan Catechism:[18]

---

[17] *Ante*, p. 178; see also Foster, p. 231; Doumergue, ii. 223, 224.

[18] *Opera*, v. 319; Cornelius, p. 133.

Whatever others may think, we certainly do not regard our office as bound in so narrow limits that when the sermon is delivered we may rest as if our task were done. They whose blood will be required of us, if lost through our slothfulness, are to be cared for much more closely and vigilantly.

It was an independent discipline, aided by the civil government when discipline had done its utmost, that there might be a trained and conscientious Christian community – the ideal of a Puritan State – that Calvin planned, but to believe that Geneva could become such a state required high idealism, intense determination to secure the result which seemed logically desirable, and a persuasive capacity to win others to his point of view. These qualities Calvin now brought to bear on the Genevan situation.

It detracts nothing from Calvin's significance as an ecclesiastical statesman that the particular device by which he and his associates proposed to secure an independent discipline, as presented in the Articles of 1537, was not original to him. At Basel, with the affairs of which city Calvin was well acquainted, three men of repute had been appointed for each parish in 1530 – two from the city council and one from the general body of inhabitants – to serve with the ministers in the supervision of the lives of their fellow citizens. This device of Ecolampadius was not successfully carried out. It encountered opposition at once. Zwingli and his successor, Bullinger, declared that excommunication was no function of a Church under pious civil rulers, but rather that discipline belonged to the State, yet the attempt at Basel was evidently the source of Calvin's plan.[19]

Besides these principal recommendations, the Articles advised the singing of the Psalms as a means of rendering public worship less cold, and the appointment of a civil commission which should judge matrimonial questions, with the aid of the ministers, in accordance with the "Word of God." The Little Council and that of Two Hundred promptly adopted the Articles, with slight reservations. The Lord's Supper was still to be celebrated but four

[19] Doumergue, ii. 224–227.

times yearly, and marriage questions were to be determined by the Little Council, though "after conference with the preachers and ministers for guidance according to the Word of God." But the plan which Farel and Calvin had presented became the law of Geneva in its essential features.[20]

The Articles had proposed a "brief outline of the Christian faith" as a basis of instruction for children, and this Catechism Calvin had either prepared when the Articles were presented or brought it speedily thereafter into readiness, for he was able to exhibit it in print in discussion at Lausanne by the February 17.[21] Composed in Latin, it was printed in French translation as *Instruction et confession de foy dont on use en l'Église de Gèneve*, and was long supposed to be lost in this form, till a copy of the original edition was discovered in the Bibliothèque Nationale at Paris in 1877.[22] The Catechism itself is a nobly expressed and transparently stated presentation of the Christian system, as Calvin apprehended it, in substantially the same order and with the same emphases as in the first edition of the *Institutes*. From the point of view of its professed purpose, the instruction of children, it is far too long, elaborate, and minute. It should be remembered that catechism-making, so characteristic of the Reformation age, was still a novelty. Luther's catechisms were only seven years old. Calvin, moreover, had had little experience as a teacher. He would have written far otherwise had he taught the young. It has been well described as a résumé of the *Institutes*,[23] and, as such, it is a compact and serviceable creed, presenting the system with the skill of a master-hand.

---

[20] *Registres du Conseil*, January 16, 1537, xxx. 151, 152; *Opera*, xxi. 206, 207.

[21] Calvin to Grynaeus, Herminjard, iv. 240.

[22] Printed with elaborate introductions by A. Rilliet and T. Dufour, *Le catechisme francais*, Geneva, 1878; see also Cornelius, p. 137; Doumergue, ii. 230, 231. The Latin form was printed in 1538, and may be found in *Opera*, v. 313–362. Some official adoption at Geneva must have taken place, for the Latin edition is described as "communibus renatae nuper in Evangelio Genevensis Ecclesiae suffragiis recepta."

[23] Rilliet, ibid., p. xlii.

With this Catechism in its earliest edition, and therefore dating at the latest from February 1537, was bound up the Confession of Faith, assent to which the Articles had recommended should be asked of the officers of the Genevan government and required once for all individually of the inhabitants of the city. Its title declared it to be "extracted from the Instruction [i.e. Catechism] of which use is made in the Church of the said city," and that "all burghers, inhabitants of Geneva, and subjects of the country, are bound to swear to guard and hold to" it. The words of this brief creed of twenty-one articles are not improbably from the pen of Farel,[24] but the order and thought is essentially that of the Catechism. Whether its actual writer or not, Calvin doubtless regarded it as expressing his convictions. Its most significant aspect, from the point of view of ecclesiastical constitution-making, is that it would base membership in the Genevan Church on an individual and personal profession of faith.[25] Looked at from the standpoint of ecclesiastical politics, its chief importance is as an endeavor to secure unity in allegiance to the new evangelical Church and the exclusion of all who opposed. But the attempt to obtain the universal assent recommended in the Articles was one resulting in great difficulties for the reformers, and their efforts were delayed by internal and external conflicts at which it will be well to glance before examining the fate of the Confession.

While the Articles, the Catechism, and the Confession were in preparation, Farel and Calvin were suddenly and savagely attacked by a fellow Protestant as heretics, and heretics of what seemed to the Reformation age the blackest dye, deniers of the doctrine of the Trinity. The accusation not merely aroused in Calvin a strong sense of resentment because it was wholly undeserved, but, insofar as it was believed, it threatened not merely Farel and Calvin's whole position at Geneva, but all influence anywhere. It was peculiarly galling,

---

[24] Rilliet, *Opera*, v. pp. lii–lviii, claims it for Calvin; the editors of the *Opera*, xxii. 14–18, ascribe it to Farel. The evidence is well summed up, with suspense of judgment, by Doumergue, ii. 237–239.

[25] Doumergue, ii. 236.

moreover, to one who felt profoundly convinced, as Calvin did, that he was above all else biblical and orthodox – an interpreter of the very "Word of God" – and it resulted in his first great personal antagonism.

Pierre Caroli,[26] who brought this accusation, was, like Calvin, a native of northern France, and, like him, a student at the University of Paris, where he had achieved distinction. Attracted by the semi-Protestantism of the school of Le Fèvre, he labored under Briçonnet in his native region, expounded the Scriptures at Paris, and obtained an ecclesiastical living at Alençon. Vain, disputatious, of rather easy morals, he had no considerable fixity of belief, and was to pass repeatedly from one communion to the other, and to die in that of Rome. The tumult occasioned by the placards compelled his flight to Geneva in 1535, where he fell out with Farel and Viret, and seems to have become thoroughly hostile to them. Thence he went to Basel, being there during a part of Calvin's residence, and in the spring of 1536 obtained a pastorate at Neuchâtel. He therefore knew the Genevan reformers well. Through influence with the government of Bern he was appointed chief-pastor at Lausanne in November after the establishment of Protestantism in that city, and given a handsome income, to the relative discredit of Viret, to whom much of the success of the evangelical cause in that city had been due. This discrimination in favor of one whom they deemed inferior to Viret in character and devotion to the Reformed faith aroused the protests of the Genevan ministers;[27] and their feelings were intensified, as may be imagined, when Caroli began to advocate prayers for the dead, not indeed as abridging purgatorial sufferings – he was then too much of a protestant for that – but as procuring an earlier resurrection. In Caroli on the one side and Farel and Calvin on the other, the divergence clearly appears which had grown up between the semi-Protestantism of the type of Le Fèvre

---

[26] The fullest treatment of this episode is that of Eduard Bähler, *Petrus Caroli, und Johannes Calvin*, in the *Jahrbuch für Schweizerische Geschichte*, xxix. 41–167 (1904); see also Kampschulte, i. 295–298; Doumergue, ii. 252–268. Calvin told his side of the story in 1545 in his *Pro G. Farello et collegis ejus adversus Petri Caroli calumnias Defensio, Opera*, vii. 289–340.

[27] Herminjard, iv. 107, 109.

and of many of Calvin's early associates and the logical, convinced, thoroughgoing Protestantism which Calvin had attained. The same division, under very different circumstances, was soon to cost Calvin the companionship of du Tillet, whose friendship had been so valuable in his own days of spiritual struggle.[28] Yet the weakness of French Protestantism had been the large number of its adherents who had but partially broken with the ancient system. Its strength, however much our natural sympathy is drawn toward these men who did not see clearly, was unmistakably in the robuster type of which Calvin was the embodiment.

On news of this development in Caroli's teaching, Calvin went to Viret's aid at Lausanne, and the matter was brought before the commissioners of Bern, then in the city, on February 17, 1537.[29] Here Caroli turned the tables on his critics by accusing them of Arianism. Calvin presented in defence the appropriate section from the new Genevan Catechism, when, in a dramatic scene, Caroli called on his opponents to leave out of discussion the creed then hardly dry from the press, and join him in assent to the three ancient historic symbols of the Church.[30] Calvin rejected the demand and answered: "We swear in the faith of the one God, not of Athanasius, whose creed no true Church would ever have approved." Here was, to Caroli, a seeming confirmation of his charges; and the action of Calvin in refusing to approve creeds which the Church had long reverenced, at the very moment when he was demanding that all inhabitants of Geneva assent to the Confession which he and Farel had prepared, is the apparent inconsistency of which has often been remarked.[31] To understand his attitude we must remember the century in which he lived, and his convictions as to the final source of authority. To Calvin the new Genevan creed was true, and therefore rightfully to be pressed on others, because it was drawn from the "Word of

---

[28] Calvin to du Tillet, January 31, 1538, Herminjard, iv. 354.

[29] The best account of the scene is the letter of the pastors of Geneva to those of Bern, written by Calvin within a few days of the event, ibid., iv. 183–187.

[30] I.e. the Apostles', the Nicene, and the Athanasian Creeds.

[31] Kampschulte, i. 296, 297; compare Doumergue's defence, ii. 266.

God." That ascribed to Athanasius was not so derived, and was therefore not so binding. A further motive for Calvin's rejection of the ancient symbol grew out of his humanistic feeling. Its want of classic style, above all its repetitions, offended a scholarship trained by the new learning and the new historical criticism.[32] To Caroli the ancient creeds seemed a precious heritage from the past. To Calvin they were of value only insofar as they reproduced the "Word of God." The humanistic reformer and the ecclesiastical revolutionist stood face to face in conflict.

Caroli's charge of Arianism was baseless, as an examination of Calvin and Farel's writings readily shows. In his *Institutes* of 1536 Calvin had not hesitated to use the word "Trinity," and to describe the mode of existence of the Godhead in terms of historical theology.[33] But while really unsupported, Caroli's charges were given a certain plausibility by the actions and writings of the Genevan reformers and were not improbably fully believed by Caroli himself. With the wish to avoid technical theological terms in manuals for popular instruction, Farel had omitted the word "Trinity" from his *Sommaire*, and it, together with the word "person," for the same reason was absent from the Catechism and Confession which Calvin and Farel had just prepared for the Genevan Church. Moreover, Claude Aliodi, a wandering preacher whom the government of Bern had banished in 1534 for opinions essentially similar to those already presented by Servetus in his *De Trinitatis Erroribus* of 1531, had been at one time a colleague of Farel at Neuchâtel, and had affirmed to the pastors at Constance that Farel's beliefs were similar to his own.[34] He was now living at Thonon, on the southern shore of Lake Geneva. To a man of Caroli's temperament, Calvin's refusal to subscribe to the three creeds would, in any case, seem scarcely susceptible of an orthodox explanation.

[32] *Opera*, vii. 315, 316.

[33] E.g. *Institutes, Opera*, i. 71. " 'I believe in the Holy Ghost,' where we confess that we believe the Holy Spirit to be true God with the Father and the Son, the third person of the most holy Trinity, consubstantial and coeternal with the Father and the Son, omnipotent and the Creator of all things. For there are three distinct persons, one essence."

[34] Herminjard, iii. 173, 174; Doumergue, ii. 241.

From Lausanne, the matter of Caroli's prayers for the dead was carried to Bern, where, on February 28 and March 1, Caroli renewed his charges before the ministers of the Consistory, in the presence of Calvin and Viret. Calvin defended himself and Farel in an address of great passion and extreme personal invective, but also of such convincing power that Caroli promptly withdrew the charge as far as Calvin himself was concerned.[35] Calvin refused to separate Farel's cause from his own, and with Viret asked the ministers of Bern to join in procuring from the Bernese government the summons of a synod. It was obtained, though not without difficulty, for the spiritual leaders of Bern were disposed to look upon the dispute as one thrust upon them by foreigners, strangers to Switzerland, of whose orthodoxy there might be just suspicion. Before the synod met at Lausanne on May 14 under the presidency of the pastors of Bern, and members of the Bernese government, with an attendance of more than a hundred ministers of French-speaking Switzerland, Calvin and Farel appeared, accompanied by their eloquent blind colleague, Élie Coraud. As at Bern, Calvin replied to Caroli with great heat and vehement personalities, but with such solid defence of his position that success was immediately his. The Genevean reformers were pronounced orthodox, Caroli was deprived of his ministry, and even Claude Aliodi recanted his Arianism.[36] Once more the matter came to public discussion, when a synod of German-speaking pastors from the Bernese territories met at Bern on May 31st, in connection with the civil Council of Two Hundred of that city. Here Farel brought most damaging charges against Caroli's private life, and he was forbidden to preach in Bernese territory. The Genevan reformers were declared orthodox by the government of Bern.[37] As for Caroli, he speedily returned to France and to the Roman Church, only to become a Protestant once more in 1539; but, by 1543, he was again in the older communion.

---

[35] Calvin gives an outline of the address, *Opera*, vii. 309.

[36] Letter of Megander to Bullinger, May 22, 1537, Herminjard, iv. 235; Calvin's own account is in *Opera*, vii. 310–317.

[37] Herminjard, iv. 238–244; *Opera*, vii. 325–337; xb. 105.

Calvin and Farel had passed successfully through a great crisis, chiefly by reason of the real groundlessness of the charges against them, but in no small degree, also, because of the moral weakness of their opponent. Yet their establishment in public confidence was not easily secured. Suspicion and doubt at Bern, Basel, Zürich, and Strassburg, and even with Melanchthon, had to be overcome.[38] If Calvin displayed great asperity of temper in his treatment of his accuser, the seriousness of the situation and the baselessness of the charges are largely an explanation, and the loyal friendship with which he supported Farel and linked his own fate with that of his associate, when a separate defence would in some respects have been easier, is worthy of all praise. That he had been suspected of sympathy with Servetus by such men as Myconius, Bucer, and Melanchthon, even though but for a brief time, undoubtedly added intensity to his hostile feeling toward that speculative Spaniard when the two came in conflict at a much later period.

These weeks of struggle to vindicate himself to foreign opinion in consequence of Caroli's accusation were also a time of contest with foes in Geneva itself. In March 1537, two Netherlandish Anabaptists appeared in the city, demanding of its authorities the right to dispute with the ministers, whose interpretation of the "Word of God" they, of course, challenged. The Little Council deemed it dangerous that they be heard in public – the Münster catastrophe was still recent – but voted that they present their cause before the Council of Two Hundred. On Farel's insistence, however, this decision was amended and two long days of public debate – March 16 and 17 – followed, till the Council of Two Hundred, perceiving much excitement of the popular mind, ordered the dispute to cease, seized the papers on either side, declared the Anabaptists defeated, and banished them on pain of death.[39] In Colladon's *Life of Calvin* this repulse is attributed to Calvin's skill in debate;[40] but it may justly be questioned

---

[38] Letters in Herminjard, iv. *passim*. They are well summed up by Doumergue, ii. 266–268.

[39] *Registres du Conseil*, xxx. 188–193; *Opera*, xxi. 208–210; Doumergue, ii. 242–243.

[40] *Opera*, xxi. 59.

whether his arguments had so much force as the orders of hostile civil authority.

While these contests, within and without, were in progress, the enforcement of the acceptance of the Confession upon all the inhabitants of Geneva made slow advance. It was, at best, a dangerous experiment to undertake in a city where allegiance to the evangelical cause was so largely the result of political conditions, but Calvin believed it to be fundamental to the erection of a proper Church, and had persuaded Farel and Coraud to a like point of view. Geneva had already seen divisions between "Eidguenots" and "Mamelouks," resulting in the victory of the former and the expulsion of the power of Savoy. Then the contest had raged between Protestants and Catholics, till the city had become, in name at least, all Protestant. But among the adherents of the evangelical cause two points of view naturally arose. While one wing, led by such men as the excellent Ami Porral, Michel Sept, Jean Curtet, and Jean Goulaz, supported the reformers, another considerable element valued the Protestantising of Geneva more for its political than for its religious results, wished no strenuous discipline, looked upon Calvin, Farel, and Coraud as French strangers who had crowded out old Genevan leaders, and admired the Protestantism of Bern, where the Church was controlled by the State and its pastors claimed no such disciplinary powers as were being sought by the ministry of Geneva. It was inevitable that such a party of opposition should arise, and its beginnings had appeared even before Calvin had become an effective leader of Genevan affairs or the Articles had been formulated. Of this party were such men as Jean Philippe, Claude Richardet, Ami de Chapeaurouge, and Pierre Vandel. Then, too, the aristocratic constitution of Geneva gave occasion, almost of necessity, for a party of opposition. As has been seen,[41] the Two Hundred elected sixteen of the members of the Little Council, and the Little Council chose the Two Hundred. It was almost a close corporation; but there was one very important point of popular attack. The General Assembly of citizens chose the syndics and the treasurer,

---

[41] *Ante*, p. 178.

who constituted the immediate executive and the most powerful element in the Little Council. A popular opposition of sufficient strength could therefore profoundly modify the government at the annual election in February, and the hope of those out of power was now set on such a reversal.

In February 1537, less than a month after the approval of the Articles, the elections had gone in favor of the party supporting the reformers, through the choice of Curtet, Goulaz, Claude Pertemps, and Pernet Desfosses as syndics. It was therefore to a friendly government that Calvin and his associates could look for the enforcement of the Confession. Requested by Farel and Calvin, the Little Council voted, on March 13, to "cause the Articles to be observed in full."[42] But, for reasons that have been seen, the reformers were unable to press matters at the time, and it was nearly the end of April before printed copies were ordered distributed to aid in taking the assent of the citizens in groups. Opposition was evidently being encountered, however, for on May 1, the Little Council declared that it would do regarding the Articles "the best it could." On July 29, urged by Farel, Calvin, and Coraud, the Council of Two Hundred ordered the local officers of the city (*dizenniers*) to bring the groups of their several districts to the Church of Saint-Pierre to assent to the Confession. This was largely done, but many refused, and, on September 19, the Council informed such malcontents that, if persistent, "they should be told to go elsewhere to live." On November 12, the Little Council repeated the demand for assent and threat of banishment yet more emphatically, and was reinforced three days later by the Two Hundred. Matters had, however, reached a crisis. Strengthened by an unfavorable opinion of the Confession expressed by Commissioners from Bern recently present in Geneva on quite other business, the opposition forced a meeting of the General Assembly, for which

---

[42] For this and the other quotations and citations in this paragraph see *Registres du Conseil*, xxx. 189, 212, 219, 229, xxxi. 30, 32, 45, 49, 61, 81, 90, 93, 100; *Opera*, xxi. 208–217. Compare Kampschulte, i. 298–306; Cornelius, pp. 137–151; Doumergue, ii. 244–251.

political negotiations with Bern gave more regular cause. Its session was stormy. Farel in especial was attacked, and Jean Philippe, the leader of the opposition, proposed the appointment of a commission to hear all complaints. That, if carried out, would have superseded the regular officials in a fundamental part of their work. Only with great difficulty did the party in control of the government succeed in weathering the storm, and it was evident that its hold on Geneva was profoundly shaken.

Under these circumstances, had Calvin been a weaker, or possibly a more experienced man, or had his associates been less fiery and more worldly wise than Farel and Coraud, he would have modified the severity of his demands and sought to lead to the results he desired by a more gradual process. He was, however, young, convinced that his way was of obedience to God and mastered by that Gallic logic in following a principle to its full consequences which the compromise-loving Anglo-Saxon finds hard to appreciate. Yet one can but admire his courage and his disinterested loyalty to conviction. And, at first, in spite of the unfavorable results of the General Assembly, it seemed as if Calvin were making progress. With Farel he went to Bern and secured what was practically a disavowal of the unofficial criticisms passed by the Bernese Commissioners on the Confession, the approval by the Bernese ministers on its contents, and letters from the government of that powerful canton recommending "peace, union, and tranquillity" to the inhabitants of Geneva.[43] Stengthened thus, for the moment, by evidence that Bern would not then support the opposition, Farel, Calvin, and Coraud informed the Little Council that they deemed it best to exclude from participation in the January Communion "those whom they knew to be disunited" – that is opponents of the Confession – and asked the Council's support. It was granted, in part, for on receipt of a third letter from Bern, on January 4, 1538, the Two Hundred sent for two of the chief malcontents and induced them to swear assent to the Confession. Yet, to the disappointment of

---

[43] *Registres du Conseil*, xxxi. 129–146; *Opera*, xxi. 217–220; Letters of December 6, 9, and 28, 1537, *Opera*, xb. 130–134.

the reformers, the same body voted "that the Supper should be refused to no one." Though the struggle for the Confession was substantially gained, Calvin's labors to introduce an effective, independent, ecclesiastical excommunication were thus brought to naught.[44] The opposition was evidently too threatening, though its point of attack was now shifting to the question of discipline.

With the election of February 3 following, came a complete political overturn. The leaders of the opposition, Claude Richardet, Jean Philippe, Jean Lullin, and Ami de Chapeaurouge, were chosen syndics. The next day ten new members were elected into the Little Council. Even Porral was deprived of all office. Yet, though the party critical of the reformers was now in power, and Farel, Calvin, and Coraud were jeered and derided by the more disorderly of the populace, the relations of the reformers and the government were at first officially regular and undisturbed. This state of suspense could not long continue, however, without serious modifications on one side or the other, and it was speedily changed to open warfare. Certain propositions had been made in February by a Savoyard nobleman in French service, the sieur de Montchenu, to leading men in Geneva of both parties, very possibly inspired by his sovereign, Francis I, designed to further that monarch's wish to separate Geneva from the alliance with Bern and bring the city under a French protectorate. The approaches were loyally rejected, but among those addressed had been Michel Sept, a leader among the supporters of the reformers. Party hatred saw in this negotiation with the enemies of the city an opportunity to complete the discomfiture of the defeated heads of the former government; and, at a meeting of the Two Hundred, held on March 11th, six of the party which had supported the reformers, including Sept and three of the syndics of 1537, who by custom had places in the Little Council, were suspended from office. The course of these proceedings against their friends had drawn the public denunciation of Farel and Calvin, and the same session of the Two Hundred saw them forbidden "to mix in politics, but to preach the gospel as God has commanded." This

---

[44] *Registres du Conseil*, xxxi. 146; *Opera*, xxi. 219, 220.

was a direct limitation on the freedom of the pulpit, and such men as the Genevan reformers were not likely willingly to submit.[45]

Strained as the relations between the reformers and the Genevan government were, a further action at this session of the Two Hundred was even more intolerable to men like Farel and Calvin than a prohibition to mix in politics. The Council voted to "live under the Word of God according to the ordinances of the lords of Bern." That is to say, the civil authorities of Geneva, without even consulting the ministers, determined the ritual of the Church. Their action swept away all partial ecclesiastical independence such as Calvin ardently desired and, taken as it was, it seemed well-nigh an insult to the Genevan reformers. It reveals in the clearest light the strained state of party feeling in the city.

Like most problems on which men divide, that of the Bernese "ceremonies"[46] – laying aside all question of the method of their adoption by the Genevan government – had two sides. The Reformation at Bern had not been quite so radical in its destruction of the older worship as that under the uncompromising Farel at Geneva. Bern had retained the use of the font in baptism, unleavened bread in the Supper, the festive array of brides at weddings; and the observance of Christmas, Easter, Ascension, and Pentecost.[47] At Geneva, all these had been done away. To the credit of the good sense of the reformers of Bern and Geneva alike, be it said, the matter was regarded on both sides as relatively unimportant in itself.[48] But the situation was further complicated by the fact that the success of the war of 1536 against Savoy had left Lausanne, Thonon, and in fact most of the French-speaking territories about Lake Geneva – save the small tract over which that city held control – under Bernese authority. While Bern

[45] See Cornelius, pp. 157–159, 259; Doumergue, ii. 271–272; *Registres du Conseil*, xxxii. 3.

[46] See Cornelius, pp. 161–169; Doumergue, ii. 273–277.

[47] See Doumergue, ii. 277; Herminjard gives them as Christmas, New Year, Annunciation, and Ascension, iv. 413. The contemporary documents speak of them generally as the "festivals" or "four festivals."

[48] Herminjard, iv. 106, 145; v. 3, 4.

thus held most of the French-speaking evangelical portions of Switzerland under its sway, and Bern's victories had made their Protestantism possible, it was but natural that their ministers, who were mostly Frenchmen, should look to French-speaking Geneva rather than to German-speaking Bern with sympathy, and adopt Genevan ideals of worship. In many places, as under Viret at Lausanne, the Reformation was introduced by personal friends of Farel and Calvin; and in turn, the Genevan ministers welcomed the French-speaking pastors from Bernese territories to their "Colloquium," or ministers' meeting. On the other hand, Farel and Calvin recognized the ecclesiastical supremacy of Bern in affairs concerning its own territories or ministers, as in the case of Caroli. Bern naturally wished uniform ceremonies in its territories, and, without absolutely forcing the issue, threw its influence in that direction. Meanwhile, the constant Bernese desire to possess as much control in the affairs of Geneva as possible, as well as the more laudable wish to have all southern Switzerland one in worship, inclined Bern to seek the establishment of its "ceremonies" in Geneva itself. In December 1537, the authorities of Bern had instructed the embassy they proposed to send to Geneva to raise the question of conformity to Bernese practice.[49] On March 5, 1538,[50] they had notified the Genevan government that they had thought good to call a synod to meet at Lausanne on March 31, "for the welfare and union of our preachers" – that is to discuss the introduction of the ceremonies into all Bernese territories – and asked for the presence of Farel and Calvin. It was probably the receipt of this letter that emboldened the Two Hundred to vote the introduction of the Bernese ceremonies at Geneva on March 11.

Meanwhile the hopes of Bern rose. On March 20, the council of that city, apparently in ignorance of what the Genevan authorities had done on March 11, wrote again, saying that the Genevan ministers would be admitted to the synod at Lausanne only on

---

[49] *Opera*, xb. 132.

[50] Herminjard, iv. 403, gives the date as March 5th, and Cornelius and Doumergue agree. The *Opera*, xb. 179, dates March 12th.

previous acceptance of the ceremonies.[51] At this difficult juncture Farel and Calvin behaved with equal courage and wisdom. They presented themselves at the meeting at Lausanne, but attempted no part in its affairs. They would not compromise the liberty of the Genevan Church, even if the Genevan authorities had voted in favor of ceremonies to which in themselves, as practiced at Bern and approved at Lausanne for the French-speaking Bernese territories, they had no serious objection. On the other hand, they would not alienate Bern by open hostility. Hence, when the synod was over, and not till then, they entered into negotiation with the religious and civil leaders of Bern with a view to having the question of the ceremonies postponed till the meeting of a much larger Swiss synod at Zürich, already in prospect for April 28th. Had Kaspar Megander still been the spiritual leader at Bern, they might have succeeded even now in their request; but he had been dismissed from his post in December 1537, and his successor, Peter Kuntz, a rough Swiss peasant by origin, was as little sympathetic with the more cultivated Frenchmen as they with him. The Bernese were too confident that the course of events was running as they wished, to desire to alter or postpone decisions already reached by the Genevan government.

On April 15th, the government of Bern wrote letters[52] to the Genevan authorities and to Calvin and Farel which were the immediate occasion of the final crisis. That to the reformers was of interest in that, for the first time in an official document, the name of Calvin was placed before that of his older associate. In these letters they reported the result of the synod at Lausanne, and asked conformity to the Bernese ceremonies. The Little Council, having received the communication, summoned Farel and Calvin and asked "whether they would observe the said ceremonies or not." The reformers urged that the matter rest till after the approaching synod at Zürich. Dismissed for the time by the Little Council, that body sent a messenger later in the day to Calvin and Farel, who reported that they "totally

---

[51] Herminjard, iv. 403; Cornelius, pp. 171–174; Doumergue, ii. 278, 279.
[52] *Opera*, xb. 184–186.

refused to preach or give the Supper in" the Bernese form. At the same session the Council forbade Coraud to preach till he had answered before judicial authority for his public criticisms of the government. The following day Coraud preached in defiance, and was promptly imprisoned. This seemed to Calvin and Farel insupportable, and accompanied by a number of the party favorable to them, including the ex-syndics Curtet and Pertemps, and also Michel Sept and Ami Perrin, they appeared before the syndics, protesting against Coraud's imprisonment and demanding a meeting of the Two Hundred. The government hesitated to proceed to final measures, and presented a compromise, offering to allow the question of the ceremonies to wait till the synod at Zürich, provided Farel and Calvin would consent to Coraud's deposition from his pastorate. The reformers declined thus to desert their colleague; and on Calvin's repeated refusal to use the Bernese ceremonies at the approaching Communion, they were forbidden to preach – the Council declaring that it "would find others" to take their places. Its hope was in the weak-kneed Henri de la Mare, pastor of the Genevan country parish of Jussy-l'Évêque; but, by Farel and Calvin's threats of excommunication, he was induced, for the time, to agree to remain inactive.[53]

The morning following was Easter Sunday, and amid great excitement, in spite of the prohibition, Calvin preached at Saint-Pierre and Farel at Saint-Gervais. It was Communion day, but they refused to distribute the elements, not, as they carefully explained, because they deemed the Bernese use of unleavened bread in itself wrong, but because to administer the Supper in the circumstances of such popular tumult would be "to profane so holy a mystery." The breach was now complete. The Little Council met the same day, and summoned the Two Hundred for the morrow and the General Assembly for the day thereafter. By these bodies the Bernese ceremonies were once more ratified, and by a majority vote of the General Assembly, on April 23,

[53] For these events see *Registres du Conseil*, xxxii. 31–34; *Opera*, xxi. 223–226; Cornelius, pp. 174–179; Doumergue, ii. 279–281.

Farel, Calvin, and Coraud were ordered to leave Geneva within three days.

The dry pages of the official register of Geneva glow with unwonted vividness as they record Calvin's answer to the announcement of his banishment: "Well, indeed! If we had served men, we should have been ill rewarded, but we serve a great Master who will recompense us!"[54] But neither Farel nor Calvin had any thought of abandoning the struggle without effort. They at once betook themselves to the authorities at Bern. The Bernese government lent them willing ears. Matters at Geneva had gone much too far to please Bern, however desirous of ceremonial uniformity. Bern began to fear for the Protestant cause in Geneva, but the controlling party at Geneva remained deaf to Bernese representations. Without waiting for the result of Bern's appeal, the reformers pushed on to Zürich, where the synod representative of that canton, of Basel, Bern, Schaffhausen, St Gall, and other Swiss evangelical territories, of which mention has already been made, met on April 28. Before this body they presented an elaborate statement, practically accepting the Bernese ceremonies as matters in the liberty of each church, but setting forth with unabated courage their program of ecclesiastical reform. They urged the establishment of efficient discipline, the use of excommunication, the division of the city into parishes, more frequent observation of the Supper, singing of Psalms, and a more careful order of ministerial selection and appointment.[55] Their recent Genevan experiences had not caused them to withdraw a hair's breadth from the strenuous ideal to which they had set themselves – an ideal more thoroughgoing than anything realized in practice as yet by any of the evangelical churches. The synod, under the persuasive influence of the reformers, approved their position, though urging them to use more Christian compliance toward an undisciplined people, and recommended the Bernese authorities to seek their restoration.[56]

---

[54] *Registres du Conseil*, xxxii. 36; *Opera*, xxi. 226, 227.

[55] Herminjard, v. 3–6. The reformers would have men free to work after the sermon on the four feasts.

[56] Herminjard, v. 14, 17.

Thus fortified, they returned to Bern. The aid wished was granted, but again the way was barred. Though Bern despatched an embassy toward Geneva with Farel and Calvin, the Little Council forbade them to enter the city[57] – a result to which the hostility of Peter Kuntz, the pastor at Bern, and of his correspondent, Pierre Vandel, not a little contributed.

Calvin's work at Geneva was now wholly, and, as far as could then be seen, permanently at an end. Most various judgments have been passed upon it. It is impossible to affirm that it was always wise or skillful. A slower and more educative attempt to secure the reforms which he wished, and for which Geneva was so far from ready, would probably have been much more effective. The situation was obscured by party hatred, for the origin of which Calvin was not responsible, but in which he might have treated the opposing interests with more politic skill. He showed too much of the impetuosity of youth and inexperience. It was natural that he should. But whatever judgment may have passed upon his methods, the ends which he had in view had never been uncertain or ignoble. He would have Geneva an orderly, disciplined, Christian city, and he would make its Church, to a degree yet unknown in Protestant circles, self-governing. Apparently he had failed; but it was a failure that carried no disgrace in the retrospect, however sharply Calvin was blamed by contemporary opponents, and criticised even by such friends of the past or present as du Tillet and Bucer.[58]

---

[57] *Registres du Conseil*, xxxii. 60; *Opera*, xxi. 229; Farel and Calvin to Bullinger, June, 1538, Herminjard, v. 21–29.
[58] Letters, Herminjard, v. 65, 103.

9

CALVIN IN STRASSBURG, 1538–1541

Convinced that their hope of restoration to the Genevan pastorate was vain for the time being, Farel and Calvin made their way to Basel, where they felt that, among friends, they might await further developments. Here they found a welcome in the home of Johann Oporin, the publisher of the *Institutes*. They watched eagerly for news from Geneva[1] and Calvin, perhaps even more than his less sensitive companion, felt a deep sense of injury. He was profoundly wounded in spirit by the experiences through which he had passed, and his trust was still that through the aid of friends a synod of Protestant Switzerland might be called which would effect their restoration. Bernese reports spread through the evangelical cantons that all was well under the new régime in Geneva caused these hopes to fade, but, as the days passed, Calvin began to take heart again as having received this bitter cup from an all-wise overruling Providence, which in due time would vindicate its ways.[2]

Meanwhile Calvin's two Genevan associates found other places of work. Coraud entered on a brief and unhappy pastorate at Orbe, which was closed in a few weeks by his death on October 4. The call of Antoine Marcourt from Neuchâtel by the Genevan

---

[1] Their letter to Viret and Coraud, June 14, Herminjard, v. 30.
[2] See, for these emotions and hopes, his contemporary letters, notably to Bullinger, ibid., p. 21; to du Tillet, p. 43; to Farel, p. 70.

authorities opened a pastorate there for Farel; and, before the end of July, he was laboring in that already familiar field. For Calvin the decision was more difficult. Farel wished him in continued association, but Calvin felt rightly that such a joint ministry so near Geneva would arouse their opponents, and Bucer urged that such companionship and location would but cause the wound which Calvin had received to rankle with fresh bitterness.[3] Bucer was, indeed, proving himself the wise and kindly friend that Calvin needed in this crisis. The letter that brought this advice repeated to the chagrined young scholar at Basel a warm invitation, already urged upon him, to make Strassburg his home – in which Capito and Johann Sturm also joined.[4] The body of French refugees which he might serve in that German city, Bucer told him, was indeed small, but it needed his aid, and a ministry at Strassburg might be of some service even to the cause which he had at heart at Geneva. Calvin hesitated. To take up a new work filled him with distrust. But now Bucer, as Farel had done at Geneva, urged the call as of God and cited the example of Jonah as parallel to his own.[5] Thus adjured, Calvin decided and, probably on September 8, he preached his first sermon to the French congregation in the Church of St Nicolas at Strassburg.[6]

Strassburg, where Martin Bucer, Wolfgang Capito, and Kaspar Hedio had labored since 1523, was the bulwark of the Reformation in southwestern Germany. In Bucer the city enjoyed a spiritual leader second only to Luther and Melanchthon. In Johann Sturm it possessed an educational reformer who was making its school, at the time of Calvin's arrival, a model of pedagogical method. In Jakob Sturm Strassburg had the guidance of a statesman of remarkable talents and breadth of view, and all had worked in harmony to promote a sane, moderate, and co-operant type of evangelical Reformation. The city had been noted for its friendliness in receiving those who sought refuge within

---

[3] Herminjard, v. 65, 77, 87, 88; Cornelius, pp. 197–200.

[4] Letter about August 1st, Herminjard, v. 64.

[5] Preface to the Psalms, Opera, xxxi. 28.

[6] Herminjard, v. iii.; Doumergue, ii. 358

its walls when persecuted for their allegiance to the Protestant cause. No greater good fortune could have come to Calvin, in his depressed and wounded frame of mind, nor, indeed, under any circumstances, in view of his later usefulness, than to be given three years of activity in such associations as Strassburg offered. He was to be relieved, in large part, of the conflicts which he had been called upon to sustain at Geneva. He was to be treated with full respect. Time was to be his for study and for the perfection of his theological system. He was to make the acquaintance of many of the leaders of the German Reformation. He was to marry. He was to ripen and deepen by experience, thought and contact with men, so that the years of sojourn at Strassburg must be reckoned among the most valuable, and in some aspects the most agreeable, in his experience.[7]

At Strassburg, in spite of the fact that he spoke no German, Calvin speedily felt at home. The spiritual and civil leaders of the city were cordial, and so far did he respond to the attractions of his new environment – doubly grateful after the storms of Geneva – that, in July 1539, he became a citizen of Strassburg, being enrolled in the guild of tailors.[8] This association implied no necessary working connection with the trade. Calvin's act shows his confidence in the Strassburg situation, for it was not till more than eighteen years after his return to Geneva that he was to enter the citizenship of that community.[9] But, though in friendly associations, Calvin had never been so pressed by poverty as he was to be during these months at Strassburg. His pay at Geneva had, of course, ceased. Du Tillet's aid had helped him before, and the prompt offer was not wanting now, but his old friend was now on his way back to the Roman Church, and coupled his offer with the request – under the circumstances almost the condition – that Calvin refrain from public activity.

---

[7] Compare the remarks of Kampschulte, i. 321. By far the best account of Calvin's stay in Strassburg is that of Doumergue, ii. 293–649.

[8] Ibid., ii. 350.

[9] December 25, 1559, *Registres du Conseil*, lv. 163; *Opera*, xxi. 725. The delay was for prudential reasons.

A man of Calvin's conscientious and sensitive spirit could not but refuse, and he declined the offer in words full of gratitude for the past, but positive as to the present.[10] At first he had no salary, and the recompense of fifty-two florins annually allowed him by the school board from May 1, 1539, was merely a nominal honorarium. A larger benefice Calvin seems never to have received at Strassburg.[11] Calvin's financial position was, therefore, oftentimes one of distress. It is not probable that he sold his personal library, as has often been said; though something came to him from the sale of books belonging to Olivétan's estate.[12] As a means of easing his fortunes, and doubtless, also, of extending his influence as a teacher, he took young French boarders, for the most part students, into his house.[13]

As a pastor of the French refugees gathered in Strassburg, Calvin soon found opportunity to put into practice much that he had attempted in vain at Geneva. The French exiles in Strassburg, who may have numbered from 400 to 600, cannot be said to have become a completely organized religious body before Calvin's coming. Under the supervision of the Strassburg authorities, to whom they, like all other worshippers, were responsible, they had had occasional preaching in their own language. But with Calvin's arrival they had a leader acceptable to the Strassburg pastors, and permission was now given them to celebrate the Supper. Calvin's organizing genius showed its power at once. To the "little Church," as he describes it, he preached four times a week. The Communion he administered monthly[14] – a frequency that he had vainly recommended to Geneva. In spite of criticism

---

[10] Du Tillet's letter of September 7, 1538, Calvin's reply of October 20, Herminjard, v. 107, 165; see also 292.

[11] See Doumergue, ii. 454–458, where the matter is fully discussed. The florin was worth about a dollar, though its purchasing power was of course greater than now.

[12] Ibid., Herminjard, vi. 13–26.

[13] Doumergue, ii. 458–462, has collected some facts regarding those thus received.

[14] Herminjard, v. 111, 112, 145. It was celebrated "according to the rite of the city."

and opposition, he established a vigorous ecclesiastical discipline; and, though the congregation was under the control of the civil and religious authorities of Strassburg, he succeeded, thanks doubtless to the foreign character of its membership, in rendering the exercise of that discipline an independent ecclesiastical act. So far did he carry it that he not only forbade the Communion to the unworthy, but he required all who would partake of the Supper to present themselves to him for a previous spiritual interrogation. Such an examination Calvin thought the only proper substitute for the Roman confessional.[15] He built up an orderly, disciplined congregation. Under his ministry it grew in influence, and his work was distinguished, also, by its success in winning Anabaptists not only of the city, but of the region about, to his way of thinking. Among the trophies of this zeal were one of the Netherlandish propagators of this faith with whom he had vainly debated at Geneva, and Jean Stordeur, then husband of the woman whom Calvin was later to marry.

Probably Calvin's most interesting, though not his most original, labor on behalf of the "little Church" was the development of its liturgy – a form which, established with considerable modifications in Geneva on his return, became the general model of Reformed, as distinguished from Lutheran and Anglican worship, and is the primary source from which the type of service familiar in the churches of England, Scotland, and America that trace their spiritual ancestry in large part to Calvin is derived. Here, as in much else that Calvin did, he drew from the best that was at hand rather than created outright; but the result bore the stamp of his impressive spiritual personality.[16] Recent investigation has shown that the form of public worship at Strassburg had been gradually modified, largely under the influence of Bucer, from the revised translation of the Roman

---

[15] Ibid., v. 291; vi. 200, 223; compare Doumergue, ii. 412, 413.

[16] The subject has been opened as never before by Alfred Erichson, *Die Calvinische und die Altstrassburgische Gottesdienstordnung*, Strassburg, 1894, who perhaps allows too little to Calvin though clearly making out his main contention. It is largely treated by Doumergue, ii. 488–504.

Mass introduced by Diebold Schwarz, in 1524, till it had acquired probably by 1537, and certainly by 1539, the form of which Calvin made use. Calvin's work in preparing this first draft of his liturgy was essentially that of a translator. The order is identical with that of Bucer, and the form of words is largely the same. But Calvin added not a little in brief phrases and modifications of expression which gave to the original German service a happy adaptation to the use of French-speaking worshippers.

As employed at Strassburg in 1539, Calvin's service, like that of Bucer from which it was taken, began with the Invocation and the famous Confession still in use in many of the Reformed churches of the continent, corresponding to, though far from identical with, that of the Anglican worship. Next followed the announcement of absolution to all who repent and "seek Jesus Christ for their salvation." Then the first table of the Decalogue – that is the first four Commandments – was sung by the congregation.[17] Upon this followed a brief form of prayer for forgiveness and for strength to keep the divine Law, succeeded by the singing of the remaining Commandments. A short form of prayer for spiritual illumination was then followed by the central feature of the service, the reading of the "Word of God" and its exposition in the sermon. That completed, there followed the long, liturgical petition of general supplication, ending in the Lord's Prayer. This was succeeded by the singing of the Apostles' Creed or of a Psalm, and the service concluded with the Aaronic benediction.[18]

It may be well to note the principal changes made in this service by Calvin when introduced into Genevan use on his return to that city[19] – the more that they illustrate a principal characteristic of his thought on liturgical usages. Most of these modifications were in the direction of approximation to the relatively undeveloped, yet more radically non-Roman, service which Farel had established in Geneva when the Reformation

---

[17] Doubtless in the rhymed form to be found in *Opera*, vi. 221.

[18] Numbers vi. 24–26. Text in part in *Opera*, vi. 174, 175; Erichson and Doumergue, op. cit.

[19] Full text, *Opera*, vi. 161–224.

gained control in 1536, and that doubtless continued in use till Calvin's return. With this end in view, against his own preference,[20] he omitted the promise of absolution, as offensive by its apparent Romanism to some more strict than he. He substituted the singing of a Psalm for the twofold chanting of the Commandments and the intermediate prayer. As Farel had done, he now gave room for extempore prayer, saying of the petition before the sermon, "The form is at the discretion of the minister." At first he substituted an enlarged paraphrase of the Lord's Prayer in the body of the general petition following the sermon for its literal repetition at its conclusion, but later restored it. For the chanting of the Apostles' Creed he substituted that of a Psalm.[21] These modifications are not inconsiderable, though they do not affect the general order, dignity, and simplicity of the service, or its resemblance to the Strassburg original to which Calvin was indebted, but they show that, within the limits imposed by the rejection of what he deemed unscriptural or superstitious, Calvin felt that public worship might be modified and adjusted to meet local needs and even prejudices. As between a fixed liturgy and free prayer he evidently had none of the scruples which later controversy was to develop among his spiritual disciples in England, Scotland, and America; and his Genevan form of worship, at least, was a happy combination of both.

A service of a yet more wide-reaching character done by Calvin for the Strassburg congregation of which he was pastor, and through it to the Reformed churches generally, was the establishment of the singing of Psalms in French. The part that the hymns of Luther played in the German Reformation is well known. But not all reformers had so recognized the value of song. Zwingli had wholly done away with it at Zürich, and the earliest French Protestants made no use of hymns.[22] Farel's circle felt the

---

[20] *Opera*, xa. 213; Doumergue, ii. 502. Doumergue remarks: "it was accommodated to the worship of Geneva to such a degree that the liturgy deserves the title of Genevese much more than of Calvinist."

[21] Doumergue, ii. 746, shows that the Apostles' Creed was recited at Geneva at the close of the Lord's Prayer, ending the general petition.

[22] Doumergue has an admirable discussion of Calvin's relation to music in worship, ii. 505–524.

value of songs, at least as a means of attacking Roman beliefs, if not of public worship, and a little volume of such popular compositions was printed at Neuchâtel in 1533.[23] But the most positive step toward the introduction of the hymn into French-speaking Protestant worship was that taken by Farel and Calvin in the Articles of January 1537.[24] Not till he came to Strassburg was Calvin able to carry the intentions therein expressed into practice. He acted with his accustomed vigor, aided doubtless by the example of the German-speaking churches of the city, in which singing was the rule. Within two months of the beginning of his pastorate, the "little Church" was singing Psalms; and in 1539, he published a brief collection, containing eighteen Psalms and three other compositions in French verse, eight of them by Clément Marot, whose poetic gifts were to make him the Psalm-translator above all others of French Protestantism; but seven of the pieces were from the pen of Calvin himself.[25] Calvin's own composition, if not of high poetic order, was dignified, clear, and far removed from doggerel. Indeed, in his own estimate, he had something of the poetic spirit, and in youth, like many another young man, tried his hand at verse.[26] But, as later editions of the Psalter were issued, Calvin's critical taste led him to substitute increasingly Marot's more inspired compositions, as they were put forth, for his own. Though chiefly drawn from the Psalms, Calvin would not confine the service of song to the rhymed words of Scripture. The Genevan liturgy of 1545 contains, besides nine Psalms, the *Nunc Dimittis* of Simeon, the Ten Commandments versified, and a free hymn of "salutation to Christ."[27] The later Puritan restriction to the words of the Bible was evidently not Calvin's making. On the other hand, whatever may have been Calvin's feeling toward the organ as an instrument of music, he did not regard its use as appropriate in public worship because

---

[23] Ibid., p. 506; Rilliet and Dufour, *Le catéchisme francais de Calvin*, p. c.

[24] *Ante*, p. 192.

[25] Doumergue, ii. 511.

[26] Ibid., p. 510, quoting *Opera*, xvi. 488.

[27] *Opera*, vi. 211–224.

of its tendency to take the thought of the congregation from the words of the hymn.[28] Far from being an enemy of song in Christian worship, Calvin was the great supporter and advocate of the use of the Psalm in the Reformed churches. While Calvin was thus busily engaged in Strassburg as a pastor, he was developing a like activity as a teacher, so that, with the additional burden of a large correspondence and his constant struggle with poverty, his days must have been full indeed. Theological lectures had been given at Strassburg[29] since the introduction of the Reformation, and since 1532, in formal fashion, by Bucer, Capito, and Hedio in the choir of the cathedral. As systematized by Johann Sturm, in the month of Calvin's arrival, the school curriculum of Strassburg included not merely elementary teaching, and advanced courses in Greek, Latin, Hebrew, mathematics, and law, but was crowned by instruction in theology given by the Strassburg ministers of whom mention has been made. The orderly, thorough, and progressive educational constitution of Strassburg must have impressed Calvin profoundly and have influenced his later action at Geneva. Naturally the Strassburg pastors, to whom theological instruction was committed, wished the aid of the author of the *Institutes*, and in January 1539, Calvin began his work,[30] at first without compensation, and from May onward with the modest honorarium of which mention has been made. The form of instruction in theology was by biblical exposition, and the natural supposition would be that the first theme of Calvin's public interpretation was the Epistle to the Romans. His *Commentary* on this letter of the Apostle to the Gentiles, the preface of which is dated October 18, 1539, was published at Strassburg by Wendelin Rihel in March 1540,[31] and inaugurated the long series of biblical expositions which were to give to Calvin the first

---

[28] Doumergue, ii. 521, quoting *Opera*, xxx. 259.

[29] Here again the sources and literature have been well summarized by Doumergue, ii. 428–440.

[30] Letter to Farel, Herminjard, v. 230; Doumergue, ii. 434. He was invited by Capito.

[31] *Opera*, xlix. 1–296; Herminjard, vi. 74–78; compare ibid., v. 230.

rank as an exegete among the leaders of the Reformation age. But adequate testimony seems to make it evident that Calvin's first work as a public instructor was the interpretation of the Gospel according to Saint John, and that this teaching was followed by the exposition of Corinthians.[32]

The lectures attracted wide attention, and drew Calvin's fellow countrymen of evangelical sentiments in considerable numbers from the homeland to Strassburg, as well as added to his rising fame in the city of this residence. And to all who came he was able to show an example, in miniature it is true, but of striking clearness, of a Christian community as he believed such a community should be – his Church of earnest-minded exiles for their faith, well disciplined, clearly taught, and knit together in common worship, while their pastor bore his share in the larger religious interests of Strassburg and extended his influence far beyond the city's walls.

This multiform activity as pastor and teacher was accompanied by a productivity in authorship that reveals the strength and concentration with which Calvin was able to work, in spite of frequent physical disability, chiefly manifested in attacks of headache, indigestion, and nervous irritability[33] – a condition of health largely due, doubtless, to his overstrain as a student in Paris and Orléans, and the anxieties and burdens borne at Geneva. In August 1539, he brought out a carefully revised and much-enlarged edition of the *Institutes*.[34] Though still lacking much of the logical perfection of arrangement which this treatise was to acquire in the final edition of 1559, it may be said that with the edition of 1539, the *Institutes* attained their doctrinal completeness. The treatment was everywhere more ample, and the second edition now published immediately superseded the relatively brief handbook of 1536. In particular, the opening sections, on the knowledge of God and of ourselves, were greatly enlarged. The distinctions between natural

---

[32] Johann Sturm, *Quarti Antipappi*, p. 20; Herminjard, v. 231; Doumergue, ii. 434.

[33] Letters to Farel, Herminjard, v. 88, 270; vi. 312, 313.

[34] Text, *Opera*, i. 253–1152.

and revealed theology were clearly set forth. The final authority of Scripture was firmly based on the inward testimony of the Holy Spirit witnessing to the reader that it is God who speaks through words. The original state of man and the consequences of the fall were discussed with much greater amplitude. Election and reprobation were now much more fully and sharply set forth, and were elaborately defended as taught in the divine revelation. In a word, without essentially departing in any fundamental respect from the theological system set forth in the edition of the *Institutes* published in 1536, this Strassburg revision of three years later reveals a mind of greater maturity, more elaborated thought, and sharper definition of the doctrines commonly called Calvinistic. The theologian had come to his full stature.

In the *Institutes* of 1539, the doctrine of the Lord's Supper, that burning point of contention between the Lutherans and the older reformers of Switzerland, is so treated that, without alteration of his fundamental view, Calvin's language is less opposed to the conception of Luther than in the earlier edition. This irenic spirit, anxious to present a basis of mutual agreement between the contending factions, is well illustrated in the *Petit Traicté de la saincte Cene*[35] – an exposition designed especially for those without technical theological training. Written in Strassburg, it was published at Geneva in 1541, and was doubtless designed for circulation in France quite as much as in Switzerland. Even more than thus far at Geneva, Calvin's work in Strassburg was revealing to him the possibility of exercising a moulding influence on the course of the evangelical movement in his homeland such as he had always desired.

As compared with his life at Geneva, Calvin's sojourn at Strassburg was free from personal controversies, but an exception is worthy of mention. Caroli, whose accusations against Farel and Calvin have already been described, had returned to the Roman Church after his failure to make good his charges at the synods of Lausanne and Bern in 1537. His restless spirit – and we may believe

---

[35] Text, *Opera*, v. 429–460. See especially his remarks about Luther, Zwingli, and Ecolampadius, ibid., 457–460. Compare Henry, i. 261–285.

his semi-Protestantism – was not satisfied, however, and in July 1539, he sought Farel and Viret, by whom he was once more received into friendship.[36] Armed with a letter of commendation from Simon Grynaeus, professor at Basel, to Calvin, he came to Strassburg, about the beginning of October, and set about to win the approval of its ministers and professors. At Bucer's request, as having been already in controversy with Caroli, Calvin did not meet him face to face,[37] and Caroli, anxious to excuse his recent reconciliation with Rome, brought up in discussion with the Strassburg divines Farel and Calvin's refusal to sign the three ancient creeds. On Caroli's retirement from the conference room, Calvin told his side of the late controversy to the Strassburg ministers and teachers.

The ministers and teachers regarded Calvin as innocent of any wrong to Caroli, though his refusal to subscribe the creeds met with their disapproval. A long Act of Reconciliation was drawn up for signature by Caroli and the Strassburg divines, in which he assented to the Augsburg Confession, but specified many peculiarities of his, at best, fluctuating beliefs. This document was not sent to Calvin for signature till late at night, and before being seen by him, it had received the approval of his colleagues. As he read it, he saw that it permitted Caroli to say that he left to God's judgment "the offences by which he had been forced to desertion" of the evangelical cause. That implied that Farel and Calvin were blameworthy for his lapse. It was an aggravating and unjust accusation; Calvin had a right to resent it. But he did much more. He lost all control of himself. He sought Sturm and his colleagues, Bucer and Matthias Zell. In words of the utmost excitement and bitterness he declared that he would die before he would sign. He rushed, so he tells Farel, from the room, but Bucer followed and in a measure calmed him, though his return home was succeeded by what must be called an attack of hysterics. In the letter which recounts these events, he blames himself severely for his ungoverned conduct; but he blames his friend Farel no

---

[36] The letters regarding this incident may be found in Herminjard, v. 352, 355, 370; vi. 35, 40, 52. It is suggestively treated by Doumergue, ii. 397–405.

[37] Calvin's letter of October 8 to Farel, Herminjard, vi. 52–58, is our source.

less as the cause of his woes. Farel's acceptance of the apparently repentant Caroli should not have been so hasty. Indeed, in the mood in which he wrote, the fault seemed to him more that of Farel than of Caroli, who having been received into favor must now be treated with kindness. Calvin succeeded in having the objectionable clause erased, and signed the Reconciliation, but the incident is one to be borne in mind in a consideration of his later controversies. He was liable to violent anger, and was easily aroused to high nervous excitement, and in this state was unguarded in the extreme in what he said, or to whom he expressed his wrath. He clearly recognized his own fault;[38] but it was one which many times overcame him, and obscured too much in his own lifetime and in later recollection other, and much more attractive, qualities of mind and heart.

It is pleasant to turn from this incident of Calvin's life in Strassburg to one of a more intimate and personal nature – his marriage. His life of study and of exile, followed by the stormy months at Geneva, had not been such hitherto as to turn his thoughts toward the establishment of a home. He had not been without companionship. His younger brother, Antoine, and his half-sister, Marie, had accompanied him to Geneva, and the former, after a few months' delay, followed him to Strassburg, arriving in December 1539, and continuing thenceforth, as had probably been the case at Geneva, a member of Calvin's household as long as he remained in the city.[39] In the comparative quiet of Strassburg, notwithstanding his poverty – and perhaps in the eyes of some of his friends, though not of Calvin himself, by reason of that poverty – the question of marriage soon began to assume importance. His former associate Viret had married in October 1538. That example, and that of the Strassburg ministry, together with the advice of Bucer, may have had weight. At all

---

[38] Doumergue, ii. 401–405, makes this incident the text of a discussion, with other examples, of this side of Calvin's nature.

[39] Marie seems not to have gone to Strassburg. She ultimately married Charles Costan, probably of Geneva (*Opera*, xx. 300), and may have been married before Calvin left Geneva.

events, it was the desirability of marriage in itself considered rather than affection for any one person that awoke the thought of his own union in Calvin's mind. He apparently first presented the matter to his bachelor friend, Farel, in a letter now lost, and writing, a little later, to that intimate correspondent in May 1539, he thus described the wife that he desired:[40]

> I am not of that insane class of lovers who, once captivated by beauty, kiss even its faults. The only comeliness that attracts me is this: – that she be modest, complaisant, unostentatious, thrifty, patient, and likely to be careful of my health.

To appreciate the unromantic and rather self-centered ideal here set forth by a man who had not reached thirty years of age, we must remember the century in which he lived, with its low estimate of the position of women as compared with their place in our own, and the absorption which Calvin felt in the reformatory task that was before him. Such as it was, his ideal was to be realized, but not immediately.[41] Nine months later, in February 1540, Calvin informed Farel[42] that marriage had been proposed to him on behalf of a well-to-do and nobly born young woman – the agents being apparently the girl's brother and brother's wife, who were devotedly attached to him and wished their sister married to one they so much admired. Calvin insisted that she learn his native French. She asked time to think it over – a request which he seems to have looked upon as a divinely appointed way of deliverance from a marriage in which inequality of birth and education might have clouded the prospect of happiness. Calvin took a prompt way to break off further negotiations. He sent his brother, Antoine, to ask on his behalf the hand of another and much poorer young

---

[40] Herminjard, v. 314; Doumergue, ii. 448. Doumergue, ibid., pp. 441–478, has treated Calvin's marriage with characteristic thoroughness. See also Henry, i. 407–423; Bonnet, *Idelette de Bure*, in *Bulletin de la Soc. de l'hist. du Prot. francais*, iv. 636–646 (1856); A. Lang, *Das häusliche Leben Johannes Calvins*, in the *Allgemeine Zeitung*, June 16–22, and separately, Munich, 1893.

[41] Apparently Farel came to Strassburg in June 1539, for some marriage project of Calvin of which we have no definite knowledge. Herminjard, vi. 168.

[42] Ibid., vi. 167.

woman, "who, if she answers to her reputation, would bring dowry enough without any money." So hopeful was he that this vicarious wooing would prosper that he wished Farel to plan to perform the ceremony not later than the 10th of the next month. Such confidence was, as may readily be imagined, unwarranted. The young woman delayed, and when at last in the following June she consented to an engagement, Calvin heard such reports of her that he speedily released her.[43] In all this there seems little sentiment save an honest fear lest he marry above his station in life and with one unsympathetic with his aims. But the search was evidently continued, for on August 17, 1540, Christopher Fabri wrote Calvin from Thonon, bidding him salute the wife whom they had heard he had recently married.[44] The wife to whom he was at last joined, "with the aid and advice of Bucer," was "a grave and honorable woman," Idelette de Bure, widow of Calvin's Anabaptist convert, Jean Stordeur of Liège, who had died, some time before, of the plague.[45] The ceremony was probably simple, and Farel himself, there is reason to believe, officiated.[46]

Calvin's married life has left fewer traces than could be wished in his correspondence, but enough remains to show that husband and wife lived on terms of cordial affection and of mutual trust. In character and devotion she was to him all that his ideal of a wife had pictured. To Viret he wrote of her immediately after her death:[47]

---

[43] Herminjard, vi. 191, 199, 238. It is possible that the person to whom he became engaged in June is not identical with the poor girl sought in February, but I have followed what seems the more probable interpretation of Calvin's letters.

[44] Ibid., vi. 275. Herminjard and Doumergue seem justified in regarding this letter as fixing the month of the marriage, though many earlier scholars placed it a month or more later.

[45] Colladon, *Life*, *Opera*, xxi. 62. Lefranc conjectures that she may have been of the family of de Bures of Noyon, and hence that the marriage may not have been "the result of a meeting wholly due to chance." *Jeunesse*, p. 191. There were Bures, however, at Liège, Doumergue, ii. 463. Idelette had a son and a daughter by her first husband.

[46] Doumergue, ii. 463.

[47] *Opera*, xiii. 230; compare ibid., viii. 73, "*singularis exempli femina.*"

> I have been bereaved of the best companion of my life, who, if our lot had been harsher, would have been not only the willing sharer of exile and poverty, but even of death. While she lived, she was the faithful helper of my ministry. From her I never experienced the slightest hindrance.

That she was a woman of unusual Christian faith, and not without force and some degree of individuality, the story of her deathbed bears witness.[48] But we know far less of her and of her influence on her husband than we desire. At best, she stands in the shadow of his much clearer-seen personality.

Calvin's married life, though happy in mutual companionship, was one of sorrow through the trials incident to human experience. His only child,[49] Jacques, born July 28, 1542, lived but a few days, and his wife's health was always feeble after the birth of their son. On March 29, 1549, she too was taken from him. In spite of the severe repression of Calvin's references to his affliction – a fortitude of mind worthy of admiration in the judgment of his intimate friends at the time[50] – it would be an injustice to regard his sense of bereavement as other than profound and lasting. His marriage, though having little of romance in its beginnings, had in it much of the satisfaction that comes from mutual trust, and of loving absorption, at least on the part of the wife, in the other's interests and work.

The years of Strassburg, so fruitful in the development of Calvin's intellectual life, his religious program, and his personal experience, were no less significant in their enlargement of his acquaintance with the men and affairs of the Reformation in its broader aspects. He was now reckoned as one of the leaders in an influential German Protestant city, trusted by its authorities, and accredited as its representative in discussions of the highest importance. As such he now came into intimate contact with

---

[48] Calvin to Farel, ibid., p. 228.

[49] Many writers, among them Bonnet and Lang, have thought that Calvin had three children; but Doumertue, ii. 470–473, shows conclusively that there was but one.

[50] E.g. Viret to Calvin, April 10, 1549, *Opera*, xiii. 233.

the problems which pressed for solution in the land of the Reformation's birth, and gained the lasting friendship of one of its earliest champions – Philip Melanchthon.[51]

Calvin's stay at Strassburg coincided with the period when the Emperor Charles V, long hindered from crushing Protestantism by the wars with France and with the Turks, as well as by the strength of the Schmalkaldic league, and not yet ready for the open attack which was to bring him seeming victory in 1547, was attempting to secure a basis of compromise between the divided wings of Christendom. Preliminary to the Frankfort Reichstag of April 1539, an imperial conference was held in the same city in February. At the Reichstag it was agreed that a friendly discussion looking toward "Christian union" should be held between the representatives of both types of faith. In compliance, after a futile meeting at Hagenau in June 1540, eleven champions from each side debated at Worms in November, and after adjournment in January 1541, the discussion was continued in April under the presidency of the Emperor himself at Regensburg. The outcome was a failure. No agreement was reached, but the attempt is one of the reckoning points of the German Reformation, and at all these meetings, except that of the Reichstag, Calvin was present. In the two last mentioned he bore a prominent part.

Calvin's visit to the Frankfort conference, for which he left Strassburg in company with Johann Sturm and other friends on February 21, 1539, was undertaken partly to secure aid for his persecuted French fellow believers, on whose behalf Bucer was already laboring at Frankfort, and partly to make the acquaintance of Melanchthon.[52] He went in no official capacity. In the endeavor on behalf of French Protestants he had little,

---

[51] The chief source for this episode are Calvin's letters to Farel. A brief sketch is that of Kampschulte, i. 327–342. Doumergue, ii. 525–649, in a much ampler treatment sharply criticises Kampshculte, and points out errors into which he fell. For Calvin's tracts growing out of these experiences, see *Opera*, v. 461–684.

[52] He described his experiences and observations in a long letter to Farel, March 16, 1539, Herminjard, v. 247–260.

if any, success, but he began a friendship with Melanchthon which was to be one of the most winsome of his relationships. Unlike in so many characteristics, and differing more and more on the theological doctrine of predestination, the severely logical, courageous, firm young Frenchman, and the more timid, cautious, and compromising elder German scholar, found much in common. Their correspondence, though not frequent and not without expressions of disagreement, shows, especially on Calvin's part, great consideration, affection, and respect; and this continued Calvin's feeling always. Calvin's patience and confidence in his friend are exhibited in a most attractive light. To Melanchthon he dedicated his reply to Pighius in 1543, and, three years later, he published and commended a French translation of Melanchthon's *Loci Communes*.[53] In any judgment of Calvin's character, his friendships not only with such intimates as Farel, or with such fellow workers as Bucer and Sturm, but with a man with whom possible points of disagreement were as numerous as with Melanchthon, must be no less regarded than such scenes as have been narrated in connection with Caroli.

Calvin's letters describing his observations and experiences at Frankfort and Hagenau[54] reveal him as a keen observer and a penetrating critic of persons and parties in Germany, and, indeed, of the whole European religious situation. He was evidently using his opportunities for acquaintance to the full; and a man of such statesmanlike grasp of conditions as Calvin shows himself could not long remain without fitting employment for his abilities in a representative capacity. At the Colloquy in Worms, Calvin appeared, therefore, not as a spectator, but as a delegate of Strassburg, and a representative, also, of Duke Ernst of Lüneburg. Here he did much to prepare the Protestant case in preliminary

---

[53] *Opera*, vi. 229, ix. 847. Their relations are interestingly discussed by Philip Schaff, *History of the Christian Church*, vii. 385–398; Doumergue, ii. 545–561; and Lang, *Melanchthon und Calvin*, in the *Reformirte Kirchen-Zeitung*, February 21–March 28, 1897.

[54] Notably those in Herminjard, v. 247–260; vi. 234–241, 256–261. Compare the remarks of Kampschulte, i. 329.

discussion.[55] In the brief public debate permitted before adjournment to Regensburg he bore no part, the chief disputants being Melanchthon and Luther's old enemy, Eck, of whom the cultivated Frenchman formed a most unfavorable opinion.[56]

To the final Colloquy, that at Regensburg, Calvin went with Bucer and the others of the Strassburg party, arriving on March 10, 1541. Melanchthon had urged the willing Strassburg authorities to send him, as having "a great reputation among learned men,"[57] but he went with reluctance. He felt himself unfitted for the task,[58] and he probably had become convinced, also, that little good was to be expected from the discussions. His stay was a time of grievous anxiety. The news from home distressed him. That scourge of the age, the plague, devastated Strassburg, and in March, cost the lives of two of the young members of his household to whom he was greatly attached, Claude Feray, a promising Greek scholar, and Feray's pupil, a Norman nobleman, Louis de Richebourg. No one can read the touching Christian letter which Calvin wrote to the father of the boy without being impressed with Calvin's warmth of feeling and genuine affection for those who stood in intimate relations with him.[59] His grief was profound, and his distress was increased by anxiety for his wife and brother yet in peril. Yet through these weeks of sadness and anxiety, Calvin's keenness of observation of men and things continued unabated. He was somewhat in the background of the more public discussions. Anxious to secure conciliation, if possible, the Emperor had obtained the appointment of the moderate Cardinal Gasparo Contarini as papal nuncio, and as negotiators for

---

[55] *Opera*, xxi. 269–271.

[56] "Picture to yourself the figure of a barbarous sophist, vaunting himself stupidly among the unlearned, and you will have half of Eck," letter to Farel, Herminjard, vii. 10. For Calvin's account of his experiences at Worms see ibid., vi. 405–415; vii. 8–12.

[57] *Opera*, v. lvi; Doumergeu, ii. 626.

[58] To Farel, Herminjard, vii. 41. Calvin's letters continue of great interest. See ibid., pp. 48–51, 55–64, 87–90, 105–107, 111–116, 150–152; also Bucer's p. 157. On the course of the Colloquy see Paul Vetter, *Die Religionsverhandlungen auf dem Reichstage zu Regensburg*, Jena, 1889.

[59] Herminjard, vii. 66–73 (to Richebourg); see also ibid., pp. 55, 63 (to Farel).

the Protestant side, Melanchthon, Bucer, and Johann Pistorius – all conciliatory men. Opposed to them were Eck, Johann Gropper, and Julius Pflug. The Protestant representatives were ready to concede much – too much to suit Calvin's strenuous evangelicalism – but, though their plans displeased him, for Melanchthon and Bucer as men of good intention he had the highest regard.[60] But the Colloquy failed of its purpose. Agreement could not be reached, and Calvin gladly obtained permission to leave before its close. On June 25, 1541, he was once more in his home in Strassburg.

Throughout the discussions at Regensburg, which he followed so eagerly, Calvin was engaged in an effort to obtain some relief for the persecuted Protestants of France. Just what this involved has been debated by historians with a good deal of diversity of opinion. But there seems no reason to doubt that he regarded the cultivation of cordial relations between the German Protestants and Francis I as one of the most promising means of aid to his French fellow believers.[61] Such relations almost of necessity implied an alliance with France as against the Emperor, and it was because of efforts to this end that Calvin was thanked in the name of the King as well as in her own in July, 1541, by no less a personage than Marguerite d'Angoulême.[62] His endeavors, joined with those of the magistrates of Strassburg, and of the Swiss Protestants, secured from the evangelical leaders and forces of Germany gathered at Regensburg a letter to the French King – Calvin had wished an embassy – protesting against the persecution of the Waldenses and of others of the Reformed faith.[63] While not so conspicuous at Regensburg and the other Colloquies as Melanchthon and Bucer, no French Protestant had so fully become a figure of European significance as had this exile for his religious convictions. Though his real stature had not yet been reached, the events from the publication of the first edition

---

[60] Herminjard, vii. p. 115. Contrast Kampschulte's interpretation, i. 337, with that of Doumergue, ii. 637.

[61] Ibid., p. 151.

[62] Ibid., pp. 198–202.

[63] Herminjard, vii. pp. 126–128.

of the *Institutes* to the Colloquy at Regensburg had made Calvin beyond comparison the most conspicuous representative of the evangelical interests of his native land.

Calvin's labor at the Colloquies brought him into intimate acquaintance with the conditions and with many of the chief men of German Protestantism. Luther, indeed, he never met; and that greatest of the German reformers seems to have known comparatively little about him. Calvin treasured highly, however, a word of greeting and of approval of his letter to Sadoleto – of which mention will be made in the next chapter – which came to him through Bucer in October 1539[64] and there were a few other evidences of goodwill on the part of the elder reformer. His own high estimate of Luther, Calvin often expressed, even when making evident the differences between his point of view and that of the Saxon reformer.[65]

Yet Calvin's acquaintance with Germany probably confirmed, rather than weakened, his confidence in his own program for a proper regeneration of the Church. He admired many of the leaders of the German Reformation but he disapproved of its want of ecclesiastical discipline, the low estimate in which the ministry was held, and the extent to which the churches were dependent on civil authority.[66] He had learned much during his years in Strassburg, but his fundamental principles had remained unaltered.

---

[64] *Opera*, xb. 402. The whole subject is discussed by Doumergue, ii. 562–587.
[65] E.g. Calvin to Bullinger, November 25, 1544, "I have frequently said, even if he should call me a devil, I should, nevertheless, render him the honor of recognizing him as an eminent servant of God." Herminjard, ix. 374. See also *Opera*, vi. 250; xii. 7.
[66] Compare Kampschulte, i. 339.

10

CALVIN RETURNS TO GENEVA –
ITS ECCLESIASTICAL CONSTITUTION, 1541–1542

Calvin left Geneva in the spring of 1538, burning with a sense of personal wrongs.[1] He felt that he had been cruelly thrust out of a position in which he had stood by divine appointment, and that his place, and those of Farel and Coraud, were being occupied by "traitors under the mask of pastors." These ministers, Henri de la Mare and Jacques Bernard, though to serve the Church of Geneva after Calvin's return, were weak and inferior men; and while Antoine Marcourt and Jean Morand, whom the city authorities associated with them, were men of greater abilities, and Marcourt certainly of superior if not always judicious character, all were to show themselves inadequate to the task before them. From the first, their difficulties were many. They had been put in office by a reaction against the strictness and independence

---

[1] His letters, Herminjard, v.–vii., or *Opera*, xb., xi., with the extracts from the *Registres du Conseil*, of Geneva, *Opera*, xxi. 227–282. The most recent thorough discussions are those of Cornelius, pp. 192–353, and of Doumergue, ii. 653–713. See also J. A. Gautier, *Histoire de Genéve*, completed in 1713, but published vol. ii. in 1896, and vol. iii. in 1898; J. B. G. Galiffe, in *Mémoires et Documents publiés par la Soc. de l'Hist. De Genéve*, xix. 262–283; Kampschulte, i. 342–412; A. Roget, *Histoire du peuple de Genéve*, 1870–1883, i. 113–315; ii. 1–84. A good brief sketch is that of Eugene Choisy, *La théocratie à Genéve au temps de Calvin*, pp. 36–62.

of their predecessors, and such a reaction was, in the nature of things, followed by a greater license of conduct on the part of the populace. In spite of stringent governmental enactments and good advice given by the new preachers, there can be no question that the moral condition of Geneva was decidedly lower – at least in outward manifestation – than under Farel and Calvin. The government, moreover, treated the ministers as its creatures, and they in turn looked up to it, as in the other Swiss cantons, as the authority regulative of Church practice.[2] The ecclesiastical independence which Calvin had sought was gone.

To render a difficult situation more trying, the party differences which had been so evident before Farel and Calvin's banishment still persisted with unabated intensity. That of Michel Sept, which had supported the old ecclesiastical régime, was now nicknamed the "Guillermins" – a title borrowed from Farel's Christian name, and it included, undoubtedly, the more religious elements of the Genevan population.[3] That such a party was arrayed against the new preachers made their position doubly difficult, and the more determined "Guillermins" proposed, by absenting themselves from the Christmas Communion, to disown the existing Genevan ministry. Though Farel would express no opinion, he evidently thought well of the plan, but at this juncture Calvin showed his superiority to mere party leadership. He urged that schism be avoided, "and the ministry and sacraments be held in such reverence that wherever they [i.e. Christians] perceive them to exist, they should judge the Church to be."[4] It was most Christian advice, and not without cost to himself, for it was anything but popular with many of his personal friends, as well as with a large part of the "Guillermins." For the time being, however, the party in power in Geneva showed itself master of the situation. The chief intellectual center of the "Guillermin" faction was the

---

[2] E.g. regarding Christmas and feasts, *Opera*, xxi. 239. Compare Doumergue, ii. 661.

[3] Cornelius, p. 203.

[4] Herminjard, vi. 168, 169. Letter to Farel of October 24, 1538. See ibid., p. 449.

Collège, taught by Antoine Saunier, by Calvin's old instructor, Mathurin Cordier, and others friendly to the banished pastors. Two of its younger teachers, having shown themselves hostile to the preachers and the new ecclesiastical administration, were exiled on September 26, 1538; and a similar fate overtook their older colleagues, for the same reason, on December 26.[5] By this drastic action and other banishments the "Guillermin" cause was greatly lamed, and the position of the party in power and of its preachers much strengthened – though the effect on the school was most damaging. Yet their hold on the Genevan community was unsatisfactory from a religious point of view and, on December 31, the four preachers offered their resignations to the Little Council, "since we can no longer have fruit such as we desire in this place, matters being in such disorder." The Council refused their dismission and took measures for active support by further punishing their critics.[6]

The policy of refusal to accept the Supper at the hands of the new preachers, which was the immediate occasion of the "Guillermin" defeat, had met with Calvin's disapproval, and time was overcoming his sense of personal injury. Bad as the Genevan situation seemed to him, it seemed worse to him and to Farel that a serious division in the ecclesiastical forces of Switzerland should continue. The vindicatory council for which both reformers had hoped was evidently unattainable without the aid of Bern. Farel accordingly, at considerable sacrifice of personal feeling, approached the Bernese pastor, Peter Kuntz. Kuntz's views had altered. Farel, settled at Neuchâtel, and no longer merely a Genevan exile, was a power in the French-speaking churches of the Bernese territories, and his friendship was now worth much to Bern. And so, under Bernese auspices, there came about, on March 12, 1539, not the desired council, but a meeting at Morges between the Genevan pastors, ministers from French Switzerland and Farel, under the presidency of two ministers of Bern, by which a reconciliation of the French-speaking Protestant

---

[5] *Registres du Conseil*, xxxii. 144, 248, 251; *Opera*, xxi. 236, 240.
[6] *Opera*, xb. 304–306; xxi. 243.

pastors was effected.[7] The Genevan ministers acknowledged that they should have consulted Farel, Calvin, and Coraud before taking their places. The exiles were declared to have been faithful pastors, and their successors promised to do their best to strengthen discipline, care for the poor, and aid the school. Not all that the exiles wished had been secured, but Calvin from his Strassburg home wrote to Farel:[8]

> We have in part obtained that which we have chiefly sought – that those evil dissensions between brethren which were wholly devastating the Church should be adjusted. We can never sufficiently render thanks to the Lord who by His goodness so surpasses our hope.

To show this re-established goodwill, Viret and Fabri now preached in Geneva. Farel, whom banishment still held away, declared his readiness to help in any manner in his power and, on June 25, Calvin wrote to the Genevan Church a calm yet most earnest letter, without a trace of personal resentment, but breathing the utmost goodwill and pastoral solicitude. He deplores their divisions and urges the sacredness of the pastoral office; declares that the trying circumstances of his own departure were due to the work of Satan, but that the appointment of their new pastors was "not without the will of God," who has preserved the Reformation and not left them to the papacy; and urges the cordial support of their ministers as the only course pleasing to God.[9] If Calvin in the heat of sudden temper or personal resentment would often speak with regrettable rashness, none have been able to express themselves, in the quietness of sober judgment, more nobly or unselfishly.

Calvin followed this service to the cause of religion in Geneva by one of even greater conspicuity not merely to the Genevan Church, but to the whole Protestant cause. The revolution of 1538, which had driven Farel and Calvin from the city, had been

---

[7] Herminjard, v. 243–246.

[8] April, 1539, Herminjard, v. p. 290.

[9] Ibid., pp. 336–341.

in no sense a Romanizing movement; the new ministers and the government were thoroughly Protestant, but the very fact of religious division in Geneva was enough to arouse the hopes of its discarded bishop and the friends of the older Church. Something might come to their advantage out of the troubled situation. Whether meetings of bishops were held at Lyons to discuss measures for Catholic restoration is doubtful,[10] but at the request of such a gathering if held or on his own initiative, the learned, moderate, and humanistic Bishop of Carpentras, Cardinal Jacopo Sadoleto (1477–1547), sent an appeal to Geneva to return to the ancient faith, which was delivered with a letter to the Little Council on March 26, 1539.[11] Courteous, rhetorical, but superficial in its appreciation of the questions involved, it attacked the Reformation as without justification, urged the charge that the reformers were actuated by disappointed personal ambition, commended humble obedience to the Church as a prime Christian duty and asked:[12]

> Whether is it more expedient for your salvation, and whether you think you will do what is more pleasing to God, by believing and following what the Catholic Church throughout the whole world, now for more than fifteen hundred years ... approves with general consent; or innovations introduced within these twenty-five years, by crafty, or, as they think themselves, acute men.

Written in Latin, and without attempt to make it popularly available by translation into French, it had no apparent effect save possibly to encourage Roman sympathizers by its existence. The Genevan government was little disturbed by it. It sent the appeal to Bern and in July, apparently after having thought of committing

---

[10] Herminjard (v. 266) regards it as historically unsupported; Cornelius (p. 247) believes the report; Doumergue (ii. 678) holds his judgment in suspense. It was believed in Geneva in December, 1538, *Registres du Conseil*, xxxii. 252.

[11] Registres du Conseil, xxxiii. 57; *Opera*, xxi. 245. The text of Sadoleto's appeal is given in *Opera*, v. 369–384.

[12] Opera, v. 378; Henry Beveridge's translation, *Tracts*, i. 13. Sadoleto's letter and Calvin's reply are admirably characterised by Cornelius, pp. 249–252.

the task to Viret, the Bernese authorities, at the suggestion of Peter Kuntz, asked Calvin to reply. The request was itself evidence of the better state of feeling that had come to exist between the ministry and government at Bern and the exiled pastors of Geneva.

Calvin received the request in August, and urged by his Strassburg friends, he undertook the answer. If, as he regarded it while at work upon it, it really proved a task of six days only, it is certainly a marvelous evidence of Calvin's mental alertness and readiness with the pen.[13] In any case, it was quickly done. Printed copies were in Geneva on September 5. But Calvin's Answer to Sadoleto had much more than a local significance. As in his letter to Francis I, he now spoke for the whole movement in which he was a leader. It was the most brilliant popular defence of the Protestant cause that had yet appeared or that the Reformation was to produce. With great courtesy for a writer of the sixteenth century, yet with profound depth of feeling, with thorough grasp of the doctrinal questions involved, Calvin first defends his ministry and that of Farel from the charge of self-seeking. He then invokes the authority of the Word of God against that of a Church which Christian antiquity shows has not been always one and the same. With immense effectiveness he presents, following the example of Sadoleto, two confessions, one of a layman and the other of a minister, before the judgment seat of God, which were doubtless drawn from Calvin's personal experience, and as such have been largely quoted in these pages in describing his conversion.[14] Obedience to God, and to God's revelation of Himself and of His truth rather than to the teaching of men, Calvin presents with tremendous power as the Protestant justification. Undoubtedly the Reply made friends for him at Geneva among those who had been his opponents, but it voiced the feelings of Protestantism everywhere.[15]

---

[13] Letter to Farel, Herminjard, v. 373. Text of reply, *Opera*, v. 385–416.

[14] *Ante*, pp. 73–75.

[15] Its translation into French was immediately begun. Pignet to Calvin, October 4, 1539; Herminjard, vi. 37. Luther's opinion has already been noted, *Ante*, p. 243.

While these friendly acts unquestionably greatly increased the prestige of Calvin at Geneva, they were not, in themselves, sufficient to bring about efforts to secure his return to the pastorate from which he had been expelled. For that result a new revolution was responsible that was to thrust from power the party that had won the election of 1538, and put the leaders then defeated once more in control. The immediate causes of that revolution grew out of the involved political relations of Geneva with Bern. The war of 1536, which had secured Geneva's release from danger of control by Savoy, had been won by Bern, and left Geneva in a difficult position in relation to its aggressive protector. Bern, in the flush of triumph over Savoy, had asserted possession of the political rights over Geneva once held by its bishop and by the duke of Savoy; but the determined resistance of the little city had brought about the treaty of August 7, 1536, by which Bern abandoned these pretensions and turned over to Geneva not merely the churches, monasteries, possessions of the vicedominus, and estates of the bishop and Chapter, but also the property and temporal powers of the prior of Saint-Victor, reserving only an ill-defined right of appeal in the administration of justice. It is evident that in the provision last named there was fuel for constant disputes, especially regarding those properties of the Chapter and of Saint-Victor which lay at a distance from Geneva and were adjacent to or surrounded by territories in which Bern held undisputed sway. Quarrels were constant, and the question was one involving interests which a large portion of the inhabitants of Geneva deemed vital to the independence of the city.

The election of February 1539, but strengthened the hold upon the government of Geneva of the party victorious in 1538, by which the reformers had been exiled. In March, that government sent three of its own members – Jean Lullin, Ami de Chapeaurouge, and Jean Monathon – to Bern to attempt a new treaty. In three days their task was done. They had signed the agreement, and Bern had approved the result. The reason of this prompt acquiescence by Geneva's powerful neighbor in a treaty which was designed to settle questions so vexed as those in dispute was that the three Genevan representatives had abandoned a large share of the Genevan claims. They had transgressed their instructions,[16] and no adequate explanation of their conduct is apparent. Nor is the attitude of the Little Council easier to understand. Though signed March 30, the agreement was not laid before that body till June 27, and then, though contrary to the instructions of the Little Council itself, simply "not accepted."[17] No vigorous denunciation of the treaty and prosecution of its authors immediately followed. Though Bern was asked to explain certain sections, and negotiations were carried on, it was not till November that the Bernese government was officially informed that Geneva rejected it. Certainly great incompetency, if nothing worse, was exhibited in this transaction, and an amazing blindness to the probable effects on the party in power. From the articles into which the treaty was divided, its framers were nicknamed "Articulants," a title which the populace transformed into "Artichauds" and attached not merely to the negotiators, but to the whole party of which they were members.

These events gave the "Guillermins" their opportunity. Under the lead of Sept, Perrin, and Pertemps they attacked the party in power, and on August 25, 1539, the two last named secured a vote from the Two Hundred that the hated treaty should never be sealed. A General Assembly, on November 16, ordered Bern informed that Geneva refused the treaty. Bern insisted on its maintenance. Party division in Geneva, in spite of the fact that both sides were now arrayed against the treaty, grew worse, though, in January and February 1540, it seemed for a little as if a compromise could be effected between the "Guillermins" and "Artichauds." By popular demand in a General Assembly, the rivals, Sept and Philippe, shook hands in token of reconciliation on January 27, and at the election of February 8 two syndics were chosen from either party. Though the majority in the Little Council remained to the "Artichauds,"

---

[16] The latest discussion is a careful note by Alfred Cartier, Doumergue, ii. 766–768.

[17] *Régistres du Conseil*, xxxiii. 186. See Cornelius, pp. 268, 273; Doumergue, ii. 684.

Sept and Pertemps were given seats in it. But Bern's action made any adjustment difficult. On April 18, a Bernese embassy declared in the General Assembly at Geneva that that city had no right to repudiate a treaty made by its duly appointed negotiators. Geneva once more refused and four days later, a new General Assembly broke forth in stormy wrath against the three to whom the treaty was due – or "three traitors," as they were now styled – and demanded their punishment. A wave of popular feeling was now in control of the city; the government was nearly powerless. The negotiators fled and on May 20, their places in the Little Council were taken by three "Guillermins," giving to that party for the first time in more than two years a majority in that body. Under the impulse of popular passion, on June 5, in spite of Bern's efforts on their behalf – or perhaps the more because of those efforts – the three negotiators were condemned to death – fortunately for them in their absence from Geneva. But worse followed. A street fight took place on the evening of the day following between members of the rival factions. It would appear that the "Artichauds" were the aggressors and at all events, the quick-tempered and impetuous Jean Philippe, leader of that party, and captain-general of the city, was drawn into the riot, which resulted in two deaths. In its heat he and Michel Sept, his opponent, who was looking on the scene from a window, exchanged recriminations. Popular fury turned against Philippe, and the next day his trial began, if such it can be called. Under threat of torture he confessed himself the cause of the death of one of the rioters – an allegation which he had previously denied. In spite of the efforts of the representatives of Bern on his behalf, popular excitement overcame all governmental scruples and on June 10, he was beheaded, dying, whatever may have been his faults, a victim of judicial murder, forced by the will of the multitude.[18]

---

[18] The death of Philippe is naturally one of the most debated points in Genevan history, and its motives and merits have been judged with much divergence by Galiffe, Kampschulte, Roget, Cornelius, and Doumergue. Of the main facts and of its consequences there can be no question. The chief points of divergence are as to his deserts, and as to the seriousness of the riot.

With the death of Jean Philippe the leaders of the "Artichauds" were broken; his associate, Claude Richardet, fled the city the night following the execution. Two of the four syndics under whom Calvin had been banished had been condemned to death as traitors for negotiating the unhappy treaty; the third had been beheaded (Philippe) and the fourth, as has just been mentioned, was in flight. This result had come about, however, not so much through the skill of the "Guillermin" leaders as through the excitement of the populace. In spite of their majority in the government, the "Guillermins" were unable to exercise efficient control of the turbulent city. But, during the summer of 1540, Bern and Geneva stood on the brink of war. By August and September, Geneva was making preparations for defence; and the danger, together with the efforts to meet it, gradually brought about order and governmental control. Fortunately the war cloud passed. During this period of anarchy, however, two of the pastors, Jean Morand and Antoine Marcourt, dropped their work and left the city without seeking dismission. The religious situation of Geneva was, therefore, one imperatively demanding a much stronger leadership than Henrí de la Mare or Jacques Bernard could exercise. The government was in the hands of the party that had supported Farel and Calvin and on news of Marcourt's demission of his pastoral office, the Little Council, by vote on September 21, 1540, instructed Ami Perrin "to find means, if possible, to make Master Caulvin come"[19] back to Geneva. It would be an error to ascribe this action to a popular demand. Even as long after it was taken as October 17, Jacques Bernard had no knowledge of an attempt to secure Calvin's return.[20] It was rather the plan of the "Guillermin" leaders, who thus sought to strengthen the fallen religious state of the city and establish their own position.

Calvin's return to Geneva had long been wished by Farel and Farel's friends. Indeed, mention had been made of it as possible in the correspondence of the reformers as early as April 1539, and

[19] *Registres du Conseil*, xxxiv. 452; *Opera*, xxi. 265.
[20] His letter to Calvin, Herminjard, vii. 23.

again in March 1540; but Calvin had declared to Farel that he would rather endure "a hundred other deaths than that cross."[21] It must have been clear to those who knew him that Calvin could not easily be persuaded to leave the quiet, the usefulness, and the growing honors of Strassburg for the inevitable struggles of Geneva. In order to ascertain his probable action before making the matter more public, and to bring as much pressure to bear on Calvin as possible, the desire of the Little Council was made known to some of Calvin's friends in the ministry of French-speaking Switzerland. Christopher Fabri, of Thonon, discussed the matter at Geneva and wrote to Farel of what had been done;[22] and the warmhearted Farel, in spite of his natural chagrin that no mention of his own possible restoration to Geneva had been made, became at once the most indefatigable of workers in the cause.[23] To him, more than to any other, Calvin's return, like that reformer's original settlement in Geneva, was to be due. Farel himself journeyed at once to Strassburg, and with him went urgent letters from Antoine Marcourt, Mathurin Cordier, and André Zébédée, pastor at Orbe. Soon Viret's appeal followed.[24]

To Calvin the call, pressed by Farel, caused great mental perturbation, but he gave answer that his immediate duty was attendance on the Colloquy at Worms, of which some account has already been given. As for his work at Geneva, he shuddered when he thought of a return, nor would "any bond have held [him] there so long, save that [he] did not dare throw off the yoke of the calling which [he] knew had been laid upon [him] by God."[25] Still, he did not absolutely refuse, for a reason that throws much light on his own view of duty. As he said to Farel: "If I were given the choice, I would do anything rather than yield to you in

[21] Herminjard, v. 290; vi. 199, 217. The letters of the reformers and the *Registres du Conseil* continue the chief source. Recent discussions are those of Cornelius, pp. 316–353; and of Doumergue, ii. 694–710.
[22] Herminjard, vi. 309.
[23] Ibid., pp. 311, 388. Compare Cornelius, p. 326.
[24] Ibid., pp. 317–324, 329.
[25] Letter to Farel of October 21, 1540, ibid., pp. 325, 326; see also Calvin's letter to the Little Council, ibid., p. 334.

this matter; but since I remember that I am not my own, I offer my heart as if slain in sacrifice to the Lord."[26]

There is no reason to doubt the thorough honesty of Calvin's expression of his inmost feeling to his intimate correspondent, nor to question that obedience to the will of God was his highest motive in this decision. Equally plain is it, here and earlier, that, strong-willed as he was himself, he was highly susceptible to representations as to his duty by those he loved and trusted. The decision was, indeed, a hard one. Strassburg offered peace; the agreeable companionship of Bucer, Capito, and Hedio, with whom, especially with Bucer, he had much in common; a pastorate from which he could influence France; a professorship which touched students from many lands; acquaintance with the leaders of Germany; and a growing fame and influence. Geneva meant the renewal of weary struggles and, at best, doubtful success; but it meant, too, greater influence on the evangelical cause in France than Strassburg afforded, and, above all, an opportunity to put in practice his programme for the organization of a well-disciplined Church, and therefore an ideal commonwealth, which he had, indeed, realized in his congregation at Strassburg, but which he could never hope to apply to that city as a whole. He might well doubt which was the path of duty; if he looked for comfort and repute – save from a pecuniary standpoint, and there is no evidence that this consideration weighed with him in the matter – his prospects at Strassburg were the brighter.

The Genevan leaders hoped, however, for a favorable decision, and now took more public action. On October 19 and 20, the Two Hundred and the General Assembly formally invited Calvin to return, and the next day, the Little Council appointed Ami Perrin "with a herald" to seek him with the message.[27] The formal notice of his honourable recall reached Calvin at Worms. It must have been a moment of high satisfaction. The disgrace of 1538, if such it can be called, had been thoroughly removed. But it was a day of great perplexity, also, for the Strassburg authorities, and

---

[26] Letter of October 24, 1540, Herminjard, vi. p. 339.

[27] *Registres du Conseil*, xxxiv. 483–487; *Opera*, xxi. 267. The letter is in Herminjard, vi. 331.

the ministers of that city made evident to him, as never before, how great was their desire that he should continue the work there begun. Calvin could only reply undecidedly to the Genevan request.[28] As time went on, in spite of constant urgency from Farel and all whom Farel could influence, Calvin's inclination seemed to turn increasingly toward Strassburg till late in February 1541, when he received from his fiery friend a "thundering" letter which, according to the testimony of Claude Féray - the young member of Calvin's household who was to die a few days later of the plague - turned Calvin's wavering mind Geneva-ward.[29]

Though almost certainly decided in Calvin's own thought at this juncture that he would return to Geneva, at least for a time, he was long detained at the Colloquy in Regensburg. Farel knew no rest. He stirred up the pastors of Zürich to urge on Calvin the importance of Geneva for the evangelical cause in France and Italy. Geneva asked the aid of Zürich and Basel, and pleaded its cause with the authorities of Strassburg. At last Calvin fully resolved, that whether his stay should be brief or permanent, he would go to Geneva, and attempt the restoration of Church-order as he understood it. He hoped to go with Bucer's companionship; failing that, he desired aid from Basel and Bern; but, in the end, he had to enter on his work alone.[30] On September 13, 1541, apparently, he re-entered the city which was thenceforth to be his residence, simply and unostentatiously.[31]

---

[28] See the letter of (1) Calvin to Geneva, (2) the ministers of Strassburg and Basel in attendance at Worms to Geneva, and (3) Calvin to Farel, from Worms November 12 and 13, 1540, Herminjard, vi. 352-367.

[29] Farel's letter to Calvin is not known to exist. Calvin replied from Ulm on his way to Regensburg, Herminjard, vii. 40-42. Féray's letter of March 8 is given ibid., p. 46. He died about the middle of the same month, see *Ante*, p. 241.

[30] Cornelius, pp. 350, 351.

[31] In spite of Beza's statement (*Opera*, xxi. 131) that he was received with the greatest congratulations of all the people and of the Council, Fabri's letter to Farel of September 18th (Herminjard, vii. 260) gives no impression of a popular demonstration. Doumergue (ii. 710) shows reasons for believing there was none. Beza gives the date.

With businesslike directness, and perfect clearness of vision he entered on his task. On the day of his arrival, he presented himself before the Little Council, explained his long indecision, asked that the Council choose a committee to aid in preparing a written constitution for the Genevan Church, and declared his wish to serve the city.[32] The Strassburg episode was past. Calvin's Genevan work had once more begun.

It was undoubtedly Calvin's feeling that he had been restored to Geneva by the hand of God. He treated his banishment as a mere interruption. Therefore, when he resumed his preaching, apparently on the Sunday following his return, instead of the sensational discourse which his hearers eagerly expected, he spoke not a word about the recent past but, after a brief definition of his office and of his motives in undertaking its duties, he began his exposition of the Scriptures at the passage with which he had closed when banished.[33] He made no effort, at the time, to have his fellow ministers removed, though they were thoroughly unsatisfactory to him, and he expressed his dislike of them freely in letters to confidential correspondents. He was conciliatory toward former opponents. He acted with wisdom and prudence, and for one of so impulsive a temperament, with great self-restraint. This attitude was made all the easier by the honorable treatment that he received from the government. He was provided with a house and garden that had once belonged to one of the canons of the cathedral;[34] his wife and household

---

[32] *Registres du Conseil*, xxxv. 324; *Opera*, xxi. 282.

[33] Calvin's letter of January, 1542, is full of interesting details, Herminjard, vii. 408–413; see also ibid., pp. 249, 350, 438.

[34] *Registres du Conseil*, xxxv. 297, 327, 352, 368; *Opera*, xxi. 281–284. The house had been purchased of the government by de Fresneville, Sieur de Sansoex, in 1539, and was bought back by the Genevan authorities in 1543. It stood on the site of the present No. 11 Rue de Calvin. Calvin's house has disappeared, the site having been built upon anew early in the eighteenth century. Not being ready at once, Calvin occupied for a few months the house adjoining (on the site of No. 9). From 1543 to his death, No. 11 was his home. The facts are fully presented by Doumergue, iii. 491–508. It was very meagrely furnished, in part at governmental expense.

goods were brought from Strassburg at the expense of the city, a salary of 500 florins was voted him, the sum being considered large partly because of his necessary entertainment of passing visitors, and allowances were made him of wheat, wine, and clothing. His income was probably equivalent to the present purchasing power of $800 to $1,000, aside from the worth of his house.[35] At best it was a frugal living for one in his position, though he was henceforth relieved from such poverty as he had borne in Strassburg.

Calvin's return to Geneva had for its object, from his point of view, the establishment of an ecclesiastical constitution which should make of the city a model Christian community. The party now in power in Geneva was weary of civil disorders, convinced of the ill estate of the Church, and of the insufficiency of its ministers. The moment was therefore ripe for the work. Yet very little evidence appears of anything that can be called a popular religious awakening, such as is witnessed in the story of English Puritanism.

In accordance with Calvin's request, on the day of his arrival, the Little Council appointed a committee of six to cooperate with Calvin and the other ministers of the city, among whom was Viret, then on leave of absence from Lausanne. Four of this committee, Claude Pertemps, Ami Perrin, Claude Roset, and Jean

---

[35] The purchasing power of Calvin's salary has been most variously estimated, from the computation of Jules Bonnet, who valued the 500 florins at $50, to that of Galiffe, $1200; and of Marcel Suès-Ducommun, $1500. Doumergue (iii. 449–477) discusses it amply, and while admitting that the subject is one on which an exact decision is impossible, he values Calvin's 500 florins at 3000 to 3500 francs, and his total compensation, aside from his house, at 4000 francs. It was double that of an ordinary minister. If these payments seem small, it must be remembered that Geneva was a little, and not very wealthy city, and that ministerial compensation in all non-prelatical Protestant lands was then meagre, partly because pre-Reformation incomes had been gauged to the needs of a celibate clergy, but even more because governmental confiscation of Church properties, abolition of fees, etc., had operated universally to the financial disadvantage of the Church. Calvin was, of course, paid from the city treasury.

Lambert, were from the Little Council itself; two, Ami Porral and Jean Balard, were from the Two Hundred. All, save Balard, had been determined "Guillermins." Of Balard's reluctant acceptance of Protestantism in 1536 mention has already been made,[36] and his evangelicalism was afterwards in doubt. Three days later the Little Council voted that the *Ordonnances*, when drafted, should be submitted successively to itself, the Two Hundred, and the General Assembly. The work moved rapidly. On September 26, it was laid before the Little Council, which proceeded, three days later, to examine it article by article – a process which was completed at the cost of much discussion and of strenuous labor on Calvin's part, on November 3. Six days later, the draft as modified by the Little Council was laid before the Two Hundred, and slightly altered by its action. On November 20, the General Assembly approved the ecclesiastical constitution without dissent. The tenacity with which the Genevan government held to its right to initiate and establish an ecclesiastical constitution, even in the days of first enthusiasm over Calvin's return, is shown, however, in the refusal of the Little Council to let the ministers see the changes which it had made in their draft before transmitting it to the Two Hundred.[37] It would have Calvin as an adviser, but not intentionally as a ruler.

The *Ordonnances* of 1541 show great advance over the Articles of 1537 in elaboration and preciseness, yet there is no essential alteration of the thoughts that underlay the less mature and definite document of nearly five years earlier. That of 1541 was much more minute and circumstantial, but its prime purposes, like those of the earlier Articles, are to give a measure of self-government elsewhere unknown in Protestant lands to the Church, while maintaining helpful relations with the State, and

---

[36] *Ante*, p. 178. The text of the first draft of the *Ordonnances*, and its various modifications till adopted, is given in *Opera*, xa. 16–30. Much of the pertinent government action is recorded in the *Registres du Conseil*, xxxv. 324–410, is printed in *Opera*, xxi. 282–287. The fullest discussion is that of Cornelius, pp. 353–387.

[37] *Registres du Conseil*, xxxv. 383; *Opera*, xxi. 286.

to put into operation an effective discipline whereby the Church might fulfill that which Calvin regarded as its most urgent duty, the initiation of its members into, and their maintenance in, right doctrine and right living. They gave to the Church no control over the State in political concerns or in the infliction of civil punishments.

As finally passed, the *Ordonnances* were not, indeed, in all respects what Calvin desired.[38] Some of the regulations that he wished were rejected on grounds of religious conviction or even of prejudice. More were modified lest the control exercised by the government be too much diminished. The principal illustrations will be mentioned in giving an outline of the document.

The *Ordonnances* begin with the declaration that Christ has instituted in His Church the four offices of pastor, teacher, elder, and deacon. The pastors of the Genevan city church are designated as five, with three assistants – a number afterwards increased. For the dependent villages pastors are also to be appointed. Their office is to preach, admonish, and reprove in public and in private, to administer the Sacraments; and, in conjunction with the elders, to make "fraternal corrections." They enter office by election by their fellow ministers, and approval by the government. This provision was modified from Calvin's draft by the reservation that the Little Council should be made cognisant of the election at the time of its occurrence, and should accept the one chosen to office only "if it seems to be expedient," thus strengthening governmental control. To the people was assigned only a right of "common consent," which amounted to little in Genevan practice.[39] Election was to be preceded by the examination of the candidate by the ministers as to doctrine and life. Calvin would have preferred induction into office by laying on of hands, but this ancient ceremony was omitted as tending to foster superstition. As provided in the *Ordonnances*, entrance upon the pastoral office

---

[38] "Not indeed quite perfect, but passable considering the difficulty of the times," Calvin said of them, Herminjard, vii. 409.

[39] In the revision of 1561, this was defined as a right to enter protest between election and installation. *Opera*, xa. 94.

was, therefore, by ministerial initiative and magisterial approval, and its twofold relation of fidelity to God in all spiritual matters and obedience to the government in all temporal concerns is indicated in the oath required of each minister.[40]

As Calvin had vainly sought during his earlier Genevan ministry, the city was now divided into three parishes: those of Saint-Pierre, Saint-Gervais, and La Madeleine; the first named being the ancient cathedral and Calvin's regular place of preaching. Sermons, to modern thinking in excessive abundance, were prescribed for Calvin, like the leaders of the Reformation generally, had a hunger for the exposition of the "Word of God." Sundays saw discourses at daybreak in two churches, at nine in all three. At noon there was instruction in the Catechism – on which Calvin laid great weight – in all the churches at three, sermons in each church once more. On Monday, Wednesday, and Friday there was further preaching and, before Calvin's death, a daily sermon had been instituted in each church of the city. Calvin wished a monthly celebration of the Supper, but, as in 1537, he was now unable to carry public opinion with him, and the Communion continued to be observed four times a year. No child was to partake till he was familiar with, and had made profession of faith set forth in the Catechism. Baptisms and marriages had place only in the public congregation. Calvin would have admitted the Bernese custom of the font – a fresh evidence that his opposition, in 1538, was not so much to the Bernese ceremonies, as to their imposition by governmental authority – but here "Guillermin" prejudice would have none of it. Visitation of the sick was an important ministerial duty, and no inhabitant was to be bed-ridden for more than three days without information being given to one of the pastors.

A most important provision of the *Ordonnances* was that requiring all the ministers of the city and as many as possible of those in its dependent villages to meet weekly for discussion of the Scriptures. These assemblies were the natural successors to the

---

[40] Oath of 1542, *Opera*, xa. p. 31.

informal *Colloquia* inaugurated in 1536; they took place on Fridays and were soon popularly known as the *Congrégation*. The exegetical exercises were open to the public. But beside these learned deliberations, the ministers collectively, or *Vénérable Compagnie*, as they were soon called, were charged with the examination and election of ministerial candidates, and with mutual supervision. Every three months they were required by the *Ordonnances* to meet for criticism one of another. A list of offences discreditable to or intolerable in a holder of the ministerial office was enumerated, and the *Ordonnances* provided that if the ministers themselves proved unable to end a contention in their ranks, recourse should be had to the aid of the elders, and then to the magistrates. This left the city government the court of final resort in questions of doctrine as well as of conduct. The object of Calvin's provisions regarding the ministry was evidently to secure a body of pastors of learning, character, and mutual helpfulness. A purely ministerial body, the *Vénérable Compagnie*, soon had an influence in Genevan affairs much greater than that indicated by its constitutional rights, though impossible of exact definition, for it had the force that comes from frequent discussion and consequent united opinion.

Calvin viewed the office of teacher as of divine appointment,[41] having as its highest duty that of educating "the faithful in sound doctrine" from the Old and New Testaments. But he felt no less strongly that before the learner "can profit by such lessons he must first be instructed in the languages and worldly sciences."[42] Calvin therefore sought to develop the Genevan school system under this ecclesiastical conception of the teachership. A "learned and expert man" was to be appointed as head of the school, and teacher-in-chief, with "readers" to give secondary instruction, and "bachelors" to teach the "little children" under his control. The teacher was reckoned in the ministry, put under its disciplinary regulations, and, in Calvin's intention, was to be installed on ministerial approval – an exercise of ministerial authority which

---

[41] Ephesians, iv. 11.
[42] *Ordonnances, Opera*, xa. 21, "sciences humaines."

the jealous Little Council modified by the provision that he first be "presented" to the government and examined in the presence of two of its members. In Calvin's judgment, the school was an integral factor in the religious training of the community.

No section of the *Ordonnances* was more important than that having to do with the third order of Church officers – that of elders. Here Calvin made a great advance upon the undeveloped recommendation of the Articles of 1537. The office of the eldership is defined as involving the duty "to watch over the life of each individual, to admonish affectionately those who are seen to err and to lead a disorderly life and, where there shall be need, to make report to the body which shall be appointed to make fraternal corrections." It was, therefore, the chief disciplining office – and was lay, not ministerial. The *Ordonnances* provided that the Little Council should choose twelve elders, subject to consultation with the ministers, and final approval by the Two Hundred. Of these officers, two were to be taken from the Little Council itself, four from the Council of Sixty, and six from that of the Two Hundred. There was no popular share in their appointment; and governmental jealousy of possible growth of ecclesiastical power is here illustrated by the addition to the simple designation "elders," given them by Calvin, of their further definition as "commissioned or deputed by the *seigneurie* to the consistory."

In the *Consistoire* just mentioned, composed of the twelve elders, and members of the regular ministry of Geneva, four to twelve in number, is to be seen the heart of Calvin's disciplinary system. As provided in the *Ordonnances*, it met every Thursday under the presidency of one of the syndics. Calvin was not its president – though he presided a few times, and may possibly have been regarded as an informal, non-elected vice-president.[43] Of the preponderance of his influence in this body, the first session of which was apparently held on December 15, 1541, there can be no question. As defined in the *Ordonnances*, the

---

[43] E.g. he presided three times in 1547, though Hudriot du Molard was president for the year. Editorial note to *Opera*, xxi. 396.

Consistory could summon for examination, censure, and ultimate excommunication any who opposed "received doctrine," neglected Church attendance, rebelled against ecclesiastical good order or were of evil life, but all was so to be done "that the corrections should be naught but medicines to bring back sinners to our Lord." This ecclesiastical power of admonition and excommunication had its background of civil authority, however. Perverse and contumacious offenders were to be reported, as less definitely recommended in the Articles of 1537, to the Little Council, which should deal with them as it deemed best. It was in regard to this question of the relation of the power of the Consistory to that of the civil government that Calvin had his severest struggle in connection with the adoption of the *Ordonnances* and won his most decided victory. He had no wish to take from the Little Council any of its civil police power or its rights as the final punisher of contumacious ecclesiastical offenders, but he desired to give the Consistory independent authority in its own ecclesiastical field. In the debate on the *Ordonnances*, the Little Council secured the insertion of the declaration:

> We have ordered that the said ministers shall have no jurisdiction in this province, but simply should hear the parties and make the aforesaid remonstrances. And on their report we [magistrates] can deliberate and render judgment according to the merits of the case.

That would have been greatly to lame Calvin's cherished ecclesiastical independence and, before the adoption of the *Ordonnances*, he procured a final modification, which may be regarded as expressing in classic form not merely Calvin's conception, but the whole sixteenth- and seventeenth-century Puritan thought, of the relations of Church discipline to the co-operant authority of a friendly government:

> That all this [i.e. discipline] shall be done in such fashion that the ministers shall have no civil jurisdiction and shall use none but the spiritual sword of the Word of God as Saint Paul directs them; and that the authority of the government and of ordinary

justice shall in no way be diminished by the Consistory, but that civil authority shall remain unimpaired. And, in particular, where it shall be necessary to make some punishment or constrain the parties, the ministers with the Consistory, having heard the parties and made remonstrances and admonitions as shall be fitting, shall report all to the Council, which shall deliberate on their report and order and render judgment according to the merits of the case.

Calvin's establishment provided, therefore, for an independent ecclesiastical exercise of discipline up to the point of excommunication, with the further punishment of refractory or gross offenders by the friendly magistrates as beyond the scope of churchly remedy. As the members of the Church included all baptized inhabitants of a given territory, discipline was for all. The Christian life, in Calvin's conception far more than in Luther's, is one of dependence on the training and repressing power of the Church and, in so viewing it, Calvin carried over to the Reformed congregations, in highly modified form, a principle characteristic of the Roman Church. Yet the basis of that discipline and the rule of its application, was not to be the wisdom of the Church, but the "Word of God." God has revealed the proper ordering of all right human life. It is the duty of the Church and of the State alike, each in its separate but mutually helpful sphere, to make men conform to His Law. The transgression of one part of that divine rule, by error in faith, for example, is no less and no more heinous than the breach of another part, by sin in conduct. Each is to be corrected, if possible, by the Church, and where the Church has done its utmost without avail, is to be remedied or punished by the State.

The fourth, and final, class of Church officers named by the *Ordonnances* was that of deacons. These included not merely those specially charged with poor-relief, but the four trustees of the city hospital, and they were to be chosen in the same way as the elders. The hospital provided care not merely for the sick, for whose relief a physician and surgeon were ordered, but a refuge for the superannuated, for indigent widows, and orphans. Begging was to be strenuously repressed.

Side by side with the preparation and discussion of the *Ordonnances*, and his ministerial activities, Calvin found himself impelled to other labors for the Genevan Church, the sum total of which rendered the closing months of 1541 so busy that one may readily credit his statement that he had worked unsparingly and had not since his return enjoyed two hours without interruption.[44] He prepared a revised liturgy based on that which he had made use at Strassburg, but conformed in many important respects, as has already been pointed out, to the existing Genevan usages.[45] He drafted a *Catechism* to take the place of that of 1537, and to serve as the basis of the Sunday noon instruction of children on which he laid great stress. Calvin had learned much as to the teaching of young people during his Strassburg sojourn, and instead of the pedagogically ill-adapted form of his earlier Genevan ministry, the new *Catechism* presented a series of brief and simple questions and answers. From a modern standpoint, it is far too long and minute and demands for its thorough comprehension a theologic insight beyond childish years, but it shows great improvement in teachable qualities, and its length and elaboration is largely to be accounted for by the fact that it was designed not merely for learning, but for pulpit explication.[46]

Two other services rendered by Calvin to Geneva in the months immediately following his return are worthy of mention not merely as significant in themselves, but as showing his relations to the civil administration. The first had to do with a recodification of the Genevan laws and constitution. Fifteen days after Calvin's return, but as far as the evidence goes, without impulse from him, the Little Council appointed a commission of laymen for this task.[47] In May 1542, the work thus begun was

---

[44] Letter of January, 1542, Herminjard, vii. 410.

[45] *Ante*, p. 223. Text, *Opera*, vi. 161–210.

[46] Text, *Opera*, vi. 1–134. On its date see Calvin's letter just cited, Herminjard, vi. 410.

[47] The passages from the *Registres du Conseil* are given by Cornelius, pp. 394, 395. The resultant revision by H. Fazy, *Constitutions de la République de Gènéve*, pp.289 et seq.; further see roget, *Hist. du Peuple de Gènévé*, ii.62–70; F. Tissot, *Les relations entre L'énglise et j'etat à Genève au temps du Calvin*, Lausanne, 1875, pp.73–75

intrusted to the syndic, Claude Roset; to Dr Jean Fabri, a lawyer of Evian; and to Calvin. In September following, Fabri being apparently unavailable, Calvin and Roset were directed to take upthe work, and to afford leisure, Calvin was released by the government from some of his duties as a preacher. Like all that Calvin undertook, the work was promptly done and on January 28, 1543, the results were essentially approved by the General Assembly. An examination of the work shows that the intention of giving to Geneva a new political constitution was entirely foreign to Calvin's mind. Practically nothing of importance was changed. Calvin's aristocratic and anti-demagogic feeling doubtless appears in the recommendation in which he and Roset joined, that only two of the four syndics should be elected in any one year, the other two holding over. The intention was evidently to prevent such an overturn of the government as had taken place in 1538, but the General Assembly, jealous of its privileges, rejected it. Doubtless the Genevan government was glad to avail itself then and often of the legal training of its chief minister, but the observation is essentially correct, "that it was in the capacity of a draughtsman and not of a legislator"[48] that Calvin did this work.

The second service related to the long and complicated disputes with Bern which had nearly resulted in war during the summer of 1540. As a means of escaping that calamity, the points of difference had been laid before arbitrators from Basel, and the report of those investigators, on reaching Geneva, was referred on January 19, 1542, by the Little Council to a committee of which Calvin was appointed by it a member.[49] Thanks to his conciliatory spirit, the Little Council, the Sixty, and the Two Hundred were brought, after long negotiation, to an agreement, only to have the whole prospect of a settlement frustrated for the time being by the opposition and threats of the popular leader, François Paguet. Negotiations were carried on afresh for a year

---

[48] Roget, *Histoire du peuple de Genéve*, ii. 68.

[49] See E. Dunant, *Les relations politiques de Genève avec Berne et les Suisses*, Genèva, 1894, pp. 15–184, for Calvin's relations to the foreign politics of the city; also Rogeet, ii. 85–109; Cornelius, pp. 398–414.

till, in September 1543, chiefly through Calvin's efforts in favor of moderation,[50] all the Genevan councils were won, in spite of the hostility of Paguet, who escaped punishment for his violent opposition only by flight. Even now the task was not done. It needed all Calvin's influence at Basel, as well as in Geneva, to bring the matter to a successful issue. At last, on February 3, 1544, the treaty was achieved, and good relations re-established between Geneva and her powerful neighbor. By the leaders of Geneva and of Bern alike, this agreement, only a few of the steps preliminary to which have been indicated, was looked upon as due in high degree to the patience, skill, and moderation of Calvin.

Enough has been said, however, to make evident Calvin's position in Geneva in the period immediately following his return. He was its most influential resident. He was everywhere recognized as its chief religious leader. He was regarded as the foremost interpreter of the "Word of God" in a community which professedly made the Scriptures its guide. As such, and by reason of his learning, legal training, and the high esteem in which he was held by the other leaders of Protestantism, his opinions commanded great respect, while his singleness of purpose, iron will, and definiteness of aim made opposition difficult. But he was in no official position of rulership, he held no civil office, he usurped none of the powers of government, however strongly he influenced their exercise. In the adoption of the *Ordonnances* he could by no means have all to his liking. In civil concerns he took part as an advisor, and not as a magistrate. What was true of these opening years continued to be characteristic of his whole Genevan work. But while Calvin had thus no civil office, and did not interfere with the ordinary machinery of government, it would be absurd to deny that he was really a ruler. His power was that of the spirit. It was the force of intellect, of persuasion, and of will, but it was none the less compelling.

It has often been affirmed and denied that the system established by the *Ordonnances* deserves the name of theocracy. If

---

[50] See Calvin's letter to Viret of September 16–20, 1543, Hermijard, ix. 34.

by this term is meant that Calvin intended to submit all Genevan life to clerical rule, and make the minister dominant over the State, that designation is incorrect.[51] Calvin would abridge none of the civil powers of government, and he left to it, partly because he must, large influence in churchly affairs. But if by theocracy is meant that all government, whether in Church or State, should be but the expression, as nearly as human imperfection will admit, of the will of the divine Lawgiver, then Calvin's ideal for Geneva was a theocracy. His system implied that there is a definitely ascertainable rule of faith and practice in the Scriptures.[52] His sole authority was as interpreter of that rule. The dangers of his position were that not all would accept his cardinal principle of scriptural authority or, accepting it, would agree with his interpretation, and that, while Church and State had theoretically their separate spheres, in the exigencies of contest appeal would be made to the stronger – and that was usually the State – to enforce his interpretation by its characteristic weapons. These perils were to have their abundant illustration in the story of Geneva under Calvin's rule, but none can deny the simplicity and grandeur of his conception, though its truth as an interpretation of the gospel is more than doubtful, and its extensive application to complex, individualistic modern life is utterly impossible.

---

[51] Roget, *Histoire du peuple de Genève*, ii. 18; compare Choisy, *La theocratie à Genève*, p. 51.

[52] Choisy well says, p. 55: "The calvinistic theocracy established the rule of the Bible, the statute book of divine law. Religion is thus conceived ecclesiastically, not as a principle of life, but as a government, and man becomes the subject of an absolute sovereign whose will is expressed by ordinances. That these be observed there is need of a body to keep watch, as a police force, regarding the divine law."

11

STRUGGLES AND CONFLICTS, 1542-1553

Undoubtedly a considerable part of the relative ease with which Calvin established his ecclesiastical constitution in Geneva, in spite of difficulties which have been mentioned, was due to the loss of several conspicuous leaders of the city life just before or soon after his return. Not to speak of the death of Jean Philippe and the collapse of the "Artichauds," which alone made that return possible, the chief "Guillermin" leader, Michel Sept, died in the autumn of 1540, while Calvin was still at Strassburg. The religious-minded, Ami Porral, followed him two years later, and in 1544, the end came to the vigorous Claude Pertemps. Ami Perrin, upon whom the "Guillermin" leadership may be said to have devolved, was by no means their equal. The time of Calvin's opening work was one of relative weakness among the older leaders of both parties in Genevan affairs.

Under these circumstances, the introduction of the new ecclesiastical discipline was easier than it might otherwise have been. The Consistory began its work promptly. No age or distinction exempted one from its censures. Men and women were examined as to their religious knowledge, their criticisms of ministers, their absences from sermons, their use of charms, their family quarrels, as well as to more serious offences.[1] Other examples, from the later activity of the Consistory in Calvin's

---

[1] Excerpts from the *Registres du Consistoire*, 1542, in *Opera*, xxi. 292-305.

time, show disciplinary procedure against a widow who prayed a *"requiescat in pace"* on her husband's grave; for having fortunes told by gypsies;[2] against a goldsmith for making a chalice; for saying that the incoming of French refugees had raised the cost of living and that a minister had declared that all those who had died earlier (i.e. before the Reformation) were damned; for dancing;[3] for possessing a copy of the *Golden Legend*; against a woman of seventy who was about to marry a man of twenty-five; against a barber for tonsuring a priest; for declaring the pope to be a good man; making a noise during the sermon;[4] laughing during preaching; criticizing Geneva for putting men to death on account of differences in religion; having a copy of *Amadis des Gaules*; or singing a song defamatory of Calvin.[5] Of course these instances are illustrative of only the more curious part of its work. It had to do, much of the time, with offences which any age would deem serious, but they exhibit its minute and inquisitorial interference with the lives of the people of Geneva.

The more flagrant faults detected by the Consistory were called by it to the attention of the magistrates, while really serious cases of crime and of error of doctrine appear to have received direct judicial cognizance without consistorial intervention. In their dealings with the accused, whether brought to them from the Consistory or in the ordinary course of justice, the magistrates acted with great severity. Torture was freely used, as in most European states of that day. There seems to be no adequate ground to hold that Calvin's influence increased the rigors with which occasional penal cases had previously been handled – one remembers the proposed torture of Jean Philippe – and it is to his credit that he made a successful protest against the cruelty with which death sentences were executed,[6] but when this has been said, it must be equally recognized that Calvin's spirit favored

---

[2] 1548, ibid., pp. 422, 428.

[3] 1550-1551, ibid., pp. 466, 489, 506.

[4] 1556, 1557, ibid., 653, 657, 664, 669.

[5] 1558, 1559, ibid., pp. 700, 701, 712, 723.

[6] March 9, 1545, *Registres du Conseil*, xl. 42; *Opera*, xxi. 348.

the full and stringent execution of the laws, and the increase of penalties for offences having to do with breaches of chastity and similar infringements of moral order. The sum total of persons punished and the breadth of the incidence of punishment, were doubtless very considerably augmented under his influence. Between 1542 and 1546, fifty-eight persons were condemned to death and seventy-six to banishment, but it must be remembered that the frightful panic of 1545 which alleged the plague to have been spread by witchcraft and conspiracy, and led to thirty-four executions, falls in this period.[7]

Undoubtedly the Consistory, as new and as limiting the authority of the magistrates, was the least popular, as it was in Calvin's judgment the most essential, of his reformatory measures. By March 1543, public hostility made itself manifest. The Council of Sixty voted "that the Consistory has no jurisdiction or power to refuse [the Supper] but only to admonish and then report to the Council so that the government may judge the delinquents according to their demerits."[8] This would have been to take from the Consistory its power of excommunication, and to have broken down Calvin's system at a vital point. Calvin's energetic protest that he would taste exile or death rather than yield, won the day, for the time being, but the action of the Sixty was ominous of contests to come.

Next to the difficulties involved in the adoption of the *Ordonnances* in the form in which Calvin wished, his first trials were from want of sympathy on the part of his ministerial associates. Henri de la Mare and Jacques Bernard could not be expected to give him more than a grudging support. The same was true of Aimé Champeraux, whom the Genevan magistrates had called before Calvin's coming. He would gladly have secured Farel and Viret, but though Viret obtained permission from the

---

[7] These figures are from the investigations of J. G. B. Galiffe – *Mémoires de l'Inst. nat. genevois,* for 1863, pp. 1–116; and Kampschulte, i. 422–428. The conclusions drawn by these authors do not, however, do full justice to Calvin.

[8] *Registres du Conseil,* xxxvii. 37; *Opera,* xxi. 309; Calvin to Viret, Herminjard, viii. 298.

Bernese authorities to come to Geneva for a few months, and greatly aided Calvin at the time of his return, it was impossible to secure Calvin's two friends for a permanent ministry at Geneva. The claims upon them of Neuchâtel and Lausanne, and the importance of holding those posts for the general cause, proved insurmountable obstacles. Gradually, however, Calvin effected a change in the complexion of the Genevan ministry, but worthy and effective ministers were rare – still rarer were those who sympathized with his strenuous zeal. It was not till he had done his training work that his spiritual disciples were to become abundant. Bernard was glad to exchange his city pastorate for a similar post in one of Geneva's country dependences early in 1542. In April 1543, a like transfer removed Henri de la Mare. Meanwhile, in July 1542, four Frenchmen, of varying degrees of satisfactoriness to Calvin, and of differing merits – Philippe de l'Église, Pierre Blanchet, Matthieu de Geneston, and Louis Treppereau – were added to the Genevan ministry.[9] Blanchet soon died under circumstances which, as will be seen, bore witness to his courage and pastoral fidelity. De l'Église and Treppereau were removed to the country in 1544, while Geneston proved acceptable to Calvin. Two other pastors, both Frenchmen of opinions sympathetic with those of Calvin, were next added to the Genevan ministry: Abel Poupin in April 1543, and Jean Ferron in March 1544. By the time of Ferron's accession, therefore, thanks to these rapid changes, Calvin was surrounded by a fairly congenial group of fellow workers, but the older inhabitants of the city may be pardoned for looking upon this foreign-born and rapidly shifting ministry as something imposed on Genevan life, even if established in each instance by the Genevan government. The most permanent and the most powerful factor was Calvin himself.

Nor did this ministry, strenuous in its demands as far as Calvin could make it, command the full respect of the community. The

---

[9] *Registres du Conseil*, xxxvi. 65; *Opera*, xxi. 298. Calvin to Farel and Viret, Herminjard, viii. 79, 105.

plague, the ravages of which at Strassburg have already been noted, reached Geneva in the autumn of 1542. Blanchet courageously offered his services at the hospital, where the magistrates required a minister; but such was the reluctance of his colleagues, that Calvin felt, not without apprehension, that should Blanchet die, he must step into the breach lest the members of his flock be left unconsoled in their extremity.[10] The test soon came. In April 1543, the plague broke out again, and before the month was over the Little Council ordered the ministers to send one of their number to the hospital. They shrank back. It was reported to the Council that some declared they "would rather be with the devil." Sébastien Castellio, the head of the school, of whom more will be said later, offered himself, but for some reason, perhaps because the government did not wish to leave the school without his oversight,[11] was not finally sent and Blanchet once more took the task, only to fall a victim to the pestilence less than three weeks later. The Little Council ordered the ministers to choose his successor, excepting Calvin as "necessary for the Church"; but five days later the pastors presented themselves before the government and declared that while they recognized the task as a duty, "God had not yet given them grace to have force and constancy to go to the hospital." They presented, instead, a French lay refugee, Simon Moreau, who took the burden, but who, in discharging it, laid himself open to grave charges of wrongdoing.[12] Calvin's action, at least, can hardly be charged to cowardice. When in Basel, just after his banishment from Geneva in 1538, he had visited Farel's nephew then dying of the same dread disease.[13] He had lofty ideas of pastoral duty,[14] and it may be that Beza was correct

---

[10] *Registres du Conseil*, xxxvi. 151, 153; *Opera*, xxi. 304; Calvin's letter to Viret, Herminjard, viii. 163. See also, Kampschulte, i. 484; F. Buisson, *Sébastien Castellion, sa vie et son oeuvre*, Paris, 1892, i. 184; Cornelius, p. 436.

[11] So Cornelius suggests, p. 437.

[12] *Registres du Conseil*, xxxvii. 80, 82, 89, 110, 113, 117; xl. 72, 79; *Opera*, xxi. 312–314, 350, 351.

[13] Calvin to Farel, August 20, 1538, Herminjard, v. 88. See also Doumergue, ii. 294, 295; iii. 147–150.

[14] Herminjard, viii. 164.

in affirming that Calvin reluctantly received exemption now from this service,[15] though nothing in the contemporary records supports his statement. The more natural interpretation is that Calvin shared the feeling of the Little Council that his life was too valuable for the larger service of the city to be risked. Such a cool judgment, however unattractive, probably bore the stamp of wisdom. Granted that the organization and discipline of the Genevan Church was a work of God – and Calvin firmly believed it so to be – it was well that the leader on whom all depended should not be exposed to danger. But the incident shows in how great a degree the larger aspects of his work outweighed the sense of responsibility for the individual souls committed to his charge. Calvin's feeling was that of a general in battle rather than of a pastor toward a suffering flock.

The pest had its melancholy sequel in 1545 when popular rumor, charging its spread to conspiracy and witchcraft, resulted in a series of cruel tortures and executions. Calvin was not in advance of his age. He believed the allegations to be facts,[16] but his plea for more merciful executions has already been noted.

Unfortunately a conscientious difference of opinion led Calvin, while these untoward events were happening, into a dispute that cost Geneva the services of one who had showed himself courageous when most displayed cowardice, Sébastien Castellio. Castellio (1515–1563), who was six years younger than Calvin, was a Savoyard by birth, had risen from very humble origins to distinction in humanistic learning at Lyons, had fled to Strassburg by reason of his Protestant sympathies and, while there, had for a brief time been a member of Calvin's household.[17] Impetuous and rather arrogant of his scholarship, he was courageous and kindhearted. At Farel's recommendation he had become a teacher of the Genevan school on June 20, 1541, nearly three

---

[15] *Life* of 1575, *Opera*, xxi. 134.

[16] *Registres du Conseil*, xl. 42, 60; *Opera*, xxi. 348, 349; Calvin to Myconius, ibid., xii. 55.

[17] The best account of Castellio is that of Buisson, already cited, p. 286. See also R. Stähelin, in Hauck's *Relencyklopädie für prot. Theol. u. Kirche*. iii. 750; Cornelius, pp. 438–445; Choisy, pp. 63–76.

months before Calvin's return. It was natural that Calvin should prefer the restoration of his old friend Mathurin Cordier to the rectorship in the school which that teacher had occupied before Calvin's banishment, but when it proved impossible to draw Cordier from his new home in Neuchâtel, Castellio was given the place in permanency, in April 1542, with the understanding that he should maintain two sub-teachers and preach at the village of Vendovre.[18]

The time was one of great scarcity in Geneva, and his salary proved all too small for his needs. This, and possibly other considerations, added to a real desire for the pastorate, led him to propose to exchange his teachership for the active ministry. The Little Council favored the plan on December 17, 1543, but Calvin opposed, since on his examination by the Vénérable Compagnie Castellio he had criticized the inspiration of Solomon's Song, holding it to be illustrative of that monarch's less reputable characteristics, and also the current Genevan interpretation of the clause in the Apostles' Creed, "He descended into hell," which taught that it means that Christ on the cross suffered vicariously the pains of hell. For these reasons, Calvin declared to the Little Council that Castellio ought not to enter the pastorate.[19]

In Calvin's judgment, the chief point at issue was Castellio's rejection of an accepted book of the Old Testament. It is easy to see why he so felt. The Scriptures were to him the corner-stone of faith and practice. In them the Holy Spirit speaks with unquestionable authority. From the vantage ground of an absolute acceptance of them – whole, and entire – as the "Word of God" and from that only, in his judgment, could the papacy be resisted and a Christian community be built up. In an age when no doctrine of progress in revelation or of the coloration of divine truth through its human interpreters had yet commanded assent, Castellio's position seemed extremely dangerous. The attack thus

---

[18] *Registres du Conseil*, xxxv. 543; *Opera*, xxi. 294.

[19] *Registres du Conseil*, xxxviii. 10, 30, 45; *Opera*, xxi. 326–329; Calvin to Viret, February 11, 1544, Herminjard, ix. 156; the certificate given by the Genevan ministers to Castellio, ibid., pp. 157–160.

begun might end in destroying the authority of all Scripture, and what evangelical foundation would then be left? Yet the Genevan ministers, led by Calvin, treated Castellio with what, for the time, was moderation. On his expressed intention to remove to Basel they gave him a certificate over Calvin's signature, stating frankly the points at issue, but testifying also:[20]

> He resigned the headship of the school voluntarily. In that office he so bore himself that we judged him worthy of the sacred ministry; but that he was not admitted was not on account of any faults of life, nor any impious dogma regarding the chief points of our faith, but this one reason prevented which we have set forth.

Castellio felt, naturally enough, that Calvin had stood the one barrier to the realization of his hopes. He complained to Viret that Calvin "had never admonished him save with temper and reproaches"[21] and, doubtless, as he brooded over the matter, his sense of antagonism grew to hostility toward the whole Genevan ministry. At its regular meeting on May 30, 1544, he drew an unflattering comparison between the conduct of the Genevan pastors and that of Paul as set forth in the sixth chapter of II Corinthians. The whole bitterness of a disappointed man spoke in his words. Calvin reported his conduct to the Little Council, which heard all parties at length and, on June 12, dismissed Castellio from his small charge at Vendovre "during the good pleasure of the government."[22] He left Geneva at once to begin a career harassed by distressing poverty at Basel, and these Genevan experiences led to a lifelong hostility between Calvin and Castellio. In Castellio the use of compulsion in matters of religion in general, and its employment in the case of Servetus in particular, was to find a manly and able opponent, who stood in advance of the spirit of his age.

---

[20] Herminjard, ix. 159, 160.

[21] So Viret told Calvin in a letter of February 16, 1544, in which he urged considerate treatment of Castellio, ibid., p. 164.

[22] *Registres du Conseil*, xxxviii. 231, 237, 246; *Opera*, xxi. 336–338; Calvin's letter of May 31, 1544, to Farel, Herminjard, ix. 264.

On the whole, however, Calvin was strengthening his position in Geneva. By the autumn of 1545, he had succeeded substantially in completing the transformation of the city ministry. Nicolas des Gallars and Michel Cop, the latter a brother of the one-time Parisian rector and both hearty supporters of Calvin, were added to the Genevan pastorate in 1544 and 1545. The place of the deceased Geneston was filled, in the last named year, by Raimond Chauvet. Champereaux, the only remaining representative of those in office at Calvin's return, was removed to the country in July, 1545. The Genevan ministry thus became a fairly homogeneous body, of which Calvin was the ruling spirit. Thus strengthened, Calvin turned his attention, in 1545, to a more strenuous administration of discipline, especially in breaches of chastity. The supervision of the Consistory was intensified in regard to such offences, and the zeal of the magistrates stimulated. It was ordered that, after having received punishment from the civil authorities, those guilty of such wrongdoing should be required to appear before the Consistory for proper ecclesiastical admonition[23] – a proceeding which appeared to many an added and unnecessary disgrace. To Calvin, it was an assertion of the just disciplinary powers of the Church.

Though Calvin had been thus far, on the whole, successful in his work, it is evident that elements in abundance existed for the growth of an opposition party in Geneva, and the forces unfriendly to him had been strengthened by the results of the peace made with Bern in February 1544, in obtaining which he bore so honorable a part. As one of its consequences, the survivors of the "Artichauds" and their sympathizers had returned to swell the ranks of those hostile to Calvin's ecclesiastical constitution. This opposition was made up of most various forces. Some were simply representatives of old Genevan families, not opposed to the Reformation, but disinclined to view with favor the strict rule which Calvin had imposed, and disposed to look upon him, the other ministers, and the French refugees whom he attracted to Geneva, as so many intruders into a city which had won liberty

---

[23] *Registres du Conseil*, of October 13, 1545, quoted by Cornelius, p. 456.

for itself only to come under the spiritual bondage of foreigners. Others were hostile to any kind of ecclesiastical or governmental discipline that would limit the free life and abundant amusements for which Geneva was noted. To be forced to hear sermons and to be reprimanded by the Consistory was not that for which they had thrown off the power of Savoy and withstood Bern at such cost. But neither element produced a really worthy and efficient leader, and to the incompetence of the opposition, in the face of Calvin's iron determination, rather than to its want of numbers, his success in the conflicts from 1546 to 1555 was to be due.

Many writers have deduced the chief features of this opposition, the principal causes of which have just been noted, from the alleged prevalence in Geneva of religious Libertinism. The ascription of hostility to this source has indeed become almost a Calvinistic tradition.[24] The Libertins or, as they preferred to call themselves, the "Spirituels," were a pantheistic antinomian sect which had its origins in the preaching of a certain Coppin, at Lille about 1529, and by 1545, was considerably widespread in France, where its supporters obtained protection for a time from Marguerite d'Angoulême, though there is no evidence that she shared their views. Calvin had encountered two of its principal representatives, an enthusiast named Quintin soon after his acceptance of the Reformed faith at Paris, and an ex-priest, Antoine Pocquet, in Geneva itself, probably in 1542. To their thinking, all is but a manifestation of the one Spirit – all is God. Nothing can be really bad, and the common distinction between good and evil acts is baseless, since all are alike the work of God. Anything more repugnant to Calvin's strenuous morality it would be hard to imagine. Early in 1545, Calvin wrote against the holders of these views one of his most vigorous and effective tracts, that *Contre la Secte phantastique et furieuse des Libertins qui se nomment Spirituels*,[25] which caused displeasure to Marguerite,[26] but seems to

---

[24] E.g. Henry, ii. 398–446; E Stähelin, *Johannes Calvin: Leben und ausgewählte Schriften*, 1863, i. 383; Schaff, vii. 498–501; R. Stähelin, in Hauck's *Relencyklopädie*, iii. 669.

[25] *Opera*, vii. 145–248.

[26] See Calvin's letter to her of April 28, 1545, *Opera*, xii. 65.

have done much to check the spread of these opinions in France. Yet neither in this tract nor in his letters of this and the immediately subsequent time does Calvin seem to feel that the Spirituels were a Genevan peril. He tells Marguerite d'Angoulême that it was the ill wrought in the Netherlands, Artois, and Hainault that induced him to enter the lists against them. Though he speaks of Pocquet's sojourn at Geneva and attempt to win approval from him, the characteristic incidents of Spirituel teaching which he relates in the tract have to do with Quintin and his stay in Paris.[27] True, some incidents of the time show sporadic examples of opinions and practices at Geneva which were essentially those of the Spirituels.[28] There were doubtless occasional spiritual Libertines in the city, but to ascribe any considerable weight to them in the opposition to Calvin is to give them an importance not their due. They did not constitute a party.[29]

Calvin's first conspicuous conflict with the elements in opposition came early in 1546. Pierre Ameaux[30] was a member of the Little Council, though not sprung from any Genevan family of prominence. His ancestral business of manufacturing playing cards had been broken up by the new discipline; he seems to have been embittered by the protracted litigation necessary before he could secure a divorce from his unworthy wife, and he

---

[27] *Opera*, vii. 160, 163, 185. He says of Pocquet's stay at Geneva that he had "*dissimulé sa meschante doctrine*," and gives no impression of effective labors there done by this Spirituel.

[28] Notably in the case of Benoîte Ameaux, wife of Pierre Ameaux, whose trial for divorce, sought by her husband, between January 1544, and June 1545, falls just in this period. See Henry, ii. 412; J. G. B. Galiffe, *Mém. de l'Inst. nat. genevois*, 1863, p. 14; Kampschulte, ii. 19. The opinions of Gruet do not seem to have been specially those of the Spirituels on important points, e.g. God and Christ. Compare Calvin's report on his book, Henry, ii., Appendix, pp. 120–122, and Calvin's account of the Spirituels, *Opera*, vii. 178–181, 198–200.

[29] The subject is well discussed by Kampschulte, ii. 13–19 (published in 1899). He shows, furthermore, that the application of the nickname "Libertin" to the party in political opposition to Calvin is not contemporary with the reformer.

[30] J. G. B. Galiffe, *Nouvelles pages d'histoire exacte* in *Mémoire de l'Inst. at. genevois* for 1863, pp. 1–16; Kampschulte, ii. 20–27; Cornelius, pp. 462–471; Choisy, pp. 77–80.

had been on cordial terms with the ministers, de la Mare and de l'Église, whose feeling towards Calvin was not far from one of friendliness. On January 26, 1645, at a supper-party in his own house, after the wine had circulated freely, Ameaux expressed his dislike of Calvin, declaring him to be only a Picard, a preacher of false doctrine, and an evil man.[31] He also accused his fellow counselors of undue dependence on the reformer, and affirmed that foreign residents would soon be masters of the city. It was the utterance of an embittered man to a supposedly confidential audience, but one of his hearers reported the speech at once to the Little Council and Ameaux was imprisoned. To Calvin the attack seemed more than a personal affront, it was a denial of his authority as an interpreter of the Word of God, and therefore an insult to "the honor of Christ," whose servant Calvin felt himself to be.[32] We have here an illustration of that identification of his own cause with that of God, which was a source of much of Calvin's strength, and also of much of his severity. The trial dragged. The Little Council was divided, and a considerable portion would have exacted slight punishment of the offender. The Two Hundred were called in and, after a stormy discussion, it was ordered, on March 2, that Ameaux appear before it, Calvin also being present, and ask pardon on his knees, "of God, the government, and Calvin." To Calvin's thinking this was not enough. He declared that he would neither accept the Council's invitation to be present at its session nor enter the pulpit till the "name of God" had been vindicated. At the head of the Consistory, he now appeared before the Little Council, the Sixty, and the Two Hundred, and demanded adequate punishment. Thus admonished, the Two Hundred retracted its mild sentence and ordered the Little Council to take up the case anew. In spite of popular restiveness in the Saint-Gervais district in which Amaeux lived, he was sentenced, on April 8, to make the tour

---

[31] *Registres du Conseil*, xl. 359; *Opera*, xxi. 368.Many excerpts from the *Registres* relating to this matter may be found, ibid., pp. 368–377; Cornelius also gives the chief passages.

[32] Calvin to Farel, February 13, 1546, *Opera*, xii. 284. See Choisy, p. 80.

of the city, clad in a shirt, bareheaded, torch in hand, and on his knees to beg mercy of God and the government.

Calvin had won a notable triumph, as he believed, for the cause of gospel order. A member of the inner circle of government had criticized him in his office and had paid the penalty by a humiliating penance. Nor was this all. Henry de la Mare ventured to express his dissent from Calvin's methods. He was imprisoned by order of the Little Council on March 17, and ultimately deprived of the rural pastorate that still remained to him. Yet the situation was ominous as to the future.

It has already been pointed out that the completion of the process by which the Genevan city ministry became a body in sympathy with Calvin was followed, in 1545, by a marked increase in the activity of the Consistory. Evidences of multiplied exercise of discipline continued, and, in the main, had the support of the city government. To ministerial initiative, though enacted of course by the civil authorities, must be credited the curious laws regarding taverns of April and May 1546.[33] In their place, five "abbeys" were established as religiously conducted houses of entertainment. No food or drink was to be served to any guest who refused to say grace; the Bible was to be at hand; all oaths and unseemly conversation were to be severely repressed. Worthy as was the object sought, the attempt, of course, failed, and before the end of June the impracticable new regulations were abandoned.

But some of Calvin's ministerial colleagues surpassed him in intensity of disciplinary zeal. In his own work there was not infrequently a moderation wanting in theirs. Such an instance occurred in the spring and summer of 1546. The day of morality plays, so beloved in the Middle Ages, had not yet passed. At the request of some of his flock, Abel Poupin, one of the ministers, had drawn a drama from the Acts of the Apostles, but though Calvin did not disapprove, the fiery Michel Cop opposed that theatrical representation in the *Vénérable Compagnie*, and forced a protest from that body in the name of all the ministers to the

---

[33] Roget, ii. 232, 234; Cornelius, p. 474; Doumergue, iii. 70–73. Many features were borrowed from earlier regulations.

Little Council.[34] That board of magistrates ordered Poupin to continue his work and told the ministers "not to mix in politics." Cop, not to be restrained, carried his denunciation into the pulpit. Almost a riot occurred. Calvin did his utmost to calm it, but on Cop's being brought before the Little Council, Calvin defended the rights of the ministry to freedom of expression; yet with such moderation and skill that the matter was adjusted, so that, after the disputed play had been held, further theatrical representations were suspended by the civil authorities "till the times should be more fitting." Undoubtedly Calvin found his situation in the face of the public made more trying by an over-zeal in an associate which he did not share, but could not wholly repudiate.

Not so moderate was Calvin's attitude on the dispute regarding baptismal names which arose in the month following the settlement of the controversy regarding theatrical represent-ations. Moved undoubtedly by ministerial impulse, the Little Council, on August 27, 1546, forbade the imposition of the favorite name "Claude" as showing an idolatrous reverence to a saint once revered in the Genevan territory. The order grew out of the refusal of Ami Chappius to permit the minister to substitute in the baptism of his son the name "Abraham" for that now condemned. About two months later, a similar refusal of the preacher at Saint-Gervais to give the names Aimé or Martin resulted in a riotous protest from a part of the congregation. At the suggestion of Calvin and the other ministers, the Little Council ordered Calvin "to make a list" of objectionable names. The result was the edict on baptismal names which became law on November 22 of the same year.[35] Undoubtedly much could be said in favor of its prohibition of such names as Sepulchre, Cross, Pentecost, Sunday, and that of Jesus, but by no means all were in these categories. To modern thinking, it was an unwarranted invasion of personal freedom.

On the whole, the year 1546 was one of decided success for Calvin in his task of imposing what he believed to be gospel

---

[34] *Registres du Conseil*, xli. 114, 142; *Opera*, xxi, 382, 385; Calvin to Farel, ibid., xii. 347, 355; Cornelius, p. 475.

[35] Text, *Opera*, xa. 49. For action of the Council see ibid., xxi. 386–391.

discipline on Geneva, and it must have been with satisfaction that he saw citizenship given to his brother Antoine by the Little Council on August 3, "in view of the great pains which his brother [i.e. Calvin] had taken for the advancement of the Word of God and to maintain the honor of the city."[36] Yet he did not deceive himself as to the growth of opposition or the extent to which his work lacked permanency and completion. His strength was also in a measure his weakness. From the time of his return, in spite of temporary diminution of their numbers during the ravages of the plague, refugees from lands where the evangelical cause was persecuted had been flocking to Geneva. The vast majority of these new residents were French. Most of them were men of character and industry, many were men of property. From them the whole ministry of the city had been recruited. They filled the houses which the banishments and voluntary exiles due to the long party struggles had made vacant, and they built up the trade of the city. They were a most valuable addition to the population – but they were foreigners.[37] The older Genevans resented their prominence, and this resentment directed itself especially against the ecclesiastical constitution and above all against the disciplinary activity of the Consistory which seemed to these opponents the chief yoke that the newcomers, led by Calvin, had laid on the city.

Most conspicuous at this time as a critic of the Consistory was a Genevan of wealth, and of influence by reason of his family connections, François Favre, whose ungovernable daughter, Franchequine, was the wife of Ami Perrin – the latter a man prominently identified, as will be recalled, with the "Guillermins," and instrumental in Calvin's return. Both François and his son Gaspard were of easy morals and, with the strengthening of the discipline of the Consistory, which was begun in 1545, their words and actions, prominent as they themselves were, were speedily brought under its cognizance. In February and March 1546, they

---

[36] *Opera*, xxi. 385.
[37] Compare Kampschulte, ii. 37–47. Not less than 130 of these refugees were admitted burghers in 1547.

appeared indeed before the Consistory, but criticized and as far as possible repudiated its authority "as that of another jurisdiction above the courts of Geneva."[38] Yet if Church government was to be effective it must apply to small and great alike. A fresh problem soon occurred. On March 21, 1546, Antoine Lect celebrated the betrothal of his daughter to Claude Philippe, son of the executed "Artichaud" leader. Among the guests, who included Ami Perrin and his wife, and the syndic Amblard Corne, then president of the Consistory itself, dancing was indulged, in contravention of the city ordinances. The Consistory proceeded to discipline, the offence was reported to the Little Council, and the dancers imprisoned. On the expiration of their brief sentence they were ordered before the Consistory for admonition. Corne, who had the religious interest of the city at heart, readily obeyed; but Perrin held out for nearly a month before yielding compliance, while his wife took a defiant attitude throughout the whole proceeding.[39] For the time being Perrin yielded, but in heart he had become Calvin's opponent, and from now on he, even more than the Favres, was the real strength of the opposition. Vain and self-seeking, he had not in him the stuff to make a rallying center of moral force, but he was strong enough to cause Calvin abundant difficulties, and had he been a man of more character might have won the struggle. Calvin's success in the condemnation of Ameaux, while these events were taking place, rendered opposition for the time being unpromising, and during the summer of 1546, his control seemed fairly secure. Gaspard Favre, having shown his contempt by playing bowls in a garden during service, was made to appear before the Consistory on June 27, and so heatedly replied to Calvin, that the latter, quick-tempered as has already been seen, abruptly left the meeting. The Consistory secured his imprisonment by the Little Council for his various offences.[40]

---

[38] Consistory records, quoted by Cornelius, p. 483.

[39] *Opera*, xxi. 376–381; Calvin to Viret and Farel, ibid., xii. 334; Cornelius, p. 473. On the first hearing, the sharp-tongued Franchequine cried out against Calvin: "Wicked man, you wish to drink the blood of our [Favre] family; but you will leave Geneva before we do."

[40] *Opera*, xxi. 382, 383.

With the opening month of 1547, however, came a change unfavorable to Calvin. The February election was largely won by Calvin's opponents. Just before they had taken place, François Favre had at last been punished, on January 24, 1547, by the civil authorities for his offences against the seventh commandment, and, on the expiration of his sentence, was ordered to appear before the Consistory for admonition. The war between Charles V and the German Protestants was in progress, and Calvin had been sent to northern Switzerland to ascertain its threatening course. So the admonition was spoken in the name of the Consistory by one of the most strenuous of the pastors, Abel Poupin. Favre defiantly declared that he "did not recognize" the ministers; they rejoined that they "did not recognize him as a sheep of the flock of Jesus Christ, but as a dog and excommunicate." The scene was one of recrimination. On Calvin's return, this "rebellion" was reported to the civil authorities, by whom, in spite of the results of the recent election, Favre was ordered to pay due reverence to the Consistory.[41]

He failed to appear, but his daughter, who was Perrin's wife, and his son, Gaspard, presented themselves on his behalf with loud protests against the treatment he had experienced from the ministers, insisting that the matter be carried to the Little Council. On March 7, accompanied by her husband, Favre's daughter repeated the demand before the civil authorities. Perrin was thus publicly ranged with the opposition. The question at issue was as to whether offenders punished by the government must endure further discipline by the Consistory. None disputed judicial control, but to add ecclesiastical censure to civil imprisonment was what Favre, and now Perrin also, resented. Their hostility is readily comprehensible. It was in a certain sense double punishment that was imposed. Yet to Calvin the whole maintenance of the ecclesiastical constitution seemed bound up in the preservation of this consistorial power.[42] The Little Council was divided. It inclined to the position that reference

---

[41] Ibid., pp. 395, 396; Cornelius, p. 493.

[42] Calvin to Viret, March 27, 1547, *Opera*, xii. 505; Cornelius, pp. 494, 495.

to the Consistory was only at the good pleasure of the civil authorities, but the firm attitude of the ministers, led by Calvin, worked a compromise. On March 29 the Council voted that the rebellious and obstinate should be sent to the Consistory after punishment by the civil courts, but not the repentant. On the whole, Calvin had held his own in a difficult struggle. The power of the Consistory was practically intact, though Calvin could count on no hearty support from the Little Council.

But a new peril threatened him – that of a popular demonstration. Perrin, conscious that Calvin had substantially held his own with the Little Council, determined to make use of the relations which his position as General-captain of the city might establish between him and the Arquebusiers, whose target practice was regarded as a popular festival. Just how far he planned to go is uncertain, but he evidently purposed a demonstration which should modify the disciplinary policy which Calvin upheld in Church and State. The issue took a curious turn. Slashed hose were much admired by the youth of Geneva, but had been forbidden by the government as a sign of sinful luxury. Perrin, on May 9, 1547, asked the Little Council to permit the target festival. The authorities promptly consented, but renewed therewith the prohibition of the desired garments. Here then was a lever to arouse popular feeling against the supporters of discipline in the Little Council. The Arquebusiers asked that their use be allowed at the festival. The issue was so threatening that the Little Council called the Two Hundred for the 25th – the day before the appointed parade and festival. Could Perrin succeed, he intended doubtless to push the matter much further, but before the Two Hundred Calvin's persuasive skill proved an insurmountable barrier. In an appeal of great force, Calvin urged that of itself the question of slashed hose was of small consequence, but to open the door to excess was very serious. Such would be the effect of the repeal of the recently re-enacted prohibition. It would lead to contempt of God and of the government. The Two Hundred supported Calvin's contention, and Perrin showed his feeling of defeat by a sudden journey to

Bern. As Calvin wrote to Viret, Perrin had found that the people were with the reformers far more than he had imagined.[43]

Calvin had escaped, for the time being, the imminent peril of the overthrow of his system by governmental action or popular tumult, but he was far from secure. Perrin, though defeated, had influence enough to be sent, in June, on a highly honorable embassy to the court of France to greet the new king, Henry II. His friend, Pierre Vandel, still carried on a work of opposition in the city. Though François Favre deemed it best to retire to his estates, his daughter, Perrin's wife, once more defied the ecclesiastical discipline by dancing, and after a heated interview with the Consistory, in which she insulted Abel Poupin who had once called her father a dog, she was ordered imprisoned on June 24, by the Little Council – a punishment which she avoided by flight. Three days later, a threatening placard, aimed primarily at Poupin, but including the whole body of ministers in its declaration, "When too much has been endured revenge is taken," was affixed to the pulpit at Saint-Pierre. Suspicion fell at once on Jacques Gruet, who had breakfasted that morning with François Favre.[44] A man of some education, inclined to the use of his pen for his private amusement, though not thus far for public influence, he was at heart a "free-thinker" in the modern sense, and also a man of sensual standards of morality. Arrested at once, he admitted the authorship of the placard under threat of torture. But a search of his house yielded documents to the thinking of the time of even more incriminating nature. Among his papers were drafts of an appeal to the people against the moral discipline of the community, and of a letter proposing that the King of France be induced to attempt the removal of Calvin from Geneva by diplomatic threats. On a scrap of paper were traced the words: "All laws, divine and human, are made by the caprice of men." On

[43] *Opera*, xii. 531, 532. On the whole transaction, see Roget, ii. 275–284, and Cornelius, pp. 497–501.

[44] For Gruet see H. Fazy, *Procés e J. Gruet*, in *Mémoire de l'Inst. nat genevois*, for 1886, i. 5–141; Roget, ii. 289–312; Kampschulte, ii. 59–67; Cornelius, pp. 501–505; also, *Opera*, xii. 563–568.

the margin of a passage in which Calvin had argued the truth of human immortality he had written, "All nonsense." These were private papers. No consequent act, save the placard, could be traced to him, but to the judges they seemed an attack on the majesty of God no less than of the State. The severest of tortures, however, failed to wring from Gruet any satisfactory evidences of a conspiracy or of accomplices. But the sixteenth century had only one opinion of the deserts of such an offender.[45] On July 26, he was beheaded.

Gruet was a worthless fellow. The real danger from him was slight to modern thinking, if not to the judgment of that age. But to Calvin, in the heat of a difficult struggle, Gruet's discovery and condemnation was a great advantage. He felt that the trial moved too slowly and rejoiced in its result.[46] Gruet, though denying that he had had accomplices, and himself so abhorrent to the conception of the time that none of Calvin's enemies would say a word in his defence, nevertheless seemed by his own wickedness to prove the fundamental viciousness of the opposition which the reformer had encountered and to justify the severity of Genevan discipline.

Strong as Calvin appeared after the collapse of Perrin's plans and the death of Gruet, before the end of the year he was to reach almost his lowest point of power. Perrin, as has been noted, had gone in June to the French court as an ambassador of Geneva. The time was one of distress for the Protestant cause brought low in Germany by the successes of Charles V. Switzerland feared his victorious arms. Under these circumstances of danger from Germany, Perrin made or listened to a suggestion that a small force in French pay, but under his command, be sent to Geneva to strengthen the city against the Emperor.[47]

---

[45] Some time after Gruet's death, a draft of a volume was found hidden in his former home showing his hostility to the Christian religion and attacking the characters of Christ, His mother, and the Apostles. Made a subject of judicial inquiry in which Calvin bore a part, it was publicly burned on May 23, 1550. Henry, ii., Appendix, pp. 120–124; *Opera*, xiii. 566–572.

[46] Calvin's letters, *Opera*, xii. 559, 576.

[47] For this whole controversy see Roget, iii. 1–39; Kampschulte, ii. 70–100; Cornelius, pp. 505–537.

The arrangement was not concluded, but the advantages of such a force to an ambitious party leader are evident. Before Perrin's return, the plan was made known, however, through the correspondence of a brilliant, rather spendthrift, but able French refugee resident of Geneva: Laurent Maigret, nicknamed *Magnifique* from his style of living, who had always maintained close relations with the French court, and with whom partly as a possible agent for advancing the evangelical cause in France, Calvin stood in friendly relations. Perrin's homecoming, in September 1547, was, therefore, sure to lead to questioning, but it was aggravated by the return to the city of his father-in-law and his wife, François and Franchequine Favre, both of whom had avoided governmental punishment by flight. They were now arrested, and Perrin having denounced their seizure in bitter words, was joined with them. At the request of Bern, with which canton they stood on good terms, the Favres were soon released from confinement and, on October 6, at last made their peace with the Consistory. Not so Perrin. Though aided by Bern, his trial continued.

Thus far all had gone well for Calvin, but a change now came. The Bernese ambassador denounced Maigret as much worse than Perrin, as a constant correspondent with the French authorities, a dangerous intriguant with France, and the real traitor. The result was that two trials went on side by side, that of Calvin's opponent, Perrin, and that of his friend, Maigret. Factional feeling was excited in high degree, but its most interesting exhibition for Calvin's story is that it gave him an opportunity to display a physical courage which shows how completely his strength of spirit could triumph over his natural timidity. One December 16, the Two Hundred met. The scene within was one of violence, and the crowd in the street outside seemed on the point of battle. Bern and France had their friends and foes in the throng. At imminent peril of his life, and against protest, warning, and threat, Calvin went to the Hall, at the head of the *Vénérable Compagnie*, and by the courage of his personal appearance and the skill of his words of exhortation brought at least external good order. It was a triumph of pluck and persuasive force.[48] But Calvin had little hope either of Maigret's acquittal or of his own continuance in the city. "I am broken," he wrote to Viret, "unless God stretches forth His hand."[49] Yet so evenly balanced were the two parties in Geneva that the result was compromise and partial reconciliation. Perrin and Maigret both went free, but Perrin gained most. He was restored to all his rights and honors, while Maigret remained out of office. This balance of parties was also evident in the choice of syndics at the election of February 1548. By the Perrinists and the friends of Calvin the board was evenly divided, and in this equality of power lay Calvin's danger and his hope alike.

Calvin's story during the next two or three years is one of effort to hold what had been gained, involving many petty, but none the less harassing struggles to maintain Church discipline. By the lighter-minded of his opponents Calvin was nicknamed Cain, dogs were named in derision for him, placards were posted criticizing him, ballads ridiculing him were sung; he was exposed to all the annoyances of petty attack. When discovered, the authors of these insults were disciplined by the Consistory, and reported to the magistrates, but they rendered his life uncomfortable, and increased the sense of danger which was his constant companion.

The ablest leader among Calvin's opponents was undoubtedly Ami Perrin, of whom frequent mention has been made. Self-centered, ambitious, without deep principles of any sort, he was yet an effective party leader, and proved himself, when in office, possessed of considerable gifts as a magistrate. His chief supporter was Pierre Vandel, forward in the original establishment of the Reformation in Geneva, but hostile to Calvin, as has been seen, even before the close of his stormy first ministry in the city. Vandel represented well the old Genevan spirit of independence, but his own disposition was such as to make any discipline irksome. Much

---

[48] Even Audin, *Histoire de la vie, des ouvrages et des doctrines de Calvin,* i. 394, praises his courage. For contemporary accounts see *Opera,* xii. 632, xxi. 418; Cornelius, p. 550; see also Calvin's Farewell Address, *Opera,* ix. 892.
[49] *Opera,* xii. 633.

inferior in intellectual gifts and in political talents, but popular, bold, and eager for conflict with foreign influences, as well as hostile to any form of restraint, were the two sons of the Genevan patriot-martyr of 1519, Philibert and François Daniel Berthelier, of whom the first named, in spite of his weaknesses, deserves to rank with Perrin and Vandel as the leader of the forces of opposition to Calvin. Among the common people Philibert Berthelier enjoyed the largest popularity. To him, chiefly, appears to have been due the renewal in 1546 or 1547, of the "Enfants de Genève" – an ancient association of young men professedly for the military defence of Geneva, the title of which recalled the patriots of his father's time. Berthelier's own character was weak, immoral, and ungoverned, and his temper and excesses rendered him an ally of doubtful permanent value to any cause. That it was compelled to use such instruments as the best available, reveals the fundamental inefficiency of the opposition to Calvin. It could in no way equal his determination, his intellectual strength, and least of all his character.

Yet this opposition was formidable enough, in spite of its weaknesses. In January 1548, Berthelier began a defiance of the Consistory, which was to continue, in varying forms, for years. It was to bring before the Little Council, in 1551, the much-vexed question of consistorial right to pronounce excommunication[50] and to lead, in 1553, as there will be occasion to point out, to a most serious effort to do away with consistorial independence. Calvin's situation was continually harassed. In May 1548, he was admonished by the Little Council for criticisms passed upon the magistrates in a sermon.[51] The following September one of his free-written letters to his friend Viret fell into governmental hands, and caused him much difficult explanation by reason of its criticisms of the Genevan situation.[52] The elections of February 1549, saw Ami Perrin made first syndic, and were immediately followed by a struggle for the removal of de l'Église and Ferron from the pastoral offices of which Calvin and the majority of

---

[50] *Opera*, xxi, 419, 473–479; Roget, iii. 44, 145–148.

[51] *Registres du Conseil*, xliii. 94; *Opera*, xxi. 426.

[52] Ibid., xliii. 194; xxi.434; Roget. iii. 63–67.

their associates deemed them on good grounds unworthy. In spite of Calvin's conviction that de l'Église should be dismissed, he remained in office under the protection of the Little Council. While these events were in progress, Calvin passed through the bitter personal affliction caused by the death, on March 29, of his wife. His own health was precarious. His old enemy, the severe nervous headaches from which he had long suffered, distressed him. The outbreak of persecutions in France and the apparent collapse of the defeated Protestant cause in Germany, crushed by the victories of Charles V, wore upon him.[53] His situation was painful in almost every aspect.

One feature of the situation was, however, full of promise and of menace alike. From the beginning of Calvin's ministry he had welcomed refugees for their faith. He had encouraged them to come by exhortation and by letter. His ideal, as he assured the Genevan authorities a little later, was "that your city may be a firm sanctuary for God amid these horrible commotions, and a faithful asylum for the members of Christ."[54] It was far more than local policy that dictated this resolution. Calvin would make, and in the end did make, of Geneva the bulwark of the Protestant cause in his native French, and in less degree in Italy, the Netherlands, Scotland, and England, by the cordial reception and generous aid there afforded to exiles from those lands. It was this that was to make of Geneva a training school for the reformation of western Europe. But while the purpose of Calvin was thus far-reaching, the effect of this welcome extended to refugees was in the highest degree beneficial to his ultimate position in Geneva, since they were prevailingly men of religious principle, and very generally filled with admiration for his theology and discipline. The menace of the situation was, however, that the coming of these exiles aroused the natural jealousy of the older inhabitants, and more than any other single cause fed the fires of opposition to Calvin's rule. It

---

[53] Compare Kampschulte, ii. 114, 115.

[54] Prefatory letter of 1552 to Calvin's *De aeterna Dei Praedestinatione, Opera,* viii. 256.

was to this feeling, more than to any other, that Perrin, Vandel, and Berthelier could make successful appeal. Calvin's time of chief peril was that between the realization that the refugees were a serious menace to the older forces of Geneva and their attainment of such strength as to constitute an efficient basis of his control of the city.

The accession of Henry II to the French throne was soon followed by severe persecution. By 1549, French refugees in numbers and rank such as had not previously made their way to Switzerland, were streaming to Geneva. Besides the many whose sojourn was temporary, 72 received permission to become inhabitants of the city in 1549, and 122 in 1550. By 1554, no less than 1,376 had obtained the right of residence. Among those who came to Geneva between 1548 and 1550, were such men as Laurent de Normandie, a royal officer of Noyon; Theodore Beza, to be Calvin's successor; Guillaume Trie, a wealthy merchant of Lyons; the Colladon family, eminent in Berry; and Robert Estienne, the celebrated Parisian printer. Not only did they encounter much popular ill will, but the Little Council, though granting rights of residence, was very chary in admissions to the *bourgeoisie* with its privilege of a vote in municipal affairs. This feeling resulted, in January 1551, to a proposal by the Little Council that the newcomers should not be eligible to vote in any Council till after a residence of twenty-five years.[55] No law to that effect was enacted; but the attempt reveals the fear with which these new inhabitants were viewed by the party which had Perrin, Vandel, and Berthelier as its chief representatives.

Yet it was from one of these refugees that a greater danger was to come to Calvin, in 1551, than the Genevan opponents, just mentioned, could alone have aroused. Jérôme Hermès Bolsec,[56]

---

[55] Roget, iii. 136.

[56] The documents in the Bolsec affair may be found in the *Opera*, viii. 141–248; contemporary letters and extracts from registers in ibid., xiv. 191–291; xv. 252, 320, 362; xxi. 481, 489–505; see also H. Fazy, *Procès de Bolsec* in *Mémoires de l'Inst, nat. genevois*, x. 1–74 (1866); Kampschulte, ii. 125-150; Roget, iii. 156–206; Choisy, pp. 113–120, and in Hauck's *Realencyklopädie*, iii. 281.

the source of this attack, was a former Carmelite monk of Paris, who, fleeing from the repressive action of the French government, had found a brief refuge at the court of Renée in Ferrara, and then, in 1550, a home at Veigy, a village near Geneva but under Bernese jurisdiction, where he served as physician to a refugee Protestant nobleman, Jacques de Bourgogne, Sieur of Falais, with whom Calvin had long been on terms of intimacy. A man of education, eminence in his new profession and, as far as had yet appeared, of character, he soon won much respect in the Genevan community. Interested in theological questions, he frequently attended the *Congrégation*, or public discussion, which the *Vénérable Compagnie* held each Friday. In the main he found himself in hearty accord with Calvin's theology, but on the doctrine of predestination he was in sharp disagreement. To his thinking, absolute predestination made God a tyrant, and was contrary to the Scripture representation that man's acceptance or rejection with God depends on the presence or absence of faith. These criticisms he had expressed in the *Congrégation*, in one instance on May 15, 1551, and before the ministers gathered in Calvin's house. On October 16 of the same year, he proceeded to a much more violent attack on the Genevan reformer, declaring to the *Congrégation* that Calvin's views were not merely erroneous and absurd, but that Calvin was not a true interpreter of Scripture or of the historic teaching of the Church.

Here was a criticism that struck at the basis of Calvin's whole Genevan position. As has been pointed out in speaking of Castellio, Calvin had no other post in the city than that of an interpreter of the Word of God, as pastor and teacher, and if he was, as Bolsec asserted, a false interpreter, all real claim to authority was swept away. Calvin had left no room for the admission of possible mistake on important doctrines. He must be right in all that was vital, or he must stand thoroughly discredited – a false teacher. And Bolsec's attack involved much more than a deadly thrust at his Genevian position, to Calvin's thinking. It was the rejection not merely of what seemed to Calvin, however it may appear to the modern world, a plain teaching of Scripture, but of a doctrine of special comfort to the Christian life. In that light, Calvin always viewed the dogma of predestination. Granted, as he held, that human nature is wholly bad, and of itself incapable of goodness, what assurance has any man of salvation save in the divine purpose to rescue him by all-powerful, transforming might from his sins? Nothing but the will of God, Calvin thought, gave any man rational ground for hope of salvation; but if one had reason to feel that God's will was manifested in grace, one had a confidence of divine favor and ultimate complete redemption such as nothing else could bestow. An attack upon a doctrine so important in itself, and so bound up with Calvin's own credit as a religious teacher, demanded his most strenuous resistance. While Bolsec might be the agent, the real author of the criticism, in Calvin's judgment, was Satan himself.[57]

Holding such views, Calvin not merely replied to Bolsec at length and with vehemence in the *Congrégation*; aided by his clerical associates, he caused the matter to be laid at once before the civil authorities of Geneva. It became immediately a legal trial involving the truth or falsity of his own doctrinal teaching. Bolsec was promptly arrested, and defended himself with no little skill; but he was a foreigner and as such had slight support even among Calvin's opponents.[58] Repeated hearings failed to shake his constancy, and a two days' discussion before the authorities in the City Hall being equally fruitless, the Little Council so far complied with Bolsec's requests as to agree that the opinion of neighboring churches should be sought on the question at issue. This was, indeed, something of a defeat for Calvin, implying, as it did, that his views on predestination were debatable, and the ministers under his lead met it by laying further accusations against Bolsec. In spite of his protests, and those of the Sieur de Falais, he was still kept in prison, and began to be seriously distressed as to the probable outcome of his trial. The Genevan

---

[57] Opera, viii. 254.
[58] Roget, iii, 158, and Choisy. p. 113, regard Bolsec as acting at the instance of Calvin's adversaries. Kampschulte, ii. 129, views his attack, probably rightly, as due simply to Bolsec's own liking for theologic discussion.

ministers, with Calvin at their head, now anticipated the action of the government by sending letters strongly denunciatory of Bolsec, on November 14, to their colleagues of Basel, Bern, and Zürich. The official letter of the syndics and Little Council went out a week later. Before the answers could be received, a piece of verse written by Bolsec in his prison fell into the hands of the authorities, and led to a painful examination as to the criticisms of his treatment that might be drawn from its several couplets. The whole course of the trial, both on the part of the ministers and of the magistrates, gives an impression of pressure and unseemly severity.

To Calvin, the letters which at length came from the friendly Swiss churches were exceedingly disappointing.[59] That of Basel viewed Bolsec as heretical, but its writers affirmed that they treated this "most intricate question" of predestination with "simplicity," laying stress neither on foreknowledge nor on election, but on faith. It was evident that predestination held no such place in the teachings at Basel as it did at Geneva. That of Zürich regretted the strife, but thought both sides too bitter in controversy. It treated the question at issue only in the most untechnical and general fashion. That of Bern went further, its writers declaring that they had heard that Bolsec was "not a very bad man," that his principles, even on the point in debate, had in them much that might serve as a basis of reconciliation, that the question of predestination was one of difficulty for many excellent men, and that moderation in such disputes was desirable. On the other hand, the pastors of Neuchâtel, led by Farel, though not asked, volunteered an opinion in which Bolsec was denounced as wholly profane, an instrument of Satan, and in no way to be endured.[60] The effect of the letters from Basel, Zürich, and Bern was not what Calvin wished. He protested to the Little Council, on December 14th, against showing them to Bolsec – but in vain. It was evident that the Genevan ministry must fight its own battle

---

[59] See his letter of December, 1551, to the ministers of Neuchâtel, *Opera*, xiv. 213, 218.

[60] Roget, iii. 193–195.

unaided, and in the *Congrégation* of December 18th, led by Calvin, the pastors proceeded to a long declaration setting forth the fundamental importance of right views on predestination.[61] This determined action on the part of the ministers evidently decided the magistrates to end the already long trial. On December 23, 1551, Bolsec was forever banished for "false opinions, contrary to the holy Scriptures, and pure Evangelical religion."

Calvin had won a victory. His critic had been exiled. His doctrine had been declared, by implication, "pure" by the Genevan government, then largely in the hands of his opponents; but the cost was great. The struggle had been won at the expense of an insistence on predestination as a fundamental Christian doctrine with which, it was evident, German-speaking Switzerland was far from sympathizing. His position as an unassailable interpreter of the Word of God was really more vulnerable than it had been before – though for the time being apparently strengthened. The controversy had undoubtedly been carried on with unnecessary bitterness. The gain that it had brought was temporary, rather than decisive.

As for Bolsec himself, his later conduct was such as to deprive him of much claim to sympathy. Protected for a while in Bernese territory where he continued to attack Calvin, he was driven away, in 1555, chiefly through Calvin's efforts. Returning to France, he recanted what he then styled his errors at the National Synod at Orléans in 1562. A year later he was deposed from the French Protestant ministry as an "apostate." Ultimately he returned to the Roman communion, and in 1577, when Calvin had been thirteen years dead, revenged himself on Calvin's memory by a biography of the Genevan reformer filled with the grossest calumnies and with ascriptions of moral turpitude, a peculiarly atrocious instance of which has already been discussed.[62]

With the exile of Bolsec the troubles aroused by the debate regarding predestination were by no means ended. The controversy, which at first excited little interest among Calvin's

---

[61] In full in *Opera*, viii. 93–138; see Colladon's *Life*, ibid., xxi. 75.
[62] *Ante*, p. 117.

native Genevan opponents, was gradually seen by them to afford a new ground of attack – not now upon his discipline, but upon his orthodoxy. Such a charge was pressed in June 1552, by Jean Trolliet, a former monk, whose reception as pastor had been much desired in 1545 by many of his fellow Genevans, but whose ambitions, being then defeated by Calvin, had led him to cherish a grudge against the reformer. Trolliet had become a lawyer, and had attached himself to the Perrinist party. He now affirmed that Calvin's *Institutes* were heretical, since the logical consequence of their teaching regarding predestination must be that God is the author of sin. Calvin complained to the Little Council, and both sides were heard.[63] Trolliet had many friends, and the result was undecided. On August 29, Calvin, therefore, appeared before the Little Council once more and demanded that justice be done him under threat of resigning his ministry. At the hearing which followed, Trolliet defended himself by an appeal to the well-known views of Melanchthon. Finally, on November 9, the Little Council voted that the *Institutes* present "the holy doctrine of God" and that "in future no one should dare to speak against that book or that doctrine," a judgment in which Trolliet thought it prudent to acquiesce, but all satisfaction which Calvin may have felt in this decision was dampened by the further vote of the same body, on the 15th, assenting to Trolliet's request that it declare him, officially, to be "a good man and a good citizen." The balance of forces in the government was undoubtedly the cause of this indecisive result.

Such a state of affairs could not continue indefinitely, and the situation was constantly complicated and embittered by hostility aroused by the growing numbers and influence of the refugees. The inefficiency of the government, in 1552, was pleasing to neither party. But the situation, as far as Calvin was concerned, grew rapidly worse with the opening of 1553. The February elections resulted in a sweeping Perrinist victory. Not only did Perrin himself once more become a syndic, but he could now count

[63] *Opera*, xxi. 510–527; Roget, iii. 235–248; Kampschulte, ii. 155–157; Choisy, pp. 121–126.

on fourteen votes in the Little Council. The balance of parties, which had continued since 1547, was now broken in favor of Calvin's opponents. The consequences were speedily apparent. On March 16, those ministers who, as burghers, had voted in the General Assembly were deprived of this small share in city politics while in office, in spite of Calvin's protest. The Little Council asserted increased authority in the examination of ministerial candidates. The right of the Consistory to excommunicate was once more brought into dispute. It was a time of annoyance and of petty attack not merely for Calvin, but for the whole ministerial body. Yet more positive were the measures taken by the Perrinist government against Calvin's friends, the refugees. Moved in part by fears of French plots suggested by Bern, but largely by their own hostility, the authorities ordered in April that all not burghers be deprived of arms, save swords only, and that these were not to be carried in the streets. None of the non-citizen refugees should share in the city watch.[64] These regulations increased in marked degree the ill feeling between the older and the newer inhabitants of Geneva which so largely underlay the divisions of its parties, and they made Calvin's position yet more difficult. By the summer of 1553, it seemed as if his fall and the collapse of his Genevan system could be but little delayed.

Through these years of struggle and anxiety Calvin had been busy with his preaching, his teaching, and his pen. A succession of writings, large and small, in addition to an enormous correspondence, flowed from his study. Besides careful revision of the *Institutes* in 1543 and 1550, the more important writings of Calvin during this period include his *Traicté des Reliques* of 1543, perhaps the keenest and most bitingly satirical criticism on this feature of the older worship that the Reformation age produced.[65] His treatise against the *Libertins* of 1545 has already been noted.[66] The Roman Council of Trent drew from him a vigorous *Antidote* in 1547,[67] and the Interim, by

---

[64] Roget, iii. 287–290.

[65] *Opera*. vi. 405–452. Eng. trans. by Beveridge, in *Calvin's Tracts*, i. 255–302.

[66] *Ante*, p. 294.

[67] *Acta Synodi Tridentinae cum Antidoto*, *Opera*, vii. 365–506.

which the victorious Charles V sought to regulate the Protestant churches of Germany pending their expected reconciliation with the papacy, encountered his earnest protest in 1549.[68] The next year came Calvin's treatise on those offences due to quarrels among Protestants, the unworthy lives of some who professed the evangelical faith, and other hindrances by which many were turned away from the Reformed cause.[69] The doctrine of predestination drew from him elaborate arguments in 1543, 1550, and 1552.[70] A series of significant commentaries on the Scripture, of the general character of which there will be something said on a later page, opened with his exposition of Romans, in 1540, while at Strassburg, and was rapidly continued at Geneva. In 1546 and 1547, he discussed I and II Corinthians; Galatians, Ephesians, Philippians, Colossians and I and II Timothy were explained in 1548. The next year Titus and Hebrews were added to the list; in 1550 came his commentaries on the Epistles to the Thessalonians, and James; I and II Peter, and Jude followed in 1551; then Acts and Isaiah were expounded; and the Gospel according to John was discussed in 1553. In these tracts and commentaries, Calvin made firmer and broader his claim, already established by the *Institutes*, to a position in the first rank of theologians not merely of his own age, but of the universal Church.

---

[68] *Interim adultero-germanum*, ibid., viii. 545–674.

[69] *De Scandalis*, ibid., viii. 1–84.

[70] *Defensio doctrinae de servitute arbitrii contra Pighium*, ibid., vi. 225–404; *De praedestinatione et providentia Dei*, ibid., i. 861–902; *De aeterna Dei praedestinatione*, ibid., viii. 249–366.

12

THE TRAGEDY OF SERVETUS –
CALVIN'S VICTORY OVER HIS OPPONENTS, 1553–1557

Calvin's position in the summer of 1553 was, as has been seen, almost desperate in its prospects. Famed as a theologian, revered as the real head of French Protestantism, his hold on Geneva seemed slipping. His disciplinary system met with constant, though often petty, resistance. His friends, the refugees, aroused jealousy. It seemed probable that the next election, at the latest, might secure such a combination of the elements of opposition as would drive him from the city, as in 1538. From this situation he was saved, and was placed on the sure path to ultimate victory by the unexpected coming to Geneva of one who was deemed an arch-heretic: Michael Servetus, whose martyrdom constitutes the most discussed episode of the Reformation age. As in the case of Ameaux, the identification of Calvin's opponents, in part, with the interests of one whom public sentiment condemned, gave renewed strength to his position, and seemed to the common man a proof of the identity of his cause with that of righteousness. To understand the case of Servetus and its effects on Calvin's fortunes, as well as Calvin's attitude toward it, one must so far as possible divest one's self of the prejudgments which three centuries and a half of progress in religious freedom since that time have engendered and try to look upon it from the common viewpoint of the sixteenth century. The gravest injustice to

Calvin's memory would be to minimize his share in a tragedy, which, however repugnant to modern thinking, was to him the exercise of a conscientious duty to the Church, and a means of triumph at the same time over his enemies.

Miguel Serverto[1] was almost certainly born in Villaneuva in the old Spanish kingdom of Aragon in 1509 or 1511. He was, therefore, about the same age as Calvin. He may have studied law at Toulouse, but his early life is very uncertain.[2] In 1530, however, he was in Basel, and there met Cecolampadius; from there he went to Strassburg, where he was kindly received by Capito. This favor was abruptly ended when he published, at Hagenau in 1531, his *De Trinitatis Erroribus*. This radical work, of a man but little, if at all, over twenty years of age, anticipated much not only of what Socianism afterwards asserted, but some Christological views which now have wide currency. To Protestants and Catholics alike, in that day, however, he seemed an extreme heretic, and he was, indeed, a radical of radicals. Of great speculative gifts, and high talents, he was undoubtedly a man of genius. His judgment was erratic, however, and his controversial manner was notoriously overbearing and contemptuous of opponents, even in that age of scanty regard for the courtesies of debate; but there can be no question that he sincerely believed that he had a mission of the highest importance as a reformer of historic theology.

---

[1] The documents relating to his trials are given in *Opera*, viii. 721–856; his letters to Calvin, ibid., 645–720; Calvin's critical account of him and his "errors," the *Defensio Orthodoxae Fidei*, of 1554, is in ibid., 453–644. The contemporary letters of Calvin and his friends may be found in *Opera*, viii. 857–872; xii. 283; xiv. 480, 510, 589–709. For Colladon and Beza's accounts see ibid., xxi. 57, 76, 146. The literature is voluminous. To be mentioned are: L. Mosheim, *Geschichte des berühmten spanischen Arztes Michael Serveto*, 1748; F. Treschel, *Michael Servet*, 1839; H. Tollin, *Characterbild Michael Servetus, u. das Lehrsystem Michael Servets*, 1876–1878; R. Willis, *Servetus and Calvin*, 1877; see also Henry, iii. 95–223; T. H. Dyer, *Life of John Calvin*, pp. 296–367; Schaff, *Hist. of the Christian Church*, vii. 681–796; Roget, iv. 1–131; Kampschulte, ii, 167–203; Harnack, *Dogmengeschichte*, iii. 661–698; Choisy, pp. 130–151; *The Cambridge Modern History*, ii. 411.

[2] Servetus' own statements were conflicting.

Compelled to conceal his identity, he became a student of medicine and natural sciences in Paris under the name of Villeneuve. Here he met Calvin, who strongly disapproved of his views, and it is said, sought an opportunity to refute them in a discussion before witnesses which Servetus doubtless deemed too perilous.[3] He next appears as a corrector of proofs in the publishing office of Melchoir and Gaspard Trechsel at Lyons, where he edited, in 1535, a most creditable edition of Ptolemy's *Geography*. But he was soon back in Paris, and threw himself with passionate zeal into the medical controversies of the day, winning many enemies thereby. His own keenly observant mind is revealed, however, in his discovery, three-quarters of a century before William Harvey, of the pulmonary circulation of the blood.[4] After brief sojourns in Avignon, Lyons, and Charlieu, Servetus settled, about 1540, as a physician at Vienne, still under the name of Villeneuve, and there won the goodwill of men of learning, especially of the clergy, and developed a large practice. Here he labored in secret on a new volume which he was to publish, early in 1553, as the *Restitution of Christianity*,[5] probably completing the manuscript in 1546. Servetus believed that he was bringing Christianity back to is pristine simplicity. On the basis of an essentially pantheistic view of God, he taught that Christ was truly the Son of God, and all the Godhead was corporeally manifested in Him, but that His personality was not pre-existent, save in the mind of God, and really began with His earthly conception and birth. To Servetus' thinking, the Nicene doctrine of the Trinity – "a sort of three-headed Cerberus" – the Chalcedonian Christology, and infant baptism were the three chief sources of churchly corruption.[6] He recognized, far more than his opponents, a progress in revelation from the Old

---

[3] Colladon, in *Opera*, xxi, 57.

[4] *Christianismi Restitutio*, p. 169; it is translated and criticised by Willis, himself a physician, pp. 205–213.

[5] *Christianismi Restitutio*. Two copies of this edition exist: one at Paris, the other at Vienna.

[6] The writer has taken a few sentences from his volume on *The Reformation*.

Testament to the New; he rejected predestination and attached merit to good works; and believed the end of the present age with the millennial reign of Christ to be just at hand. For that reign his *Restitution* was to be a preparation.

It was while working on this volume, in 1545, that Servetus entered into correspondence with Calvin. Begun with courtesy, though with great self-assertion on Servetus' part, it speedily degenerated into an exasperating controversy. Calvin sent to Servetus a copy of his *Institutes*, which the Spanish thinker returned filled with critical, dissenting, and contemptuous annotations. On the other hand, Servetus transmitted to Calvin a portion of the manuscript of his volume which Calvin retained. He appealed, also, to Poupin and Viret, evidently hoping to win someone of the leaders of French-speaking Switzerland for his opinions. Calvin, however, wearied speedily of so fruitless a correspondence with one whom he deemed a heretic and, writing to Farel, on February 13, 1546, he declared that, should Servetus come to Geneva, as the over-sanguine Spaniard proposed, he would never suffer Servetus to go forth alive, if his authority had weight.[7]

Many causes conspired to induce such sanguinary feelings in Calvin toward Servetus. The tone in which the Spaniard framed his criticisms, not merely of Genevan, but of all generally-accepted thinking on the Trinity, was exasperating. Calvin's own orthodoxy on the doctrine had been a tender point ever since the controversy raised by Caroli in 1537; the honor of God seemed to him even more grievously attacked than in the case of Ameaux; but deepest of all was Calvin's profound conviction that only the historic doctrine of the Trinity, taught, he believed, throughout the Scriptures, maintained the full divinity of Christ, and only as that divinity was perfect was there adequate atonement for human sin, availing intercession with the Father, or true sonship for the redeemed.[8] Servetus, to Calvin's thinking, destroyed the Christian hope and, repulsive as it seems to the modern man, he deemed it his duty to rid the world of such

---

[7] Opera, xii. 283. The letter was written in the midst of the trial of Ameaux.
[8] Compare G. Kawerau, in Meoller's *Lehrbuch der Kirchengeschichte*, iii. 432.

"impiety," should the opportunity be his, and Servetus still be unrepentant of his "errors."

Early in 1553, a copy of the *Restitution*, then just secretly printed by Balthasar Arnoullet and his head-manager Guillaume Geroult, at Vienne, reached Geneva, possibly sent by Servetus to Calvin.[9] It happened that at the time, Calvin's friend, Guillaume Trie, once a merchant at Lyons, but now a fugitive for his faith at Geneva, was in correspondence with a cousin, Antoine Arneys, who still resided at Lyons, was an ardent adherent of the Roman Communion, and was disposed to rally Trie on the alleged license in belief prevalent in Geneva. To him, Trie replied on February 26, 1553, declaring that it was in Catholic France, rather than in Geneva, that blasphemies were tolerated, and giving as his proof the *Restitution*, whose author and publisher he named. As evidence of his charges he enclosed the first few pages of the volume, and declared of Servetus, that he "ought to be burned alive, wherever he might be found." This letter was no official denunciation. It was from one cousin to another. But, in spite of the fact that, writing just a month later, Trie tells Arneys that the letter was meant for himself alone, its writer can have had no great unwillingness that it be laid before the ecclesiastical authorities at Lyons, as it was. Process was at once opened against Servetus, but he denied his identity, alleging that he was simply the physician, Villeneuve; and neither with him nor with the printers were incriminating papers found. Recourse was had to Trie for further proof, who now, on March 26, forwarded to Lyons the annotated copy of Calvin's *Institutes*, and a number of Servetus' letters to Calvin. These documents he declared had been procured from Calvin with great difficulty. Under the date of March 31, further information was furnished by Trie.

The transaction just narrated raises a difficult question. Was Calvin the instigator, and Trie simply the tool in this denunciation of Servetus to the French authorities? The affirmative opinion is that of many recent scholars.[10] It was that

---

[9] This is the opinion of Willis, pp. 231–234.

[10] E.g. Roget, iv. 25–27; Willis, pp. 235–251; R. Stähelin, p. 675.

of Servetus himself.[11] On the other hand, it had been vigorously denied,[12] and Trie's own statements already cited, are confirmed by Calvin's rejection of the imputation that he had himself delivered Servetus to the Roman ecclesiastics.[13] To the writer the simplest explanation seems to be that Trie, as a friend of Calvin, knew in general of Servetus' identity and book; that he wrote the first letter of his own motion to Arneys, thinking the opportunity of a reply to his cousin's criticisms of Geneva too good to miss; but that from the time of his second letter, and with no great difficulty in spite of his allegation, he procured from Calvin all the aid and documents that the Genevan reformer was able to furnish, so that, from the date of that letter, at least, Calvin must be deemed the chief, though indirect, agent in the denunciation of Servetus to the Catholic court.[14]

The case at Vienne moved slowly. Servetus had personal friends, though no sympathizers in his beliefs. By their connivance, it would seem, he escaped from prison on April 7; on June 17, his trial was ended by a sentence to death by slow fire, which was executed in effigy,[15] Servetus himself having fled more than two months earlier. After wandering for a number of weeks in southern France, Servetus came, for no reason that seems conclusive, to Geneva itself, intending to make it a stopping-place on his way to Naples. Though it has often been asserted that he spent a month unrecognized in the city, there is no real reason to believe his sojourn was more than a few days in length.[16] He had negotiated for a boat through his landlord of the "Rose" tavern to continue his journey when, on August 13, while listening to

---

[11] *Opera*, viii. 732, 789, 805.

[12] E.g. Henry, iii. 140; Choisy, p. 131.

[13] *Opera*, viii. 479.

[14] I owe to Rev. Nathanaël Weiss the probable suggestion that Calvin may have hoped to aid the "five scholars of Lausanne" (p. 382) by unmasking Servetus and thus doing a favor to their captors in Lyons.

[15] Opera, viii. 784–787.

[16] Compare Servetus' own statement, *Opera*, viii. 770; the notes of the Strassburg editors, ibid., xiv. 590; and Roget, iv. 41–43.

a sermon by Calvin, it is said,[17] he was recognized, and soon after arrested, undoubtedly at Calvin's instigation.[18] Had Calvin been indisposed to severity, he might have prevented Servetus' incarceration till it was evident that the Spaniard intended to remain in Geneva, but he felt that Servetus had been delivered into his hands, and that he ought to prevent further "contagion." From the first, Calvin hoped that Servetus would forfeit his life, though not by a painful death.[19]

The trial opened quite as Calvin wished. A refugee in his employ, Nicolas de la Fontaine, made the complaint, and took upon himself the liabilities of a false accuser, should it not be proved. Thirty-eight counts were alleged against Servetus before the civil court, mostly of a theological character, though embracing also his attacks on Calvin. To these Servetus replied with skill, and now a new force made itself apparent. Servetus won no converts, his theological speculations in themselves were not approved, but he was Calvin's opponent. His conviction would be a triumph for Calvin's waning authority in the city. These considerations, rather than any doctrinal sympathy, explain the support which Servetus now received from Calvin's Genevan foes. At the hearing on August 16, hot words were exchanged between Philibert Berthelier representing the lieutenant of justice, and the learned refugee lawyer, Calvin's friend, Germain Colladon, who now appeared as counsel for the prosecution. It was evident that the case was to involve much more than Servetus' heresies. It was to test the relative strength of the rival parties in Geneva, and the permanence of Calvin's control. For this new struggle, in spite of a personally hostile majority in the Little Council, Calvin had the great advantage of demanding justice on one who seemed to most religious men an intolerable heretic. Berthelier, blind with party hatred, had put himself in the precarious position of staking his success on the defence of a discredited cause, and that

---

[17] Notes to Opera, viii. 725.

[18] Calvin's letters, *Opera*, xiv. 589, 615.

[19] "I hope the judgment will be capital in any event, but I desire cruelty of punishment withheld." Letter to Farel, August 20, above cited.

not because he believed in the accused, but because he disliked the accuser. The condemnation of Servetus now became vital to Calvin's whole Genevan status.

Calvin felt the gravity of the situation. On August 17, he appeared in person before the Little Council against Servetus. The examination took a technical character. Not only were the Trinitarian attacks in the *Restitution* debated, but a criticism of the fertility of Palestine implying that it was not a land "flowing with milk and honey," which Servetus had copied into his edition of Ptolemy, was made the basis by Calvin of accusation that Servetus had brought charges of falsity against Moses, and therefore of blasphemy against the Holy Spirit by whose inspiration Moses, Calvin believed, had spoken. Calvin also pushed Servetus to the declaration consonant with his pantheistic principles, that the very floor and benches of the courtroom were "the substance of God," upon which Calvin declared, "Then the devil is God in substance," to which Servetus replied, with a laugh that must have prejudiced his case with the judges, "Do you doubt it?"[20]

The Little Council, however averse to Calvin some of its members were, could not doubt that the case was one of great seriousness. On August 17, it freed de la Fontaine from further responsibility, and the prosecution now fell into the charge of the states-attorney of the city, Claude Rigot, a friend of Calvin. Four days later, the Little Council determined to ask the advice of Bern, Basel, Zürich, and Schaffhausen, and also to obtain from Vienne the action of its court against the prisoner. There is no reason to see any plan to aid Servetus in this determination to ask outside opinion. The condemnation of one accused of heresy was a formidable step, and the Council, doubtless, desired to act with care. But this consultation undoubtedly encouraged the hopes of Servetus and of Calvin's opponents. It must have been remembered that in the recent case of Bolsec, the advice of the Swiss cantons, and their ministers, had been in favor of leniency.

---

[20] This is Calvin's account of the point last discussed, *Opera*, viii. 496. Perhaps it is to be taken with some reserve, Roget, iv. 52.

To that extent it was a rebuff to Calvin, who preferred that the court should convict the prisoner without delay. On August 23, Servetus had to answer to a new series of charges prepared by the states-attorney and of such a character that, while the trial did not cease to be for heresy, Servetus' life and the general evil influences of his teachings, rather than theological minutiae, were emphasized. The attempt to prove Servetus of unworthy life failed completely; nor could it be shown that he was an intentional turmoiler of public peace. He asserted with sincerity that his advocacy of his views had been under the impulse of a sense of duty. Undoubtedly Servetus, thus interrogated, made a much better impression on the court than earlier, and this slight success was strengthened by his plea that his discussions had always been with learned men on abstruse questions of theology, and involved no seditious actions whatever. Rigot's efforts had injured, rather than aided, the prosecution. To the demand of the authorities of Vienne that Servetus be extradited to them for execution, the Little Council, on August 31, sent a politely phrased refusal.

On August 17, the Little Council had directed that an attempt be made to show Servetus his "errors." That indicated a discussion, for which Calvin was nothing loath; and on September 1, such a colloquy was begun between the two contestants, before the judges, including Ami Perrin and Philibert Berthelier. The debate was confused and unsatisfactory. Servetus objected that the prison was no fit place, to which Calvin agreed and expressed a wish for a public disputation, but the authorities cut short all debate, ordering Calvin to present Servetus' errors in writing and the latter to reply, both using Latin. Two reasons seem to have induced this action. Perrin and Berthelier undoubtedly feared that a public disputation with so able a debater as Calvin would mean a popular victory for the reformer – a result highly displeasing to them; and the preparation of such documents would afford material, in which Servetus could make the best statement of his case possible, for presentation to the Swiss cantons, the advice of which it had been decided to ask. Calvin's opponents, though not daring to back Servetus openly, were causing all the delay they could, and making the outcome of the trial as dubious as possible, and Servetus himself took great encouragement from their support. The accusations of heresy drawn from Servetus' writings were quickly formulated by Calvin, and the prisoner was prompt with his reply – his confidence in the support of Calvin's enemies appearing in the contemptuous tone of the answer. Servetus declared Calvin to be a disciple of Simon Magus, of confused mind, who hoped by barking like a dog to overwhelm the judges. To this reply a rejoinder, couched in severe terms, was made and signed by all the Genevan ministers. Delivered to Servetus on September 15, in the course of the next two or three days he annotated the paper with replies that are marvellous in their exasperating character considering the circumstances under which they were written.[21] "You lie," "you play the fool," "you rave," "cheat," "vile scoundrel," are among the accusations and epithets which he employed. On the 22nd, Servetus sent a remarkable appeal to the Genevan government, demanding the arrest of Calvin under the *lex talionis*, as a false accuser and a heretic, and "that the case be settled by his or my death or other penalty." He asked that Calvin "be not merely condemned but exterminated" and his goods adjudged to himself. Meanwhile, on September 22, the letters of inquiry, voted on August 17, were despatched by the Little Council to the ministers and magistrates of Bern, Basel, Zürich, and Schaffhausen. The progress of events now awaited their answer.

The reasons of Servetus' defiant attitude and expectations of acquittal were largely temperamental, but they were undoubtedly greatly strengthened by a new struggle in which Calvin found himself engaged and that promised indirect advantage to the prisoner. There has been frequent occasion to note the aversion of Calvin's opponents, both of those of undisciplined life and the more worthy representatives of old Genevan independence, towards the central element of his ecclesiastical government, the Consistory, and especially towards the power of excommunication

---

[21] All these documents are given in *Opera*, viii. 501–553.

exercised by it. That power, though regularly employed, had long been in dispute, and had several times seemed on the point of being taken away by the Little Council. To Perrin, Vandel, and Berthelier the present juncture seemed a fitting time to assert the superiority of the Little Council over the Consistory. Calvin was busied with the case of Servetus; the issue of the trial depended on the Little Council and was of utmost consequence to him. Should the Little Council, in which the Perrinists had a decided majority, now withdraw the right of independent excommunication from the Consistory, Calvin might acquiesce, however reluctantly, lest his opposition should cost him the support of the Little Council in the conviction of Servetus. Berthelier seemed the fitting agent for the attack. He was courageous, fond of fighting, popular, and under excommunication by the Consistory; unfortunately for his party, however, his life was notoriously blameworthy and his discipline not undeserved. On September 1, he now appeared before the Little Council, and demanded that it supersede the excommunication of the Consistory, and admit him to the Communion to be held on Sunday, September 3. Calvin was called to express his opinion. It was a crisis as vital for his church government as it was unexpected, but he protested against the proposed action to the utmost of his power. In vain, however, for the Little Council granted Berthelier's request.[22] That result called for Calvin's utmost energy of protest. He demanded, and obtained, a meeting of the Little Council on Saturday, and declared that we would die before he would administer the sacrament to Berthelier. To all outward appearance he failed once more. The Little Council held to its decision. But really his iron firmness of will snatched success from defeat; for while reaffirming its release of Berthelier from excommunication, the Little Council advised him – secretly it would appear – not to present himself at the Lord's Table. It was a thoroughly weak compromise. Whether Calvin was aware of it is uncertain, but he was determined that

---

[22] *Registres*, and Calvin's letters, *Opera*, xiv. 605, 654; xxi. 551; Roget, iv. 61–73; Kampschulte, ii. 203–223.

there should be no popular doubt as to his position. Before the crowded congregation, gathered the next day for the Lord's Supper in Saint-Pierre, and eagerly anticipating a scene, he forbade anyone under ban of the Consistory to commune, and declared that none should do so while he had strength to oppose.

Fortunately for Calvin, Berthelier had heeded the advice and was absent. The situation was in the highest degree critical. Calvin had defied the Little Council. He was so convinced that his action would be resented that he preached, that afternoon, what was well-nigh a farewell sermon. His courage had, however, but increased the indecision of the Council. On September 7, he and his fellow ministers made formal protest to that body; again on the 15th; and on the 18th, the Little Council voted to "hold to the *Ordonnances* as before." That left the question of excommunication where it had been previous to Berthelier's attack. It was still one in dispute; but the real victory was Calvin's. Berthelier's attempt had been frustrated by Calvin's force of character.

It is not surprising, however, that Servetus took courage and gained hope of release from this struggle. Calvin's defeat would have been his advantage; but the result left him in worse case than ever. And, on October 18, the replies of the Swiss ministers and governments arrived. In marked contrast to the answers in the case of Bolsec, all now condemned the teachings of the prisoner, and approved the attitude of Calvin and his associates. While no direct recommendations as to punishment were made, all, and notably Bern, made it evident that it should be such as would "remove this pest" from the churches.[23] It was evident to all that Calvin had the support of Protestant Switzerland. His opponents were beaten. Perrin tried to delay the conclusion by absenting himself from the Little Council and by proposing an appeal to the Two Hundred,[24] but to no purpose. On October 26, the Council ordered that Servetus be burned alive the day following. Calvin sought a milder form of death – his disinclination toward cruel

---

[23] *Opera*, viii. 819. For these letters, see ibid., pp. 555–558, 808–823.

[24] Calvin to Farel, October 26, Opera, xiv. 657.

executions has already been noted[25] – but in this the court gave him no heed.

To Servetus the sentence seems to have been wholly unexpected, and its first effect was crushing. His courage came again, however, and he never appeared to better advantage than in his last hours. He sent for Calvin, and begged pardon for any wrong he might have done the Genevan reformer. He asked an easier death, not because he retracted any of his opinions, but lest in the agony of fire he should deny the truths which he championed. He went in simple dignity to the place of execution on the hill of Champel, lectured and urged to repent by Farel, who had come to Geneva for the final scene. At the sight of the flaming torch, Servetus could not repress a cry of horror, but his courage was adequate to his extremity. The unskillfulness of the executioner – not any intention as has been sometimes charged – prolonged his agony, but the last utterance that escaped his blistering lips, as the flames tortured his body, was a prayer expressive at once of his Christian hope, and of the peculiar interpretation of the mysterious doctrine of the Trinity which he had championed, and for which he died: "Jesus, thou Son of the eternal God, have pity on me!"[26]

To one whose fortune it is to live under the greater freedom of the twentieth century, such a scene, and the bitter prosecution of which it was the crown, is utterly repulsive. His sympathies, whatever his estimate of the theological questions involved, or however keenly he may recognize the many weaknesses of the sufferer, go out toward the victim of the tragedy. Calvin's eagerness to secure his conviction and the co-operation with the authorities at Vienne, however explainable, are not pleasant to contemplate. Those who erected a monument to Servetus near the place of his martyrdom on its 350th anniversary in 1903, did well.[27] That faggot-heap was a milestone from which the world's

---

[25] Ibid., see *Ante*, p. 283. The sentence is given in *Opera*, viii, 827–830.

[26] It is perhaps unnecessary to point out, even in an untheological age, that the difference between the phrases "Son of the eternal God" and "eternal Son of God," with their implications, epitomizes the dispute.

[27] See the *Monument expiatore du supplice de M. Servet*, Geneva, 1903.

progress along the pathway toward freedom of utterance may be reckoned.

The burning of Servetus did not, indeed, pass altogether un-condemned in its own time. At Basel, especially, where greater freedom existed than elsewhere in Switzerland, and where Castellio had some slight influence, voices were raised in criticism. Many of the Italian Protestant refugees, themselves for the most part radicals, dissented. Calvin felt the criticism and, in February 1554, he published, with the approving signatures of his colleagues in the Genevan ministry, his *Refutation of the Errors of Servetus*,[28] in which he gave not merely his own version of the tragedy, but a defence of the employment of capital punishment for the repression of heretics in general.[29] To Calvin's anger, this narrative drew from his old opponent Castellio, and some associates, a volume sharply criticizing the use of force in religion, and containing a widely selected collection of opinions in favor of toleration. "Christ would be a Moloch," it urged, "if He required that men should be offered and burned alive."[30]

The voices were, however, relatively few and un-influential. The general opinion in Protestant circles was that the world was happily rid of Servetus and that Calvin had done well. His Genevan associates approved; the Swiss churches favored him; even so mild a man as Melanchthon declared that it was "justly done."[31] Nor can there be any question as to its effect upon his own position and the evangelical cause. He had freed the Swiss churches from imputation of heresy; he had prevented any toleration of anti-trinitarian opinions in the religious circles that looked to him for guidance. Above all, his Genevan opponents had compromised themselves irretrievably by countenancing,

---

[28] *Defensio Orthodoxae Fidei de Sacra Trinitate*, etc., *Opera*, viii. 453–644.

[29] Ibid., pp. 461–479.

[30] It was published in March 1554, under the pseudonym of Martinus Bellius, and ostensibly at Magdeburg, as *De Haereticis, an sint persequendi?* In Calvin's opinion, Castellio was a "beast, no less virulent, than untamed and obstinate." *Opera*, xv. 209.

[31] Letter of October 14, 1554, to Calvin, *Opera*, xv. 268.

not out of theologic sympathy, but out of hatred to him, a man whom most of the world looked upon as a justly punished heretic.

Yet this enfeeblement of Calvin's opponents was not immediately evident. Scarcely had Servetus been executed when Berthelier renewed the long struggle with the Consistory. On November 7, the Little Council referred the thorny problem to the Two Hundred, which decreed that the Consistory had no power to excommunicate without orders from the Council. So energetic was the protest of the ministers, led by Calvin, however, that the Little Council and the Two Hundred weakened its position, so far as to decide to ask the opinions of the churches of Bern, Zürich, Basel, and Schaffhausen.[32] As might have been expected, from the customs of other Swiss churches, the replies were far from a complete support of Calvin's discipline. Thanks to his efforts, aided by Bullinger, those of Zürich and Schaffhausen were favorable, but Bern was distinctly hostile. Yet it shows the weakening of the opposition, that, instead of asserting their claims, the Little Council and the Two Hundred now patched up a truce that, while nominally leaving the question where it was before, was really a victory for Calvin's discipline. Even Perrin saw that his attack had failed. The events of the year 1553 had changed the balance of power in Geneva, and further evidence of the decline of the opposition was manifest in the choice, at the February election of 1554, of three of the four syndics from among Calvin's supporters. In October following, Berthelier still continuing his refusal of obedience to the Consistory, a commission was appointed to consider the problem of the right of excommunication; and finally, in January 1555, to Calvin's great satisfaction, the question which had been agitated for years was settled by the successive votes of the Little Council, the Sixty, and the Two Hundred, that they abide by the *Ordonnances*.[33] In form this was,

---

[32] *Registres du Conseil*, xlvii. 175–177; *Opera*, xxi. 559–561.

[33] Ibid., xlviii. 138, 176–182; *Opera*, xxi. 588, 593, 594; Roget, iv. 186–192; Kampschulte, ii. 254–256. See Calvin's letter to Bullinger, *Opera*, xv. 449.

indeed, inconclusive. The interpretation of the *Ordonnances* had been in dispute. But, in reality, the decision finally confirmed the existing usage, which Calvin had so long struggled to maintain. He could now rest satisfied that the power of excommunication without interference from the civil authorities was secure. The cornerstone of his Genevan ecclesiastical edifice was at last firmly laid.

While Calvin's position was rapidly strengthening in Geneva, he was subject, to a degree never before experienced, to attack from outside Genevan territories. Some of this hostility which centered in Castellio at Basel, but was by no means confined to him there, has already been noted. In that city, to be called a disciple of Calvin passed with many for a term of reproach,[34] the reason being far more Calvin's strenuous insistence on the doctrine of predestination than his action in the case of Servetus. That doctrine, as was noted in connection with the trial of Bolsec, won no hearty approval, in its strenuous Genevan form, from the other Swiss churches.[35] Bern, in particular, had dissented; and from Bern Calvin's chief troubles now came. There were many causes for Bernese hostility. Bern and Geneva had long-standing sources of quarrel in their political relations. Bern was suspicious of the growing influence of the French refugees on whom Calvin so largely depended. It preferred and supported the old Genevan element represented by Perrin and Vandel, as more pliable toward its own interests and hostile to any possible French alliances. The Bernese ministry viewed with distrust the Genevan discipline, so different from their own; and the international fame of the head of the Genevan Church was regarded with some natural jealousy. Chief of all sources of friction was, however, the state of the French-speaking territories under Bernese jurisdiction. They extended almost to the walls of Geneva, their ministry was in general

---

[34] Hotman to Bullinger, quoted by Kampschulte, ii. 225.
[35] *Ante*, p. 318. Except, of course, those, like Neuchâtel, in which Calvin's friends were in control.

sympathy with Calvin and his methods – a notable example is that of Viret, at Lausanne – yet their churches were under the Bernese government.

Since Bolsec's banishment from Geneva in 1551, he had been permitted the range of its territories by Bern, and had laboured in French-speaking Switzerland as the determined enemy of Calvin. Bolsec's attacks on Calvin's strict doctrine of predestination found hearing. André Zébédée and Jean Lange, pastors at Nyon and Bursin, sympathized with him, and Calvin was soon denounced as "a heretic and antichrist."[36] The Genevan ministers complained to the Bernese authorities, but received little satisfaction. In January 1555, the Bernese Council ordered attacks, indeed, to cease, but at the same time declared the disputed doctrine to be more fitted to awaken strife, hatred, and immorality than edification. This was painful enough for Calvin, but worse was to follow. In March, an embassy from the Genevan Little Council, in which Calvin's friends now had a majority, appeared on his behalf before the Bernese government, accompanied by Calvin himself. Bolsec's ejection from Bernese territory, as a disturber of the peace, was obtained.[37] But the Council of Bern affirmed that both Calvin and his opponents had been too contentious and too eager to pry into the hidden mysteries of the divine counsels, and they added the insulting declaration that if any books by him or others contrary to the Bernese reformation were found in their jurisdiction they should be burned.[38] Calvin was not, indeed, expressly declared a heretic on the question of predestination by Geneva's chief Protestant neighbor, but that was the interpretation naturally put upon this action by a large part of the public, and in Bernese territories heated attacks upon his orthodoxy were widely made.

Had these events occurred two years earlier there can be little doubt that, combined with the hostility of Perrin, Vandel, and

---

[36] Complaint to the Bernese government of the Genevan pastors, October 4, 1554, *Opera*, xv. 252. For the whole case see the letters in *Opera*, xv.; also Roget, iv. 171–183, 202–224; Kampschulte, ii. 232–243.

[37] Farel to Haller, March 29, *Opera*, xv. 533.

[38] *Opera*, xv. 543–549.

Berthelier, they would have sufficed to end his Genevan ministry. But in Geneva itself, Calvin's situation had been growing steadily stronger since the close of 1553. The errors of his opponents had aided him. A body of young citizens was being trained year by year under his ministry, and was increasingly influenced by his ideals. But, above all, the refugees were a steadily augmenting force in the community and their weight was almost wholly on Calvin's side. As compared with the ordinary Genevan artisan-citizen they were men of character, learning, often of wealth and high social standing. They had had the courage to leave home and country for conscience's sake. They were a picked body of men, chiefly from France, and in much fewer numbers from Italy, but also from England and Scotland, especially after Catholic Mary had succeeded Edward VI on the English throne. Such men as the Neapolitan nobleman Galeazzo Caraccioli, marquis of Vico, the Colladons, and the Budés, or Laurent de Normandie, would have been eminent anywhere – in little Geneva they were imposing. As has been well said: "There was perhaps in the Protestant world no other community that could show so many noble, distinguished, and aristocratic names."[39] Their presence in Geneva was Calvin's work. Such refugees could not but gradually win favor with the ordinary Genevan citizen, however heartily Perrin, Vandel, Berthelier, and their followers might hate them, and insofar as they commended themselves they increased Calvin's credit and influence in the Genevan community. The common Genevan was pleased alike with the distinction they gave the city, and with the added trade which they brought.

Though many of these immigrants had received the right of habitation, relatively few had been admitted burghers and become possessed in consequence of a voice in city politics. Twenty-six had been so received in 1553, and seven in 1554. But the elections, which had been favorable to Calvin in the latter year, resulted yet more satisfactorily for the reformer in February 1555, partly on account of Calvin's growing strength and partly by reason of popular weariness because of the degree to which Perrin had used

---

[39] Kampschulte, ii. 247.

his position in the government to exalt himself, his relatives, and friends. Not merely were all four syndics now decided Calvinists, but the Calvinist vote in the Little Council and the Two Hundred were greatly increased. The party favorable to the reformer now determined to make its position permanently secure by admitting a sufficient number of refugees as burghers,[40] thus rendering forever idle such opposition as the old Genevan party had hitherto made. Beginning on April 16, by May 9, sixty new burghers had thus been created, among them such men as Guillaume Trie, Laurent de Normandie, Germain Colladon, Jean and François Budé, and Jean Crespin, devoted supporters of Calvin. Perrin, Vandel, and Berthelier, at first scarcely suspicious, soon saw all too clearly what the consequence of this drastic action would be. They sought in vain to keep the new citizens unarmed, and to deprive them of the right of voting for ten years. The fears of Calvin's opponents rapidly increased. On May 13, the old-Genevan Lieutenant of Justice, Hudriot du Molard, made formal protest to the Little Council and demanded the summons of the Two Hundred. The Little Council replied by voting to continue to receive new citizens. The next day he renewed his protest, accompanied by a crowd of sympathizers, only to receive the same answer.[41]

The evident defeat of the lately powerful Perrinist party, and their inability to accomplish anything to avert the catastrophe by legal means, now led to a step which proved their ruin, the exact nature of which has been much controverted, though its results are evident.[42] On the evening of May 16, 1555, a number of

---

[40] Calvin to Bullinger, July 15, 1555, *Opera*, xv. 678, 679. He states the purpose distinctly.

[41] *Registres du Conseil*, xlix. 70–76; *Opera*, xxi. 604, 605.

[42] Calvin gave his version in a long letter to Bullinger, *Opera*, xv. 676–685; see also his letters to Farel, ibid., 617, 686, 693. Colladon and Beza treat it from a strongly Calvinistic standpoint, *Lives*, ibid., xxi. 79, 150. The defeated party's account may be found in E. Durant, *Les relations politiques de Genève avec Berne*, pp. 142–146. Among modern discussions may be mentioned Henry, iii. 374–378; J. B. G. Galiffe, *Quelques pages d'histoire exacte*; Roget, iv. 245–336; Kampschulte, ii. 258–278; Choisy, pp. 174–186. Roget in particular gives an epitome of much of the testimony at the trials.

the Perrinist party, including Perrin and Vandel, supped at two taverns and denounced with much heat the Genevan situation. They probably intended some further and more energetic demonstration against the policy of the government than that of May 14th, but no carefully thought-out course of action seems to have been decided upon. The supper parties broke up early. Perrin and Vandel had gone home by nine, but the main body of the guests proceeded through the city streets in more or less menacing and disorderly fashion. Arrived opposite the house of Jean Baudichon de la Maisonneuve, one of the partisans of Calvin recently elected to the Little Council, they cried out against the French refugees, and Claude Dumont, servant of Jean Pernet, like Baudichon one of the new Calvinist members of the Little Council, was hit by a stone thrown by the younger of the Comparet brothers, boatmen who had been of the party at the taverns. Dumont was not dangerously wounded, and his injury was the sole physical harm done in the whole affair. His cries attracted a watchmen, and also brought Henri Aubert, one of the syndics, from his adjacent drug shop. Aubert attempted to arrest the stone-thrower. The Comparet brothers resisted. A crowd soon gathered. Hot words were exchanged between the two factions. Cries of "traitors," "kill, kill," "beat down the French," and the like resounded. Perrin appeared on the scene and attempted to take from Aubert his bâton, significant of his authority as a syndic, and repeated his effort a little later with the syndic, Pierre Bonna.

The original quarrel spent its force in a few minutes, but sinister rumors ran through the city. It was declared that the refugees had been collecting arms, and that they were assembling in numbers. A crowd of Perrinists gathered in the Bourg-de-Four quarter, of which Vandel was captain, and refused to disperse when ordered by a syndic, only yielding when Vandel joined his entreaties. Many threats were uttered against the refugees, but all ended before midnight. The Comparets were arrested, and the city was once more in peaceful charge of its sixteen watchmen.

Considered in itself this event of the evening of May 16th was a very trifling affair, but it might easily have led to a bloody riot.[43] It showed a disposition, also, to go beyond legal means in expression of opposition toward further admissions of refugees to the franchise. But the facts speak too clearly against the existence of any well-planned conspiracy to overturn the Genevan government to make that interpretation tenable. Perrin and Vandel had gone home quietly and early from the supper. Vandel helped to disperse the crowd. Of any attempt to master the city by attack on the Little Council, then in evening session, there is no evidence. No barricades were raised; no organization from a military point of view was apparent. But to Calvin and his friends the affair took the proportions of a formidable attempt upon the freedom of the government. It was, they declared, a revolutionary conspiracy aimed at the slaughter of the French refugees and the overthrow of the four syndics and their obnoxious associates in the Little Council.[44] There is no reason to doubt that Calvin and most of his sympathizers sincerely believed that the affair was a deep-laid plot. He thought no good of Perrin and Vandel.[45] Their work was, and had long been, in his judgment one hostile to God. But it was a very convenient belief, also, in the existing political situation. If the Perrinists were guilty of high treason, their party could be forever swept from power. Contentions in a small city-republic like Geneva have always been bitter. The victorious side had pushed its triumph far against the "Mamelouks" and "Artichauds," in the past. It was to show itself yet more unsparing now to the Perrinists.

The brothers Comparet had been arrested at the time of the disturbance, and a general investigation of the whole affair was begun by the Little Council the next day, Perrin and Vandel taking their accustomed place among its membership. Many witnesses were heard, and the case was prolonged. On the 23rd, the Council

---

[43] To the writer the interpretation of Choisy seems better justified than the too-minimizing judgment of Roget.

[44] Calvin to Bullinger, June 5, 1555, *Opera*, xv. 681.

[45] See his description of them to Bullinger, July 15, 1555, ibid., 677, 678.

ordered further arrests. The day following the Two Hundred met, and strengthened by its action, the Little Council now decreed the arrest of Perrin and others of his party. Fortunately for them they perceived their danger, and escaped by timely flight. The Bernese authorities made representations on their behalf, but neither Calvin nor his friends were likely to give a welcome to anything that Bern had to say. On June 3, Perrin and four associates were formally sentenced to be beheaded and quartered, though happily for them not in Geneva's power. The Comparets, who were in the city prison, were now examined with cruel torture to force from them the acknowledgement of a conspiracy. The efforts were successful while the pain endured, but before their execution, on June 27, they denied that the riot had been a premeditated act. On August 27 and September 11, Claude Genève and François Daniel Berthelier, Philibert's younger brother, followed them in death by the same bloody path. Meanwhile, on August 6, Pierre Vandel and Philibert Berthelier had been sentenced in their absence to the same fate, and others involved to punishments of varying severity. Even the wives of the condemned were banished from the city, and at a meeting of the General Assembly on September 6, not only was what had been done approved, but all effort to aid the return of the fugitives to the city was forbidden under pain of death.[46] The Perrinist party, as a political force in Geneva, had been totally destroyed.

Calvin's share in these events was not official. The trials and condemnations were the work of the civil authorities. His participation in the struggle was none the less real. He visited the condemned in prison and sought to secure from them an acknowledgement of the alleged conspiracy.[47] He wrote full accounts of his version of the event to Bullinger for influence on the governments of Zürich and Schaffhausen.[48] He expressed satisfaction that torture would probably wring from two of the

---

[46] *Opera*, xv, 752.

[47] Letter to Bullinger, *Opera*, xv. 831.

[48] Ibid., p. 677.

prisoners the information desired.[49] In spite of his aversion to cruel deaths, which has already been noted, he saw a special act of God's judgment in the prolongation of the sufferings of the Comparets through an unskilfulness on the part of the executioner which the Genevan government rebuked by the banishment of that official.[50] He felt that the authorities had been, if anything, too moderate in their action.[51] It is Calvin in his hardest and most unsympathetic mood that here expresses himself, but it should be remembered in explanation that he had suffered for years almost to the shipwreck of a work which he believed to be even more that of God than his own at the hands of the party the destruction of which he now witnessed with such satisfaction.

To Calvin the fall of the Perrinists brought the cessation of serious opposition in Geneva. Refugees were freely admitted to citizenship. Before February 1, 1556,[52] one hundred and seventy had become burghers, and eighty-four more received the same right in the next twelve months.[53] The Consistory acted with a freedom and an undisputed authority that it had not yet enjoyed. Geneva had become, not the city of Calvin's ideal – that it was never to be – but a Puritan town, religious, conscientious, strict in supervision of conduct, and efficient in ecclesiastical censures. The work to which he had set his hand on his return in 1541, had been largely accomplished.

Yet Calvin's hard-won success might even now have been largely frustrated had it not been for unanticipated political good fortune. Though united at home to a degree never heretofore realized, Geneva's external relations, notably with Bern, had never been worse than at the fall of the Perrinists. To Bern's shelter of Calvin's critics already noted was now added its protection of

---

[49] To Farel, *Opera*, xv. 693. Eng. trans. *Letters of John Calvin* (Phila.), vol. iii. 206. "Before ten days we shall see, I hope, what the rack will wring from them."

[50] Ibid.; *Opera*, xxi. 610.

[51] To Bullinger, ibid., xv. 684.

[52] I.e. between February 1, 1555, and February 1, 1556. These are Roget's figures, iv. 327, v. 48; Kampschulte, ii, 285, gives somewhat different figures.

[53] In 1559 alone 1,708 received the right of habitation; between 1549 and 1559 the number of inhabitants received was 5,017. Doumergue, iii. ii, 74.

the banished Perrinist leaders. The alliance between Geneva and this powerful and politically valuable neighbor was to expire by limitation in March 1556. Geneva wished it renewed, but Bern refused consent, save on terms humiliating to the Calvinist government. Geneva therefore dropped the alliance. Yet the situation of the little city, without the political aid of Bern, was precarious in the extreme; and negotiations, in which Calvin bore his full share, were carried on at great length with other cantons and with Bern for a restoration of the confederacy. Bern's terms were too exacting and asked too much in favor of the Perrinists for Geneva to accept. A change came unexpectedly, however, in 1557, when the great victory of the Spaniards over the French at Saint-Quentin on August 10, of that year, won under the generalship of Emmanuel Philibert, Duke of Savoy, made him the most famous commander in Europe, lamed the power of France, and rendered it possible for him to lay claim to the ancient Savoyard lands. The danger both to Bern and Geneva was real, and under a common sense of peril, what negotiations had thus far failed to achieve was now quickly attained. A "perpetual alliance" in which Geneva was for the first time placed on a full equality with Bern was effected in January 1558; the Perrinists found the hopes that they had built on Bernese aid utterly frustrated, and the results of 1555 were made permanent. The party of Calvin had not merely won victory at home, but had secured that victory by the abatement of the most dangerous external perils to which Geneva was exposed, and the attainment of the political independence greater than that which their city had ever before enjoyed.

These months of anxious negotiation with Bern were a time of severe domestic trial for Calvin. The wife of his beloved brother, Antoine, long suspected of unworthy conduct, was charged with adultery committed with Calvin's hunchbacked secretary-servant, Pierre Dagnet, while all were inhabiting Calvin's house. On January 7, 1557, Calvin and his brother laid the case before the Consistory, by which it was referred to the Little Council. On February 16, the crime having been proved, the Little Council gave Antoine a divorce and ordered his former wife to leave the city. The scandal and the chagrin of the reformer were great, but the case seems to have been aggravated. It gave to his enemies, however, an annoying point of attack, especially when Antoine Calvin shocked Roman Catholic feeling by marrying again in 1560.[54] Nor was this the only trial occasioned by those of his own household and circle that Calvin was to experience. In 1562, his stepdaughter, Judith, fell into similar disgrace – a matter which Calvin felt so keenly that he left the city to seek the solitude of the country for a few days after the misdeed became public knowledge.[55]

[54] Calvin to Viret, *Opera*, xvi. 379; *Registres du Consistoire* and *du Conseil*, ibid., xxi. 658–661; Doumergue, iii. 572.
[55] Calvin to Bullinger, *Opera*, xix. 327.

13

CALVIN CROWNS HIS GENEVAN WORK, 1559

Calvin's interest in Geneva was primarily religious. He would make the city an example of a Christian community, a refuge for oppressed Protestants, and a center of influence for the spread of the evangelical cause. His own interpretation of his duties was broad, and he was keen to see that material well-being and education were essential to the realization of his ideal. A well-ordered population should be no less industrious than religious. With this aim in view, as early as December 29, 1544, he urged the Little Council to develop the weaving industry as an aid to the prosperity of the city. His efforts in this direction had very considerable success and were efficiently aided by the character and thrift of many of the refugees. Geneva prospered in a material way under his influence.[1] For this time, Calvin held liberal views on questions of trade. Though he did not approve moneylending as an exclusive profession, he believed the receipt of a fair interest on the use of money not only unforbidden by Scripture, but wise and just.[2] This growth in popular well-being is a factor to be taken into account in explaining the increasing

[1] See H. Wiskemann, "Darstellung der in Deutschland zur Zeit der Reformation herreschenden national-ökonomischen Ansichten," in the *Schriften der Jablonowkischen Gesellschaft*, for 1861, pp. 79–87. Less value, but still a decided significance, is attached to this work by Kampschulte, i. 429, 430. See Schaff, vii. 516.

[2] *Opera*, xa. 245–249.

favor with which his system was regarded by the inhabitants of the city.

Calvin's concern for Geneva was, however, far more spiritual and intellectual than material. In his estimate, religion and education were closely associated. A true faith must be intelligent. The school and the Church are necessary and mutually supplementary agencies; or rather the school is an essential part of any effective Church organization. Intelligence, not ignorance, was to Calvin the mother of piety; and no other conception characteristic of him was more fully impressed on the churches which came under his spiritual influence. France, Holland, Scotland, Puritan England, and New England were all to feel its power and to draw from it lasting benefit.

Calvin had long desired the establishment of a really efficient school at Geneva, effective in its methods, especially in instilling a fundamental basis of philological learning, and having as its crown instruction in theology, by which pastors could be trained for the service of the Church. His ideal was undoubtedly the school system of Strassburg, made familiar to him by participation in its instruction during his sojourn in that city. But circumstances had long been unfavorable to its realization.[3] Given a prominent place in the *Ordonnances* of 1541, the school was, nevertheless, long the weak point of Calvin's structure. Mention has already been made of the vain efforts to secure Mathurin Cordier for its service, and of the unhappy breach with its headmaster, Castellio.[4] The school continued, but so inefficient was its instruction that Genevan parents who desired a thorough education for their sons had to send them to other cities.[5] Theology was, indeed, vigorously taught by Calvin himself throughout his Genevan ministry.

---

[3] An admirable account of Calvin's work for Genevan education is that of Charles Borgeaud, *Histoire de l'Université de Genève*, Geneva, 1900, i. 1–83. Roget, v. 225–248; and Kampschulte, ii. 310–342, have much of value. See, also, Doumergue, iii. 372–392.

[4] *Ante*, p. 289.

[5] Beza'a introduction to the *Laws of the Genevan Academy*, 1559, *Opera*, xa. 66; Borgeaud, i. 1.

On the fall of the Perrinists, and especially after Calvin had renewed old associations by a brief visit to Strassburg in 1556, he set his hand earnestly to the regeneration of the Genevan school system. The conflict with Bern delayed the action then begun; but on its successful conclusion, in January 1558, the Little Council, at Calvin's instigation, ordered the selection of a site for a "Collège."[6] The buildings, which have survived in large part to the present day, were begun in the following April, and Calvin undertook to enlist competent teachers. Geneva was poor, and Calvin asked for gifts and legacies, with such success that the current of beneficence thus started brought more than 500 gifts to the new foundation in the course of the next sixty years.[7] Yet it was impossible, at first, to offer an adequate compensation to the instructors invited, and Calvin's efforts were hampered by this and other difficulties, till an unexpected controversy at Lausanne led to the immediate realization of his purpose.

A school at Lausanne, begun by the theological lectures of Viret in 1537, had been developed into a regular foundation by the Bernese authorities in 1540.[8] There Mathurin Cordier had taught since 1545, but was now supplemented by reason of old age by François Bérauld, a native of Orléans. With them Calvin's friend and disciple, Theodore Beza, had been associated as professor of Greek since 1549, and Jean Tagaut, like Beza a French refugee, as professor of "arts," his specialty being mathematics, since 1557. The school was flourishing and highly respected, and for some years it consisted the only seat of advanced instruction for French-speaking Protestants. The ministers and teachers at Lausanne, notably Viret and Beza, fully sympathized with Calvin's ecclesiastical discipline and, in March 1558, they tried to introduce there his independent right of excommunication. The

---

[6] *Registres du Conseil*, quoted by Roget, v. 227; see, also, Borgeaud, i. 34, 35.
[7] Borgeaud, i. 35, 36. 1074 florins were received in legacies in 1559; certain fines were also so disposed, Roget, v. 232, 233; 10,024 florins are said to have been collected in six months, Kampschule, ii. 314.
[8] Borgeaud, i. 38–42.

consequences were disastrous.[9] The Bernese government, under which Lausanne stood, would have none of it. Beza foresaw the result of the storm, and betook himself to Geneva in September of the same year. Here he was warmly welcomed, nominated to the Genevan ministry by the *Vénérable Compagnie*, and designated by it and the Little Council as professor of Greek in the Collège to be. Thenceforth Beza was to be Calvin's right-hand man. In mental equipment very like Calvin, though without his originality, Beza was devoted to Calvin's theology, discipline, and ideals, and bound to him by ties of intimate friendship. No master ever had a more apt or admiring disciple, and it was Beza who for more than forty years after Calvin's death was to carry on Calvin's work in the path and with much of the success of the older Genevan reformer. Viret, aided by his pastoral associates, maintained the struggle at Lausanne a few months longer; but, in January 1559, he was deposed from his long pastorate, and now came with many of his companions in the ministry and the school to the welcome shelter of Geneva. For the next three years, Viret was a Genevan minister.

By this exodus from Lausanne Calvin was provided with instructors for his Academy. On nomination of the *Vénérable Compagnie*, for in accordance with the principles enunciated in the *Ordonnances* of 1542, Calvin would have the school under ecclesiastical control, he presented to the Little Council, on May 22, 1559, the names of François Bérauld as professor of Greek, and of Jean Tagaut as professor of philosophy.[10] With them was joined a brilliant teacher, once the tutor in French of the Princess Elizabeth, now Queen of England, Antoine Chevalier, as professor of Hebrew. To Beza was given the rectorship of the school instead of the chair of Greek as originally intended. These teachers were, like Calvin, all Frenchmen, and all had been at Lausanne, though Chevalier only for a brief time, and unlike the others not as an instructor in its school. Below them, as teachers in the secondary department, seven *régents* of classes were appointed, of who Jean

[9] Roget, v. 207–224.
[10] *Registres du Conseil*, lv. 48; *Opera*, xxi. 716.

Randon, the headmaster, had been of the school at Lausanne. Thus equipped, the Academy was formally inaugurated under the guidance of Calvin, and with an address by Beza, in the presence of the syndics, counselors, ministers, and other dignitaries of the little city, gathered in Saint-Pierre on June 5, 1559.

On May 22, Calvin had presented, and the Little Council had approved, the translation into French of the constitution of the Academy – the *Leges Academiae Genevensis*.[11] In all probability it was his work.[12] Built in large part on what had been achieved at Strassburg by Johann Sturn, and by Claude Baduel at Nîmes,[13] the Genevan academical constitution gave Greek an equal place with Latin in the curriculum, and emphasized even more than the earlier educational reformers the value of thorough preparatory linguistic studies. The institution was divided into what would now be described as a department of primary and secondary education, and a course of higher studies of university grade. The former, the *scholia privata* or gymnasium, was strictly graded into seven classes, each under a *régent*. In each class the scholars were grouped in tens according to progress and abilities. The seventh or lowest class was taught to read in French and Latin. Grammar and exercises filled the next two years. With the fourth class Greek was begun, and with the second the elements of dialectics. The scholar finished his preliminary course in the first class, with a considerable command of Latin and Greek, some knowledge of their literatures, and a moderate acquaintance with logic. The higher instruction was given in the *scholia publica* by "public professors" of Hebrew, Greek, and Philosophy, or "Arts," and by Calvin and Beza as instructors

---

[11] *Opera*, xxi. 716; text in *Opera*. xa. 65–90.

[12] Always ascribed to him by tradition, his authorship was denied by Berthault in his *Mathurin Cordier*, Paris, 1876; and Bourchenin in his *Étude sur les academies protestantes*, Paris, 1882, p. 62, in favor of Beza and Cordier. Borgeaud has replied with effect, even if unable to furnish an absolute demonstration of Calvin's authorship, i. 45–47. Cordier, then in his eightieth year, came with the exodus from Lausanne to Geneva, and was given a lodging in one of the Collège buildings in recognition of his deserts. He was apparently in feeble health.

[13] See Borgeaud, i. 42–45.

in theology though without professorial title. Here there were no classes, the students being received by inscription and signature of a confession of faith. They were allowed comparative freedom, as in a modern German university. Instruction was free. While an annual public promotion was appointed for the *scholia privata*, the celebration of which on May 1st became an important festival, Calvin made no provision for the bestowment of degrees, nor did the magistrates feel such powers to be within their competence. The scholar of the *scholia publica* had to content himself with a certificate of attendance and character, to which the reputation of the Academy soon gave widely recognized value.[14]

Calvin's object in founding the Academy of Geneva was twofold. He would give opportunity for instruction to the children of the city, and provide training in theology for students from abroad. He would make Geneva the theological seminary of Reformed Protestantism. From the first, the addition of courses in law and medicine were contemplated; but this enlargement was not effected till after Calvin's death. Its success, in point of attendance, was immediately assured. At Calvin's death, 1,200 scholars were enrolled in the *scholia privata*, and 300 in the *scholia publica*.[15] The vast majority of those in the higher studies were foreigners, attracted to Geneva by the fame of the school as a fountain of Protestant theology. Within three years of its opening, it numbered among its scholars such names as those of Kaspar Olevianus, to be one of the two authors of the Heidelberg Catechism; of Philippe de Marnix de Saint-Aldegonde, of Netherlandish memory; of Florent Chrestien, tutor of Henry IV of France; of Thomas Bodley, the founder of the library known by his name at the English Oxford; of Francis Junius, later to be the ornament of the University of Leyden. France, England, Scotland, the Netherlands, Germany, Italy, and Switzerland had their representatives, but France most of all.[16]

---

[14] Borgeaud, i. 160–165.

[15] Ibid., p. 63.

[16] Borgeaud, i. pp. 55–63. Compare Kampschulte's interesting discussion, ii. 333–342.

The Academy was the crown of Calvin's Genevan work. It was a final step toward the realization of his ideal of a Christian commonwealth. To pure preaching and thorough discipline he now added religious education. His disciples should not merely have the evangelical faith, they should be able to give a reason worthy of the respect of every man of learning for the faith that was in them. Powerful as was the moulding force of the Academy upon Geneva, its influence was even greater outside the city's walls, for the students that it trained and inspired with the ideal that it championed, and the example that it presented, spread its spirit to France, the Netherlands, Scotland, and England. It sent out scores of earnest disciples, convinced that Calvin's message was that of God, and eager to fight and to suffer for the faith that it taught. It was the mother of the Huguenot seminaries. No other force was so powerful in disseminating Calvin's ideals, save his *Institutes*, and no school in all Protestantism ranked higher in public repute for a century after his death. Its honorable history has continued to the present day, when it has long since become in name, as it was always, one may say, in fact, the University of Geneva.

While these negotiations which resulted in the foundation of the Academy were in progress, Calvin was suffering from serious ill health. His constitution, long racked by overwork, anxiety, and excessive hours of study, was breaking, and he languished from September 1558, till the spring following, under attacks of intermittent disease then known as quartan fever. The symptoms would point to severe nervous dyspepsia. From this illness his health was never fully restored. Always extremely temperate in food and drink, from now onward he took regularly but one meal a day, and frequently in the distress of his attacks would pass forty-eight hours without food.[17] Much of his time from this illness onward he was compelled to spend in bed, going out to preach or lecture, and returning to his couch, to study, to dictate his letters, and to compose his books.

---

[17] Colladon, *Life, Opera*, xxi. 87–89, 109.

It is illustrative at once of Calvin's facility in the accomplishment of scholarly work, and of his firmness of will, that during this illness of the autumn and winter of 1558–1559, besides maintaining his enormous correspondence, and revising his commentary on Isaiah, he brought to its classic completion the perfected edition of the *Institutes*. This, in itself, was a scholarly task of great labor; and its accomplishment under circumstances of illness is doubly remarkable. The *Institutes* had now attained their growth. Issued in 1536, as has been seen, in six considerable chapters, they revealed Calvin's full theological development in the edition of 1539, but in that of 1559, under consideration, they exhibited the experienced teacher and the developed master of logical order. It was, as the title-page declared, "almost a new work." As now presented, the *Institutes* followed the sequence of the Apostles' Creed, and had grown to a compass of four books, in eighty chapters, though these chapters average much less in length than those of the original edition.[18] Designed for popular reading, as well as for scholars, the qualities of vivacity and clearness conspicuously mark this masterpiece of Reformation theology. From its publication, this edition of the *Institutes* became the standard presentation of the Calvinistic system. Its circulation was European. Before the definitive Latin edition of 1559, the *Institutes* had been repeatedly published in French, beginning in 1541, and once, in 1557, in Italian. In its final form, it appeared in French in 1560; in Dutch, during the same year; in English, in 1561; in German, in 1572; and in Spanish, in 1597. Before the close of the sixteenth century, to speak of no other versions, eight editions of the entire work had been issued in English, and abridgements in that tongue had been four times published.

Mention was made, in speaking of Calvin's labors during this illness, of his commentary on Isaiah, and earlier exegetical publications have been enumerated.[19] These series of Bible

---

[18] Text in *Opera*, ii. That of the French edition, published in 1560, is in vols. iii. and iv. The best English edition is that translated by Beveridge, 3 vols., Edinburgh, 1845–1846.

[19] *Ante*, p. 324.

expositions grew out of Calvin's theological lectures, which took largely the form of scriptural interpretation, and their publication continued as long as he lived. His commentary *Genesis and the Canonical Epistles* appeared in 1554, his *Harmony of the Gospels* in 1555, the year 1557 saw his exposition of the Psalms and of Isaiah; the Minor Prophets were explained in 1559, Daniel in 1561, the whole Pentateuch, Jeremiah, and Lamentations in 1563, and Joshua in 1564. It was not merely very extensive and rapid work that Calvin accomplished as a commentator.[20] It was the best work of biblical interpretation that the Reformation age produced. Brief, clear, of great spiritual insight, and resting on the basis of ample philological knowledge and of a sound and practical judgment, he held that each Scripture passage must be understood as containing a definite message, and not a threefold or fourfold meaning as the early Church and the Middle Ages had believed. That meaning was to be ascertained by natural grammatical and historical interpretation. The modern conceptions of a progressive revelation, and of human admixture of error, to say nothing of such views as regard the Bible as a literature embodying the religious conceptions of many ages and of a variety of writers, were of course unknown to him. The language might be the humble speech of a Paul, but the thoughts were those of the Holy Spirit. Yet, for his time, Calvin was remarkably fresh, translucent, and sensible in his comments, and the series of expositions from his Romans of 1540, to his Joshua of 1564, were second only to his *Institutes* and the Academy in the propagation of his theology.[21]

The time of the foundation of the Academy was not only one of physical distress to Calvin, it was a period of anxiety to the entire Genevan community in which the whole existence of the Reform movement there and the independence of the city seemed at stake. On April 3, 1559, the struggle between Henry II of France and Philip II of Spain was brought to a close by the peace of Câteua Cambrésis. As had been foreshadowed by the Spanish victory at

---

[20] These commentaries fill nearly all of vols. xxiii.–lv. of the *Opera*.

[21] Calvin's services as a commentator are well treated by Schaff, vii. 524–538, where references to the further literature of the subject are given.

Saint-Quentin, the results of the struggle had been decidedly favorable to Spain; and its ruler regarded the suppression of Protestantism as his God-appointed task. It was evident to all that the close of the armed contests between the two great Catholic powers would endanger the status of Protestantism, and the thirty years from 1559 to 1589 were to be the darkest period of the evangelical cause. For Geneva the situation brought about by the peace was alarming. Not only was the city justly regarded as the stronghold of French-speaking Protestantism, Calvin was, as there will be occasion to see in the next chapter, the real, though unofficial, head of the French evangelical party. His pupils were its ministers, his advice and exhortation had for years encouraged its struggles, his labors had made Geneva an asylum for its refugees. To crush Geneva would be to deal a blow to all French Protestantism, and as the event proved, though it was not then so evident, to that of the Netherlands also. The instrument seemed at hand. The victor of Saint-Quentin, Emmanuel Philibert, the young and able duke of Savoy, was restored by the peace to the territories which France had taken from his house.[22] It would be natural that he should seek also to gain what Bern had seized, and Geneva itself, in which his ancestors had had so large a stake. It was to be anticipated, too, that in this, or in some other, effort against its freedom Geneva would find itself confronted by the power of Spain and of France, eager to end an independence so obnoxious to the Roman cause.

Geneva was in anxiety, but not in panic.[23] On news of the peace, fortification was begun at once, and the month of the opening of the Academy saw, as Haller wrote from Bern to Bullinger, on June 22, all the inhabitants, "magistrates, ministers, nobles, artisans," working feverishly on its defences.[24] It was an exhibition of courage and firmness worthy of the little city which Calvin led. Yet, fortunately for Geneva, its guns and its earthworks were not

---

[22] To save French pride, this restoration was nominally subject to legal adjudication within three years. A. Armstrong, in *The Cambridge Modern History*, iii. 400.

[23] Roget, v. 249–266.

[24] Quoted, ibid., p. 254.

to be put to the test. Though Pope Paul IV urged the kings of Spain and France "to smother the snake in its nest," political and military jealousies prevented action lest one or the other sovereign gain the profit.[25] Geneva's chief deliverance came, however, through the unexpected death of Henry II, on July 10, 1559, from wounds received in a tournament. Though not immediately relieved from its fears, the turmoils and party divisions in France, begun with the brief reign of Francis II, and to lead, in 1562, to the Huguenot wars, rendered Geneva comparatively secure from any attack in which France or Spain should have a part. Though a fresh danger that was long to continue, was created when Emmanuel Philibert, after long negotiations, secured for the Savoyard House the restoration in 1564, the year of Calvin's death, of the territories on the south shore of Lake Geneva which Bern had conquered in 1536,[26] Geneva's political situation was never again so perilous during Calvin's life as in 1559 – while the intellectual influence of the city was vastly augmented from that date. It was indeed an advance-post of Protestantism, thrust into the midst of perils, but the foundation of the Academy was its noblest answer to its enemies.

The relations of the civil authorities of Geneva, now composed almost exclusively of Calvin's friends and admirers, took on increasingly an aspect of respectful reverence; but Calvin was indisposed to profit personally by their bounty. At the meeting of the Little Council, on May 22, 1559, at which he presented the statutes of the Academy about to be, he thanked the magistrates most heartily for their "great benefits" during his recent illness, but begged them not to carry out their purpose of paying the apothecary for the medicines prescribed. The Council voted "to remonstrate with him," requesting him to take it in good part, because it "wished to do that and more, if there was need."[27] Again, in June 1563, the Little Council made a donation of twenty-five *écus* to Calvin, through his brother, Antoine, to defray the cost

---

[25] Roget, ibid., pp. 255, 256, ascribes the unwillingness to Spain; Armstrong, op. cit., p. 405, to France.

[26] Armstrong, p. 405.

[27] *Registres du Conseil*, lv. 49; *Opera*, xxi. 716.

of medicines and other incidents of illness. Calvin promptly returned the gift with an expression of his grateful appreciation; and once more the Council asked him "to keep it and to spare nothing."[28] In his last illness in March 1564, the Council repeated the gift, only to have Calvin again decline it, this time with the message "that he felt scruples about receiving his ordinary salary when he could not serve."[29] Calvin was no self-seeker in financial relations, or exploiter of the bounty of others, even when freely offered, and his reserve in these cases is the more creditable since the gifts proposed were from the public treasury of a city which he had reason to feel that he had greatly served.

These endeavors to ease Calvin's increasing physical disabilities by pecuniary assistance were only a part of the expressions of governmental goodwill. On December 25, 1559, the Little Council requested him to become a burgher, an honorable invitation which he gratefully accepted.[30] In May following, it voted him a cask of the best wine to be found, "because indebted by reason of the great labors which he undertakes for the government"[31] and in his last illness, besides the money gift already mentioned, it ordered prayers on his behalf, directed the syndics to "visit him often"; and, finally, went in a body to his sick-room, on April 27, 1564, "to hear what he should wish to say, and afterwards to express to him all warm affection and friendship, even to his relatives after his decease, by reason of the acceptable services which he has performed for the government, and because he has acquitted himself faithfully in his office."[32] The message thus tersely indicated in the arid pages of the public records must have been grateful to Calvin's heart, and must have, sweetened with a sense of public recognition, achieved the recollection of many a bitter struggle and many a rebuff from the government which then did him affectionate reverence.

---

[28] *Registres du Conseil*, lviii. 67, 68; *Opera*, xxi. 804.

[29] Ibid., lix. 18, 20; xxi. 813.

[30] Ibid., lv. 163; xxi. 725.

[31] Ibid., lvi. 38; xxi. 731.

[32] Ibid, lix. 38; *Opera*. xxi. 815.

14

CALVIN'S INFLUENCE OUTSIDE OF GENEVA

Unremitting as was Calvin's struggle to make of Geneva a city answering to his religious ideal, he had always more than the reformation of that city in view. He would transform it into a model Christian community; he would render it an asylum for all who were oppressed in the profession of their evangelical faith; and, above all, by example, by hospitality, by training, by the sending forth of pastors, and by the influence of its ministers and magistrates, he would make Geneva a power for the spread of the Reformation. In all this effort he largely succeeded. Geneva was never to Calvin an end in itself. It was a means by which the conception he held of the Protestant faith should be advanced far beyond even the bounds of a single nation throughout western Europe. That non-German Protestantism, in spite of diversities of races, of governments, and of intellectual development, attained essential doctrinal unity, and so largely exhibited a common type of religious life, was primarily due to Calvin's forceful impress. Where, as in a certain section of the English Reformed party, other influences prevented the full dominance of Calvin's ideals, a divergent type of Protestantism was manifest; yet even Anglicanism felt the moulding touch of Calvin's doctrinal system for half a century after his death, and he struggled long for the mastery of England with a Puritanism that was almost wholly his own. Elsewhere in western Europe no influence was to be compared, during the latter half of the sixteenth century with that of Calvin.[1]

The prime reason for this influence was Calvin's transcendent ability as a theologian. The propagating and unifying power of the *Institutes* was due to the fact that in them the Reformation epoch received its clearest, most logical, and most characteristic presentation of Christian truth. However inadequate it may appear to our own age, there can be no question that, more than any other work, it seemed to the sixteenth century the ablest answer to Roman claims, and the most complete presentation of the gospel. Second only to the impressive power of the *Institutes* was the influence of the apparent realization of a Reformed Christian community in Geneva. Though to us Calvin's system gives the conviction of unendurable spiritual tyranny, there were thousands of his religious and earnest contemporaries to whom it seemed, as it did to John Knox, "the most perfect school of Christ that ever was on the earth since the days of the Apostles."[2] But, beside these gifts, as a theologian and an organizer, Calvin had a statesmanlike breadth of view which enabled him better than any other reformer to grasp the whole European religious situation. The only Protestant divine at all comparable to him in this quality of mind was Zwingle, and the field in which the Zürich pastor labored was relatively circumscribed.

As a preparation for Calvin's far-reaching acquaintance with the position and the possibilities of the evangelical cause, the circumstances of Calvin's life previous to his return to Geneva in 1541 were most fortunate. Acquainted as a student of law and of the humanities with a considerable circle in France outside of that moved by the religious impulse which became dominant in him by 1553, he rose to recognized leadership as the spokesman of French Protestantism by his letter to Francis I in 1536. His life at Basel brought him familiarity with northern Switzerland, his journeyings to Ferrara showed him a little of Italy, his stay

---

[1] A valuable account of Calvin's influence is that of E. Stähelin, *Johannes Calvin*, i. 505; ii. 244.

[2] In letter to Mrs Anne Locke, December 9, 1556. In *Works*, ed. Laing, iv. 240.

at Strassburg strengthened his hold upon the Protestantism of his native France, while bringing to him ample knowledge of the parties and leaders of Germany. By the time of his return to Geneva, he had become the most widely traveled and the most variously engaged of the reformers. Thenceforth his journeys were few; but Geneva became at once a city of refuge, and the future religious leaders of France, the Netherlands, England, and Scotland, in no small numbers, came thither to him.

Calvin's personal acquaintance was maintained and supplemented by the correspondence of remarkable extent. Even aided as he was by the constant employment of amanuenses, the number and importance of the epistolatory demands upon his strength, especially during the later years of his life, are such as to make evident the value which he attached to this means of serving the evangelical cause and its time-consuming burden.[3] The variety and significance of his correspondents are equally impressive. Besides his familiar and frequent letters to Farel, Viret, Bucer, Bullinger, and Beza, the roll of his correspondents contains such names of reformers as those of Melanchthon, Hedio, Brentz, Sturm, Jonas, Olevianus, and Sleidan of Germany;[4] Cranmer, Grindal, Hooper, Coverdale, Norton, Cox, and Whittingham of England; Knox of Scotland; Blaurer, Gryaeus, Haller, Musculus, Myconius, and Sulzer of Switzerland; à Lasco of Poland, Friesland, and England; the Italian refugees, Peter Martyr, Ochino, and Zanchi; the radicals Laelius Socinus and Servetus; besides many in France, including Admiral Coligny, Condé, and Anthony of Navarre. Many of his correspondents were of great social and political distinction. He wrote to Marguerite d'Angoulême, Renée of Ferrara; Somerset, the Lord Protector of England, and

---

[3] The surviving letters to, from, and about Calvin fill volumes xb.–xx. of the *Opera*, and number 4,271 pieces. Calvin's own letters, beside a number the address of which is uncertain, were directed to no less than 307 persons and bodies; and this collection must contain only a portion of those actually written.

[4] Luther should perhaps be mentioned, though Calvin's acquaintance with him was slight and they never met. *Ante*, p. 243.

Edward VI of that realm; Frederick III, the elector Palatine; Philip of Hesse, and Sigismund August, King of Poland. They are letters of a writer fully acquainted with the usages of the cultivated world: clear, tactful, energetic, seldom of much personal emotion, but penetrated by a profound conviction of the truth of his cause, a marvelous grasp of the situation, and a transparent appeal to the reason and will. He warns, he comforts, he intercedes, he gives the news of the hour, he endeavors to foster the evangelical cause, and to bring victory in the contests in which he was engaged in Geneva and beyond the borders of the city.

Calvin's thoughts turned first of all to his native France. For him Geneva was always a vantage point for French evangelism. Situated on the borders of France, and speaking the language of that land, Geneva was naturally the city toward which French refugees turned. Calvin welcomed them and, in turn he made Geneva a power for the propagation of Reformed ideas in the homeland.[5] French Protestantism had always had its large proportion of unacknowledged adherents, and toward them, in spite of their danger from persecution, Calvin directed his utmost urgency. In his *Petit traicté monstrant que c'est que doit faire un homme fidèle congnoissant la verité de l'Èvangile quand il est entre les Papistes*,[6] published as a reply to many individual inquiries in 1543, he urged the duty of complete conformity to the gospel:[7]

> I am asked what advice I would give to a believer who is thus
> dwelling in some Egypt or some Babylon where he is not allowed
> to worship God purely, but is constrained, according to the
> common fashion, to accommodate himself to evil things. First,
> that he go forth, if he is able ... If any one has not the means of
> going away, I would counsel him to consider whether it is not

---

[5] On Calvin's relations to French Protestantism, see Karl Müller, Calvin und die Anfänge der franzosischen Hugonottenkirche, in the *Preussische Jahrbücher*, cxiv. 371–389 (December, 1903); A. A. Tilley, in *The Cambridge Modern History*, ii. 287–296. Of less value is H. Diener-Wyss, *Calvin: ein aktengetreues Lebensbild*, Zürich, 1904, pp. 80–97.

[6] *Opera*, vi. 537–588.

[7] *Opera*, vi. 576.

possible for him to abstain from all idolatry ... furthermore that he make it his duty to instruct and edify the poor ignorant people as far as he is able. If he answers that he cannot do this without danger of death, I acknowledge it. But the glory of God, which is here in question, ought to be much more precious to us than this fading and transitory life.

To many French Protestants this seemed hard doctrine, and to these accommodating and halting souls Calvin replied in 1544, in his *Excuse ... à Messieurs les Nicodemites*[8] – a nickname which he coined for them. But to many, also, Calvin's insistence on the maintenance of "the glory of God," was a trumpet-call to utmost self-sacrifice.

Calvin was in no way indifferent to the course of governmental repression to which he urged such manful though wholly spiritual resistance. His efforts while at Regensburg to secure German action aimed at a mitigation of persecution in France have already been noted.[9] On his return to Geneva they were continued, when occasion demanded, though with little success. On the outbreak of the savage attack upon the Waldenses of Provence in 1545, he aroused the Genevan government to assist the fugitives and, with its countenance, journeyed to Bern, Basel, Zürich, Schaffhausen, and Strassburg to secure action by the several Protestant governments on their behalf.[10] Each case of persecution for the evangelical faith was to Calvin a matter of profound interest and, as far as possible, of effort on behalf of the victim, either by exciting Protestant attempts at intervention, or by letters of encouragement to those under suffering – though of course the fate of the majority of martyrs was too speedily determined to permit either form of attempted assistance.

One of the most notable instances of Calvin's masterly relation to the cause of the persecuted in France occurred in 1552 in connection with the "five scholars of Lausanne." Severe

---

[8] Ibid., pp. 559–644.

[9] *Ante*, p. 242.

[10] Letters in *Opera*, xii. 75–84; see also xxi. 352–354. See Baird, *Rise of the Huguenots*, i. 244–251; *The Camb. Mod. Hist.*, ii. 289.

as was the persecution under Francis I, after the placards its
intensity was increased after the accession of Henry II in 1547.
Five young Frenchmen, who had studied under Beza and Viret
at Lausanne, now on their way home to preach the evangelical
faith, were arrested in May 1552 at Lyons, and sentenced by the
ecclesiastical court. By an appeal to the Parlement of Paris their
death by fire was delayed till May 16, 1553. The government of
Bern, and of other cantons, protested to the King in vain on their
behalf, and Calvin sent to them encouragement, without a trace
of sentimentality, but breathing a spirit like that of a commander
in battle.[11] A single quotation may exhibit this quality:[12]

> It is needful that you sustain hard conflicts, that that which
> was said to Peter be accomplished in you: "You shall be carried
> whither ye would not." But you know in what strength you have
> to fight; upon which all who rely shall never be surprised and
> still less confounded. Therefore, my brothers, be confident that
> you will be strengthened according to your need by the spirit of
> our Lord Jesus that you fail not under the burden of temptations,
> however pressing they may be, any more than He who had so
> glorious a victory that it is an infallible pledge to us of our
> triumph in the midst of our miseries. If He pleases to make use
> of you even to death in His battle, He will uphold you by His
> mighty hand to fight firmly, and will not suffer a single drop of
> your blood to remain useless.

The whole evangelical cause in France drew strength from the
contagious example set by Calvin at Geneva, from the courage
of the preachers that he trained and the firmness of his system of
churchly organization. In some respects that system was at its best
outside of Geneva; for in a degree unmatched by that of any other
of the reformers it suited the needs of an oppressed cause which
had to rely on its own inherent strength. In Geneva the principles
enunciated in the *Institutes* were limited by dependence on a civil
government theoretically friendly and co-operant, but often jealous

---

[11] *Opera*, xiv. 331, 423, 469, 491, 544; Baird, i. 283–285; *The Cam. Mod. Hist.*, ii. 293.
[12] *Opera*, xiv. 423.

of ecclesiastical independence. In lands where the authorities were hostile, or of another race as at Strassburg, Calvin's Church government showed its full power. Lutheranism, Zwinglianism, and Anglicanism were dependent on the State; Calvinistic Presbyterianism secured a self-governing, intelligently served, and strictly disciplined Church – an ecclesiastical *imperium in imperio*.

Calvin discouraged the formation of churches, with the administration of the Sacraments, until the close-knit congregation after the Genevan model could be had.[13] Informal assemblies of evangelical believers had existed more or less continuously in Paris, Meaux, Nîmes, and elsewhere in France, but in 1555, the considerable organization of Protestant churches, equipped on the Genevan pattern with pastors, elders, and deacons began. In that year, the Paris congregation was definitely organized, and others were constituted in Angers, Poitiers, Loudon, and Arvert. Churches in Blois, Montoire, Bourges, Issoudun, Aubigny, and Tours followed in 1556; Orléans and Rouen were thus supplied in 1557 and in 1558, no less than twenty came into being. By the beginning of 1559, there were seventy-two in France.[14] Under Calvin's leadership, Geneva set itself to supply them with pastors, and these churches in turn looked to Calvin for their ministry. In 1559, nineteen ministers were either asked of or sent from Geneva; in 1560, twelve; while in 1561 the number of demands for such assistance rose to ninety.[15] It was, of course, impossible for Geneva to supply all this need, but between 1555 and 1566, one hundred and twenty pastors were sent by the *Vénérable Compagnie* to French churches.[16] No wonder French Protestantism was moulded by Calvin's spirit.

In spite of relentless persecution, the French Church went forward with its organization. From May 26 to 28, 1559, the first Protestant General Synod met at Paris. A firm constitution,

---

[13] Müller, op. cit., p. 384.

[14] *The Camb. Mod. Hist.*, ii. 293, 294; Müller, op. cit., p. 385. The number of Protestant gatherings, of incomplete organization, was much greater.

[15] *Opera*, xxi. 710–771.

[16] *The Camb. Mod. Hist.*, ii. 294; the same work, p. 373, gives the number as 161.

on Calvin's principles, was adopted, by which adjacent churches were grouped in a "colloquy," and the neighboring "colloquies" in a "provincial synod," while all were represented in a national synod. A confession of faith was issued, often, though apparently erroneously, attributed to Calvin, but epitomizing with great clearness his theological system, and largely the work of his devoted pupil, Antoine de la Roche Chandieu.[17] A great national Church, for the first time in Reformation history, was created independent of a hostile State, and the work was one for which Calvin had given the model, the inspiration, and the training, even though its actual accomplishment aroused, at the moment, his anxiety rather than won his approval.[18] With its churches he continued in constant correspondence. They sought his advice in difficulties and his comfort in trial. In a real sense, Calvin was a bishop to the Huguenot congregations of France and took upon himself, so long as he lived, the "care of all the churches."

As the Protestant cause developed in France, it began to attract converts from the higher classes, and by the time of the first meeting of the General Synod it was becoming a political party as well as a religious propaganda. Calvin promptly put himself in communication with these more distinguished converts. By 1558 he was writing to François d'Andelot, whose conversion to Protestantism had been wrought by Calvin's publications, to Anthony of Navarre and to Admiral Coligny. He followed with painful interest the course of persecution that marked the last days of Henry II, and the accession of the Guises to power when Francis II came to the throne in July 1559. He disapproved of the plot to break the control of that intensely Catholic family in March 1560, known as the "Tumult of Amboise."[19] He had no confidence in such illegitimate intrigues, and distrusted the use of force. Yet he was glad to have Beza do what he could to arouse the King of

---

[17] Text, *Opera*, ix. 731–752; Schaff, *Creeds of Christendom*, iii. 356–382. See also *Opera*, ibid., p. lvii; Schaff, ibid., i. 493; *The Camb. Mod. Hist.*, ii. 295; Stähelin, in *Realencyklopädie*, iii. 677; Müller, op. cit., p. 388.

[18] See Calvin's letter of May 17, 1559, *Opera*, xvii. 525.

[19] Letters to Bullinger, Blaurer, and Coligny, *Opera*, xviii. 84, 95, 425.

Navarre to put himself at the head of a proposed demonstration of a more legitimate character in the south of France which, had Anthony of Bourbon been a man of vigor, might easily have led to civil war in the summer of the same year.

With the death of Francis II on December 5, 1560, the power of the Guises was broken, and the position of French Protestantism immediately improved. Its adherents were growing rapidly in numbers, and in July 1561, the evangelicals were summoned to present their case before the new king, Charles IX. At the colloquy held in consequence at Poissy in September following, the Protestants were represented by twelve ministers, headed by Beza. They would gladly have had Calvin as their spokesman, but even his most ardent friends did not dare advise so hated a foe of the older communion to expose himself to the dangers of a journey to France, nor was the Genevan Little Council willing that he should thus imperil his life.[20] With the following March, and the massacre at Vassy, the great Huguenot wars began, but Calvin could well hope that the peace of Amboise, of March 18, 1563, by which the first of the long series of struggles was ended, was but the dawn of the triumph of Protestantism in his native land, though he disapproved its relatively slight advantages to the cause he had at heart and felt much anxiety for the future.[21] To his thinking war was a poor means of advancing the gospel. "I would always counsel," he wrote on news of the peace, "that arms be laid aside, and that we all perish rather than enter again on the confusions that have been witnessed."[22] Calvin did not live to see the renewal of the conflict.

In the neighboring Netherlands Calvin's theologic and organizing influence proved as determinative as in France, though he exercised no such superintendence as there over the churches – few of which, indeed, were founded till near the close of his life. Under the influx of preachers from France into the French-speaking southern provinces, the movement in the Netherlands in

---

[20] *Opera*, xviii. 555; xxi. 755; Baird, *Theodore Beza*, p. 136.

[21] *Opera*, xix. 687–693.

[22] Ibid., p. 688.

favor of Protestantism, which in its beginnings had been Lutheran and Anabaptist, became prevailingly Calvinistic. Most extensive at first among the Walloons, it won its strongest support, though not till after Calvin's death, in the northern territories which were ultimately to gain their independence of Spain. Guy de Bray, the Netherlandish martyr, to whom, whatever may have been the aid received from others, the preparation of the Belgic Confession of 1561 was due, had almost unquestionably come into personal relations with Calvin at Frankfort in 1556.[23] This Confession, which was to become a doctrinal basis of the Reformed Church of Holland and of its spiritual offspring in America, was modelled in large part on that adopted by the Huguenot synod at Paris in 1559,[24] and shows its author to have been a convinced disciple of Calvin. As in France, and amid even severer struggles, the Calvinistic system proved itself a discipline for battle. The State Church of the victorious northern provinces was to be one of the most eminent members of the Calvinistic family.

Calvin's relations to the leaders of the Reformation in England and Scotland were even more direct and personal. He wrote to the Lord Protector, the Duke of Somerset, in the early months of the reign of Edward VI, urging strenuous preaching of pure doctrine, extirpation of Roman abuses, and vigorous discipline. "You have," said Calvin, "two sorts of headstrong fellows who raise themselves against the King and the state of the kingdom. The one is of fantastic folk who would put all in confusion under pretence of the Gospel. The other is of persons obstinate in the superstitions of the Roman antichrist. Both will deserve to be repressed by the sword which is intrusted to you."[25] He corresponded with Cranmer. He exhorted the young King to support the Reformation cause with zeal. As Edward's brief reign advanced, his influence and the acceptance of his doctrines in England increased. But it was by reason of the cordial welcome that Calvin gave to the exiles whom

---

[23] L. A. van Langeraad, in Hauck's *Realencyklopädie*, iii. 364. For the Confession and its history see Schaff, *Creeds of Christendom*, i. 502–508; iii. 383–436.

[24] *Ante*, p. 385.

[25] October 22, 1548, *Opera*, xiii. 65–90.

the policy of Mary drove to seek shelter on the Continent, and their acquaintance with his system, at its Genevan fountainhead, that his following in England was chiefly developed. Those refugees, rejected by the Protestant cities of northern Germany on account of their non-conformity to Luther's views of the Lord's Supper, found in Calvin a warm friend. He endeavored, though without success, to heal the breach between the adherents of the English Prayer Book and their more radical opponents in the exiled congregation at Frankfort. Though his sympathies were with its critics, the English service seemed to him, at worst, to be chargeable only with "many endurable trifles."[26] When the Frankfort refugees divided on the issue, he welcomed to Geneva the critical wing, led by John Knox, and secured for their use, and that of the Italian Protestant exiles, the Church of Mary the New (the "Auditoire"), with careful definition of their rights of worship in their own languages.[27] On one day in October 1557, no less than fifty English refugees were admitted inhabitants of the city and, on May 30, 1560, when the favorable reign of Elizabeth permitted their return to England, these sojourners for their faith formally thanked the Genevan government for the hospitality they had enjoyed.[28]

The return of the Marian exiles to England was followed by a greatly increased acquaintance with, and acceptance of, Calvin's system in that land. The more eager Protestants looked upon the reform of the Church largely from his point of view. They desired its further purification from Roman observances, the establishment of an earnest, preaching ministry, and of a thorough parochial discipline. The result was the growth of the Puritan party – a movement which was only in its beginnings at the time of Calvin's death, but which was to grow all through the reigns of Elizabeth and James, to lead to the settlement of New England, and to wrest the scepter for a time from the House of Stuart. In the Confession and Catechisms of the Westminster Assembly, called in 1643, in the midst of the great Civil War, Calvinism was to be

---

[26] January 18, 1555, *Opera*, xv. 394. See also 337, 554, 776.

[27] Ibid., xxi. 619, 620 (November, 1555).

[28] Ibid., pp. 676, 732.

given a symbolic expression that is still in its essential features the recognized creed of thousands of Christians in Scotland and America. And even where Calvin's theories of Church organization and discipline were rejected, there was in England for years after his death a general use of his *Institutes* and Catechism in the theological instruction in the universities, and a wide sympathy with his theology, of which that archenemy of the Puritans, Archbishop John Whitgift, may be cited as an illustration.

Calvin's connection with the Reformation in Scotland was closely bound up with his association with the chief Scottish reformer, John Knox. The beginnings of Knox's evangelical activity in Scotland, and his imprisonment by the French captors of St Andrews, were followed by ministerial labors in England under the reign of Edward VI. Soon after the accession of Mary he had to fly to the Continent, and in 1554 was in Geneva, an eager student of theology and of Hebrew, and an enthusiastic admirer and disciple of Calvin. From Geneva he went, in the same year, to become a preacher to the mixed congregation of English and French refugees at Frankfort, only to involve that body in controversies over the use of the Edwardine liturgy, and to be forced to leave the city in March 1555. With his fellow believers he now made his way once more to Geneva. Thence, in the autumn of the same year, Knox returned to Scotland to spend a few stormy months in premature efforts to establish the Reformation. The close of the summer of 1556 saw him once more in Geneva where he now became the pastor of the English fugitive congregation – an office which he held till his final and successful return to Scotland in May 1559. The estimate in which he was held by Calvin and his Genevan friends is shown by his gratuitous admission, on June 24, 1558, as a burgher of the town – the records curiously describing him as "of Scotland in England, English minister in this city."[29]

Knox's return to Scotland was followed by the sharp battle for the establishment of Protestantism and its victorious outcome in the summer of 1560. The new Kirk of Scotland, erected with such

---

[29] *Opera*, xxi. 697.

violent overthrow of older institutions, and as a consequence of what was no less a civil than a religious revolution, was fashioned on the model created by Calvin. Its Confession, drafted by Knox and his associates in four strenuous days of August 1560,[30] was essentially Calvinistic. It emphasized true preaching, the right administration of the Sacraments, and the characteristic Calvinistic trait of discipline, as the notes of the Church; it viewed the "conservation and purgation" of religion as a prime duty of civil rulers. The worship of the Scottish Church, Knox attempted to regulate after the model of the English refugee services in Geneva. Its Presbyterian constitution, with the session of minister, elders, and deacons in each normal congregation; the stated meetings which soon developed into "presbyteries," the district "synods," and the "General assembly" of ministers and delegated elders over all, was the application to the whole kingdom of the principles of the *Institutes* as already embodied in the practice of Geneva and of the Huguenot churches of France. If Knox in his "superintendents" retained a prelatical element in his constitution, it was destined to be short-lived. In Scotland, Calvinism was to bear some of its noblest fruits. It proved marvelously adapted to the training of the nation, from the semi-barbarism of pre-Reformation days into the forceful, intelligent, able Scotland of modern history. If the great Reformation upheaval was given its form by the genius of Knox, his work was moulded and made possible by the training and inspiration that flowed from Calvin.

The Genevan reformer followed the course of Knox's work in Scotland with affection for a disciple, as well as with interest in the cause. Knox presented inquiries, signing himself *vobis addictissimus*. In replying, Calvin addressed him as *eximie vir et frater nobis carissime*. He had a word of moderation for Knox's rough-shod impetuosity, but the work as a whole must have been one of thorough satisfaction to Calvin.[31]

---

[30] Schaff, *Creeds of Christendom*, i. 680–685, iii. 437–479. Election and reprobation, though taught, are not made so prominent as they would probably have been by Calvin. Presbyterianism is not a *jure divino* polity.

[31] See letters in *Opera*, xvii. 619, 665; xviii. 434; xix. 74.

Calvin's influence penetrated even earlier to eastern Europe, with much apparent prospect of large results, though with far less permanency and ultimate success than in the countries just considered. In Poland, Calvin's teaching found a prompt hearing, not only as offering the most effective weapon against the strong Roman party, but as more acceptable than anything which savored of German origin – a source which the Polish leaders viewed with no little jealousy. By 1545, Calvinism was spreading rapidly among the nobles and educated classes of "Little Poland" about Cracow. Calvin's *Institutes* were widely read. In 1549, Calvin dedicated his *Commentary on Hebrews* to the young king, Sigismund Augustis.[32] The King, who was at heart a very tolerant Catholic, married a sister of Nicolas Radziwill, the leading Calvinist among the nobility. Calvin wrote to Sigismund and to Radziwill in 1554 and 1555, earnestly commending activity in the Reformation cause, and favoring, at least by implication, the retention of an episcopal order in Poland.[33] The next year he was invited to Poland by the Calvinistic ministers and nobles assembled in a synod at Pinczow – a request to which he returned a regretful refusal in March 1557.[34] His interest and participation by letter in Polish affairs continued unabated; but the work of organization which Calvin might have undertaken was carried on from the close of 1556 till ended by death in 1560 by John à Lasco, already distinguished in Friesland and England. It promised much. But, though Calvin did not live to witness its decline, the Protestant cause was soon weakened in Poland by internal quarrels between Lutherans, Calvinists, and anti-trinitarians. It never took strong hold upon the lower classes and, with the exception of à Lasco, never developed a champion of commanding abilities.

In yet another region of eastern Europe, Calvinism became a power, though at a somewhat later period than in Poland. In Hungary its appeal was especially to the Magyar element in

---

[32] *Opera*, xiii. 281. See R. N. Bain, in *The Camb. Mod. Hist.*, iii. 74–86; Dalton, in Hauck's *Realencyklopädie*, xv. 514–525.

[33] *Opera*, xv. 329, 428; especially, 333.

[34] Ibid., xvi. 128, 420.

the population. At a Calvinistic synod held at Czenger in 1557 or 1558, the Hungarian Confession was drafted, and by 1563, Calvinism was widespread and its characteristic discipline and organization introduced.[35] Calvinism in Hungary has survived the vicissitudes of fierce persecution, and the adherents of churches Calvinistic in origin and profession even now number two-thirds of the evangelical population of the land, or not far from one-seventh of its inhabitants.

Calvin's most difficult relations were with the churches of German-speaking Switzerland which were his nearest neighbors. Already established before he began his work, and not in the making, as were those of which mention has been made, they were not easily to be moulded to his ideas. Their constitutions all gave an ecclesiastical authority to the civil magistrates which he rejected in theory, and in practice so far as he was able at Geneva. Bern stood in constant hostility to his system of discipline, and never became wholly reconciled to his teaching in his lifetime. The freer thought of Basel looked with grave suspicion on his emphasis on predestination. In Zürich he was long regarded as too much of a Lutheran on the doctrine of the Lord's Supper. Yet he obtained an agreement, in 1549, with the Zürich divines, led by the peace-loving Bullinger, on this burning question of the Reformation age, that paved the way to more friendly relations which resulted ultimately in the general acceptance of Calvin's doctrinal system in essential, if moderate form, though not of his disciplinary peculiarities, by all the Protestant churches of Switzerland. The work of Zwingli was absorbed in the larger and abler development due to Calvin, very much as was the theological system of Bucer.

The agreement between the spiritual leaders of Geneva and Zürich shows to much advantage the skill and good feeling of both. Calvin, as has already been pointed out,[36] was far more in sympathy with Luther than with Zwingli in the conception of Christ's presence in the Supper set forth in the first edition of the *Institutes*, though denying to that presence the physical

---

[35] Schaff, *Creeds of Christendom*, i. 589–592.

[36] *Ante*, p. 142.

quality which Luther had made so essential. Bullinger, who had succeeded at Zwingli's premature death to the leadership of the Zürich ministry, had departed from Zwingli so far as to lay much greater emphasis than he on the work wrought by Christ through the sacrament in the believing recipient, and was consequently approaching Calvin's intermediate position between the interpretations of founders of German and Swiss Protestantism. Agreement on this much-disputed question was therefore relatively easy and, after considerable correspondence in 1548 and 1549, supplemented by personal conference, Calvin and Bullinger united, in the year last named, in the Consensus of Zürich.[37] Undoubtedly in this agreement, and in his desire for union, Calvin went as far as he could in the Zwinglian direction. Bullinger's decidedly modified Zwinglianism was substantially unaltered.[38] Any form of physical presence was rejected. But an emphasis wholly agreeable to Calvin, and not objectionable to Bullinger, was laid on the true spiritual union wrought between Christ and the believer by the sacrament, while a characteristically Calvinistic note was struck in the restriction of the reception of its benefits to the elect. Not printed till 1551, this Consensus was soon accepted not merely by the churches of Geneva and Zürich, but by those of Schaffhausen, St Gall, Neuchâtel, and Basel, and constituted a bond of theologic union between German and French-speaking Switzerland.

Calvin had less success, as has already been noted in speaking of the controversy with Bolsec, in securing prompt acceptance for his uncompromising presentation of the doctrine of a twofold predestination. The Genevan Consensus of 1552 on this matter failed to secure a symbolic authority outside that city.[39] But the doctrine, in Calvin's interpretation of it, even if with some caution in expression, won its way in the Reformed churches and here, as elsewhere, the mastermind of the Genevan reformer tended to

---

[37] Text, *Opera*, vii. 659–748; see also ibid., xii. 480, 590, 705, 727; xiii. 110, 164, 221, 223, 259, 278; Schaff, *Creeds*, i. 471–473.

[38] Egli and Heer, in Hauck's *Realencyklopädie*, iii. 543, 545.

[39] Text, *Opera*, viii. 249–366.

bring all non-Lutheran and non-Anglican Protestantism under its sway.[40]

The agreement of the Swiss churches on the nature and effects of Christ's presence in the Supper, brought about by the Consensus of Zürich, became the occasion of the bitterest doctrinal controversy of Calvin's later life – that with the extreme Lutheran, Joachim Westphal of Hamburg, who regarded its denial of Christ's physical presence not merely as a restatement of the hated Zwinglian heresy, but believed that by attacking it he was defending original and pure Lutheranism against secret Melanchthonian modifications. In the bitter exchange of controversial pamphlets that ensued from 1552 to 1557, and again in the dispute on the same thorny doctrine with Tilemann Hesshusen of Heidelberg and Magdeburgh in 1560 and 1561,[41] Calvin claimed Melanchthon for his doctrine, and with no little justification, though the cautious German reformer held himself as far as possible from the battle. The struggle gave to Calvin, however, a painful feeling of estrangement from the German Protestants, whose leaders he had earlier known and admired and whose interests he had defended with his pen against the emperor, Charles V.

Though Calvin's relations to the German divines of the stricter Lutheran school thus became increasingly strained during the later years of his life, he had the satisfaction of seeing his theology, though only in a very moderate degree his system of Church discipline, begin a career of conquest on German soil that was to be continued long after his death.[42] The bitterness of the attack made by the strict Lutherans upon the Philippists, as the followers of the moderate Melanchthon were styled, drew these

---

[40] A discussion of much value is that of Prof. B. B. Warfield, "Predestination in the Reformed Confessions," in the *Presbyterian and Reformed Review*, January, 1991, pp. 49–128.

[41] *Opera*, ix. 1–120, 137–252, 457–524.

[42] An excellent epitome of this theme, with references to its literature, is that of Gustav Kawerau, in the 2nd ed. of Moeller, *Lehrbuch der Kirchengeschichte*, iii. 276–292.

milder Lutherans into increasing sympathy with the Genevan reformer. Agreeing at first with Calvin principally in the essential features of his theory of Christ's presence in the Supper, and little inclined to accept his strenuous views of predestination, the exigencies of conflict with their ultra-Lutheran opponents, the force of the *Institutes*, and to some extent the influence of the Genevan Academy in attracting and impressing its students, inclined the Philippist party, especially in southwestern Germany, • to a growing appreciation of Calvinism. It was in the Palatinate that these results were most evident in Calvin's lifetime.

Frederick III, of the Palatinate, long of earnestly religious temper, was led by the controversies between the extreme Lutheran Tilemann Hesshusen, already mentioned, and the latter's deacon, Wilhelm Klebitz of Heidelberg, to a careful study of theology which left him a convinced Calvinist. He now summoned to his aid two young divines, both personally acquainted with Calvin and Bullinger: Kaspar Olevianus in January 1560, and Zacharias Ursinus in September of the year following. Olevianus had studied in the Genevan Academy, while Ursinus had been a pupil of Melanchthon at Wittenberg. Both were earnest Calvinists. By these theologians, one twenty-six and the other twenty-eight years of age, with the help of other churchly leaders of the Palatinate, the famous Heidelberg Catechism was prepared in 1562, and set forth by order of the Elector in 1563.[43] Sweet spirited, experiential, clear, moderate, and happily-phrased, the Heidelberg Catechism has always been regarded as one of the noblest presentations of the Calvinistic system in its least controversial aspects. As such, it is the most widely accepted symbol of the Calvinistic faith. Calvin himself could not possibly have written it; but Olevianus, gratefully recognizant of student days at Geneva and anxious for Calvin's help in the establishment of Church discipline, sent Calvin an early copy, with an affectionate letter in which he addresses the Genevan reformer as "*carissime pater*."[44] Calvin, in

---

[43] Text, Schaff, *Creeds*, iii. 307–355. See M. Lauterburg, in Hauck's *Realencyklopädie*, x. 164–173; Schaff, i. 529–554.

[44] *Opera*, xix. 683; see ibid., 538.

turn, dedicated his *Lectures on Jeremiah*, of 1563, to the Elector.[45] The discipline regarding which Olevianus wished Calvin's aid was introduced, though imperfectly in 1570, when elders were ordered in every parish. With greater success public worship was reduced to Genevan simplicity.

Though the Palatinate was carried back to strict Lutheranism under Frederick's son, Lewis IV (1576–1583), and more than 500 Calvinistic ministers and teachers deprived of office, the tables were turned, and Calvinism restored under Lewis' brother, John Casimir. Calvinism continued to win recognition in Germany long after Calvin's death, gaining Nassau in 1577 a strong footing in Bremen, Anhalt, Baden, and Hesse before the close of the sixteenth century, and in Brandenburg, its most important conquest after that of the Palatinate, in 1613. Yet it was Calvin's theology rather than his discipline that thus won assent, and the observation of a modern German historian that the Calvinistic churches of Germany constituted "an intermediate stage between pure Calvinism and pure Lutheranism"[46] is amply justified.

Calvin for one brief period looked beyond the bounds even of Europe, and shared in an attempt to plant the evangelical faith in the New World. Like the reformers generally, he was strangely insensitive – so it seems to the modern Christian world – to the claims of missions.[47] But when the treacherous Villegagnon sought to strengthen his ill-fated and mismanaged colony in Brazil, in 1556, by securing Protestant recruits and Protestant preachers, Calvin provided two ministers from Geneva with letters to him and encouraged them on their enterprise, which, though having the spiritual welfare of the settlers primarily in view, did not wholly forget the needs of the natives.[48] The colony was soon ruined by Villegagnon's own duplicity and

---

[45] Ibid., xx. 72.

[46] Kawerau, op. cit., p. 277.

[47] Ibid., p. 409; G. Warneck, in Hauck's *Realencyklopädie*, xiii. 127–130; ibid., *History of Protestant Missions*, Eng. trans., pp. 19, 20.

[48] See letters of Villegagnon and of the ministers from Brazil to Calvin, March, 1557, *Opera*, xvi. 433–443. On the colony, see Parkman, *Pioneers of France in the New World*, pp. 16–27.

cruelty, and with it ended Calvin's only direct connection with efforts to establish Protestantism beyond the Atlantic. Calvin's system was to be a powerful influence in moulding the religious history of America. The English Puritans, the Scotch and Irish Presbyterians, the Hollanders, and the Huguenot exiles of France were to establish his faith, and to a large extent his polity, wide over the North American continent; but this work was yet far in the future when he died.

Calvin would gladly have secured a more visible and effective evidence of the spiritual union of Protestantism and its fellowship in doctrine and in opposition to Rome than proved feasible under the conditions of the sixteenth century. When the English archbishop, Thomas Cranmer, proposed to him in March 1552, that a council of learned Protestants should be gathered, to promote the unity of the evangelical churches, and to offset the Roman council then meeting at Trent, Calvin welcomed the plan with enthusiasm, and declared his readiness to support it to his utmost;[49] but it remained only a pious wish.

In this wide extended influence is to be seen one of Calvin's largest claims to permanent remembrance. He knit the forces of non-Lutheran Protestantism into a real spiritual communion animated by similar ideals and dominated by one view of the Christian life. The ill-related Reformation movements of France, of the Netherlands, of Scotland, to a less degree of Poland and Hungary, found in him their unifying force. He gave them creed, discipline, and organization. He formulated their theology. He inspired their martyr-courage. He taught them how best to oppose Rome. He trained many of their leaders, provided them a city of refuge in persecution and an example of the disciplined Christian community which attracted their admiration and imitation. Over all this vast region he exercised an unofficial but far-reaching episcopate. By constant correspondence, by personal acquaintance and appeal to those whom he never met face to face, by the labors of those who had been his pupils and reproduced

---

[49] Letters in *Opera*, xiv. 306, 312.

his spirit, he moulded the growth and determined the form of the Reformation movement to a degree comparable with the work of no other among the reformers save Luther. But for him the story of the Reformation outside of the land of its birth would have been vastly different. He has been called "a pope,"[50] but the designation is apt only in its indication of the geographical extent of his authority. That authority was not due to office or peculiar advantage of station. It was purely one of mind over mind. But it was all the more real and long-enduring. Calvin so impressed his interpretation of Christian truth and of the Christian life upon men that they thought his thoughts after him, and his ideas became part of the mental fabric of a large portion of the inhabitants of central and western Europe, and ultimately of North America.

The influence of Calvinism, for more than a century after the death of the Genevan reformer, was the most potent force in western Europe in the development of civil liberty. What the modern world owes to it is almost incalculable. Yet Calvin was never by intention a political reformer. His interest was always overwhelmingly religious, and the results of Calvinism in the cause of religious freedom were the indirect and unexpected, rather than the anticipated, consequences of his work. They were the effect of the logic of Calvin's principles, rather than any conscious part of his reformatory aim.

Calvin's views on civil government are succinctly stated in the *Institutes* and come to their fullest expression in the final form of that work issued in 1559. Its object is,[51]

> that no idolatry, no blasphemy against the name of God, no calumnies against His truth, nor other offences to religion, break out and be disseminated among the people; that the public quiet be not disturbed, that every man's property be kept secure, that men may carry on innocent commerce with

---

[50] E.g. W. H. Frere, *The English Church in the Reigns of Elizabeth and James I*, p. 78.
[51] *Inst.*, IV. xx. 3; Beveridge's translation, Edinburgh, 1846. See also W. A. Dunning, *A History of Political Theories from Luther to Montesquieu*, pp. 26–33.

each other, that honesty and modesty be cultivated; in short, that a public form of religion may exist among Christians, and humanity among men.

In Calvin's opinion and practice the preservation of religion is an even more important function of the State than the maintenance of order. As to the various types of government, each has its characteristic dangers. No one is absolutely best:[52]

> Monarchy is prone to tyranny. In an aristocracy, again, the tendency is not less to the faction of a few, while in popular ascendancy there is the strongest tendency to sedition.

His own preference, characteristic alike of his temperament and of his Genevan environment is for "aristocracy, either pure or modified by popular government"; but no one form is adapted to all times and places, nor ought changes to be agitated, for,[53]

> if it has pleased Him [God] to appoint kings over kingdoms, and senates or burgomasters over free states, whatever be the form which He has appointed in the places in which we live, our duty is to obey and submit.

To Calvin's mind the obligation of obedience even to bad rulers is no less complete:[54]

> If we have respect to the Word of God, it will lead us farther, and make us subject not only to the authority of those princes who honestly and faithfully perform their duty toward us, but all princes, by whatever means they have so become, although there is nothing they less perform than the duty of princes.

Diets and parliaments, indeed, have the duty of restraining the tyranny of unworthy rulers; but the private citizen must submit, save with one fundamentally important exception:[55]

---

[52] Ibid., IV. xx. 8.
[53] Inst., IV. xx. 8.
[54] Ibid., IV. xx. 25.
[55] Ibid., IV. xx. 32.

We are subject to the men who rule over us, but subject only in the Lord. If they command anything against Him, let us pay the least regard to it, nor be moved by all the dignity which they possess as magistrates.

There is little in these utterances of Calvin's mature judgment, except in that last quoted, to stimulate civil freedom; but the principle that when God commands, all obedience to human rulers ceases, is of far-reaching influence. It struck a note already sounded by Zwingli that, more than any other, served to interpret the intellectual individualism of the Renaissance and the religious individualism of the Reformation in terms of political freedom. Who shall decide whether a command of a ruler is contrary to the will of God, if not each thinking man, weighing it by the tests of his own divinely implanted judgment? Calvin formulated no such conclusion, but his principle inevitably tended to make men question the rightfulness of human statutes and institutions, and to demand some other justification for obnoxious laws than the mere fact of their enactment by those in authority.

Calvin's ecclesiastical constitution, moreover, made for civil freedom, especially in the conditions of his age. His insistence that the Church, though served by the State, was yet independent of it, gave a place – as in Scotland and in France if not so fully in his own Genevan practice – for the development of a system of representative ecclesiastical institutions largely free from State control. In the Scottish General Assembly, for instance, rather than in the Scottish Parliament, was to be found throughout the latter portion of the sixteenth and the whole of the seventeenth centuries the truer embodiment of the wishes and hopes of the people of Scotland. French Protestantism, from 1559 onward, found expression in a series of national synods held in the face of a hostile government.

The system of Church discipline characteristic of Calvin, executed in the congregation, or in Geneva as the work of the united Church of the city, by an aristocracy of the minister or ministers and his associated lay elders, made every Calvinistic parish a school of government in a sense true of no other communion of the Reformation age, while his principle that officers should serve only with the consent of the congregation over which they were placed, however imperfectly worked out under Genevan conditions, had in it the germ of a real responsibility of ecclesiastical governors to those whom they ruled. Calvin did not carry the principle to its logical consequences, but it is impossible for men long to hold one theory in ecclesiastical and another in civil government. If Church officers are responsible to the people they serve, why not kings and magistrates? Scotland and Puritan England asked the question and wrote the answer large in the history of the seventeenth century. King James I of England, voiced the results of this aspect of Calvinism, and its effects on such theories of the absolute monarchy as he entertained, when he declared at the Hampton Court Conference in 1604:[56]

> A Scottish Presbytery as well agreth with a Monarchy, as God and the Devill. Then *Jacke*, and *Tom*, and *Will*, and *Dick* shall meet, and at their pleasures censure me and my Councell, and all our proceedings.

Calvin's aristocratic soul might have revolted as much as the Stuart King's from the democratic freedom thus satirized, but it was none the less a natural fruit of his system.

The Calvinistic theory of the Church furnished, moreover, the only effective system in the Reformation age for the organization of an oppressed Protestant party. Lutheranism, Anglicanism, and Zwinglianism were all dependent upon the State; Calvinism could be effective without State support, as France, Holland, Scotland, and England were to bear abundant witness. But it was only where Calvinism did its work as a discipline as well as a theology that its services to civil liberty were considerable. Where, as in Germany, its position was that of a representative of a certain type of doctrine, and not also of a peculiar conception of the Christian life, its effect on political thought was inconspicuous.

---

[56] W. Barlow, *The Summe and Substance of the Conference*, London, 1638, p. 81.

15

CALVIN'S THEOLOGY

Within the brief compass allotted to this volume no adequately comprehensive treatment can be given to so extensive a theme as Calvin's theology, but its salient features must at least be cursorily described. As has already been pointed out, Calvin built on the general foundation laid by the reformers who had preceded him. To Luther and to Bucer he owed the basal elements of his own theologic structure. Without their antecedent work – certainly without that of Luther – his would never have been accomplished. Yet he so clarified and systematized evangelical theology, and so stamped his own genius upon its presentation, that he ranks pre-eminently as the theologian among the reformers, and as one of the three or four greatest expounders of religious truth in Christian history. This work has its illustration in his commentaries, and minor treatises but above all in the *Institutes*, which came to its completeness in the classic edition of 1559.[1] Foremost in Calvin's system was his emphasis on the great thought of God. His sovereignty extends over all persons and events from eternity to eternity. His will is the ground of all that exists. His glory is the object of all the created universe. He is the sole source of all good everywhere, and in obedience to Him alone is human society or individual action rightfully ordered. His

---

[1] *Opera*, ii. The quotations in this chapter are from Beveridge's translation, Edinburgh, 3 vols., 1845–1846.

honor is the first object of jealous maintenance by the magistrate, or of regard by the citizen. Good laws are but the embodiment of His will; and complete surrender to Him is man's prime duty and only comfort. His kingly sovereignty, His glorious majesty, His all-perfect and all-controlling will are the highest objects of man's adoration, and the prime concern of all human interest. By His permission kings rule, and for each member of the human race He has an unalterable and supremely wise plan from all eternity. Infinitely transcending the world of created things, in honor, dignity, and power, God touches it, and all human life, at every point with His righteous law and majestic sway. "Our very being is nothing else than subsistence in God alone."[2] To know Him is the supreme object of human attainment.

But how is God to be known? Calvin answers that sufficient knowledge of Him is implanted in the human mind to leave the wicked without excuse, but this natural theology is supplemented and made clear by "another and better help" – that of the divine revelation in the Scriptures, the writers of which were "sure and authentic amanuenses of the Holy Spirit."[3] By these alone is God adequately made known. "There is an inseparable relation between faith and the Word, and these can no more be disconnected from each other than rays of light from the sun."[4] "The full authority which [the Scriptures] ought to possess with the faithful is not recognized, unless they are believed to have come from heaven, as directly as if God had been heard giving utterance to them."[5] This conviction can, indeed, be fortified by arguments drawn from their arrangement, dignity, truth, simplicity, and efficacy; "still it is preposterous to attempt, by discussion, to rear up a full faith in Scripture." Our confidence "must be derived from a higher source than human conjectures, judgments, or reasons; namely, the secret testimony of the Spirit."[6] The Bible is therefore

---

[2] *Institutes*, Bk. I, chapter i, section 1.
[3] IV. viii. 9.
[4] III. ii. 6.
[5] I. vii. 1.
[6] I. vii. 4.

no arbitrary body of truth to be accepted on the authority of the Church or of external miracles. It approves itself to men by its own clear illumination, by the response of the soul enlightened by the Spirit of God to the voice of the same Spirit speaking through its pages. That testimony carries with it acceptance of all that the Scriptures contain. "Those who are inwardly taught by the Holy Spirit acquiesce implicitly in Scripture."[7] It is no mere Christian consciousness selecting and appropriating truth wherever truth can be found; it is Truth itself awakening recognition of its clear, ample, and final authority in the divinely enlightened soul. In this doctrine of the absolute and unique authority of the Word of God, Calvin stood on ground common to all the reformers, and his teaching as to the immediate witness of the Holy Spirit had been anticipated, though less clearly by Luther.[8] But his presentation of this cardinal principle of the Reformation is the amplest that it had yet received, and may be said to be its classic expression. Far more than Luther, however, Calvin treated the Scriptures as a new law regulative of the Christian life.

While God is thus the source of all that is good, man in his present fallen state is in himself wholly bad. As created in Adam – and Adam with Calvin, as with Augustine, is a personage of great significance – man was made in the image of God, with all the good endowments and qualities therein implied; but he fell by "infidelity," ambition, and pride, together with "ingratitude," and that fall involved all the race in original sin: "a hereditary corruption and depravity of our nature, extending to all the parts of the soul, which first makes us obnoxious to the wrath of God, and then produces in us works which in Scripture are termed works of the flesh."[9] The consequences are a total depravity of all human nature. "The soul, when plunged into that deadly abyss, not only labors under vice, but is altogether devoid of good."[10] As with Augustine, so in Calvin's conception, man is absolutely unable to

---

[7] I. vii. 5.
[8] F. Loofs, *Leitfaden zum Studium der Dogmengeschichte*, 3rd ed., pp. 373, 431.
[9] II. i. 4, 8.
[10] II. iii. 2.

aid himself in his fallen estate, nor has he even a co-operant part, as with Melanchthon, in a salvation begun and made possible by God. "The will is enchained as the slave of sin, it cannot make a movement towards goodness, far less steadily pursue it. Every such movement is the first step in that conversion to God, which in Scripture is entirely ascribed to divine grace."[11] True, God has not so left man in his ruin as to deprive him of all aid to righteous action. "Whatever excellent endowments appear in unbelievers are divine gifts ... He visits those who cultivate virtue with many temporal blessings ... [but] those virtues, or rather images of virtues, of whatever kind, are divine gifts, since there is nothing in any degree praiseworthy which proceeds not from Him."[12] In an evil plight, all men are incapable themselves of real good; their condition is one of deserved, yet helpless, condemnation.

From this hopeless state some men are undeservedly rescued by the mercy of God. The means by which this deliverance is effected is by the work of Christ, by which in His threefold office of Prophet, Priest, and King He wrought salvation for them. "Christ, in His death, was offered to the Father as a propitiatory victim." "Not only was the body of Christ given up as the price of redemption, but that which was a greater and more excellent price – that He bore in His soul the tortures of condemned and ruined man."[13] He paid the penalty due for the sins of those in whose behalf He died. Yet this propitiation of the Father implied no diversity of feeling between the Persons of the Trinity. With Scotist emphasis on the unconditioned will of God as the highest object in the universe, Calvin declares that even "Christ could not merit anything save by the good pleasure of God."[14] His sacrifice was of value because the Father chose to put value on it, and to order it as the way of salvation. Hence Father and Son were at one in providing, offering, and accepting the ransom. "The love of God" is its "chief cause or origin."[15]

---

[11] II. iii. 5.

[12] III. xiv. 2.

[13] II. xvi. 6, 10.

[14] II. xvii. 1.

[15] II. xvii. 2. Compare G. B. Stevens, *The Christian Doctrine of Salvation*, pp. 153, 154.

But all that Christ has wrought is without avail unless it becomes man's personal possession. "So long as we are without Christ and separated from Him, nothing which He suffered and did for the salvation of the human race is of the least benefit to us." "He must become ours and dwell in us." He is "our Head."[16] This indwelling is effected by faith on man's part; but this faith, which, as with Paul and Luther, is no mere acceptance of historic facts or of a system of belief, but a vital union in a new life between the believer and Christ, is due to nothing in man, but has its origin in "the secret efficacy of the Spirit."[17] Its consequence and inseparable accompaniment is repentance. While genuine disciples may at times be assailed by doubts, "full assurance" is a proper attribute of this faith, doubts must be temporary, and "he only is a true believer who, firmly persuaded that God is reconciled and is a kind Father to him, hopes every thing from His kindness, who, trusting to the promises of the divine favor, with undoubting confidence anticipates salvation."[18]

The consequence of this faith is the Christian life. "Christ cannot be known without the sanctification of His Spirit, therefore faith cannot possibly be disjoined from pious affection."[19] That life, far more than in Luther's conception of it, is one of struggle and effort in which the Law, though no longer the test of acceptance with God, is the stimulus to endeavor. "The whole lives of Christians ought to be a kind of aspiration after piety, seeing they are called unto holiness. The office of the Law is to excite them to the study of purity and holiness by reminding them of their duty."[20] Calvin thus saves himself, in spite of his doctrines of election, irresistible grace, and perseverance, from any possible antinomianism. He leaves room for a conception of "works" as strenuous and as effort-demanding as any claimed by the Roman communion, though very different in relation to the accomplishment of salvation.

---

[16] III. i. 1.
[17] Ibid.
[18] III. ii. 15, 16.
[19] III. ii. 8.
[20] III. xix. 2.

"We are justified not without; and yet not by works, since in the participation of Christ, by which we are justified, is contained not less sanctification than justification."[21] "If the end of election is holiness of life, it ought to arouse and stimulate us strenuously to aspire to it, instead of serving as a pretext for sloth."[22]

Calvin is next confronted by the evident fact that men are very unalike in their reception of the gospel. "Among a hundred to whom the same discourse is delivered, twenty perhaps, receive it with the prompt obedience of faith; the others set no value upon it, or deride, or spurn, or abominate it."[23] Holding, as Calvin does, that all good is from God, and viewing man as helpless to initiate or resist his conversion, Calvin can but ascribe this dissimilarity to "the mere pleasure of God." He was not peculiar in this view. The Reformation age was markedly one of revived Augustinianism. In its essential features the doctrine of election had been equally the property of Luther and Zwingli. Melanchthon, under the influence of his belief in the power of the human will to cooperate with or resist the divine leadings, was swinging away from it, and was ultimately to lead the Lutheran churches in the direction that he pointed out, but an acceptance of predestination was widely characteristic of the theology of the age. Yet the use which Calvin made of the doctrine is far more vital than that of Luther, for example. To Luther the prime question was always, how are men saved? When he asked why, and he did not often ask the question, he gave the Augustinian answer. To Calvin, as to Bucer before him, the problem of the origin of salvation was of much more fundamental importance, and this significance was strengthened by his controversies with Bolsec. Yet it is an error to describe predestination as the "central doctrine" of Calvinism,[24] though it became so under his successors and interpreters. Its prime value for him was always its comfort as giving assurance of salvation to the Christian believer.

---

[21] III. xvi. 1.

[22] III. xxiii. 12.

[23] III. xxiv. 12.

[24] A Schweizer, *Die protestantischen Centraldogmen*, i. 57; see R. Seeberg, *Lehrbuch der Dogmengeschichte*, ii. 397.

Calvin advanced beyond Augustine in two ways. The great African theologian had represented God as active in election to life only. The lost were simply passed by and left to the deserved consequences of sin. To Calvin's thinking, election and reprobation are both alike manifestations of the divine activity. In Augustine's estimate, not all believers are even given the grace of perseverance. With Calvin all in whom God has begun the work of salvation would have it brought to complete fruition. Calvin's severe logic, insistent that all salvation is independent of merit, led him to assert that damnation is equally antecedent to and independent of demerit. The lost do indeed deserve their fate, but "if we cannot assign any reason for His bestowing mercy on His people, but just that it so pleases Him, neither can we have any reason for His reprobating others but His will." The sole cause of salvation or of loss is the divine choice:[25]

> The will of God is the supreme rule of righteousness, so that everything which He wills must be held to be righteous by the mere fact of His willing it. Therefore, when it is asked why the Lord did so, we must answer, Because He pleased. But if you proceed further to ask why He pleased, you ask for something greater and more sublime than the will of God, and nothing such can be found.

Whether this Scotist doctrine of the rightfulness of all that God wills by the mere fact of His willing it leaves God a moral character, it is perhaps useless to inquire. The thesis here advocated has always had its earnest supporters and its determined critics. But of the comfort which Calvin and his disciples drew from the doctrine of election there can be no question. To a persecuted Protestant of Paris it must have been an unspeakable consolation to feel that God had a plan of salvation for him, individually, from all eternity, and that nothing that priest or king could do could frustrate the divine purpose on his behalf. Nor was it less a source of strength to one profoundly conscious of his own sinfulness to feel that his

---

[25] III. xxii. 11; xxiii. 2.

salvation was based on the unshakable rock of the decree of God Himself. Reprobation, too, gave an explanation for the hostility of rulers to the evangelical cause, and for the great number of those who, in that age, as in any epoch, were notoriously irreligious of life. Calvin was far too political a man to suggest that a Henry II or a Catherine de' Medici were of the reprobate, but it must have been a grim satisfaction for those under their persecuting sway to believe that they and others like them "were raised up by the just but inscrutable judgment of God, to show forth His glory by their condemnation."[26]

Calvin's doctrine of the Church has often come under our notice in this volume. It is the means by which we are nourished in the Christian life. "To those to whom [God] is a Father, the Church must also be a mother."[27] Following the line already marked out by Wyclif, Huss, and Zwingli, Calvin defines the Church in the last analysis as "all the elect of God, including in the number even those who have departed this life."[28] But, besides its application to this invisible fellowship, the name "Church" is properly used of "the whole body of mankind scattered throughout the world who profess to worship one God and Christ, who by baptism are initiated into the faith, by partaking of the Lord's Supper profess unity in true doctrine and charity, agree in holding the Word of the Lord, and observe the ministry which Christ has appointed for the preaching of it."[29] Whoever alienates himself from it is a "deserter of religion." Yet to leave the papacy is in no sense to leave the Church, for "it is certain that there is no Church where lying and falsehood have usurped the ascendancy."[30] Calvin admits, however, that even in the Roman communion some vestiges of the Church exist, though in ruins.

This visible Church is properly governed only by officers of divine appointment made known in the New Testament. These

---

[26] III. xxiv. 14.
[27] IV. i. 1.
[28] IV. i. 2.
[29] IV. i. 7.
[30] IV. ii. 1.

are pastors, teachers, elders, and deacons – partly clerical and partly lay office-bearers, for in Calvin's system the recognition of the rights of the layman, characteristic of the whole Reformation movement, comes to its completest development. This recognition receives further illustration in that the officers of the Calvinistic churches, unlike those of the Roman, Anglican, Lutheran, and Zwinglian communions, properly enter on their charges only with the assent of the congregation that they serve. Their "call" is twofold: the secret inclination which has God as its author, and their election "on the consent and approbation of the people."[31] Peculiar circumstances at Geneva disposed Calvin to regard that "consent of the people" as there expressed by the city government; but elsewhere, especially where Calvinism was face to face with hostile civil authority, the system developed its more normal form.

One main object of the establishment of Church officers is discipline, the importance of which in the Calvinistic system, as contrasted with other theories of the Church current in the Reformation age, there has been frequent occasion to point out. "As the saving doctrine of Christ is the life of the Church, so discipline is, as it were, its sinews." It "is altogether distinct from civil government," and belongs "to the consistory of elders, which [is] in the Church what a council is in a city." "The legitimate course to be taken in excommunication ... is not for the elders alone to act apart from others, but with the knowledge and approbation of the Church, so that the body of the people, without regulating the procedure, may, as witnesses and guardians, observe it, and prevent the few from doing anything capriciously."[32]

This ecclesiastical independence which Calvin emphasized more than any other of the reformers and for which he fought with such intensity and persistence at Geneva was very far, however, from implying that civil government had no duties toward the Church. Minister and magistrate were alike charged with the administration of government in the name of God. Further than

---

[31] IV. iii. 15.
[32] IV. xi. 1, 6; xii. 1, 7.

excommunication the Church could not go. When that failed or was insufficient for the enormity of the offence, as in the case of flagrant heresy or crime, the magistrate, as equally charged with maintaining the honor of God, must apply his civil penalties. His duty it was to defend, support, and care for the Church, though in its proper sphere the Church was to be independent of his control. Calvin thus took up into his system the characteristic theory of the Middle Ages regarding this matter, carefully guarding it, however, from becoming, as the mediaeval contention too often was, an assertion of the supremacy of the Church over the State. It was to become the view of Puritanism and to have ample illustration, for instance, in the early history of New England.

Characteristic of Calvin is his doctrine of the Sacraments, and of the Lord's Supper in particular. Nowhere was his desire for the union of divided Protestantism more evident than in the treatment of these vexed questions, in spite of the heat of his later polemic with Westphal and Hesshusen.[33] He stood, as has already been pointed out, in an intermediate position between Luther and Zwingli. To Calvin the value of a sacrament is that of a seal attesting God's grace. "It is an external sign, by which the Lord seals on our consciences His promises of goodwill toward us, in order to sustain the weakness of our faith, and we in turn testify our piety towards Him."[34] Baptism "is a kind of sealed instrument by which He assures us that all our sins are so deleted, covered, and effaced that they will never come into His sight."[35] The benefit is not wrought by the sacrament itself; it accompanies it, and is received only by the predestinate. "From this sacrament, as from all others, we gain nothing, unless in so far as we receive in faith." To them it is a perpetual witness to forgiveness, so that there is no room for the Roman doctrine of penance. "The godly may ... whenever they are vexed by a consciousness of their sins, recall the remembrance of their baptism, that they may thereby

---

[33] *Ante*, p. 398.
[34] IV. xiv. 1. See a most valuable brief treatment of Calvin's views in Seeberg, *Lehrbuch der Dogmengeschichte*, ii. 401–409.
[35] IV. xv. 1.

assure themselves of that sole and perpetual ablution which we have in the blood of Christ."[36] The rite, Calvin argues at great length, and with much use of the analogy of circumcision, is to be administered to infants as well as to those of years of intelligence.

In Calvin's conception, as in that of the Roman and Lutheran Communions, whatever else the Lord's Supper may signify, it is "a spiritual feast, at which Christ testifies that He Himself is living bread on which our souls feed for a true and blessed immortality."[37] The heart of the discussion in the Reformation age was, however, as to the nature of Christ's presence in this sacrament. Luther had insistently asserted, in substantial agreement with the older Church, that that presence is physical. Zwingli rejected all physical presence, made the chief value of the Supper its memorial character, and reduced the nourishment of the participating soul to a stimulation of faith in His death for us. To Calvin's thinking, as to Zwingli's, it seemed impossible that Christ's physical body could be at the same time in heaven and in many places on earth. "Let no property be assigned to His body inconsistent with His human nature."[38] But Calvin's religious feeling revolted, no less than Luther's, from any representation that did not imply a true presence of Christ in the Supper and that "only makes us partakers of the spirit, omitting all mention of flesh and blood." "By the symbols of bread and wine, Christ, His body and His blood, are truly exhibited to us."[39] Yet this participation is spiritual and by faith. "It is enough for us, that Christ, out of the substance of His flesh, breathes life into our souls, nay, diffuses His own life into us, though the real flesh of Christ does not enter us."[40] Christ "breathes" into the disciple "power"; He "feeds" him. But only the disciple receives. "I deny," said Calvin, "that it can be eaten without the taste of faith, or, (if it is more agreeable to speak with Augustine), I deny that men carry

---

[36] IV. xv. 4, 15.
[37] IV. xvii. 1.
[38] IV. xvii. 19.
[39] IV. xvii. 7, 11.
[40] IV. xvii. 32.

away more from the sacrament than they collect in the vessel of faith."[41] Calvin's relations to Luther and Zwingli have been well defined by a recent writer:[42]

> If one asks whether Calvin's doctrine approaches nearer to Luther or to Zwingli, the decision is usually rendered, through credal interests, in favor of the latter. But if one observes that, in contrast to the purely subjective commemorative interpretation of Zwingli, Calvin accepts a special presence of the living Christ, together with the religious inworking thereby caused, in the manner of Luther, we may, nevertheless, conclude, – while recognizing the permanent dissimilarity – that in religious comprehension of the sacrament Calvin stands nearer to Luther than to Zwingli.

The doctrinal positions just enumerated contain the main emphases and chief peculiarities of Calvin's theology, though they by no means exhaust the round of his teaching. On such themes as the judgment, the resurrection, or future rewards and punishments, he stood on the common basis of the religious thought of his age, and had little, if anything, novel to offer for their elucidation.

In Calvin's exposition the theology of the Reformation age rose to a clearness and dignity of statement and a logical precision of definition that have never been surpassed. A logician of critical acumen, a lawyer by training, a master of Latin and of French expression, a humanist, a student of history and of Christian antiquity, Calvin brought to the service of Christian theology gifts which must always make the *Institutes* a classic presentation of doctrine. But to recognize the transcendent qualities of his work is by no means to assert its perpetuity. His system has been no exception to the general rule of modification and supersession which seems essential to all progress even in the apprehension of the deepest of Christian verities. Calvin's system has stood the test of time better than most expositions of religious truth,

---

[41] IV. xvii. 33.
[42] Seeberd, op. cit., ii. 404.

but it has suffered a general attrition, and though the degrees in which its various aspects are now rejected are very unequal, it is nowhere held in its pristine integrity; while the larger part of the Protestant world, even in the churches which most honor his memory, has turned far aside from it.

Most universally abandoned is Calvin's conception of the duty of civil rulers to guard the purity of the Church. A trial like that of Servetus has happily long been impossible, and the first name on the list of subscribers to Servetus' monument at Geneva is that of the Consistory of the present Genevan Church which traces its historic continuity from his foundation. His doctrines of election and reprobation aroused profound dissent in the early seventeenth century, and Arminianism preserves the memory and the results of the protest then initiated. Even where these explanations of God's ways with men are nominally maintained they are held in reality with far less than his rigor and with little of his sense of satisfaction. His valuation of discipline has been wholly rejected. No modern Christian community would tolerate the iron inquisitorial rule which he laid on Geneva; and discipline, even in its milder forms, instead of being thought of as a prime duty of the ministerial office, is now regarded as one of the most difficult and seldom-to-be-employed means of Christian edification.

More widely accepted in theory, perhaps, but none the less generally abandoned by modern Christian thinking, is his view of human nature as utterly depraved. The appeal of evangelists and the training of the Sunday school and of the catechetical class alike now addresses itself to those whom they regard as indeed enfeebled by sin and in grievous need of divine aid, but not hopelessly incapable of turning to or of accepting the light. Much modern thinking in churches which still regard Calvin as their spiritual ancestor, denies that men are, even in their worst state, other than wandering children of God, needing to be made conscious of their sonship, but in no sense useful in their destruction only. Nor has the modern Christian world followed Calvin in confining all revelation to the Scriptures. The protest begun by the Quakers in the seventeenth century has become common property. The thought of the Reformation age that a God who rules the world by the constant activity of His providence, and whose Spirit works how and when and where He will, has yet confined all revelation to long-closed Scriptures, is recognized as inconsistent. The light is seen to have been and to be much more widely diffused than Calvin imagined, and to have shone not merely in ages but among peoples who, to his thinking, had been consigned by God's decree to utter darkness.

Nor is Calvin's estimate of the Scriptures themselves that of the modern Christian world. Their writers are almost nowhere now viewed as "amanuenses" of the Holy Spirit. The human element in them, though in very varying degrees of apportionment, is everywhere recognized as real. A degree of progress in revelation, of which he never dreamed, is universally admitted. With many, even their inspiration, in the sense in which he understood it, is denied. His interpretation of patriarch, psalmist, and prophet is inconsistent with that evolutionary philosophy under the light of which the present age believes that it has come to truer and worthier views of man's religious development. His ideal Adam, so marvelous in endowments, and so fateful in relation to the race, has been very generally relegated to the legendary explanations of the origin of evil; his restriction of salvation to those under the light of the gospel little accords with the modern sense of the extent of the divine compassion. His theory of the atonement gives to it a significance as a penal satisfaction now widely abandoned. His emphasis on the sovereignty of God has been increasingly displaced by a clearer conception of the divine Fatherhood.

To the present Christian world Calvin's representations of the divine dealings with men seems not without considerable elements of hardness and even of cruelty. That they so appear is, it may be hoped, to be ascribed to clearer apprehensions of the gospel and of the message, life, and significance of Christ.

But while Calvin's system as a whole can no longer command the allegiance it once claimed, its value in the progress of Christian thought is not to be minimized or forgotten. It laid a profound emphasis on Christian intelligence. Its appeal was primarily to the intellect, and it has trained a sturdy race of thinkers on the problems of the faith wherever it has gone. It has been the foe of popular ignorance, and of shallow, emotional, or sentimental views of Christian truth. Equally significant as an educative force has been its insistence on the individual nature of salvation. A personal relation of each man to God, a definite divine plan for each life, a value for the humblest individual in the God-appointed ordering of the universe, are thoughts which, however justly the social rather than the individual aspects of Christianity are now being emphasized, have demonstrated their worth in Christian history. Yet perhaps the crowning historic significance of Calvinism is to be seen in its valuation of character. Its conception of the duty to know and do the will of God, not, indeed, as a means of salvation, but as that for which we are elected to life, and as the only fitting tribute to the "honor of God" which we are bound to maintain, has made of the Calvinist always a representative of a strenuous morality. In this respect Calvin's system has been like a tonic in the blood, and its educative effects are to be traced in the lands in which it was held sway even among those who have departed widely from his habit of thought. The spiritual indebtedness of western Europe and of North America to the educative influence of Calvin's theology is well-nigh measureless.

16

CALVIN'S LAST DAYS – HIS PERSONAL TRAITS AND CHARACTER, 1564

As has already been pointed out, Calvin's position in Geneva was absolutely assured from the time of the defeat of the Perrinists in 1555. Whatever dangers thenceforth threatened him and his system were from without the city, not from within. He had triumphed within its walls. His conception of a city obedient to the will of God in Church and State, served by an educated body of ministers, disciplined by ecclesiastical watch and strict magisterial supervision, and taught by excellent schools, had been largely realized. Not but that there was much for the Consistory to reprove and for the Little Council to punish in the lives of the citizens. The iron discipline and drastic inquisitionary inspection of Genevan morals were now given their fullest development; but the ideal of a perfected society for which Calvin had striven was now clear, and to many, seemed to have been more fully realized than at any previous time in Christian history. Geneva stood in the thought of a large section of evangelical Christendom as a model Christian commonwealth.[1]

Calvin was now almost universally honored by the inhabitants of the city not only as its most eminent resident, but as a well-

---

[1] Calvin's last days are well described by Colladon and Beza, who were contemporary witnesses, *Opera*, xxi. 95–118, 160–172. A careful, though too critical, estimate is that of Kampschulte, ii. 354–387.

nigh infallible interpreter of that Word of God which the new generation of citizens had been taught by him to regard as the ultimate law of public and private conduct and belief.

By his critics outside of Geneva he was called its "pope," "king," or "calif." A simple-minded refugee, who spoke of him as "Brother Calvin," was quickly reminded that in Geneva "Master Calvin" was the only fitting form of address.[2] His voice oftenest spoke the disciplinary sentences of the Consistory. It was he who expressed the wishes and the criticisms of the ministers to the Little Council. He was largely consulted in affairs of State. His advice greatly influenced the political relations of the city.

Yet Calvin's ripened fame and power brought no change in title or in official position. He was still simply one of the city pastors, a preacher at Saint-Pierre, and a teacher of theology. His clothing was very plain, his house scantily furnished for one in his station.[3] Though considerable sums of money passed through his hands, especially in the form of gifts for needy refugees, his administration was to the utmost scrupulous; he refused presents even from the city government, and his salary barely sufficed to meet the very modest demands of his own living and the cost of a freely bestowed but exceedingly simple hospitality. His whole estate amounted to less than 200 écus, the equivalent in value perhaps from $1500 to $2000, including the worth of his library.[4] He had enough, however, for his modest wants and was satisfied with his thoroughly unostentatious ménage.

In personal appearance, Calvin "was of medium height, of a rather pale and dark complexion, with eyes clear even to his death, which evidenced the sagacity of his mind." Greatly emaciated in later life by illness, his face was little changed to the last.[5] The slight figure, with the strongly marked features, broad,

---

[2] Kampshculte, ii. 376, 387.

[3] Colladon, Opera, xxii. 113. An inventory of furniture allowed him by the city, made in 1548, may be found, ibid., xiii. 135. The whole matter is carefully discussed by Doumergue, iii. 491–508.

[4] Colladon, Opera, xxi. 113; see also, the notes of the Strassburg editors, ibid., xx. 301; and Doumergue, iii. 481–483. Calvin's will named 225 écus of bequests.

high forehead, bright eyes, and rather scanty beard, must always have carried an impression of scholarly refinement; but Calvin's chief graces were those of intellect and spirit – vivacity, clarity, impressive earnestness, keen penetration, felicitous and striking characterization. Men felt an intellectual and moral masterfulness in him, perhaps the more strongly because its physical embodiment so imperfectly bespoke its greatness. Calvin's capacity for work was prodigious. When not in extreme ill health,[6]

> he preached every day of each alternate week; he lectured three times each week on theology; he was at the Consistory on the appointed day, and spoke all the remonstrances; what he added at the Conference on the Scriptures every Friday which we call the Congregation ... was equal to a lecture; he was not neglectful in the visitation of the sick, in special remonstrances, and in other innumerable concerns having to do with the ordinary exercise of his ministry.

Beza reckoned his sermons at 286 annually and his lectures as only 100 less in number.[7] To these must be added his constant work on his *Institutes* and other theological treatises, his long and frequent consultations with those who sought his counsel, and above all his correspondence, some account of the voluminous extent of which has already been given.[8] Such a multiplicity of duties left scanty opportunity for special preparation. He worked with great rapidity and, even in expository lectures, took nothing but the text of the Scriptures into the desk. Here his retentive memory stood him in good stead. All that he had ever read was at ready command. Nor was he less observant of men. Though he mingled little in familiar intercourse with the people of Geneva, and must have been to most of them rather a remote and awe-inspiring figure, he constantly surprised his associates in the Consistory by his recollection of past offenders and his minute accuracy as

---

[5] Colladon, ibid., xxi. 105; Beza, ibid., p. 169.

[6] Colladon, ibid., p. 66.

[7] Kampschulte, ii. 376, from Beza, *Tract. theol.*, ii. 353.

[8] *Ante*, p. 378.

to previous censures. A large proportion of his letters and of his scholarly writing was dictated, and interruptions seemed rarely to break the chain of his thought or compelled him to read over what he had said before the visit or the new demand upon his attention compelled the suspension of his task.[9]

While he could at times display much oratorical skill, as in the crisis of December 1547, of which some account has already been given,[10] Calvin in general spoke with great simplicity, brevity, and directness. He avoided rhetorical ornament. Clarity and logical strength added an intellectual impressiveness to the weight of his thought, while his evident earnestness of conviction lent an emotional force to his quiet delivery. He spoke slowly, and could therefore easily be followed by those who would take notes. Much of his work as a commentator owed its preservation to the zeal of his auditors, who wrote from his oral delivery what he afterwards prepared for the press.[11] His sermons and lectures always commanded a crowded congregation.

Calvin kept long hours in his study. "He slept little"; by five or six in the morning his books were brought to him in bed and his amanuensis was ready. Much of the morning, even on days on which he preached, he lay on his couch, believing a recumbent position better for his weak digestion – but always at work. After the single meal which constituted his daily repast in the latter part of his life, he would walk for a quarter of an hour, or at most for twice that time, in his room and then return to the labors of the study. Sometimes, chiefly when urged by his friend, he would play a simple game – quoits in his garden, or "clef" on the table in his living room.[12] He was not indisposed to good humored chaffing. He was not insensible to a pleasant garden or a cheerful outlook from his windows, but his few recreations were briefly enjoyed.

---

[9] Colladon, *Opera*, xxi. pp. 108, 109.

[10] *Ante*, p. 309.

[11] *Opera*, xxi. 70, 132; xxix. 238; Kampschulte, ii. 376–378.

[12] Colladon, *Opera*, xxi. pp. 109, 113. Doumergue, ii. 527–563, has made the utmost possible of this side of Calvin's character. In the game of "clef" the keys were pushed on a table, the aim being to bring each contestant's nearest to the further edge without falling off.

Calvin's acquaintance was vast, but his intimate friends were few. With Farel, Viret, and Bullinger, he remained for years in constant correspondence. Beza was to him as a son in his last days.[13] His brother Antoine, the Colladons, Trie, des Gallars, Michel Cop, Laurent de Normandie, a few of the refugees, and magistrates, enjoyed his full confidence. His fascination of manner for his friends was always marked. If he had none of the genial *bonhomie* of Luther, he was no misanthrope. His comparative isolation of spirit was that of a man compelled to husband his strength to the utmost, of aristocratic tastes, and with little leisure or inclination for anything which did not bear on the accomplishment of his task. With his few familiar friends, however, he stood on terms of cordial intimacy.

From the time of his prolonged illness in the autumn and winter of 1558–1559, Calvin's health, never vigorous at best, and long undermined by overwork, anxiety, and want of exercise, was evidently greatly impaired. That illness left its mark in a lameness that at times involved distress; and a yet more serious sequence was manifest in pulmonary hemorrhages. The severe indigestion from which he had suffered since the days when he was an unsparing student at Paris and Orléans now increased so as to compel the rigidly abstemious diet, the long hours on the bed, and the semi-invalid life of which some account has been given. His old enemy, protracted headaches, doubtless the result of his digestive weakness, often attacked him.[14] By 1563, Calvin's feeble frame was rapidly breaking. In the autumn he was for two months confined to the house. His indigestion was now marked by severe attacks of colic. He suffered from renal calculus and gout, and other distressing symptoms appeared.[15] He still

---

[13] *"Optimus ille meus parens,"* Beza styled him. Letter to Bullinger, March 6, 1564, *Opera,* xx. 261.

[14] E.g. letter of October 14, 1560, to Bullinger, *Opera,* xviii. 217; Colladon, *Opera,* xxi. 89, 94.

[15] Calvin himself gave a minute account of his symptoms in a letter of February, 1564, to the physicians of Montpellier, ibid., xx. 252; see, also, Colladon, ibid., xxi. 94. Doumergue discusses them fully, iii. 509–526.

laboured at his books and correspondence, he still preached and lectured – but with increasing difficulty. The brave spirit was master of the feeble body and he was carried to the familiar pulpit in a chair when no longer able to walk. But a shortness of breath that seemed to his contemporaries an indication of advancing pulmonary tuberculosis was now manifest. On February 2, 1564, he lectured for the last time in the Academy; four days later he preached his last sermon. For a little longer he attended the Friday "Congregation" where he was not obliged to speak at length. On March 27, he was carried to the City Hall and appeared before the Little Council to present his friend, Nicolas Colladon, as rector of the School. At the April Communion, which fell on the second, he was present, borne in a chair, and not only partook of the consecrated elements, but joined in singing the psalm as much as his feeble voice would permit.[16]

Calvin felt that his end was near. He was ready and even eager to go. "Lord, how long!" was the exclamation constantly on his lips. He seemed continually in prayer.[17] On April 25, he made his will, leaving most of his little property to his brother, Antoine, and Antoine's children, but remembering the School and the relief of poor strangers.[18] Two days later, the Little Council appeared before him in his sickroom and heard from the familiar voice a characteristic exhortation, expressive of gratitude for what they had done for him, of friendship, and of desire for forgiveness for any faults and excess of vehemence on his part, but pointing out clearly their shortcomings, since "each has his imperfections," and urging humble dependence upon God.[19] The day following he received the Genevan ministers, and spoke to them a farewell remarkable for its biographic allusions:[20]

---

[16] Colladon, *Opera*, xxi. pp. 96–98; Beza, ibid., p. 161.

[17] ibid., pp. 96, 104.

[18] In French, *Opera*, xx. 298; in Latin, ibid., xxi. 162; in English trans., Schaff, vii. 828.

[19] *Opera*, ix. 887; xxi. 164; Schaff, vii. 831.

[20] *Opera*, ix. 891; xxi. 166; Schaff, vii. 833.

When I first came to this Church it had well-nigh nothing. There was preaching and that is all. The idols were sought out and burned; but there was no reformation. All was in confusion. That good man Master Guillaume [Farel] and the blind Coraud were indeed here... I have lived in marvelous combats here. I have been saluted in mockery of an evening by fifty or sixty gun-shots before my door. Fancy how that could shock a poor student, timid as I am and as I confess I have always been. After that I was hunted from this city and betook myself to Strassburg. Having dwelt there some time, I was recalled, but I had no less difficulty than before in seeking to fulfil my office. They set dogs on me, crying, "Scoundrel," and my cloak and legs were seized. I went to the Council of Two Hundred when they were fighting[21]... and when I entered they said to me, "Sir, withdraw, it is not with you we have to do." I said to them, "No, I shall not! Go on, rascals, kill me and my blood will witness against you, and even these benches will require it" ... I have had many faults which you have had to endure, and all that I have done is of no value. The wicked will seize upon that word, but I repeat that all I have done is of no value, and that I am a miserable creature. But, if I may say so, I have meant well, my faults have always displeased me, and the root of the fear of God has been in my heart. You can say that the wish has been good; and I beg you that the ill be pardoned, but if there has been good in it that you will conform to it and follow it.

As concerns my doctrine: I have taught faithfully, and God has given me grace to write. I have done it with the utmost fidelity, and have not to my knowledge corrupted or twisted a single passage of the Scriptures; and when I could have drawn out a far-fetched meaning, if I had studied subtilty, I have put that [temptation] under foot and have always studied simplicity. I have written nothing through hatred against any one, but have always set before me faithfully what I have thought to be for the glory of God.

These are the words of one already much broken by illness, dwelling in memory on the perils of the past, which had burned their bitterness into his soul; but they speak forth Calvin's characteristic humility before God, his conscious rectitude toward men, and his ruling motive to exalt the divine will.

---

[21] He refers to the tumult of December 1547, *Ante*, p. 309.

The sensitive, easily wounded spirit, and the unbending determination of purpose, so curiously combined in him, equally appear in them.

From this farewell address to his ministerial associates to his death nearly a month elapsed. On May 2, Calvin wrote to his well-tried friend Farel the last letter he was ever to send to any correspondent:[22]

> Farewell, best and truest brother. If God wills that you remain the survivor, live mindful of our union, which has been useful to the Church of God, so that its fruit abides for us in heaven. I am unwilling that you weary yourself for my sake, for I draw breath with difficulty, and constantly await its failing me. It is enough that I live and die unto Christ, who is gain to those who are His in life and in death. Again, farewell [to you], together with the brethren.

In spite of the infirmities of age,[23] of which Calvin showed such tender consideration in this letter, Farel could not let his younger associate pass from earthly companionship without looking upon Calvin's face once more. He hastened from Neuchâtel, visited and supped with Calvin, and preached, under the burden of his grief, to the people of Geneva. But the sands of Calvin's life had not yet quite run out. On May 19, the day when the Genevan ministers fulfilled the curious quarterly duty of mutual criticism which Calvin had made part of the ecclesiastical constitution, he had them assemble at his house, was carried to them in a chair, spoke briefly with them, and feebly tried to join in the common meal with which it was the amicable custom to close the trying session. It was a final effort to discharge his ministerial duty and to express his fraternal regard. He never rose from his bed again.

On Saturday, May 27, 1564, about eight in the evening, the end came. Conscious and intelligent to the last, he fell peacefully asleep. The next day, as the *Ordonnances* provided,[24] they buried

---

[22] *Opera*, xx. 302.
[23] Farel was 75, but seemed older to his friends, e.g. Colladon, *Opera*, xxi. 103.
[24] *Opera*, xa. 27.

his body about two in the afternoon, wrapped in a shroud and encased in a plain wooden coffin, without pomp or elaborate ceremony "in the common cemetery called Plain-palais," his grave being marked by a simple mound like that of his humbler associates in death. It was his wish that his burial should be thus modest, and that no gravestone should mark his resting-place. But he could not prevent, nor would he have desired to prevent, the spontaneous outpourings of the inhabitants of Geneva – pastors, professors, magistrates, and citizens – to do him honor at his burial.[25] And there in some now undeterminable spot in the ancient Genevan acre of God rests all that was mortal of the reformer.

Calvin was not fifty-five years of age. The thought is natural that his career was prematurely cut short, and that had he lived he might have done much more. Yet, to a degree unusual even in the experience of long-lived men, his was already a completed work, and it may well be doubted whether a score of years of added life would have increased materially its power and significance. His theological system had long been complete. His conceptions of the Church and of its relations to the State had not merely long been familiar to the public, but had been as fully realized in Genevan practice as it was possible to anticipate that they would ever be. His system of discipline was in high efficiency. The Genevan schools had been crowned by the Academy. His ideal of the Reformation had become that of a large part of western Europe, and had extended to Germany, Poland, and Hungary; but its guidance had passed beyond the control of any one man, however gifted. Even in Geneva, it was probably desirable that the further direction of the ecclesiastical life of the city should come under more conciliatory leadership. The battle had been fought, as he alone could fight it. Another, devoted to his ideals but less warlike, such as Beza, could now better maintain what had been won. Calvin's work was essentially finished.

---

[25] Colladon, *Opera*, xxi. 106; Beza, ibid., p. 169. A comparatively modern stone bearing the letters J. C. has been placed as a memorial.

Calvin's character is one of lights and shadows. He was the son of his age and of the land of his birth. He was a lawyer by training. With the clarity of mind native to the Frenchman, he combined the skill of the advocate and the reverence for system of the jurist. He made all his experiences and learning tributary to his development. As a recent biographer has well said of him:[26]

> Few men may have changed less; but few also have developed more. Every crisis in his career taught him something, and so enhanced his capacity. His studies of Stoicism showed him the value of morals; and he learned how to emphasize the sterner ethical qualities as well as the humaner, and the more clement by the side of the higher, public virtues. His early Humanism made him a scholar and an exegete, a master of elegant Latinity, of lucid and incisive speech, of a graphic pen, and historical imagination. His juristic studies gave him an idea of law, through which he interpreted the more abstract notions of theology, and a love of order, which compelled him to organise his Church. His imagination, playing upon the primitive Christian literature, helped him to see the religion Jesus instituted as Jesus Himself saw it; while the forces visible around him – the superstitions, the regnant and unreproved vices, the people so quickly sinning and so easily forgiven, the relics so innumerable and so fictitious, the acts and articles of worship, and especially the Sacraments deified and turned into substitutes for Deity – induced him to judge the system that claimed to be the sole interpreter and representative of Christ as a crafty compound of falsehood and truth.

That he was a creative theologian of the highest rank may well be questioned. He owed much to Augustine, and to the type of thought which Scotus had impressed on the later Middle Ages. His debt to Bucer was large. Without Luther his work could not have been done. But as a systemizer of Christian truth he stood without a rival in his century. He best taught men the answer to make to Roman claims and, under his logic, theology attained once more a classic presentation. Yet he was much more than a theologian. As an organizer he was at his best, at least in

---

[26] A. M. Fairbairn, in *The Cambridge Modern History*, ii. 363.

intention. To quote Fairbairn's happy phrase, he sought to answer the question: "How could the Church be made not simply an institution for the worship of God, but an agency for the making of men fit to worship Him?"[27] His answer had its evident faults. His methods were largely those of inquisitorial discipline, of State support, of force; but his answer was the best given in his age.

Calvin's own judgment of himself was that he was shy and timid by nature. To this opinion he often gave expression,[28] and there is no reason to doubt its truth as an analysis of his inward feeling. But his moral, and even his physical, courage is beyond doubt. Once convinced of the rightfulness of a course of action, no perils led him to swerve from its pursuit. His chief faults were a supersensitive self-consciousness which led him to feel slights and criticisms far too keenly, and a quickness of temper which often overcame him to the loss of self-control. Of this infirmity a characteristic example has already been cited.[29] He was himself fully conscious of the weakness, and it was no less clearly recognized by his friends.[30] His nerves, racked by constant struggle and by long illness, were easily rasped. In his lightly aroused exasperation, he often expressed himself, even to his intimates, with acerbity. To his enemies, for example to Castellio and Servetus, he was hard and vindictive. Much of this asperity was the result of semi-invalidism, but much, also, was the fruit of the conviction – a source, indeed, in no small degree of his strength – that his work was fully that of God. So intense was this identification of his own interests with those of the Master he would serve, that he thanked his physician for the aid in recovery from illness less on his personal account than as a service rendered to the Church, and he regarded attacks upon himself as a danger to the cause of the gospel.[31] It was easy for such a temperament to see in a criticism a serious offence and in an opponent an enemy of God.

---

[27] *The Cambridge Modern History*, ii. p. 364.

[28] E.g. *Opera*, xxi. 102; xxxi. 21–24.

[29] *Ante*, p. 232.

[30] e.g. Colladon, *Opera*, xxi. 117; Beza, ibid., p. 170.

[31] *Opera*, xii. 68; xiii. 598; compare Kampschulte, ii. 383.

Calvin undoubtedly appeared in different aspects to his contemporaries, and this diversity has led ever since his time to widely various estimates of his character. To his opponents he was the stern, unrelenting enemy – the "king," "pope," or "calif." To the majority of his supporters he was the admired leader, the matchless logician, the wise commander in a great cause, the inspirer of courage and of martyr-zeal, but a figure somewhat distant and awesome. To his intimates, he was the affectionate, if quick-tempered and sometimes censorious friend – a man to be loved as well as reverenced.

But whether friend, disciple, or foe, none could fail to recognize Calvin's transcendent ability. He might be slandered, the worst of motives might be imputed to him by traducers, but none who knew him could doubt his devotion to his cause. With all his frequent arrogance towards men, Calvin's spirit was humble towards God. To do and to teach His will was undoubtedly his prime intention; and if Calvin too often identified the divine purpose with his own wishes, the error does not detract from the sincerity of his consecration. He submitted to his long bodily enfeeblement as from the wise hand of God. In the crises of his life, his conversion, his first settlement in Geneva, and in his return to the difficult ministry in that turbulent city, he sacrificed ease, scholarly honours, and personal inclination to what he deemed the imperative voice of God. He put God first. In the strength of the conviction that God had chosen his task, he fought his battles and did his work. It is this crowning trait that was expressed in the declaration of the Genevan Little Council, standing under the shadow of his recent death: "God gave him a character of great majesty"[32] – and that must ever remain Calvin's highest claim to personal regard.

---

[32] R. Stähelin, in Hauck's *Relencyklopädie*, iii. 683.

OTHER BOOKS OF INTEREST
FROM
CHRISTIAN FOCUS PUBLICATIONS

HISTORY MAKERS

GEORGE MÜLLER

DELIGHTED IN GOD

Roger Steer

GEORGE MÜLLER

Delighted in God

Roger Steer

George Müller's life is a powerful answer to modern scepticism.

His name has become a byword for faith throughout the world. In the early 1830s he embarked upon an extraordinary adventure. Disturbed by the faithlessness of the Church in general, he longed to have something to point to as "visible proof that our God and Father is the same faithful creator as he ever was."

Praying in every penny of the costs, he supervised the building of three large orphanages housing thousands of children. Under no circumstances would any individual ever be asked for money or materials. He was more successful than anyone could have believed possible and is as much an example to our generation, as he was to his.

Roger Steer is an acclaimed writer and broadcaster. He lives in the West Country with his family.

Other subjects in the HistoryMakers series include D. L. Moody, John Calvin, Gordon of Khartoum, Robert Murray McCheyne, Hudson Taylor, Pastor Hsi Sheng Mo, and Major-General Sir Henry Havelock.

ISBN 978-1-84550-120-4

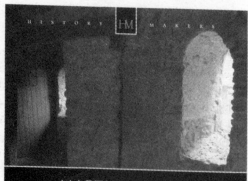

MARTIN LUTHER

THE MAN WHO STARTED THE REFORMATION
Thomas Lindsay

HISTORY MAKERS

MARTIN LUTHER

The Man Who Started the Reformation

Thomas Lindsay

Martin Luther's father was a miner with ambitions – he wanted to better himself and provide his children with a good education. Martin upset his father's plans by becoming a monk rather than a lawyer, but by the age of 29 he was a Professor of Theology. In addition to his Collège duties he preached almost every day and visited people on pastoral duties – he kept two secretaries very busy.

Luther's father, meanwhile, became a town councillor, the part owner of six mines and two foundries, and owned a large house in the main street.

What happened to make this son of the upwardly mobile establishment into a revolutionary who nailed 95 Theses onto the church door at Wittenberg, affecting not only the whole of the Christian Church but also breaking the power of a European superstate? This is the story of a passionate, flawed, and courageous man who loved his family and the people around him; a man who went further in challenging the status quo than any other in history, the man who started the Reformation.

THOMAS LINDSAY was a distinguished Professor at the United Free Church Collège, Glasgow. He had an international academic reputation and the ability to communicate his learning in a readable style. His biography of Luther manages that difficult balance of being a book for both historical students and popular readers.

ISBN 978-1-85792-261-5

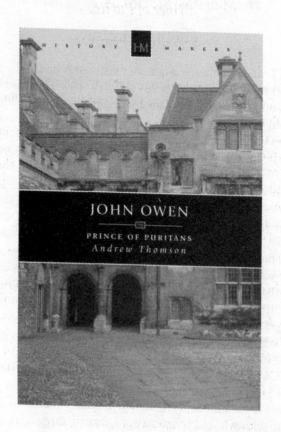

JOHN OWEN

PRINCE OF PURITANS
Andrew Thomson

JOHN OWEN

Prince of Puritans

Andrew Thomson

John Owen (1616–1683) was one of the defining theologians of the Christian era. His books have been continually in print and are still influential today.

Educated at Queen's Collège, Oxford, he was a moderate Presbyterian who became a Congregationalist after reading a book by John Cotton. He later helped draw up the Savoy Declaration, the Congregational Basis of Faith.

During the English Civil War Owen was wholly on the side of the Parliamentarians, accompanying Cromwell on expeditions to Scotland and Ireland as Chaplain. Owen was influential in national life and was made Vice-Chancellor of Christ Church, Oxford. After the Restoration of the Monarchy he was ejected from this position and devoted his energies to developing "godly and learned men," in writing commentaries and devotional books, and in defending nonconformists from state persecution.

Andrew Thomson was a popular biographer from the nineteenth century. He also wrote about the lives of Thomas Boston (see overleaf) and Richard Baxter (Richard Baxter: The Pastor's Pastor ISBN 978-1-85792-380-3).

The Mortification of Sin – *A Puritan's View of How to Deal with the Sin in Your Life* (ISBN 978-1-84550-977-4) by John Owen

ISBN 978-1-85792-267-7

HISTORY MAKERS

THOMAS BOSTON

HIS LIFE & TIMES
Andrew Thomson

THOMAS BOSTON

The Gentle Saint of Ettrick

Andrew Thomson

Few British pastors can claim to have written a book that is amongst the "life-books of their generation," yet Boston is one. His *Fourfold State of Man* has been the instrument of countless conversions and could be said to have changed the zeitgeist of his era as effectively as Luther's *Commentary on Galations*, Alleine's *Alarm to the Unconverted*, Bunyan's *Pilgrim's Progress*, Edwards' *Sinners in the Hands of an Angry God*, Wilberforce's *True Christianity*, or Lewis' *Mere Christianity*.

His autobiography has been compared in its simplicity and truth to Augustine's.

Thomson shows that Boston was not only a dedicated and adept Pastor-Scholar but also someone whose influence has lasted through the Victorian era until the present-day revival in his theological writings. A Hebrew Scholar of the first rank, Boston was also fluent in Greek and Latin and competent in French and Dutch.

He was a humble man, a compassionate pastor, and a stern man when principles were at stake. Boston disliked controversy yet took a central role in the major controversies of his time. Above all, however, his life was characterized by his heart of service to his church. When he could no longer stand, his sermons were delivered from an armchair in the pulpit, when he could no longer get to the church, he preached from the open window of the manse. This is the remarkable story of one of the key figures of the eighteenth century church who influenced nations from a small rural parish, and continues to do so today.

ISBN 978-1-85792-379-7